D0871829

Africa in World Politics

AFRICA
IN WORLD POLITICS

VERNON McKAY

Professor of African Studies
School of Advanced International Studies
The Johns Hopkins University

GREENWOOD PRESS, PUBLISHERS
WESTPORT, CONNECTICUT

Library of Congress Cataloging in Publication Data

McKay, Vernon.
   Africa in world politics.

     Reprint of the ed. published by Harper & Row,
New York.
     Bibliography: p.
     1. Africa--Politics--1960-   2. World politics
--1955-1965. 3. United Nations--Africa. I. Title.
DT30.M24 1974   327.6   73-11866
ISBN 0-8371-7100-8

Originally published in 1962 by Harper & Row, Publishers, New York

Reprinted with the permission of Harper & Row, Publishers, Inc.

Reprinted in 1974 by Greenwood Press,
a division of Williamhouse-Regency Inc.

Library of Congress Catalogue Card Number 73-11866

ISBN 0-8371-7100-8

Printed in the United States of America

To
Congressman Frances P. Bolton
Friend of Africa, Africans, and Africanists,
for her pioneering work in stimulat-
ing American interest in Africa dur-
ing her long service in the House
Committee on Foreign Affairs.

Preface

IN contrast to many volumes on conditions inside Africa, this book is devoted to Africa's relations with the outside world. It highlights the major African issues in international relations, bringing into focus a wide variety of subjects and source materials. Since this approach has led me far afield, even to the point of becoming my own Sovietologist for three chapters, I have been happy to raise questions but modest in supplying answers. Africa's future relations with Europe, Asia, and the Americas are of cardinal importance, and it is my hope to stimulate others to devote more attention to the nature and significance of these rapidly multiplying contacts.

My work on Africa began in 1934 with the study of the history of European imperialism. In 1945 I turned from the history of Africa to current African issues, and the present volume is essentially a narrative of contemporary history since 1945. The trouble with writing contemporary history is that one finds it extremely difficult to be either contemporary or historical, particularly for a continent as volatile as Africa has been since World War II. The passing of time and the opening up of other source materials will make possible many new perspectives on African controversies in world politics today. It is always interesting, nonetheless, to analyze issues during the heat of the battle.

After an introductory chapter on the combination of internal and external pressures which stimulated the quick rise of Africa to prominence, the book is divided into four related parts dealing with (1) the impact of the United Nations on Africa, (2) Pan-African, Afro-Asian, and Eurafrican movements, (3) the policies of India and

the Soviet Union on Africa, and (4) American interests and policies in Africa. The two chapters which I originally planned on
American policy became so absorbing that they grew into seven. A
final chapter attempts to synthesize the many aspects of Africa's
impact on international relations. A major theme running through
many chapters is the striving of Africa's new leaders to develop foreign policies of their own, independent of either the Soviet or Western blocs.

Although footnotes have been restricted to citations for direct
quotations, my sources are listed, chapter by chapter, at the end of
the volume. In the chapters dealing with the United Nations and
with American policy, the story is based in part on my own participation in the events described, especially during the period from 1948
to 1956 when I worked for the Department of State on African issues
in the United Nations, and served on many U.S. Delegations at
U.N. meetings.

I gratefully acknowledge the help of many specialists on African
areas and subjects. My thanks are also due to the editors of numerous
publications in which I have presented earlier versions of certain
ideas. My own graduate students in the Program of African Studies
at the Johns Hopkins School of Advanced International Studies have
been sympathetic listeners, discerning critics, and willing helpers in
assembling data. My deepest appreciation is reserved for my research
assistant, Mrs. Sally Hanger Willcox.

Contents

Part IV American Policy in Africa

List of Tables

1

The Rise of Africa
in World Politics

THE rise of Africa was dramatized for the entire world by the turmoil at the fifteenth session of the United Nations General Assembly in 1960. The first appearance of a galaxy of leaders from 16 new African states brought many presidents and prime ministers to the U.N. to welcome the newcomers. As delegates plunged into the hectic Congo crisis, the cold war mounted, and it appeared for a time that the rise of Africa might precipitate the decline of the U.N. Soviet leader Nikita Khrushchev will long be remembered for the table-pounding pyrotechnics he displayed when he entered the Assembly to launch a startling verbal assault on U.N. Secretary General Dag Hammarskjold.

This U.N. interest in Africa was not new, however. The annual agendas of the General Assembly were studded with African problems almost from the beginning. By 1953, in fact, quarrels over the colonial question had become so bitter that Walter Lippmann wrote in his daily column on January 12: "The U.N. is being torn apart by the formula that almost anyone can put almost any claim before . . . [it], and then can compel all the nations to align themselves pro and con, black or white. This is a perfect formula for failing to make peace, for dividing mankind, and for fomenting bad will." This worldwide interest in Africa's affairs places its peoples in a position unique in their history. Although they live in the least developed of all the continents, and therefore have little physical power, their new place in the ideological struggle between Western and Soviet blocs gives them unusual significance. Their ultimate decisions regarding the merits and weaknesses of the Western democratic tradition could have a powerful influence on the destiny of mankind.

Although Africa seldom attracted universal attention until the turbulent years after World War II, it had a more substantial role in the past than is generally acknowledged; the myth that Africa is a continent without history dies hard. Yet any observant traveler should realize that the great variety of physical types he sees indicates a fascinating history of migrations and mixtures of peoples. A few highlights of this past will counteract the impression that Africa had no role in world affairs before the twentieth century.

AFRICA IN THE PAST

Whether man originated in Africa, as recent evidence suggests, or whether Africa's earliest peoples came from Asia, the continent was the scene of countless migrations which ultimately carried some people westward through the flatlands of the Sudan and into the forest regions, while others journeyed eastward and southward through the scenic highlands and great lakes of eastern Africa. The Pygmies of the equatorial rain forest and the Bushmen and Hottentots of southern Africa, who may be the modern descendants of Africa's earliest Homo sapiens, still survive in small numbers. Most of Africa's remaining 250,000,000 inhabitants may be classified racially as either Caucasoid, in the north and northeast, or Negroid, in most of the rest of the continent. Linguists have identified perhaps 12 language families, two of which include those languages spoken by the vast majority of Africans. These are the Afro-Asiatic languages, of which the Semitic and Hamitic languages of north and northeast Africa are representative, and the Niger-Congo or Nigritic languages, spoken in most of sub-Saharan Africa from the west coast to the southern cape. The Bantu languages of central, eastern, and southern Africa are a subgroup of this great family, which includes about 800 distinct languages. These sub-Saharan vernaculars became written languages only where Western missionaries introduced the familiar Latin alphabet and prepared dictionaries and grammars. By 1961 more than 350 African languages were in written form, the complete Bible having been translated into more than 60 of them and the New Testament into 117. However, fewer than one out of every five Africans had learned to read and write, although literacy rates varied from as high as 55 percent in Basutoland to less than 5 percent in Angola.

From the sparse records of early Arab travelers and the later work of archaeologists and other scholars, it nonetheless appears that remarkable societies flourished in the early Kingdoms of Ghana and Mali and the Songhai Empire in the western Sudan, beginning at least a thousand years ago, Ibn Batuta, the celebrated traveler of Islam who visited the western Sudan in the fourteenth century, expressed deep appreciation of the organization, justice, and security he found in the Kingdom of Mali:

There is complete security in the country. Neither traveler nor inhabitant in it has anything to fear from robbers or men of violence. They do not confiscate the property of any white man who dies in their country, even if it be uncounted wealth. On the contrary, they give it into the charge of some trustworthy person among the whites, until the rightful heir takes possession of it. They are careful to observe the hours of prayer and assiduous in attending them in congregations, and in bringing up their children to them.[1]

The progress of these early Kingdoms was partly stimulated by contacts between Sudanic peoples and the Arabs of North Africa through camel caravans across the Sahara which brought trade goods, including precious salt, into Timbuktu and other towns in exchange for alluvial gold produced in the Sudan. The attraction of gold was also a factor in the civilization which produced the massive granite structures of the Great Zimbabwe Ruins which still stand in Southern Rhodesia as an imposing vestige of a past culture that apparently thrived 600 to 800 years ago.

A new era in African history began 500 years ago when the com-

---

[1] Ibn Batuta, *Travels in Asia and Africa, 1325–1354,* trans. H. A. R. Gibb, London, 1957, pp. 329–30.

mercial revolution brought European trade out from inland seas and rivers to the oceans of the world. Since the fall of Rome a thousand years before, Europe had slowly worked its way out of a dark age of isolation when life was similar in some respects to that in much of Africa until the twentieth century. The search for gold was a spur to the new nation-states of Europe when they began to push their way around the west coast of Africa. Although disappointed in this search, they soon established trading posts, and local demand for European trade goods quickly developed.

The European rivalries culminating in the great colonial wars of the eighteenth century between France and England were fought primarily in America and India rather than Africa. Simultaneously, however, as African leaders still point out, American and other slavers were "robbing Africa of Africans," an evil practice that was supplemented a century later by the imperialist scramble when Europe "robbed Africans of Africa."

IMPACT OF THE WEST

The slave trade was the first great impact of the West on Africa. The nature and results of this corrupt traffic have been well summarized by J. D. Fage in his *Introduction to the History of West Africa*. Perhaps 15,000,000 to 20,000,000 slaves were landed in America between the sixteenth and nineteenth centuries, and another 3,000,000 or 4,000,000 may have died in slave ships. Including those killed in slave raids and in other ways as a direct result of the slave trade, this appalling loss of African manpower may have totaled as much as 40,000,000. The average annual loss over this 300-year period may have been less than 1 percent of the population, but the slaves were taken whenever possible from among the youngest and fittest Africans available, two-thirds men and one-third women. In addition to the actual loss of manpower, fear and uncertainty retarded the normal development of the area. African middlemen developed a monopoly of slave-raiding and selling slaves to Europeans. They first sold their own domestic slaves and then raided other tribes. It should not be forgotten, moreover, that an Arab slave trade with Africa had already been underway for several centuries, and had not entirely ended even by 1960. Despite these human tragedies, however, some of the most advanced and densely populated parts of Africa today, as Fage reminds us, are areas where the slave trade was most active, the Gold and Slave Coasts and southern Nigeria—which suggests that the trade with Europe, even in slaves, sometimes stimulated the growth of population and the development of political institutions.

With the demise of the slave trade in the nineteenth century came the clamor for "legitimate" trade, followed soon by the European scramble to partition Africa into colonial empires. Africa entered world politics in a major way when the clash of rival colonial ambitions came to the council tables of Europe. In William L. Langer's excellent two-volume study of European alliances and the diplomacy of imperialism, no less than 10 out of 36 chapters are devoted largely to the African rivalries of the European powers between 1871 and 1902. Germany sought to absorb "Mittelafrika" by linking the Cameroons, Tanganyika, and South-West Africa into a solid block. France sought to swallow up northern Africa by linking its North African territories with its holdings all the way from Senegal to French Somaliland. Portugal tried to obtain a solid band of territory all the way across from Mozambique to Angola. Leopold II, King of the Belgians, managed to carve out a vast empire in the Congo. Imperialist zeal not only fostered direct clashes between some of these powers, but it brought all of them into conflict with Britain, which was simultaneously trying to paint the map red all the way from Cape Town to Cairo. As Harry Rudin has suggested, however, this colonial rivalry did not cause war; it actually prolonged the peace in Europe for another generation by making it possible for European governments to maintain friendly relations for short periods by compensating each other with territory belonging to others.

The role of Africa in nineteenth-century world politics differs sharply, nonetheless, from its position after World War II. Before 1900 the partition of Africa was of primary concern to governments in Europe. Although public opinion had already begun to play a role in international relations, it did not yet have the power it was later to acquire. After World War II, the attraction of Africa appealed to peoples as well as governments, and to America and Asia as well as Europe. Moreover, in the heyday of imperialism, Europe had both the power and the will to handle many African problems as it saw fit. By the end of World War II, however, Europe had lost much of its power and its will to *dispose* of Africa's business. Instead, it had to learn to *deal* with Africans.

Europe's earlier imperial power is well illustrated by an episode in African history vividly described by Roland Oliver in his biography of Sir Harry Johnston. In a notable encounter at a dinner party one night in May, 1889, Cecil Rhodes and Harry Johnston met for the first time, "a chance event, which Johnston was to regard as a turning-point in his life and a landmark in the history of the British Empire."[2] The two men were so fascinated by each other's views on Europe's destiny in Africa that they went to Rhodes's hotel suite after the dinner party and talked all night. It was during this talk that Johnston gave Rhodes the Cape-to-Cairo idea which Rhodes later made famous. In return, as dawn was breaking, he gave Johnston a check for £2,000 for a treaty-making expedition to Nyasaland.

Johnston went off to Nyasaland shortly afterward with Lord Salisbury's blessing and Rhodes's money, and, with the aid of English and Scottish missionaries, began signing treaties with Nyasa chiefs. The chiefs did not give up their territory or get British protection, but simply agreed not to make cessions of territory to other powers without British consent. The primary purpose of the treaties was "to prove at the council tables of Europe the priority of British interests over those of other powers. . . ." Johnston found a hunter named Alfred Sharpe in Nyasaland and engaged him as a temporary vice-consul. Johnston and Sharpe then marched out in two long arms west of Lake Nyasa, one westward and the other northward, signing treaties and "trusting to luck that no European rival would make a better showing in the middle." When a chief refused to sign, "they simply moved on, leaving, as it were, a gap in the chain."[3] It made no difference, because when the British government later established a protectorate over Nyasaland, it did so without referring

[2] Roland A. Oliver, *Sir Harry Johnston and the Scramble for Africa*, London, 1957, p. 152.
[3] *Ibid.*, p. 160.

to the treaties, arbitrarily including in the protectorate the territories of all the chiefs, whether or not they had signed treaties with Johnston and Sharpe.

In the late nineteenth century, Europe thus had the power and the will to rule. The role of Africa in world politics was a passive role. However, the word *passive* is appropriate only in the context of European diplomacy. In Africa itself, the inhabitants of many areas engaged in active though ultimately unsuccessful armed resistance to Europeans. This fact is well demonstrated by the Nigerian historian K. O. Dike in his book *Trade and Politics in the Niger Delta—1830–1885*, which challenges those authors who tend to write as if African opposition to European penetration did not exist.

After World War II, Africa was transformed from a passive into an active force in world politics. Redrawing the map of Africa was no longer left to Europeans like Salisbury, Johnston, and Rhodes, but became the prerogative of Africans like Prime Ministers Kwame Nkrumah and Sékou Touré. When they formed the Ghana-Guinea union in November, 1958, it was Europe which passively accepted their decision.

AFRICA'S QUICK TRANSFORMATION

What are the causes of this profound change? What factors or combination of factors made possible such a quick transformation of Africa from a vast colonial domain into a continent of independent states? Since this will undoubtedly prove to be one of the major revolutions of the twentieth century, the problem of its causation is certain to intrigue historians. From time to time they will no doubt reinterpret the causes of the revolution in the light of the preconceptions of their own age.

In the future, scholars may conclude that the emergence of Africa was primarily a natural culmination of 400 years of contact with the West. In 1960, however, the underlying cause of the rapid rise of African issues in world politics appeared to be the profound change in relative strength among the great powers. After World War I, Western Europe, even though crippled, was still the strongest power factor in politics. But World War II shifted the centers of world power away from Western Europe to the United States and the Soviet Union. The emergence of these two rival centers precipitated an ideological struggle for Asia and Africa. A weakened Western Europe therefore found itself confronted simultaneously by the demands of African leaders, by the newly independent Arab-Asian states which strongly supported African aspirations, by the threat of Soviet imperialism, and by a variety of direct and indirect pressures from the United States.

A second and obviously basic factor was the rapid development of nationalism, using the term loosely to cover anticolonialism and other types of protest movements, including some which do not fall within the traditional Western concept of nationalism. In the search for a less inaccurate word than nationalism, Lord Hailey, in the 1956 revision of his *African Survey*, coined the term *Africanism*. James S. Coleman, seeking still more precise terminology, divides African resistance into three types of protest movements against colonial rule—*traditionalist, modernist,* and *syncretistic* (a blend of traditional and modern elements). Thomas Hodgkin in his *Nationalism in Colonial Africa* prefers to retain the word *nationalism*, terming it *incipient* in some territories and *mature* or *developed* in others.

One does not need to choose one or the other of these three concepts. Each of them helps to clarify what is meant by African nationalism and therefore refines our knowledge of it. Whatever they are called, Africa's modern political movements originated as protests against colonial domination. Those African leaders who were taught in Western schools to exalt nationhood naturally sought to develop it in their own countries. Before political agitation could become really effective, however, Africa needed a larger number of educated leaders, and a greater number of town dwellers and wage earners to follow them. This condition began to be fulfilled in certain territories before the outbreak of World War II, when the expanding education system was graduating more and more potential leaders and urbanization was bringing more Africans into the towns.

To this political nucleus were added many disgruntled war veterans from the hundreds of thousands of Africans who served Allied armies loyally in World War II. The contacts and experiences of those who served overseas awakened new aspirations, and many soldiers were unwilling to return to the life they had led before the war. The British alone enlisted about 400,000 Africans, nearly half of whom served abroad. Restive and ambitious, these veterans were easily influenced by political leaders whose hopes for self-government had been raised by the Atlantic Charter and other wartime declarations.

Meanwhile, a spectacular growth of towns was under way all over Africa, accompanied by a remarkable increase of educational opportunities, including the provision of higher education for thousands of Africans in Britain, France, and the United States.

In French territories, the granting of French citizenship, the widespread extension of the right to vote, and the increase in the number of African representatives at home and in France gave a new impetus to the development of political parties. Many leaders were still too attracted by French traditions and culture, or at least an Afro-French blend, to follow the nationalist pattern of British territories. The same resentment of paternalism was everywhere present, however. As Sylvanus Olympio told the United Nations Trusteeship Council in 1947 when he first arrived as an African petitioner from French Togoland, what Africans particularly dislike is the "Daddy knows best" attitude of their rulers.

In the Gold Coast, unrest precipitated an outbreak of violence on February 28, 1948, when war veterans and other African demonstrators staged a protest march on the governor's residence. When stones were thrown, the police responded with gunfire and tear gas, setting off several days of rioting in which 26 Africans were killed and 242 others, including 15 Europeans, were injured. It was this outburst which spurred the crucial chain of British decisions culminating on March 6, 1957, when the Gold Coast became the independent state of Ghana. Since the Gold Coast was the first African colony south of the Sahara to attain independence after World War II, Britain's action set a vital precedent the repercussions of which were immediately felt in French territories, a short time later in the Belgian Congo, and then in Portuguese territories.

The British decision forced the French to quicken the political advance of neighboring Togoland, which became to some extent a "pilot project" for other French territories. The late Governor Pierre Ryckmans, an outstanding colonial official who spent a generation in Ruanda-Urundi and the Congo before he became Belgian representative in the United Nations Trusteeship Council, was among the first to realize the significance of all this for the Congo. He remarked to me in 1950 that Britain's action meant independence for British territories in 10 years, French territories in 20, and the Congo in 50. When independence came, he lamented, the Belgian Congo would have a government worse than that of Haiti which, at the moment, he seemed to regard as the most misgoverned country on earth. Although history quickly bypassed Ryckmans's timetable, his views were a considerable advance in the thinking of Belgians, many of whom were still talking in terms of 200 years for Congo independence. In any case, Britain's decision to grant quick independence to the Gold Coast rather than hold the line during a period of further gradual preparation ranks as one of the most important and influential decisions in postwar Africa.

The Asian revolt against the West was a third factor stimulating the rise of African issues in world politics. The hopes of African leaders were quickened by the successes of nationalist strivings in Asia, where more than half a billion people won their independence after World War II and formed a dozen new states. In Toynbee's view of history, the non-Western majority of mankind was once again besieging the Western fortress after an interval of almost three centuries in which the West was on the offensive in an unsuccessful attempt to conquer the world through the conquest of the ocean. It is these last three centuries which made the great non-Western majority think of Westerners as habitual aggressors. The world was inclined to forget that the West itself was subjected to a long and dangerous Arab siege until the tenth century, to a perilous Mongol siege in the thirteenth century, and to a 300-year Ottoman siege which ended only under the walls of Vienna in 1683.

Whatever the validity of such an interpretation of history, it is, clear that colonialism became a hated symbol of centuries of Western domination. The Arab-Asian attack on Western control of Africa was motivated by genuine sympathy for Africans, but it was also obvious that the Asians found a vicarious enjoyment in using the symbol of colonialism as a stick with which to beat their former rulers. The passion of this onslaught on colonialism was magnified by memories of white racialism, because the personal humiliations suffered by colored people at the hands of arrogant or thoughtless whites were often so vivid that it would be difficult to exaggerate their significance. The racial superiority complex of Westerners was perhaps more responsible than any other factor for the ground swell of anti-Westernism and the new images of "neocolonialism" in the minds of many Asians and Africans after their countries attained independence. They often seemed to become not more but less friendly after they were free.

In any event, the United Nations, by bringing the Arab-Asian peoples of the world together, gave them an additional sense of power which they were able to use persistently and effectively in presenting African grievances and demands before the United Nations.

Mention should be made of still another facet of the revolt against the West. It was a revolt against economic hardship. Even if, by some stroke of magic, colonialism, paternalism, and racialism could have been wiped off the face of the earth, it was clear that conflicts of interest and ideas would continue between the relatively well-to-do industrial peoples and the poorer peoples of the predominantly agricultural countries.

A fourth important factor in the rise of African issues in world politics was the expansion of the principle of international accountability for colonial administration. Although the non-Western states became the driving force behind the movement to make the colonial powers more and more accountable to the international community, it should not be forgotten that this was the goal of many liberal groups in Western countries at the end of World War II. The Atlantic Charter, the "four freedoms," and the three chapters of the United Nations Charter dealing with colonial peoples carried forward Woodrow Wilson's principle of self-determination and the mandates system of the League of Nations. The comparative calm with which the League of Nations treated the colonial question was a reflection of the League's composition. Led by Britain and France, the League never had more than eight members from the continent of Asia, some of whom were subject to varying degrees of European influence. In sharp contrast, the United Nations by 1960 had 22 Arab-Asian and 25 African members, and the whole tone of international relations had changed. Constant U.N. pressure to help Africa was both a cause and a result of the rise of African issues in world politics.

Communist influences on African issues constitute a fifth factor. Since three later chapters are devoted to Soviet policy in Africa, it is mentioned only in broad outlines here. It is deliberately placed toward the end of this list of causes in order to avoid the error of those who exaggerate the extent of communism in Africa during the 1950s. By 1958 communism had still made relatively little headway. Party membership was for the most part limited to the areas in which industry had developed and Europeans lived in large numbers, particularly North Africa. Nonetheless, Soviet pressure was not only real but growing stronger. Although communism was rarely the cause of disturbances in Africa, the Communists often stepped in to exploit trouble spots.

The Russians used many channels other than Communist parties. In addition to trade unions, student groups, front organizations, and political and other movements, they found in the United Nations a ready-made forum for wooing African nationalists and for subverting the friendship of the Western allies. African leaders found that it was Soviet delegates who said the things they liked to hear and Western representatives who did not. The happy lack of restraint in the Russian position made it extremely difficult if not impossible for the West to compete with Soviet appeals to colonial peoples. Moreover, many nationalists are impressed by what they read and hear about Soviet achievements in the quick economic development of backward areas and by the reputed lack of color prejudice among Russians. When Soviet leaders set aside the doctrinaire Stalinist call for Communist revolutions in favor of more flexible tactics, Russian prospects improved. The advent of new states provided numerous opportunities for the expansion of Russian influence, which had been curtailed by the colonial powers. In addition, by 1960 Chinese Communists had developed an interest in Africa.

There is still abundant evidence, however, that African leaders have no desire to substitute Soviet domination for Western rule. Moreover, in contrast to the scanty footholds of communism in Africa, the West has numerous valuable bridgeheads where university-trained Africans have been exposed to democratic ideals and have had rudimentary experience with parliamentary institutions. If the West will make every possible effort in the coming years to help these emerging peoples develop African institutions and attain higher living and educational standards, there is reason to hope that they will develop non-Communist states.

A sixth powerful factor encouraging Africans and irritating Europeans has been the influence of the United States. The variety of American interests and policies in Africa are elaborated in Part IV of this volume. Although conflicting interests committed the United States to a restrained policy, in contrast to the unrestrained tactics of the Soviet Union, American pressure on African events has been exerted in many ways—through diplomatic persuasion in Europe, through our votes on African issues in the United Nations even when we abstained, through "The Voice of America" and other propaganda media, through the educational exchange programs of the State Department and other agencies, both public and private, and through economic and technical assistance to Africa. The development of many new air routes after World War II enabled thousands of Americans to make their way through much of Africa—journalists, teachers, students, scholars, technicians, clergymen, philanthropists, congressmen, businessmen, tourists, labor leaders, and numerous American political leaders including Vice-President Richard M. Nixon in 1957 and Vice-President Lyndon Johnson in 1961. Many Americans were meanwhile attacking the cautious attitude of their government toward African demands for liberation.

The reality of American pressure for African advance is clearly reflected in the reaction of Europeans. Their mingled uneasiness and irritation was expressed by André Siegfried in the *Figaro* on February 7, 1949, when he suggested that the United States, by fomenting colonial revolts, was as dangerous a revolutionary force as the Soviet Union.

A final factor quickening the emergence of Africa was a notable change in the colonial policies of the European powers after World

War II. Politically, the nineteenth-century policy of establishing law and order was supplanted by the twentieth-century aim of promoting self-government. Economically, the laissez-faire policy of letting each colony support itself largely from its own revenues was altered by substantial financial aid from metropolitan treasuries and by the extension of state activity in economic affairs. In their origins, these new policies were not the result of the external pressures already described, but were developed under the leadership of men who headed European colonial ministries, among them Arthur Creech Jones of the United Kingdom, Marius Moutet of France, and Jan Anne Jonkman of the Netherlands. All three were Socialists or Laborites whose parties came to power in postwar political overturns, and who had devoted intensive study to colonial problems and had long been advocates of reform. At the very least it was their goal to accelerate the old policy of gradualism.

Although they were not yet responding primarily to external pressures, they were nonetheless aware of the trend of things to come. After visiting Soviet Moslem republics in Central Asia, Colonel C. E. Ponsonby, a Conservative member of the British Parliament, reported to a joint meeting of the Royal Empire and Royal African Societies on May 30, 1945:

Twenty-one years ago the literacy . . . in Uzbekistan was 7 per cent, practically the only teaching being in the Mohammedan schools, and very few women could write at all. There were one or two small irrigation schemes on the Czar's estates—there were no factories and no hydroelectric plants. What is the situation after twenty-one years? Now 98 per cent of the population can read and write; there are 4,000 schools, two universities and several technical institutes; there are large efficient factories; huge irrigation schemes; 20 hydroelectric plants, and, amongst other things, a wonderful ballet and opera.[4]

Although Colonel Ponsonby had no sympathy with Soviet methods, he did use the comparison to ask whether the British government could not have spent more money and initiated more reforms, a sentiment echoed by Lord Hailey who concluded the meeting by suggesting that Britain should try to benefit by the Soviet example with-

[4] C.E. Ponsonby, "African Colonial Administration," United Empire, September–October, 1945, pp. 167–172.

out departing from the British policy of "respecting the traditions and customs of the African people."

The mounting barrage of criticism from the outside world, accompanied by increasingly vehement African demands, gradually undermined the confidence of the major colonial powers in the justice, righteousness, and practicability of gradualism. The resulting decline of the "will to rule" is graphically portrayed in the following words of J. H. Huizinga in the *Manchester Guardian* of August 5, 1949:

> To believe that you know better what is good for your subjects than your subjects themselves, to refuse to be swayed by their self-appointed spokesmen, to remain unaffected by their imputations of selfish intent, to render them harmless when that becomes necessary in order to avoid . . . force—all this requires such courage of one's autocratic conviction as does not come easily to the ruler bred in the democratic tradition.

The negative tendencies of the colonial powers to resist premature African demands therefore began to be replaced, or at least supplemented, by a new form of pressure—positive offers of inducements to persuade Africans to remain in the Western fold when they obtained self-government.

These new influences included the grant of several billion dollars by European taxpayers for development and welfare programs; the British decision to move the Gold Coast rapidly to self-government, with Nigeria and others soon to follow; the concessions made by France in the effort to persuade the people of west and equatorial Africa to accept a new form of autonomous relationship; the British attempt to induce Kenya and the new Federation of Rhodesia and Nyasaland to adopt a multiracial pattern of political evolution; and the Eurafrican movement to include non–self-governing territories within the new European Economic Community.

The most perceptive European leaders recognized the need for new political relationships freely arrived at in the fullest possible cooperation with African wishes. All the colonial powers except Portugal and Spain therefore began to publicize self-government in one form or another as the goal to be achieved sooner or later. To an increasing extent, rapid advance to political independence began to be viewed as the best means of preserving economic and other links. In the words of Patrick Gordon-Walker, a Labor member of the British

Parliament, in 1947: "If Mr. Churchill were in power, he would throw away the Empire as George III threw away the thirteen colonies. The aim of the Labour Government is to save it. This will be accomplished by giving the colonies self-government. If this plan comes off, the Empire will be a very powerful affair indeed."[5]

French taxpayers began to contribute $250,000,000 a year for the development of France's territories south of the Sahara. The French financial contribution to Africa was actually greater than that of Britain, although the latter received better publicity. The relative magnitude of French economic aid was in itself a form of political pressure on African leaders to maintain this profitable relationship. As the September, 1957, conference of the Rassemblement Démocratique Africain at Bamako showed, more and more Africans in French territories were already using the word *independence* to describe their goal, but they were thinking in terms of an association with France somewhat like Puerto Rico's relationship with the United States since 1952—a kind of "divorce with alimony" which granted local autonomy and maintained the economic benefits of the old relationship, but left the burden of defense and foreign relations to Washington. It was not long, however, before the magic of independence swept these pragmatic arguments aside, and the French territories also joined the march.

SUMMARY

Seven causes of the rise of Africa in world politics have been outlined—the shift of world power centers from Western Europe to the United States and the Soviet Union; African nationalism and anticolonialism; the growing principle of international accountability for colonial peoples; the Asian revolt against the West; the pressure of communism; the pressure of the United States; and the new colonial policies adopted in Western Europe. Gaining strength through mutual support, this combination of nationalist pressures within Africa and external pressures from overseas proved so powerful that it bore fruit more quickly than anyone expected. Finally, it should be recalled that all seven of these factors were further stimulated by

[5] *U.D.A. London Letter*, March 8, 1947.

World War II. If they are underlying causes which, in their origins, antedate the war, the war nonetheless served as their catalyst. Among its most significant results was the establishment of the United Nations which, as the next four chapters show, was to have a powerful impact on Africa.

Part I

Africa and the United Nations

2

Africa in the United Nations

EARLY in its history, the United Nations Trustee-
ship Council received a petition which attracted widespread amuse-
ment. It came not from Africa but from St. Joan's Social and Political Alliance, an organization of Catholic women in England who
complained that the Fon of Bikom, a chief in the British Cameroons,
had 600 wives! When the Council sent its first visiting mission to
West Africa in 1949, its members trudged up a Cameroons moun-
tain to investigate the complaint. The mission received a frosty reception from the Fon and many of his people who, resentful of inter-
ference with an accepted tribal tradition, obviously thought the
United Nations ought to mind its own business. In any case, the mission reported, the Fon had only 110 wives, 44 of whom were of advanced age, having been inherited from a previous Fon. Moreover,
although 30 wives had already left him, the rest remained voluntarily,
the Fon's polygamy providing them a form of social security. The
mission therefore contented itself with recommending legal safe-
guards for wives in polygamous marriages, along with education toward the gradual abandonment of the custom.

The Fon soon discovered, nonetheless, that the impact of the
United Nations on Africa was greater than he realized. The story of
how other wives began to leave him has been graphically related in

21

Rebecca Reyher's *The Fon and His Hundred Wives*, a readable account of her visit to the old chief's compound. However, according
to a later report with an apocryphal ring, the Fon's gloom ultimately
turned to joy. He decided the United Nations was marvelous, since
it enabled him to make a fortune by recovering a £40 dowry for every
wife who left him!

IMPACT OF THE U.N.

The Fon of Bikom is not the only person who, at one time or another, has felt that the U.N. ought to mind its own business. The
method of U.N. intervention in the grave Congo crisis which erupted
in 1960 angered many Africans, not only in the Congo but in other
African states. Africa's 5,000,000 whites also turned against the
United Nations because of its stimulus to the independence movement which gave birth to 22 African states between 1956 and 1960.
In Europe, some of the best-known and most respected authorities
on Africa were highly critical. If only the United Nations did not
exist, they said, Europe and Africa might be able to iron out their differences and disagreements in a way advantageous to the peoples of
both continents and to the nations of the free world. This attitude
attracted numerous sympathizers as U.N. quarrels over Africa widened
in scope and increased in bitterness. Although it was largely irrelevant,
since the facts of life can't be dealt with by wishing they didn't exist,
it was nonetheless an interesting view because of its basic assumption that the United Nations, even in its early years, had a profound
impact on Africa.

To analyze the nature and extent of this impact, many questions
must be asked. How did recommendations by the United Nations
Trusteeship Council affect the seven African trust territories which
contained about 10 percent of Africa's population and 7 percent of
its area? In what way did the Committee on Information from Non–
Self-Governing Territories help the 100,000,000 inhabitants of 19
other African territories under its annual review? These are only the
most obvious questions.

By 1950 it was becoming apparent that a second type of question
was more significant. In November, 1949, the General Assembly had

adopted a resolution of major political import to make Libya independent, to federate Eritrea with Ethiopia, and to establish a 10-year timetable for independence in an Italian-administered trust territory of Somaliland. The Somali precedent foreshadowed Africa's "year of decision" in 1960, and soon raised a number of pertinent political questions. To what extent were United Nations activities stimulating African political activity? How was African behavior affected by the visiting missions sent by the Trusteeship Council to study the trust territories on the spot and to listen to the views of the inhabitants? What was the total impact of the thousands of petitions and other communications from Africans examined by the Council, and of the steadily mounting number of oral hearings in New York granted to Africans by both the Council and the General Assembly?

Did this awakening of Africans to their opportunities and capacities for advancement prove helpful by bringing the colonial relationship to a quicker end and enabling Africa to rise more rapidly to its full potentialities? Or did the unbridled attacks on the colonial powers in the United Nations play into the hands of extremists by jeopardizing orderly evolution toward self-government and by weakening the spirit of cooperation necessary to make the U.N. work effectively?

By 1960, when Africa took the biggest step in its transformation from a vast colonial domain into a continent of independent states, questions of a third type became more vital: those involving the growing potentiality of the United Nations and its many specialized agencies as multilateral instruments for the provision of technical assistance and capital to new states. Because the United Nations stimulated the march to independence, many members believed it had a special responsibility to help strengthen the economic, social, and educational foundations of the new political entities. In any event, the new nations themselves besieged the U.N. with many more requests for economic and technical assistance than had come from their colonial rulers in the past decade.

To evaluate the total impact of the United Nations on Africa, one must subject these many and varied questions to systematic analysis. First of all, however, it is essential to explain two important facts about the U.N.'s evolution. One of these is the remarkable proliferation of U.N. machinery affecting Africa, and the other is the emotional and highly political atmosphere in which this machinery operated.

THE BACKGROUND OF THE TRUSTEESHIP QUESTION

When the United Nations Charter was signed in San Francisco in 1945, many observers believed that most U.N. work regarding Africa would be undertaken by the Trusteeship Council. This view clearly underestimated the depth of the disagreement at San Francisco, and failed to anticipate the powerful emotions generated by the idea of colonialism in the next decade. The rigid negativism with which the colonial powers were to resist expansion of United Nations activities in Africa is easier to understand if one bears in mind its historical background.

The conflict of views at San Francisco was at times so deep as to seem irreconcilable. No trusteeship proposals were ripe for discussion because the colonial question had been postponed during the Dumbarton Oaks conversations from August 21 to October 7, 1944. At Yalta four months later, President Roosevelt, Prime Minister Churchill, and Marshal Stalin had agreed on certain basic principles to guide the draftsmen of the Charter: (1) the Big Five should meet prior to the San Francisco Conference to agree on trusteeship proposals to be presented to the United Nations; (2) trusteeship should be applied to League of Nations mandates, to territory taken from the enemy as a result of World War II, and to any other territory voluntarily placed under trusteeship; (3) all specific territorial settlements were to be a matter for subsequent agreement, and were therefore not to be discussed either in the preliminary meetings of the Big Five or at San Francisco. After President Roosevelt returned from Yalta, an interdepartmental committee worked out a revision of United States trusteeship proposals, which was approved by the President on April 10, two days before his death. But the preliminary meeting of the Big Five, which was to have been held in Washington, was delayed until too late by a controversy in the United States on the issue of whether to annex or to place under trusteeship the Pacific islands taken from the Japanese.

The major source of controversy, however, was the reluctance of colonial powers to accept the idea of a trusteeship system with extensive powers of international supervision. Many influential Europeans opposed any international trusteeship system at all. Although such views did not prevail, they illustrate the complexity of the problem. Several months before the San Francisco Conference, Britain's Secretary of State for the Colonies, Colonel Oliver Stanley, declared that the mandates system "was a conception which belonged more to the old theory of colonial trusteeship than to the modern conception of colonial partnership; more to the passive era of colonial administration than to the present dynamic age."[1] Jean de la Roche, a leading spokesman for the French, expressed the similar belief that the narrow tutelage involved in the concept of trusteeship was outmoded by a formula of association which brings the colonies and mother country closer together. Britain's distinguished Africanists, Lord Lugard and Lord Hailey, whose extensive colonial experience entitled them to a hearing, wrote in a similar vein. Lugard, noted for his "indirect rule" in Nigeria and for his work in the League of Nations Permanent Mandates Commission, opined in January, 1945, that the present mandates may have served their purpose and should be annexed by the mandatories providing the latter continued to issue annual reports on their work. Lord Hailey, widely known for his monumental *African Survey*, suggested that the relations between colonial powers and colonies should be as senior and junior partners rather than as trustees and wards.

Postwar internationalism proved too strong for those views, however. After many stormy private meetings and numerous gloomy predictions of impending failure, the disputants finally agreed to the compromises embodied in the three chapters of the Charter devoted to the advancement of colonial peoples. The ambiguities and loopholes in the Charter which made this agreement possible were subsequently bared in headlong conflicts over their interpretation by colonial and anticolonial members of the United Nations. For example, Article 2(7) attempts to ban U.N. intervention in "matters which are essentially within the domestic jurisdiction of any state," but Article 10 authorizes the General Assembly to discuss and make

[1] *British Information Services*, Press Release R4286, January 19, 1945.

recommendations on any questions or matters within the scope of the Charter. And Article 77 makes provision for but does not oblige states to place any of their dependent territories under trusteeship. To the disappointment of many observers, only seven African and four Pacific island territories taken from Germany in World War I or from Italy or Japan in World War II were placed under trusteeship. The population of these territories, as shown in the *United Nations Demographic Yearbook for 1960*, is listed in Table 1.

TABLE 1.   Territories Under the U.N. Trusteeship System

Trust Territory	Administering Authority	Area	Population	Date
Tanganyika	United Kingdom	360,000	9,238,000	1960
British Cameroons	United Kingdom	34,081	1,652,000	1960
British Togoland	United Kingdom	13,041	436,000	1956
French Cameroons	France	166,489	3,225,000	1959
French Togoland	France	21,893	1,442,000	1959
Ruanda-Urundi	Belgium	20,535	4,780,000	1959
Somaliland	Italy	178,000	1,990,000	1959
New Guinea	Australia	93,000	1,376,000	1959
Nauru	Australia	8	4,000	1959
Western Samoa	New Zealand	1,133	104,000	1959
Trust Territory of the Pacific Islands	United States	829	76,000	1960

SOURCE: *United Nations Demographic Yearbook for 1960*, New York, 1961. Table prepared from various data on pp. 99–150.

Because the placing of these territories under trusteeship was somewhat delayed, it was not until 1947 that the trusteeship system went into operation. From that time onward anticolonial members engaged in a more or less constant if not systematic campaign to extend the African activities of the United Nations throughout the whole U.N. system in a manner which went far beyond what the colonial powers thought they had agreed to in the Charter. The proliferation of African discussions in almost all U.N. organs, councils, commissions, committees, and agencies was a development of major significance. To illustrate it, let us highlight the Africa work of the six principal organs of the United Nations—the Trusteeship Council, the Economic and Social Council, the Security Council, the International Court of Justice, the Secretariat, and the General Assembly.

OPERATIONS OF THE PRINCIPAL U.N. ORGANS

The most intensive study of African territories was carried on in the Trusteeship Council. Although the seven trust territories in middle Africa represented a relatively small proportion of the continent's total area and population, they nonetheless afforded the United Nations an opportunity for detailed scrutiny and comparison of the colonial objectives and methods of Britain, France, Belgium, and Italy. During its semiannual sessions, the Council made many recommendations to these administering authorities—many more, in fact, than its predecessor, the Permanent Mandates Commission. At least every three years each territory was also studied on the spot by one of the visiting missions, usually of four members, sent out annually by the Council. When the petitions that trickled into the Council in the early days increased to a flood, the Council had to create a Standing Committee on Petitions to meet between as well as during Council sessions. A Committee on Administrative Unions was also created to examine annually those administrative arrangements which provide common public services for a trust territory and an adjacent territory under the sovereignty of the same power. From time to time, the Council also appointed special committees to deal with other matters, including higher education and rural economic development.

The study of annual reports and the sharp questioning of special representatives from each trust territory enabled the Council to measure the territory's progress during the year, to appreciate more fully the difficulties of the administering authority, to praise its achievements, and to single out its failures for criticism. As the trust territories neared independence, the United Nations in several instances sent commissioners with teams of Secretariat officials to supervise plebiscites ascertaining the freely expressed wishes of the inhabitants regarding their political destiny. Thus, after a decade of accountability to the United Nations, the African trust territories began to attain self-government or independence—British Togoland as an integral part of Ghana on March 6, 1957; French Cameroons as the Republic of Cameroon on January 1, 1960; French Togoland as the Republic of Togo on April 27, 1960; the northern British Cameroons as an integral part of Nigeria on June 1, 1961; the southern British Cameroons as a part of the Republic of Cameroon on October 1, 1961; Tanganyika on December 9, 1961; and Ruanda-Urundi on July 1, 1962, as two states, the Republic of Rwanda and the Kingdom of Burundi.

A second principal organ of the United Nations is the Economic and Social Council (ECOSOC), which deals with a multitude of economic, social, cultural, educational, health, human rights, and related activities of the United Nations and the specialized agencies. Through its many subsidiary commissions it began to initiate programs for Africa as the movement to aid underdeveloped areas grew. The effort to expand these African activities led to the establishment of an Economic Commission for Africa, which first met in Addis Ababa in December, 1958. Another of the Council's subsidiary organs, the Human Rights Commission, devoted many heated discussions to Africa, particularly during controversies over the right of self-determination.

Delegations desirous of attacking colonialism as a denial of the right of self-determination could thus do it not only in the Trusteeship Council but in the Human Rights Commission, which reports to the Economic and Social Council; then in ECOSOC itself; and finally in the General Assembly, where the reports of ECOSOC and the Trusteeship Council are discussed. Clyde Eagleton, writing on "Excesses of Self-determination" in the July, 1953, issue of *Foreign Affairs*, contends:

The speeches go far beyond anything hitherto thought of in connection with self-determination; it is not merely independence which the speakers demand, but perfect satisfaction for all human desires. Furthermore they would limit the claims to self-determination to colonial peoples only; and thus self-determination is made the basis of combination against the colonial powers and against the domination of the white race.

In the Security Council, aside from an early discussion of the Anglo-Egyptian Sudan, African questions did not come to the fore until 1960, when the nationalist storm had reached the stage of major physical violence in South Africa, the Belgian Congo, and Angola. On April 1, 1960, the Security Council for the first time adopted a resolution censuring South Africa, 10 days after the Sharpeville riot of March 21 in which 68 Africans were killed and 186 wounded by police fire. The first Security Council resolution on the Congo crisis was adopted on July 13, 1960, and its first resolution on Angola on March 12, 1961. The bloody conflict in Algeria, which was discussed annually in the General Assembly from 1955 onward, was drawn to the attention of the Security Council on several occasions beginning in 1955, but the Council decided not to discuss the substance of the problem.

A fourth of the principal United Nations organs into which African questions gradually made their way was the International Court of Justice, which gave three advisory opinions on South-West African issues between 1950 and 1956, and a decision in 1952 in the dispute between France and the United States over the rights of the latter in Morocco. When South Africa persisted in defying U.N. resolutions regarding South-West Africa, a move which might prepare the way for sanctions against the Union Government was initiated. Liberia and Ethiopia, as former members of the League of Nations, submitted to the Court in 1960, under Article 7 of the mandate, a complaint that the Union of South Africa had failed to comply with the terms of its mandate over South-West Africa. This step was made possible by Article 37 of the Court's Statute, under which it assumes certain functions of the Permanent Court which existed during League days. The forging of the final link in this legal chain would be up to the Security Council. If the Union failed to "perform the obligations incumbent upon it under a judgment rendered by the Court," Article 94 of the United Nations Charter provides that "the other party may have recourse to the Security Council, which may, if it deems necessary, make recommendations or decide upon measures to be taken to give effect to the judgment." This might include economic or even military sanctions to force the new republic to comply with the Court's decision on the South-West African issues raised by Liberia and Ethiopia. And if Security Council action were blocked by the veto of one or more of the five permanent members, the opponents of South Africa might seek a two-thirds vote of the General Assembly for sanctions. Many members of the General Assembly, however, would undoubtedly question whether the South-West African issue is the type of threat to "international peace and security" which would justify the grave precedent of invoking sanctions.

The U.N. Secretariat, the fifth principal organ, has also played a significant role in helping to expand U.N. activities affecting Africa. Secretariat officials have proved themselves not only competent but indispensable in enabling the United Nations to carry on its work. Over the years they have produced voluminous and invaluable documentation on Africa. It has not been an easy task, partly because of the difficulty in obtaining accurate and up-to-date information, and partly because of the conflicting pressures exerted on the Secretariat by colonial and anticolonial powers.

In the first decade of the United Nations, these international civil servants had to walk a tightrope on the emotional colonial issue. The delicacy of their position was indicated by the fact that when some of them exercised their individual initiative to assist anticolonial delegates in the preparation of speeches and draft resolutions, they were criticized by delegates of the administering authorities. Secretariat officials like to play a creative part in expanding the role of the United Nations in Africa. On a number of occasions some of them went so far that certain administering authorities felt they violated their obligation under Article 100 of the Charter to "refrain from any action which might reflect on their position as international officials responsible only to the Organization." In 1960, ironically, they were under attack from a new quarter. The Soviet bloc accused them of being pro-Western in the Congo crisis. Another significant development after 1960 was the increasing number of Africans appointed to the Secretariat.

The sixth principal organ of the United Nations and the most important of all in expanding its African activities is the General Assembly. Its African discussions and recommendations steadily grew from year to year until they touched upon nearly all the continent's areas and problems—the disposition of the Italian colonies; the Tunisian, Moroccan, and Algerian questions; the unification movements in Togoland, the Cameroons, and Somalia; the granting of oral hearings to many African petitioners; the three perennial South Africa agenda items; the Angola rebellion and other Portuguese Africa problems; the Congo crisis; and many others.

The Assembly carries on its work through seven main committees, each of which is composed of delegates from all U.N. members. Although the Fourth or Trusteeship Committee, often confused with the smaller Trusteeship Council, is the main body dealing with colonial questions, African issues arise with greater or lesser frequency in all the other committees as well. In fact, anticolonial members, after an unsuccessful move in one committee, occasionally make a similar effort in another.

The Fourth Committee was responsible for a major constitutional evolution in the relations between the Trusteeship Council and the General Assembly. Since the membership of the Trusteeship Council was evenly divided between administering authorities and nonadministering members, the anticolonial group was unable to persuade the Council to adopt measures to which the colonial powers took strong exception. As a result the Council was sometimes attacked as a tool of the colonial powers, and the anticolonial members brought more and more African issues into the Assembly, where they held a voting majority. This led the Assembly to take over functions which, in the view of the colonial powers, should have been concentrated in the Trusteeship Council. A good example is the important practice of granting oral hearings to Africans from trust territories.

Another major constitutional evolution in the United Nations was the Assembly's creation of the Committee on Information from Non–Self-Governing Territories. Since the Charter provides no specific machinery to help Africans who live in colonies outside the trusteeship system, the noncolonial powers used Article 73(e) as an entering wedge. They persuaded the Assembly to create a committee to examine the information transmitted under this article to the United Nations by the colonial powers on dependent territories outside the trusteeship system. Despite strong contentions that the Committee was unconstitutional, the next step of the anticolonial group was to press for extension of its tenure and terms of reference with a view to making it eventually into an organ such as the Trusteeship Council. This, of course, was partly motivated by the failure of the administering authorities to place any territories other than former League of Nations mandates under the international trusteeship system.

Proposals emanating from the Fourth Committee have also led the General Assembly to create numerous other committees affecting Africa, including committees on South-West Africa, on Angola, on administrative unions, and on the problem of defining a non–self-governing territory. At the twelfth session of the Assembly in 1957 the presence of new members from Africa gave additional impetus to this movement to expand U.N. activities. By 1957, the majority of noncolonial members over the colonial powers was 72 to 10, a notable increase over the old ratio of 52 to 8 which prevailed for nearly a decade. As a result the rigid attitude of the colonial powers began to show occasional signs of bending, whether consciously or unconsciously, under the weight of this anticolonial preponderance and, in particular, under the pressure of the growing number of African states with which they had to deal.

A particularly revealing example of the proliferation of U.N. activities affecting Africa is the Assembly's resolution of November 26, 1957, recommending that the Economic and Social Council "give prompt and favorable consideration to the establishment of an Economic Commission for Africa." This resolution, adopted by a vote of 78 to 0 with Belgium abstaining, is significant because it marks a sharp reversal in the attitude of the colonial powers and the United States, which had opposed earlier proposals for the establishment of an Economic Commission for Africa. At the time of these earlier proposals, the colonial powers were launching the six-power Commission for Technical Cooperation in Africa South of the Sahara (CCTA), and it was argued that a U.N. Economic Commission would duplicate CCTA efforts. The CCTA was then, however, little more than a name. By 1957 it had built up a widespread organizational network in many fields of economic and social cooperation, had admitted Ghana and Liberia to membership, and had invited other African states to join. One might therefore think that a U.N. Economic Commission for Africa would be even more repetitious and unnecessary than it was said to be in 1950.

Such an assumption overlooks one important fact. The earlier proposals came from non-African states. In 1957, however, it was Ghana which made the proposal, supported by Egypt, Ethiopia, Liberia, Libya, Morocco, the Sudan, and Tunisia—all African states—as well as 21 other cosponsors. The United States boarded the bandwagon early, and the United Kingdom, after abstaining in the Fourth Committee, switched to an affirmative vote in the plenary session of the General Assembly with the weak explanation that it did not consider the resolution mandatory on ECOSOC.

Finally, mention should be made of the growing African activities of the specialized agencies, among them the World Health Organization (WHO), Food and Agriculture Organization (FAO), International Labor Organization (ILO), U.N. Educational, Scientific, and Cultural Organization (UNESCO), and the International Bank for Reconstruction and Development (IBRD). Their relations with the U.N. are governed by special agreements which vary with each agency. By 1960 their programs for Africa had greatly expanded, and three of them had established regional offices in Africa south of the Sahara—WHO in Brazzaville, the ILO in Lagos, and the FAO in Accra. Their operations will be described in Chapter 4.

CONFLICTING EMOTIONS

The second important fact about the evolution of the United Nations is the increasingly emotional atmosphere in which much of this expanding machinery operated. Time and again the depth of feeling of both colonial and anticolonial delegates has affected U.N. discussions even on technical and procedural questions. In a classic speech to the General Assembly on November 14, 1951, Chaudhri Mohammed Zafrullah Khan of Pakistan condemned colonialism as a vicious and evil relationship which degrades both the dominator and the dominated. Citing examples of personal indignities suffered by his countrymen under British rule, he contended that the spirit of the whole system was impregnated with a lack of courtesy and an insulting arrogance which demeaned the dignity of the human person. "As an indispensable measure for the upholding of prestige and the maintenance of authority," he said, "those who are dominated cannot be accepted as . . . equals by the instruments through which domination is exercised. On occasion, arrogance may be tempered with condescension, but the mixture is even more nauseating than the plain article." It is this spirit, he concluded, which makes subject peoples resent alien domination with such fierce passion, and makes them regard the abolition of colonialism as the biggest political problem of the day.[2]

National and personal pride are also deeply felt by the rulers, as is evident in the remarks made to the General Assembly on October 21, 1952, by British Minister of State for Colonial Affairs Henry Hopkinson. "My own feeling in this matter," he said, "is one of intense pride in our achievements in what may be described as the colonial field over several hundreds of years."[3] The emotions which U.N. disputes are capable of arousing are also well illustrated in Sir Alan Burns's 1957 book, *In Defence of Colonies*. At the end of a distinguished career of more than 40 years in the British colonial service, Sir Alan was appointed in 1947 to a quite different post as United Kingdom Representative on the Trusteeship Council. His lifetime of experience, he hoped, would enable him to play a constructive role in the tradition of Lord Lugard in the Permanent Mandates Commission of the League of Nations. For nine years, however, he had to listen too often to what he regarded as a "venomous" berating of the major ideas and ideals of his life. This experience, he writes, "completely disillusioned" him regarding the value of the U.N.'s efforts to help colonial peoples. Sir Alan's account of this ordeal is less a defense of colonies than a provocative attack on anticolonialism. It tells us as much about his own emotions as it does about the United Nations.

Lest the wrong impression be conveyed, however, a word of caution is in order. These emotions, while deeply felt, are expressed relatively seldom in open debate. One who attends a session of the Trusteeship Council or even of the less-restrained Trusteeship Committee of the General Assembly usually finds the proceedings quite prosaic and tedious after the novelty has worn off. In the art of "trusteeman-

---

[2] United Nations General Assembly, *Official Records*, Sixth Session, 343rd Plenary Meeting (A/PV.343), 14 November 1951, pp. 114–115.

[3] U.K. Delegation to the U.N., mimeographed text of speech to the Fourth Committee, October 21, 1952.

ship," much time is spent by delegates in carefully calculated maneuvering to put their opponents at a procedural disadvantage. Both the colonial and the anticolonial groups have their private meetings behind the scenes in which their strategy is planned. The anticolonials, with the advice of friends in the Secretariat, maintain constant pressure to extend the system of international accountability. But they are not so emotional that they cannot beat a coolly rational retreat, if they consider it desirable, when they push the administering authorities to the point of boycotting U.N. machinery.

Controversy over colonialism nonetheless weakened the United Nations, at least in the short run, by shaking the confidence and cooperation of its members. The colonial powers signed the Charter in good faith, and subsequently did much to advance dependent peoples on the road to self-government. But they soon found they did not have the protection they thought Article 2(7) gave them; they found that the protection inherent in the evenly divided membership of the Trusteeship Council was inadequate because the Council was responsible to the General Assembly where they were greatly outnumbered; they found that the protection they had in the wording of Article 73(e) disappeared when the Assembly appointed an extraconstitutional committee to discuss non–self-governing territories; and they found that every year they were confronted with new proposals to extend the system of international accountability, which they regarded as illegal attempts to amend the Charter by General Assembly resolutions. That is why they came to regard the colonial activities of the United Nations as a "necessary evil," and to fight any extension of these activities as a slippery slope to something worse. This rigid negativism naturally irked the enemies of colonialism and enhanced their suspicions of Western motives.

The intemperate partisanship of numerous United Nations members led some observers to call for a return to the use of impartial experts, following the practice of the Permanent Mandates Commission of the League of Nations. Pierre Ryckmans, Belgium's first representative on the Trusteeship Council, had appeared a generation earlier before the members of the Mandates Commission to answer their questions on Belgian administration of Ruanda-Urundi. Since he respected the Commission experts and their criticism, he felt not only an official but a personal need to be able to show improvements in Ruanda-Urundi when he returned the following year. His experience in the Trusteeship Council, however, led him to contend that the motives of its members were too political to merit this kind of respect from local administrators.

The idea of returning to League practice was nonetheless impractical because it disregarded the profound changes that have taken place in the composition and political climate of the society of nations since the days of the League. Impartial experts could not have insulated themselves from this new political climate without being ignored. Moreover, even if the recommendations of the Mandates Commission experts were less resented than those of Trusteeship Council politicians, it does not necessarily follow that they were more effective. The occasional biting edge in trusteeship recommendations provoked emotional reactions, but it had an indirect psychological effect in prompting the colonial powers to move faster, if only to show that criticisms in the United Nations were sometimes unfair.

3

The United Nations in Africa: Political Influence

WITH this account of U.N. behavior in mind, we can now evaluate the impact of the United Nations on Africa during its first 15 years by focusing on the general questions raised at the beginning of the last chapter. First, have Africans made tangible gains as a direct result of U.N. recommendations? Second, how have U.N. activities affected the political behavior of Africa's peoples? And third—this question to be discussed in Chapter 4—how much has Africa benefited from technical assistance and economic aid from the United Nations and the specialized agencies?

THE EFFECT OF RECOMMENDATIONS ON AFRICA'S ADMINISTRATORS

At the outset it should be recalled that the U.N. is not a world government but a democratic society of more than 100 sovereign nations. Generally speaking, these nations have only been willing to let the General Assembly make recommendations which, as the word implies, are not obligatory. Only with respect to threats to the peace, breaches of the peace, and acts of aggression does the Charter, in Articles 41 and 42, provide for the use of economic, military, and

37

other sanctions to maintain or restore international peace and security.

It is therefore difficult to find evidence of direct results of U.N. recommendations, if only because the administering authorities often contend that sooner or later they would have taken a particular step whether or not it was recommended by a U.N. body. In fact, many U.N. resolutions only "invite," "request," "urge," or "recommend" that "as soon as practicable" or "at the earliest possible moment" the administering authorities take steps that are already in their development plans.

The mechanical method by which the Trusteeship Council turned out annual recommendations on each trust territory was perhaps inevitable. Instead of concentrating on a few outstanding problems and giving the administering authority a limited but workable number of suggestions which hard-pressed administrators could seriously consider during the year, the Council members made suggestions on a wide variety of subjects and then appointed a drafting committee for each territory to combine these suggestions into recommendations that could win a majority vote. Almost invariably the result was a series of recommendations, often repetitive and redundant, on each of the four general fields into which the Council divided its business —political, economic, social, and educational. However, even if recommendations had been fewer in number, it is not certain that busy officials would have given them more attention.

Nonetheless, numerous examples can be cited of steps taken by administering authorities after the Trusteeship Council has recommended them, and of steps which the administering authorities did not take because of the watchful eyes of the Council. Changes sometimes result from the initiative of a colonial administrator who has been pressing his government toward a particular course of action and who cites U.N. recommendations as additional arguments for his cause.

Europeans and Africans alike have praised the constructive influence of the mandate and trusteeship systems on race relations in Tanganyika. In his autobiographical *African Afterthoughts*, Sir Philip Mitchell, who served in numerous Tanganyika posts from 1919 to 1935, writes that "not a little of the credit" for the model race relations in Tanganyika belongs to the terms of the mandate, under which all forms of discrimination were illegal "except such protective discrimination as backward people must have until they are able to stand on their own feet."[1] Other observers have contended that its mandate status retarded Tanganyika's economic development before World War II because potential investors feared the territory might be sacrificed to meet the colonial demands of Nazi Germany. Sir Philip, however, avoids criticism of the mandate on such grounds. In his view, economic development was slow because Tanganyika had poor communications, poor land, tsetse fly, and unreliable rainfall. In another of his interesting afterthoughts he suggests that perhaps it was just as well that material development was slow because it provided time for the territory to develop good human relations among all the races living there.

The helpful influence of international supervision on Tanganyika's race relations is also stressed by an African, B. T. G. Chidzero, in his scholarly 1961 analysis *Tanganyika and International Trusteeship*, which points out that in Tanganyika there is no system of land reservation and no unchecked alienation of land in favor of the economically stronger section of the population. Moreover, in contrast to Kenya and Southern Rhodesia, there is no "legally sanctioned, or administratively condoned," residential segregation of races. Sharp questioning in the Trusteeship Council regarding the ambiguity of "multiracialism" as a political doctrine for Tanganyika led the special representative of the United Kingdom in 1956 to reply that Tanganyika was nonracial rather than multiracial, a position explained in 1957 by the Governor, Sir Edward Twining, as follows:

Although we have called our policy a multi-racial policy, I think it can be better described as a non-racial policy, by which I mean that all the peoples of Tanganyika, no matter what their origin, will be given equal opportunities, will be treated in exactly the same manner, and will achieve positions on their own merits and not because of any racial consideration.[2]

Tanganyika also provides a good example of the effectiveness of the United Nations in deterring an administering authority from steps

[1] Sir Philip Mitchell, *African Afterthoughts*, London, 1954, p. 67.
[2] *Tanganyika Standard*, May 19, 1957.

it might otherwise take. The clearest case in point is the influence of Tanganyika's mandate and trusteeship status in helping to prevent the success of the white settler movement in establishing a closer political union between Kenya, Uganda, and Tanganyika; both the Permanent Mandates Commission and the Trusteeship Council carefully insisted on safeguarding the distinct international status of Tanganyika until it attained self-government or independence. When the movement for a political union failed, the government of the United Kingdom created an administrative union of the three territories after World War II to provide common services in such matters as customs, posts and telegraphs, railways and scientific research. In response to this and comparable arrangements in other territories, the Trusteeship Council established a Standing Committee on Administrative Unions to serve, in the words of United States Representative Francis B. Sayre, as a "watchdog" to undertake an annual review of the operation of all administrative unions to ensure that they did not obstruct the separate development of trust territories as distinct entities.

Belgium, while reacting strongly against many U.N. views, also modified its trust territory policy partly in response to U.N. pressure. The first visiting mission to Ruanda-Urundi and Tanganyika in 1948, which was severely criticized by both the Belgians and the British, made a deeper impression than was acknowledged at the time. The Trusteeship Council commended certain economic and social developments in Ruanda-Urundi, but it called on the Belgian government to provide higher education for Africans and to give them responsible posts in the government. Council discussions publicized the fact that while the British and French had many Africans studying in universities overseas and working in responsible administrative posts, the Belgians did not. This publicity alone was a form of pressure on the Belgians, even if the Council had not adopted recommendations on the subject.

In Belgian theory the best way to advance Africans was to begin with social and economic development and primary education. When the Belgians were confronted, however, not only with U.N. criticism but also with the example of their British and French allies, the combination was too difficult to resist. The influence of the United

Nations was therefore one of the factors that induced Belgium in 1951 to begin sending the first Ruanda-Urundi students to Belgium for higher education, to bring the two African rulers of Ruanda and Urundi into the Vice-Governor General's Council, to develop institutions of local government further, and to establish two universities in the neighboring Congo in 1954 and 1956.

Unfortunately, as the Congo debacle of 1960 proved, it was another case of too little and too late. Unlike most British and French territories, neither the Congo nor Ruanda-Urundi had enough Africans with higher education and modern political experience when independence came. The Belgians clung too long to the mistaken conception that their evolutionary Africa policy could be pursued in isolation from the powerful revolutionary currents stimulated by the pressure of world opinion. Portugal and South Africa not only made the same mistake, but drew the wrong lesson from the Belgian experience by insisting that it only proved the evil of going too fast.

The recommendations of the Committee on Information from Non–Self-Governing Territories, which was created to deal with territories outside the trusteeship system, were less effective than those of the Trusteeship Council because of constitutional limitations on the Committee's powers. Unlike the Trusteeship Council, it was not a principal organ of the U.N. but a subsidiary committee of the General Assembly. It could not send visiting missions into Africa or examine petitions from Africans. Moreover, it could not direct a recommendation to a particular government on a situation in a single territory; the Assembly limited it to making general recommendations on economic, social, and educational—but not political—conditions in non–self-governing territories.

Committee members often did refer to conditions in individual territories, however, and they sometimes crossed the indefinable borderline to discuss political conditions. In several cases in which an administering authority ceased to transmit information to the U.N. on a particular territory on the grounds that it had achieved self-government, the Committee engaged in a detailed debate on the political and constitutional status of the territory. Perhaps the most interesting example of this development was the trouble the United States had in 1953 in persuading the Assembly to accept, by a vote of 26 to 16 with 18 abstentions, the decision of the United States to stop sending information on Puerto Rico to the United Nations—Puerto Rico having decided that it wanted self-government in a new form of association with the United States.

Because of its limited terms of reference, the Committee's discussions often dealt with general principles rather than particular situations, and it is difficult to point to any specific action, other than the provision of additional information, taken by the administering authorities as a result of the Committee's work.

Attempts by the anticolonial group in the Assembly to extend the Committee's powers were met with determined opposition by certain administering authorities, who regarded the very existence of the Committee as unconstitutional. Belgium withdrew from the Committee in 1953, and others threatened to do so. Evidently believing that the best defense is a strong offense, the Belgians accompanied this withdrawal from the Committee by further elaborating their complaint that all members, not just the colonial powers, should report to the United Nations under Article 73(e) on the aboriginal populations under their jurisdictions. This Belgian thesis, as it came to be known, was elaborated in detail by Fernand van Langenhove, Belgium's Permanent Representative in the United Nations, in his book *Le Problème de la Protection des Populations aborigènes aux Nations Unies.* Under the Belgian thesis, the United States would have to report to the United Nations on the American Indians, and a large number of states without colonies would have to report on aboriginal peoples within their "metropolitan" territory. Whatever merits the Belgian thesis may have had, it was regarded in the United Nations as a defensive smoke screen for Belgian policy. It won no approval from the anticolonial group and little support from the colonial powers.

Withdrawals or threats of withdrawal also occurred in the Assembly's Fourth or Trusteeship Committee over the question of whether the Assembly itself had the right to discuss political (as opposed to economic, social, and educational) conditions in territories not under trusteeship. While the anticolonial group contended that the General Assembly did have this right, a view shared by many delegations because of the Assembly's broad powers under Article 10 to discuss anything within the scope of the Charter, they did not force the issue to a showdown, evidently because they feared that certain administering authorities would cease to cooperate with the Assembly.

The nature and significance of this problem was strikingly illustrated in the Fourth Committee's treatment of the Central African Federation issue in 1953. Britain's federating of the two Rhodesias and Nyasaland was one of the most notable African developments since World War II. This action went against the wishes of a large majority of those African leaders in the area who took part in the controversy, several of whom requested the Reverend Michael Scott, an Anglican clergyman, to make their opposition known to the United Nations. He did so in a written communication to the chairman of the Fourth Committee. The Committee decided to circulate the communication as an official document, and the representative of India precipitated a crisis by asking that delegations wishing to discuss the problem should be given the opportunity. The issue was critical because the Central African Federation was not an item on the agenda; because certain administering authorities believed the Fourth Committee did not have the legal competence to discuss political conditions in non–self-governing territories; and because the communication from the Reverend Scott concerned a non–self-governing territory rather than a trust territory, and the Charter makes no provision for the consideration of petitions from the former. In addition to these legal objections, the United Kingdom was strongly opposed to any United Nations action which might inspire further political agitation in the three territories and weaken its efforts to make the Federation a success.

The British Delegation therefore not only refused to discuss the substance of the issue, but served notice that the United Kingdom might be "unable to continue to cooperate in the work of the Committee" if the matter were made the subject of debate. The Committee then adopted a face-saving Indian motion which, in effect, kept the debate open on the subject in the event that any delegation wished to revert to it later. The strong British stand accomplished its purpose, for the subject was not mentioned again until the last meeting of the Committee six weeks later when the representative of India read a brief statement criticizing the establishment of the

Federation, and referring also to the Mau Mau crisis in Kenya and the deposition of the Kabaka of Buganda. The incident was closed when the British representative replied that he had no comment to make on an episode which was, in substance, outside the scope of the Committee's work.

These events were significant partly because they illustrated one of the limitations on U.N. action affecting Africa and partly because they indicated that the British feared a U.N. discussion might have a strong impact on a critical African problem.

EFFECT ON AFRICAN POLITICAL BEHAVIOR

The second general question raised in this analysis is how U.N. activities have affected the political behavior of Africa's peoples. Although more intangible, this question is easier to answer, and is more significant than the problem of demonstrating that U.N. recommendations brought specific benefits to Africans. In the perspective of history, it will probably appear that the most powerful impact on Africa of the United Nations during its first 15 years was its stimulation of political agitation among colonial peoples.

In the trust territories the widely heralded visits of the Trusteeship Council's visiting missions conveyed to the people the feeling that the outside world wanted them to advance. It was the establishment of the United Nations which revived the abortive Ewe and Togoland unification movement. The coming of the first visiting mission to the Ewe area in 1949 gave local politicians a unique opportunity to arouse mass interest in the movement. In its report to the Trusteeship Council, the mission has related how an Ewe propapanda barrage began even before the mission landed at Lomé airport, for as their plane descended members could see at a long distance huge placards inscribed with the word *Unification* borne by a large crowd. The mission reported that it felt "it was in the presence of a rather highly organized and intelligently conducted movement not unlike movements in their own countries."[3] As the mission traveled through

[3] United Nations Trusteeship Council, Official Records, Seventh Session, 1 June–21 July 1950, *Reports of the United Nations Visiting Mission to West Africa and Related Documents*, Supplement No. 2 (T/798), p. 86.

the two Togolands it was met by large gatherings, and, if an unofficial report is correct, some of the faces seen among demonstrators in southern Togoland appeared again among northern crowds.

Like most petitioners to the United Nations, the Togolanders who asked for either Eweland or Togoland unification failed to get precisely what they asked for. When the Trusteeship Council found that there was no form of unification on which a majority would agree, it avoided any recommendation for unification, proposing only certain steps to facilitate freedom of movement across the Anglo-French frontier. Indirectly, however, the resulting political agitation induced the administering authorities, particularly the French, to inaugurate a number of political reforms. The widespread publicity given the problem encouraged those Togolanders who supported France and opposed the unificationist party to ask for faster progress toward self-government. When this pro-French party, whose sympathies France wanted to hold, added its demands to already existing pressures, Paris was really under fire. The resulting changes made Togoland something of a pilot project for self-government in other French African territories.

Meanwhile, unfortunately, bitter feelings were aroused particularly among French Togolanders, whose disagreements led to occasional outbursts of violence, in one of which seven Africans were killed. Even in the U.N. thinly veiled threats of violence were made by unificationist leaders in the hope of winning support. The disillusionment resulting from the inevitable discouragement of the unificationists for a time strengthened the hand of younger and more radical leaders.

The Ewe and Togoland unificationist movement also set a questionable precedent by encouraging unificationist movements in other areas of Africa where ethnic and political boundaries do not coincide. Local politicians were able to exploit a unificationist movement in the two Cameroons by whipping up support for rival parties. When the U.N. stepped in to supervise plebiscites in 1960 in the northern and southern sections of the British Cameroons, 60 percent of the northerners voted to join independent Nigeria, while 70 percent of the southerners voted to join the independent Republic of Cameroon formerly under French administration. This divided vote precipitated one of the bitterest wrangles in United Nations history at the fifteenth session of the General Assembly in 1961. A flood of African petitioners descended on the Assembly to challenge the fairness of the vote despite the careful supervision by the U.N. itself. The former French Cameroonians denounced the British and Nigerians for fraudulent electoral maneuvers in the northern section. In the U.N. corridors they spread the private rumor that unless the U.N. plebiscite were reversed the Cameroons would go Communist. When the Fourth Committee rejected their appeal after a long and heated debate, the Cameroon delegates walked out in high dudgeon at 2 A.M. followed by the French and Belgian Delegations and the African delegations of a number of French Community states. The key to this hectic quarrel lay in the realities of political power in the Republic of Cameroon, where the government of Premier Ahidjo depended heavily on the support of Moslem northerners and therefore needed additional voters from the northern British Cameroons.

In view of the fireworks over the northern vote, the turbulence in the south was a rather sad and whimsical anticlimax. Here the defeated minority, which had voted to join Nigeria, unsuccessfully petitioned the U.N. to divide the southern Cameroons. With an African interpretation of self-determination which challenged majority rule, a Balondo petitioner whose minority group had voted 22,495 to 9,454 to join Nigeria rather than the former French area said to the Assembly: "If five people were asked to choose between eating rice or eating potatoes for their dinner, and three chose rice while two chose potato, you do not compel the two who don't like the taste of rice to eat rice because more people had chosen rice." In an impassioned peroration he concluded that "we are irrevocable *never* to accept union with the Cameroun Republic. If on this we have to be killed to the last man it should rather be better that history records how a race of men died to the man fighting for freedom."[4] The Assembly did not wish to upset its own plebiscite, however, and voted to approve the results in both the northern and southern Cameroons under British administration.

The impact of the United Nations in stimulating political agita-

[4] Mimeographed statement by N. N. Mbile, distributed in accordance with the decision taken by the Fourth Committee at the 1142nd meeting.

tion is also clear in Tanganyika. The Tanganyika Africa National Union, led by Julius Nyerere, grew rapidly after 1954 when a visiting mission angered the British by affirming that self-government was within the reach of the people of Tanganyika much earlier than the 20 to 25 years the same mission suggested for the Belgian trust territory of Ruanda-Urundi. While the United Nations did not create Tanganyika nationalism, it certainly encouraged it by giving Africans new confidence in the validity of the demands made by their nationalist leaders. The U.N.'s close scrutiny also tended to restrain the inclination of British authorities to restrict political agitation. British policy favored gradual evolution toward self-government, and the pace of political progress in Tanganyika had long been slow. After 1954, however, the combination of international pressure and nationalist demands was too great for the United Kingdom to resist. Political advances came in rapid succession, culminating in Tanganyika's independence on December 9, 1961, far sooner than Tanganyika nationalists had thought possible five years before.

Another vital U.N. activity which helped to stimulate politics in the trust territories was the increasing practice of granting oral hearings to enable petitioners to express their grievances in person at the United Nations. By the end of 1961 the Trusteeship Council had granted 41 of 71 appeals for oral hearings, and the General Assembly had granted 177 of 179 requests. Although they rarely got what they asked for in New York, these petitioners stimulated much political excitement at home, both while raising money to pay for their trips and in recounting their experiences upon their return. Several of them later became prime ministers or presidents, including Abdullahi Issa in Somalia, Sylvanus Olympio in Togo, and Julius Nyerere in Tanganyika. In the beginning they appealed to the Trusteeship Council, but as time passed practically all of them came to the General Assembly where they could plead their cases before all members instead of only the 14 in the Trusteeship Council.

Outside the trust territories, evidence of U.N. stimulus to political activity is less tangible but nonetheless real. No visiting missions may enter other areas, and no regular channels for petitions are available except for the inhabitants of South-West Africa. It is therefore more difficult for their problems to reach the United Nations. Items for discussion in the General Assembly must be formally proposed by states rather than individuals, and must be approved by a majority of U.N. members before being placed on the agenda.

Nonetheless, Algerian, Moroccan, and Tunisian nationalists in North Africa waged from the beginning a persistent campaign for U.N. help. Tunisian leader Habib Bourguiba first came to New York in November, 1946. Until 1951, the North Africans were disappointed because no state would formally present their case to the U.N. Meanwhile, however, the Assembly decided to make neighboring and less-developed Libya an independent state, thereby providing the nationalists in French territories an additional argument for their cause. Finally, in 1952, the Moroccans and Tunisians succeeded in getting their demands on the Assembly agenda at the instigation of 13 Arab-Asian states. Only four years later, to the surprise of even the nationalists themselves, Morocco and Tunisia were granted independence by France. The Algerians, however, had to resort to arms and to fight more than six years longer before they were allowed to determine their own political status.

France contended that North African questions were outside the Assembly's competence and refused to participate in certain Assembly debates. French anger at U.N. intervention at first stiffened the French position, and nationalist leaders were punished with jail or exile. Once again, however, the combination of nationalist demands and international pressure proved too difficult for long resistance. It is often argued that the French did not capitulate because of U.N. pressure, but it cannot be denied that the sympathy of world opinion expressed through the U.N. was a continual encouragement to the nationalists to struggle until the French gave in.

At the southern end of the continent, as will be seen in Chapter 5, "The Impact of World Opinion on South Africa," a similar process was under way although the eventual outcome was less clear. Every year for many years, three South African items appeared on the Assembly agenda. Like the French, the South Africans boycotted some of the discussions, contending that the Assembly had no legal competence to intervene.

Moral judgments as to whether the political agitation encouraged by United Nations activities was helpful or harmful are largely influenced by individual bias. Some observers contend that it was harmful because it upset the orderly evolution of Africa toward self-government based on adequate economic, social, and educational foundations. Others argue that Africa could be remade only by its own people, and that anything which awakened their consciousness of their capacity for advancement was therefore constructive. Possibly both views are irrelevant, since the ferment in Africa began before the United Nations was created and would have quickened even if there had been no U.N. to encourage it.

4

The United Nations in Africa: Economic Aid

THE third aspect of U.N. impact on Africa consists of the slowly but steadily growing program to provide technicians and capital to help build enduring economic and educational foundations for political freedom and stability. On December 19, 1961, during its sixteenth session, the General Assembly adopted two resolutions, 1710 and 1715, calling for an intensified program of international economic cooperation. Resolution 1710 designated the current decade as "United Nations Development Decade," with the objective of attaining in each under-developed country "a minimum annual rate of growth of aggregate national income of 5 percent at the end of the decade." Resolution 1715 asked member states to raise the combined budgets of the Expanded Program of Technical Assistance and the Special Fund to $150,000,000 in 1962.

The remarkable expansion of aid programs and activities within the framework of the U.N. in the 17 years since World War II was largely unexpected and therefore followed no preconceived plan. Technical assistance is provided not only through numerous programs within the U.N. itself, but also by most of the 12 specialized agencies and, since 1958, by the International Atomic Energy Agency, each of which has its own constitution, membership, secretariat, rules of procedure, and budget. The scope, trends, and costs of these various programs and the problem of coordinating their overlapping efforts are dealt with at length in a consolidated report for the U.N. Economic and Social Council (E/3347/rev.1). This document also contains a valuable chart, shown in Figure 1, which indicates the budgetary growth pattern of the major agencies between 1947 and 1960.

Millions of dollars

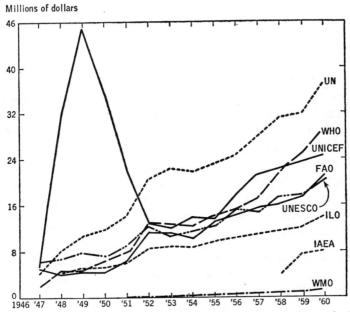

Fig. 1.   Total expenditure estimates (regular budget and extrabudgetary funds) for economic and social activities, 1947–1960. Source: United Nations, Department of Economic and Social Affairs, *Five-Year Perspective, 1960–1964,* E/3347/rev.1, Geneva, 1960, p. 116.

With the advent of 16 new and needy African members in 1960, the U.N.'s opportunities in this area soared, giving rise to the hope that its major influence in the Africa of the future might be its activities as a multilateral aid agency. Its potentialities were clouded, however, by political instability in the new states, along with the simultaneous intensification of the ideological struggle between the Western and Soviet blocs. The Congo crisis raised in many minds the question of whether the U.N. could even survive. It is worth recalling, therefore, that in February, 1961, while the U.N. was still reeling under the shock of "Afro-American" rioters screaming "Lumumba! Lumumba!" in the packed public gallery of the Security Council, the U.N. Economic Commission for Africa was calmly exchanging ideas on the economic development of Africa at its third session, in Addis Ababa. Time and again delegates emphasized their desire to have more aid channeled through multilateral agencies, especially the United Nations.

THE GROWTH OF ASSISTANCE PROGRAMS

For the first 15 years, United Nations technical assistance to Africa was understandably small in contrast to the major development programs of the colonial powers. It was even smaller than the limited technical assistance program of the United States in Africa, which totaled only $13,000,000 as late as 1956. The U.N.'s Expanded Program of Technical Assistance, which budgeted a mere $444,891 for four African territories in 1950–1951, had risen to only $2,200,000 in 1956, serving 22 African territories by sending 156 Africans to study overseas and sending 288 technical experts to Africa. The slow growth of these early years is indicated in Table 2 on direct project costs for Africa in the Expanded Program.

TABLE 2. Direct Project Costs for Africa in the Expanded Program of Technical Assistance

Year	Costs
1950–1951	$ 442,000
1952	1,347,000
1953	1,497,000
1954	1,279,000
1955	1,799,000
1956	2,244,000
1957	2,915,000
1958	3,387,000
1959	3,746,000
1960	4,278,000
1961–1962	20,088,000

SOURCE: United Nations Office of Public Information, *The United Nations and Africa*, New York, February, 1962, p. 17.

TABLE 3. Total Number of Expert Assistantships and Fellowships[a] Provided for Africa Under the United Nations Expanded Program of Technical Assistance Between 1950 and 1960

Country	Experts	Fellows	Country	Experts	Fellows
Libya	738	576	Congo (Leopold-ville)		25
Egypt	599	471	Bechuanaland	13	
Ethiopia	319	115	British Somaliland	7	5
Liberia	205	187	Mali		12
Sudan	204	127	Basutoland	5	5
Tunisia	165	104	Gambia	7	2
Morocco	146	73	Swaziland	8	
Ghana	117	52	Chad	5	1
Somalia	63	56	Ivory Coast	2	4
Tanganyika	95	15	French Equatorial Africa		5
Nigeria	47	57	Senegal		5
Federation of Rhodesia and Nyasaland	15	34	Dahomey		4
Cameroon	12	34	Ruanda-Urundi	4	
Kenya	19	24	Congo (Brazza-ville)		3
Sierra Leone	29	9	Niger		3
French West Africa	10	27	British Cameroons	2	
Uganda	10	25	Spanish West Africa		2
British East Africa	28	6	Upper Volta		2
Togo	16	18	Mauritania		1
Guinea	19	13	Spanish Guinea		1
Portuguese Territories	1	28	French Somaliland		
Algeria	6	20	Gabon		
Zanzibar	21	5			

[a] Those serving more than one year are counted for each year they served.

SOURCE: Prepared by the author from various Annual Reports of the Technical Assistance Board and other U.N. sources.

A striking perspective on the limited scope of the U.N.'s early activities was given to the Committee on Information from Non–Self-Governing Territories by the representative of Belgium on October 1, 1952. By the end of March, 1952, he pointed out, the

United Nations and its specialized agencies had recruited only 1054 technicians for the 1,500,000,000 people in all the underdeveloped countries, while Belgium had 4673 full-time European officials, most of whom were of the expert caliber sought by the U.N., serving the 11,500,000 Africans of the Congo. While the U.N. Food and Agriculture Organization had 271 experts and a budget of less than $6,000,000 for its world program on January 1, 1952, the Belgian Congo agricultural service had 633 European technicians and $14,600,000 for its 1952 program.

In the early years the bulk of U.N. assistance went to the independent states of Libya, Egypt, Ethiopia, and Liberia, partly because they needed and asked for help and partly because they had no colonial rulers to provide them assistance. The initial coolness of the colonial powers toward U.N. assistance projects for their own territories began to diminish as the practical value of U.N. assistance for agricultural, educational, health, and other projects was demonstrated. Since the U.N. was partly responsible for the rapid advance of economically weak territories to self-government, most of its members began to feel an increasing responsibility to provide them material aid as well as moral support. As Table 3 (p. 53) shows, however, independent states continued to be the principal recipients of aid throughout the 1950s.

"PARTICIPATING ORGANIZATIONS" AND TYPES OF PROGRAMS

The bureaucratic ramifications of U.N. technical assistance activities are difficult to clarify because of the numerous "participating organizations," which include the United Nations Technical Assistance program (UNTA) under the direction of the Bureau of Technical Assistance Operations and 7 of the 12 specialized agencies—the International Labor Organization (ILO), Food and Agriculture Organization (FAO), United Nations Educational, Scientific, and Cultural Organization (UNESCO), International Civil Aviation Organization (ICAO), World Health Organization (WHO), International Telecommunications Union (ITU), and World Meteorological Organization (WMO). The International Atomic Energy Agency (IAEA) is also a participating organization.

Moreover, several different types of programs have developed over the years. These include (1) the Regular Programs carried out by the UNTA, the ILO, UNESCO, WHO, and the IAEA, and financed by annual assessments on their numbers; (2) the larger Expanded Program of Technical Assistance, established in August, 1949, financed by the voluntary contributions of governments and administered by a Technical Assistance Board composed of the Secretary General and the heads of the participating organizations; (3) the Special Fund, also financed by voluntary contributions of governments, which went into operation on January 1, 1959, under Managing Director Paul G. Hoffman to undertake projects larger in scope than those aided by the Expanded Program; and (4) the OPEX program, financed out of the UNTA's regular budget, which was started in 1959 to provide "operational and executive personnel" who work not as U.N. employees but as part of the civil service of the underdeveloped countries which request them.

The distinction between the Regular and Expanded Programs is based primarily on budgetary considerations and is somewhat artificial in terms of their operational activities. Both concentrate on (1) sending experts to advise, teach, or work in underdeveloped countries, and (2) granting fellowships to enable technicians or prospective technicians in the underdeveloped countries to attend schools or do on-the-job training, usually overseas. Where necessary, equipment may be provided to assist the expert technician or fellowship holder. In 1960, the budget for Regular Programs in Africa totaled $2,900,000, while the total for the Expanded Program was $4,200,000.

Under these programs the United Nations Bureau of Technical Assistance Operations carries out a wide range of activities, like sending UNTA experts to establish Public Administration Institutes in Egypt in 1953 and Ethiopia in 1956 and a School of Public Administration in Libya in 1954. More recently, advisory services have been made available to the majority of independent African countries on such matters as industrial development and productivity,

natural resources development, fiscal policy and financial institutions, housing, community development, and social welfare. Another
type of project is a valuable training program for African economists
begun in 1957, under which a number of African civil servants each
year are given six-month fellowships to broaden their experience in
problems of economic development by study at U.N. headquarters
in New York.

The OPEX program, which provides U.N. operational, executive,
and administrative personnel to work in developing countries, grew
from a small $200,000 budget in 1959 to a modest $850,000 in the
U.N. budget for 1961. The number of appointees is therefore limited.
Each officer enters the service of the requesting government to perform specific duties assigned to him by that government; in other
words, rather than serving as an adviser responsible to the U.N., he
works for and is paid by the local government the same salary a national of that country would receive. His salary is supplemented by
the U.N. to bring it into line with the pay of internationally recruited experts. An OPEX appointee is also obligated to train local
personnel to take his place as soon as possible. By mid-1961 only
$88,000 had been allocated for four African countries—Libya, the
Sudan, Ethiopia, and Guinea—but the program has much potential
for the future.

The inauguration of the Special Fund in 1959 marked the begin-
ing of a new, improved, and expanded U.N. program for African
development. The aim of the Special Fund is to raise production
and productivity through "preinvestment" activities which carry the
work of technical assistance programs a step forward and lay the
groundwork for capital investment. The Special Fund has only a
small staff to review requests for aid. It utilizes the administrative
machinery of the Expanded Program. When it approves a project it
appoints an executing agency, usually one of the specialized agencies,
to carry it out. The Special Fund differs from the Expanded Program
in that it concentrates on a smaller number of comparatively large
projects, and provides a larger amount of supplies and equipment.
Another improvement is the fact that the Managing Director of the
Special Fund has greater executive authority and is more independent
of Economic and Social Council politics. The Fund is also strength-

ened by a new requirement that recipients make counterpart contributions to its projects. And it is able to make longer term aid commitments, up to five or six years. The possibility of merging the U.N.'s other technical assistance operations with the Special Fund is being studied, but the Specialized Agencies prefer the older system which makes additional money available to them.

By March 31, 1962, the Special Fund had approved commitments of $173,352,300 for 205 projects.

Geographical Area	Number of Projects	Special Fund Allocation
Africa	53	$ 42,551,900
The Americas	57	50,520,500
Asia and the Far East	64	55,589,900
Europe	7	5,321,400
Middle East	23	15,502,600
Interregional	1	3,866,000
Total	205	$173,352,300

SOURCE: United Nations Special Fund, *Status of Projects Approved by the Governing Council as of 31 March 1962,* SF/Reports, Series A., No. 19, New York, March 31, 1962.

With the counterpart contributions of local governments, the total budget for these projects was more than doubled. They included the establishment of secondary schoolteacher training institutes in several African countries, vocational training programs in others, an Institute of Public Administration in Ghana, and numerous soil, water resources, fishery, and other surveys.

Most of these are projects of several years' duration. For example, the Secondary Schoolteacher Training Institute for the Republic of Cameroon is a six-year project supported by a Special Fund allocation of $1,174,800 and a Cameroon Republic counterpart contribution of $1,518,000. Cameroon needs 1500 secondary schoolteachers during the next decade to meet the expected increase in secondary school enrollment from the present 7000 to 31,000. The Special Fund project will assist in establishing and operating, at least initially, the teacher training institute by providing teaching staff, fellowships, and equipment. Located at Yaoundé, the Institute will have a capacity of 200 students and will include a documentation and research center.

THE WORK OF THE SPECIALIZED AGENCIES

To explain more precisely how the specialized agencies fit into the African technical assistance activities of the United Nations family, let us examine each of them in turn.

UNESCO provides technical assistance mainly through its program of "special activities" to meet specific needs of member states in free and compulsory education; fundamental education; racial, social, and international tension problems; mutual appreciation of the cultural values of East and West; and scientific research aimed at improving standards of living. On February 8, 1962, the Ghana Parliament voted a credit of $182,000 to build an office in Accra for a UNESCO Regional Center for Africa.

Since 1958, UNESCO's Regular Program has been more closely integrated with the Expanded Program, and technical assistance activities are now formulated as a whole, regardless of the budget to which they will eventually be charged. The educational needs of new states sparked a major expansion of UNESCO's African activities after 1960. As of February, 1961, its Africa program totaled $15,639,534, divided among the following budgets:

Regular Program	$2,500,000
Expanded Program	4,012,359
Emergency Program	2,250,000
Special Fund Projects	2,782,500
ONUC (Congo)	4,094,675

UNESCO held Africa Conferences at Addis Ababa in February, 1960, and May, 1961, the latter under joint auspices with the U.N. Economic Commission for Africa. The 1961 Conference, which stressed the need to relate educational development closely to economic growth, set ambitious goals to achieve universal primary education in Africa by 1980, as is shown in the following schedule giving the percentage of school-age students in school:

	1960	1965	1970	1980
Primary	40	51	71	100
Secondary	3	9	15	23
Higher	0.2	0.2	0.4	2

The Conference also projected the estimated costs of African educational programs for the next 20 years, including the amount needed from foreign aid. The costs shown are in millions of dollars.

Year	Total Cost	Needed from External Financing
1961	$ 580,000	$ 140,000
1962	650,000	150,000
1963	820,000	260,000
1964	940,000	310,000
1965	1,150,000	450,000
1970	1,180,000	1,010,000
1980	2,600,000	400,000

Since most African countries have yet to complete a comprehensive analysis of their education needs, the above figures can only be regarded as "guesstimates." Whether the needed external aid will be forthcoming and whether economic development will generate the revenues necessary to meet local costs are imponderables which make this statistical house of cards even shakier. Setting up such goals is nonetheless a useful way to illustrate the magnitude of the problem.

The World Health Organization, which has a large regional office in Brazzaville, has concentrated on the control of communicable diseases. The budget for 1962, however, shifted to an emphasis on the strengthening of national health programs in Africa, allocating 63 percent of its funds for this purpose. In the field of disease control, the most encouraging successes by the end of 1959 were achieved in the control of yaws (17,000,000 people examined in Africa and 8,000,000 treated), leprosy (more than 1,000,000 of the estimated 2,300,000 cases brought under treatment), tuberculosis, and smallpox. Malaria and bilharziasis have proved more expensive and more difficult to control. WHO has established a Malaria Eradication Special Account for contributions to help in the fight against this widespread disease. In recognition of its responsibilities to the new African states, the thirteenth World Health Assembly increased the 1961 effective working budget by $200,000 for newly independent or emerging states. It has been estimated that the total budget for all

WHO activities in Africa in 1962 is about $4,300,000, not including Special Fund projects.

The Food and Agriculture Organization, which established an African regional office in Accra in 1959, does not pursue separate technical assistance activities under its Regular Program. However, many of its Expanded Program projects originate in the work conducted under the Regular Program. It has sponsored several regional meetings in Africa on technical subjects, and held its first FAO Regional Conference in Africa from November 3 to 12, 1960, in Lagos to review food and agricultural policies and programs. The organization concentrates on measures to increase the production of crops, livestock, fish, and forests, with attention also given to general problems of land and water use.

Africa has benefited from several FAO Special Programs, such as the World Seed Campaign of 1957-1961 and the Freedom from Hunger Campaign, which began in 1960. In 1961, with an appropriation of $200,000, a Special Africa Program was undertaken to assess the main problems and first priorities for agricultural development in selected African countries. In his Program of Work and Budget for 1962-1963, the Director General stressed the need for generous supplementary appropriations to launch a Special Program for Education and Training in Africa similar to that envisaged by UNESCO and other specialized agencies.

The International Labor Organization, which established a field office in Lagos in 1959, has a small regular budget for operational activities. Its first African Regional Conference, held in Lagos in December, 1960, was attended by delegates from 36 African countries. It should not be forgotten that the ILO has a long-standing interest in Africa. It appointed a Committee of Experts on Native Labor in 1926, which was replaced by a Committee of Experts on Social Policy in Non-Metropolitan Territories in 1947 and by its present African Advisory Committee in 1959. The technical assistance work of the ILO was largely confined to North Africa until 1958. Since then its activities have been carried on throughout the continent, and include such projects as the operation of industrial productivity centers, vocational training, rural industry and handicraft training, rural cooperative work, and assistance in the field of social security and labor administration.

Unlike the other specialized agencies, the ILO has sometimes functioned as a quasi-political body. During the struggles for Moroccan and Algerian independence, French colonial policies were discussed at ILO meetings. And in June, 1961, the ILO Conference adopted by a vote of 163 to 0 with 89 abstentions a Nigerian proposal to expel South Africa because of that country's racial policies. It is possible that ILO conventions regarding freedom of association may cause friction with those African governments in which a dominant political party has sponsored a single national labor federation, such as Guinea, Ghana, and the Ivory Coast.

The International Civil Aviation Organization has developed a Regional Plan for Africa which includes 117 airports, 139 established air routes, 200 radio circuits between stations on the ground for specifically aeronautical purposes, 328 electronic aids to air navigation, and 127 meteorological forecasting stations for aeronautical purposes. The ICAO's technical assistance program concentrates on the training of technical and administrative personnel for these air facilities. In February, 1961, there were 43 ICAO technical experts serving in six African states.

The World Meteorological Organization budgeted $527,400 for 39 technical assistance projects in 17 African countries for 1961–1962. In the Congo, for example, a chief meteorological expert was appointed in August, 1960, and was joined by 12 other experts by mid-1961. In this case the experts actually did the work, mainly forecasting, rather than acting only as advisers. The WMO has also drawn up a five-year plan to train Congolese nationals to assume practically all professional functions in the Congolese Meteorological and Geophysical Service.

The International Telecommunications Union also has a limited technical assistance program, which it began to expand in Africa in 1961-1962. For example, it is the executing agency for a Special Fund project in Libya—a Radio and Telecommunications School in Tripoli to include courses for radio technicians, telephone technicians, and radio and telephone mechanics. It is a five-year project with a total budget of $1,183,600, about half of which was allocated by the Special Fund.

The International Atomic Energy Agency, which functions with respect to the U.N. Technical Assistance program in much the same manner as a specialized agency, undertakes a wide variety of projects connected with the mining, production, and use of nuclear materials. The Africa program of the IAEA has been small—involving 10 fellowships and one expert assignment in 1960—but considerable expansion is expected in the future. In 1960 a special mission visited Africa and the Middle East to study the possibility of establishing a regional training center for the area, and training courses were organized in the use of radio isotope techniques, including their application to medicine and agriculture.

The United Nations Children's Fund (UNICEF), which also cooperates with but is not one of the specialized agencies, has brought vital help to Africa. Converted in 1950 from an emergency operation, it is now concerned mainly with the long-range needs of children. By January, 1961, UNICEF had allocated $22,715,000 for Africa, which has been matched in recent years by recipient government contributions of $2 or more for each $1 allocated by the Fund. UNICEF aid concentrates on three types of projects: control or eradication of communicable diseases, maternal and child health and welfare services, and nutrition. UNICEF not only establishes and equips village and other health centers, but it provides or aids in the local production of insecticides, antibiotics, vaccines, and serums, and it distributes to school and preschool children and pregnant and nursing mothers rations equivalent to a large cup of milk daily and sometimes vitamin A and D capsules. Its disease control projects in Africa have helped to reduce malaria, yaws, syphilis, leprosy, and trachoma. It also has a small emergency aid program which, for example, provided blankets for Algerian and other refugees in Tunisia and Morocco in 1959. UNICEF is provided certain technical assistance and consultative services by other U.N. agencies.

Finally, in addition to technical assistance, Africa needs capital. Major help in meeting this need has been provided by still another specialized agency in the United Nations system, the International Bank for Reconstruction and Development or World Bank, which established a new Department of Operations for Africa on April 12, 1962. By February 8, 1962, the World Bank had made 41 loans totaling $929,000,000 in 16 African areas as indicated in Table 4. This was about 15 percent of all loans made by the Bank.

TABLE 4.   World Bank Loans to Africa Through February 8, 1962

Country	Number of Loans	Amount
Algeria and Sahara	2	$ 60,000,000
Congo (Leopoldville)	5	120,000,000
East Africa	1	24,000,000
Egypt	1	56,500,000
Ethiopia	5	26,000,000
Federation of Rhodesia and Nyasaland	5	146,600,000
French West Africa	1	7,500,000
Gabon	1	35,000,000
Ghana	1	47,000,000
Kenya	2	13,600,000
Mauritania	1	66,000,000
Nigeria	1	28,000,000
Ruanda-Urundi	1	4,800,000
South Africa	10	211,600,000
Sudan	3	74,000,000
Uganda	1	8,400,000
Total	41	$929,000,000

SOURCE: Prepared by the author from International Bank for Reconstruction and Development, *The World Bank in Africa*, Washington, July 1961, p. 72, and from other data supplied by Bank officials.

World Bank loans are made for a wide variety of projects in agriculture, communications, electric power, general development, highways, industry, irrigation, mining, oil pipeline, ports, and railroads. More than half the amount lent has gone into transportation projects, with power development second. One impressive achievement aided by the Bank with an $80,000,000 loan in 1956 is the Kariba Dam across the Zambezi River, a few hundred miles downstream from Victoria Falls. This 420-foot-high dam has created the largest man-made lake in the world, and its generators transmit electric power to industries in Southern Rhodesia and to the copper belt of Northern Rhodesia. Another notable example is the $66,000,000 loan for the development of high-quality iron ore deposits in the desert country of Mauritania, which will involve the building of a township at Fort Gouraud to mine the ore, the construction of a railway to the sea, and the building of port and other facilities at Port Etienne on the Atlantic Coast. In addition to its lending operations, the World Bank provides considerable technical assistance. This is also true of two other specialized agencies, the International Monetary Fund, whose primary function is to promote international monetary cooperation, and the International Finance Corporation, which invests directly in private enterprise, without government guarantees.

In the fall of 1960, an affiliate of the World Bank, the International Development Association, came into existence to provide capital on easier terms for projects unsuitable for World Bank loans. By the end of June, 1961, it had made "development credits" of $100,000,000 available, including one Africa credit of $13,000,000 for the Roseires Dam on the Blue Nile in the Sudan. IDA credits are repayable over 50 years with no interest; the recipient pays 75 percent for administrative expenses.

THE ROLE OF THE ECA

In addition to the above analysis showing the role of the specialized agencies in Africa, special mention must be made of the United Nations Economic Commission for Africa (ECA). This new organization provides an institutional means to enable Africans to play an effective role in programming U.N. technical assistance. Established in 1958 with permanent headquarters in Addis Ababa, the ECA corresponds to the other U.N. regional economic commissions established in Europe, Latin America, and the Far East. In February, 1962, its membership consisted of 29 independent African states and 5 European powers which still administered dependent areas in Africa. It was staffed by about 70 professional officers headed by Executive Secretary Mekki Abbas. Consultative status at its meetings has been accorded to several other U.N. members, including the

United States and certain specialized agencies and private organizations. ECA's growing range of activities includes projects to survey resources, to develop and improve statistical services, to train development planners, and to develop inter-African transportation and trade. It is also considering the establishment of an African Development Bank.

At its third annual meeting in 1961, delegates expressed the opinion that the Commission was an African organization and that as such its membership should be confined as soon as possible to African countries. A resolution sponsored by 14 independent African states was passed requesting that the non–self-governing territories in Africa participate in the work of the Commission as associate members and that they be represented by Africans at its next meeting. However, one of its operative paragraphs, which would have ended the membership of Belgium, France, Portugal, Spain, and the United Kingdom, was defeated.

BILATERAL GRANTS AND LOANS

By mid-1961 the African efforts of the U.N. had attained a new dimension. Africa had risen to first place among the five regions of the world receiving U.N. aid. For the two-year period 1961-1962, the Expanded Program of Technical Assistance budgeted more than $20,000,000 aid to Africa, a sharp rise over the $4,000,000 budget for 1960. In 1961 alone, all U.N. economic and social assistance to 42 African countries totaled over $30,000,000, plus $63,200,000 in World Bank loans. In addition, the Civilian Operations Mission in the Congo was authorized to spend $14,000,000 between July, 1960, and May, 1961.

To place these statistics in perspective, however, it must be pointed out that 90 percent of the aid to Africa in 1960, which totaled $1,400,000,000, was bilateral assistance. According to estimates in *The United Nations and Africa*, published by the U.N. Department of Public Information in February, 1962, the major bilateral sources of aid in 1960 were $732,000,000 from France, $231,000,000 from the United States, and $144,000,000 from the United Kingdom.

SUMMARY

These three chapters on African issues in the United Nations have dealt mainly with the years between 1945 and 1960 when Africa was still predominantly colonial. The form of the problem has substantially changed since 1960 when 16 African states joined the U.N. The most recent African crises in South Africa, the Congo, Angola, and elsewhere and their far-reaching impact on international relations will be highlighted in later chapters.

In summary, the impact of the U.N. on Africa during the first 15 years after World War II was many-sided but often intangible. It is misleading to overconcentrate on evaluating the direct results of U.N. recommendations. The manifold pressures, tensions, and demands fostered or encouraged by the U.N. are more significant. The U.N. proved to be more than a "mirror" and to have more than "nuisance value." U.N. discussions forced governments and peoples to recognize that the future of Africa had become a vital problem in international relations. By encouraging African demands for faster political advance, the U.N. upset the policy of gradualism advocated by the colonial powers. It indirectly helped African petitioners to become prime ministers. It served as a useful training school in diplomacy for future African leaders. It had a unique effect in international relations by enabling new African states to enter the U.N. family of nations almost automatically, or at least without having to establish themselves according to the old pattern of diplomacy before their entry into international affairs. And the U.N. performed a valuable service by collecting and publishing a massive documentation which stimulated and assisted the serious study of Africa.

As for U.N. recommendations and resolutions, they are often redundant and frequently ignored. This is inevitable and in fact inherent in the nature of international organizations. Nonetheless, the trust territories and indirectly the other territories in Africa as well did benefit from the fact that every year the colonial powers presented their records and defended their policies before the United Nations. This system of international accountability, even when its excesses angered and disillusioned the administering authorities, continually prodded them to reappraise and perfect their colonial policies and methods. Even the African inhabitants of South-West Africa have benefited in material ways, despite the South African government's rigid defiance of U.N. resolutions. Perhaps U.N. criticism has the indirect psychological effect of provoking governments to further action, if only to prove their integrity to themselves.

The future of the U.N. in Africa will, of course, depend on its general effectiveness, which seemed in jeopardy in 1962 when 14 members were refusing to pay their share of the cost of the U.N. operation in the Congo, and many other members were in arrears. The U.N. will also be affected by the future of race relations, that is to say, by the ability of white and nonwhite peoples to cooperate despite the racial attitudes, suspicions, and tensions that are reflected in the U.N. The crucial importance of this racial factor makes the explosive tension in South Africa so dangerous to the rest of the world. Because South Africa has been subjected to a barrage of U.N. resolutions and other external pressures for more than 15 years, it provides an unusually interesting case study of the impact of world opinion on Africa.

5

The Impact of World
Opinion on South Africa

MOST South African whites are adamant in their rejection of U.N. criticism. Prime Minister D. F. Malan, addressing a congress of his Nationalist Party followers on October 21, 1953, denounced the U.N. as a failure and "a cancer gnawing at world peace and tranquility." South Africa has boycotted numerous U.N. General Assembly discussions, contending that the Assembly has no legal competence to intervene in South African affairs. Irked by UNESCO's stand for racial equality, the Union withdrew from it in 1955. Foreign Minister Eric Louw told the South African House of Assembly on May 5 that UNESCO was "a sort of Mecca . . . for academic theorists, for unemployed intelligentsia and . . . quite a number of cranks. . . . South Africa cannot afford to spend £30,000 for flights into cloud cuckoo-land." Prime Minister Hendrik F. Verwoerd, in his 1962 New Year broadcast to the nation, declared that the destruction of confidence in the U.N. as a result of the Congo, Goa, and other crises held much promise for his new republic.

The angry reactions of Malan, Louw, and Verwoerd were shared not only by most Afrikaans-speaking supporters of the Nationalist Party, which has controlled the government since 1948, but also by most English-speaking supporters of the opposition United Party.

The English-language press, despite its strong attacks on the Nationalists, frequently joined them in attacking foreign meddling in South African affairs. Even courageous liberals, who appreciate the moral support of the outside world, often complain about the ignorance and occasional malice of South Africa's critics. Under the continuous pressure of world opinion, however, most South African whites seemed to develop a kind of mental armor which protected them, at least until 1960, from external criticism.

South Africa's whites numbered 3,067,638 in the 1960 preliminary census. They enjoy one of the highest standards of living in the world, and their prosperity has indirectly benefited the country's 10,807,809 Africans or Bantu, 1,488,267 Coloreds of mixed blood, and 477,414 Asians. The budget of South Africa in 1960 was approximately $1,400,000,000, which was roughly equal to the combined budgets of all other African countries excluding Egypt. That is why South Africa's nonwhites are more advanced in material ways than the blacks in any of the new states south of the Sahara. Precisely for this reason they find racial discrimination all the more frustrating and embittering.

THE SHOCKS OF 1960

The three main disputes over which South Africa's whites have been subjected to a constant barrage of U.N. recommendations since 1946 are (1) the refusal of South Africa either to place South-West Africa under trusteeship or to accept its obligations for South-West Africa as defined by the International Court of Justice, (2) the treatment of peoples of Indian origin in South Africa, an issue described in Chapter 10, and (3) the broader question of race conflict in South Africa which developed out of an Indian announcement at the sixth Assembly that it would bring the whole issue of *apartheid* before the next Assembly in 1952. The details of the U.N.'s treatment of these three issues have been described by others; my purpose is to analyze South African reactions to the United Nations and to other external pressures as well.

In the spring of 1960, after 15 years of U.N. attacks, a series of shocks reverberated through South Africa with such force that many observers believed the Union's fiftieth anniversary might prove to be a turning point in its history. South Africans had been upset since mid-1959 by a spreading movement in the outside world to boycott South African goods. Then, on February 3, 1960, after many months of concern over the boycott, they were deeply disturbed by British Prime Minister Harold Macmillan's celebrated "wind of change" speech to South African parliamentarians in Cape Town. The weeks of heated controversy precipitated by Macmillan were followed on March 21 by the devastating jolt of the Sharpeville riot, in which 67 Africans were killed and 186 wounded by police fire; a startling condemnation by the United States State Department less than 48 hours after Sharpeville; the unexpected seizure and imprisonment without trial of 2000 South Africans, including about 100 whites, under a state of emergency proclaimed on March 30; the first intervention by the United Nations Security Council to denounce South Africa on April 1; and the attempt to assassinate Prime Minister Hendrik F. Verwoerd, a unique event in South African history, on April 9. Meanwhile, the value of shares on the Johannesburg stock exchange had plunged £501,000,000 since January 1.

The big question during April and May was whether these shocks would at last crack the segregationist walls of *apartheid*. It was not until May 20 that the world learned the answer was no. Minister of Finance T. E. Donges, speaking on behalf of the Prime Minister, who was still recovering from two bullets fired into his cheek by an allegedly deranged English-speaking gentleman farmer, informed Parliament that the government saw no reason to depart from its policy of separate development of the races. The Prime Minister's rigidity prompted Alan Paton, noted author and national President of the small integrationist Liberal Party, to say: "It is not easy for a white South African who has grown up with a love of his country and a respect for democracy to welcome the existence of pressure from outside on his country. But what alternatives have the Nationalists left us?"[1] Other enemies of the government felt, however, that external pressures only helped the Nationalists win votes by patriotic denunciations of foreign intervention. Both conservatives and liberals from Johannesburg to Stellenbosch were inclined to ask

[1] *Die Transvaler*, May 28, 1960.

whether foreign attacks on *apartheid* really produced any lasting effect, and, in particular, whether they were strong enough to force a change in government policy. It is not an easy question to answer.

MACMILLAN'S "WIND OF CHANGE"

Considering Alan Paton's plea for more external pressure, the reactions of South Africans to foreign criticism are worthy of detailed examination. At the peak of the 1960 crisis there were four major external pressures on South Africa: the boycott movement, the Macmillan speech, the U.S. State Department criticism, and the Security Council resolution. Of these four, the blow with the greatest impact came from Great Britain. This was only natural because of South Africa's long-standing historical, cultural, economic, and other links with the British. After 15 years of hostility from the United Nations General Assembly, South Africans were partially inured to the first attack from another U.N. organ, the Security Council. The unexpected State Department criticism proved quite disturbing; but since it came within 48 hours after Sharpeville, it was generally regarded as a premature and immature judgment of the situation and as a power-politics play in the American popularity contest with the Russians for Afro-Asian favor. The boycott movement, after arousing initial alarm, had moved off the front pages; the public was evidently tiring of seven months of boycott news since the Ghana Trades Union Congress, following a Jamaican lead, announced on July 14, 1959, its plans to boycott South African goods. But British Prime Minister Macmillan's celebrated February 3 speech was big news for more than six weeks. Numerous observers contended that the impact of the speech was so great that South Africa would never be the same again. It therefore provides an intriguing case study of the effect of external pressures on the country.

The text of the speech gives little indication of why it aroused such a tempest.[2] It is a delicate balance of sympathy and criticism which begins with praise, turns to warning, and ends on a note of friendship. After praising the beauty of the South African country-

---

[2] The following quotes are taken from the mimeographed text of the Macmillan address released by the Office of the High Commissioner for the United Kingdom in South Africa on February 3, 1960.

side and the warm friendship and affection of its people, Macmillan emphasized the "immense material progress" the Union had achieved, and expressed pride in the fact that British capital had provided "nearly two-thirds of the overseas investment outstanding in the Union at the end of 1956." Our economies, he added, "are now largely interdependent," with Britain taking one-third of all South Africa's exports and supplying a third of its imports. "Britain has always been your best customer," he said, "and as your industries develop we believe we can be your best partner too."

Having thus put the parliamentarians at ease, the Prime Minister then began to tread on their toes. In words which acquired worldwide fame, he declared that "the wind of change is blowing throughout the Continent." Of all the impressions he had formed in Africa, he found the most striking to be the strength of the "African national consciousness." "Whether we like it or not," it is a political fact. "We must all accept it as a fact," and "we must come to terms with it." Unless we do so, "we may imperil the precarious balance of East and West on which the peace of the world depends." The granting of independence "is the only way to establish the future of the Commonwealth and of the free world on sound foundations."

To this clear statement of the British attitude toward nationalism in Africa, Macmillan now added a diplomatic but blunt commentary on South Africa's racial policy. The old saying, "Mind your own business," he began, should be expanded so that it runs, "Mind how it affects my business too." The aim of the United Kingdom was to create in its territories societies "in which individual merit, and individual merit alone, is the criterion for a man's advancement, whether political or economic. . . . We reject the idea of any inherent superiority of one race over another." Finally, in his most pointed remark of all, the Prime Minister declared:

As a fellow member of the Commonwealth it is our earnest desire to give South Africa our support and encouragement, but I hope you won't mind my saying frankly that there are some aspects of your policies which make it impossible for us to do this without being false to our own deep convictions about the political destinies of free men. . . .

After this straightforward warning, the Prime Minister returned to the sympathetic vein of his earlier remarks. He paid a pleasant tribute to his fellow Scots in South African history, and reminded his listeners that even the United States had found that it could not "live for itself alone." In conclusion, he moved from sympathy to outright support by an unexpectedly strong condemnation of the overseas boycott of South African goods.

SOUTH AFRICA'S REACTIONS TO MACMILLAN'S ADDRESS

The immediate reaction to Macmillan was one of calm, but it was calm before the storm. Prime Minister Verwoerd, in an impromptu but moderate reply, called for justice for the white man too. In its leading editorial the next morning, the government organ, *Die Transvaler*, quietly dismissed the subject by noting that two distinguished statesmen with different backgrounds had spoken and that their views had naturally varied. Three days later, the storm broke in a flamboyant and exaggerated banner headline in South Africa's most widely read newspaper, the Johannesburg *Sunday Times* on February 7: "MAC CHANGES POLITICAL FACE OF AFRICA—SHATTERING IMPACT OF VISIT ANALYZED." Calling Macmillan's address "the gravest international setback the Nationalist Government has suffered since it came to power in 1948," the *Sunday Times*, in three leading articles, exploited to the limit one new "fact" it claimed to have discovered, namely, that "Mr. Macmillan told Dr. Verwoerd that Britain would no longer be able to vote for South Africa at the United Nations."

South Africans of all opinions had meanwhile been thinking over the implications of what Macmillan had said. Dr. G. D. Scholtz, editor of *Die Transvaler*, decided to find out the opinions of his readers. In a leading editorial on February 9 he called on them to express their views as a "moral duty" because the maintenance of white civilization was at stake. This unusual appeal produced such a flood of letters that the paper announced, 13 days later, that it could publish only those letters already received. Seldom in the history of South African journalism, *Die Transvaler* said, had there been such a shining and overwhelming reaction, which "underscores again the truth of the old saying that good is born out of bad."

What was the "good" that came out of the "bad" Macmillan speech? A change of policy? Indeed not! It was the fact that the episode had awakened South Africans to the danger threatening them, and would therefore strengthen their determination to make the sacrifices necessary to make *apartheid* work. This was called South Africa's only possible salvation. *Die Transvaler* even suggested that Dr. Verwoerd invite other British Cabinet members out, in particular Colonial Secretary Iain Macleod, to help frighten awake any remaining ignorant or recalcitrant South Africans. Shortly afterward, Minister of External Affairs Eric Louw added that he knew of nothing in recent years which had "contributed so much to bringing right-thinking English- and Afrikaans-speaking South Africans nearer to each other."[3]

Letters in response to *Die Transvaler*'s appeal were not all hostile to Macmillan, but no sentiment for abandoning *apartheid* was expressed. The only hope for the white man, the letters contended, was to make *apartheid* work. When the English press entered the fray, the Johannesburg *Star* hopefully praised a moderate reaction to Macmillan by the Afrikaner industrialist Anton Rupert, but its most interesting letter was from J. C. Smuts, son of the late Prime Minister, accusing Macmillan of falling into "the classic pitfalls that blind all overseas people who do not live with the problem." Calling himself an "inveterate opponent of the Nationalist government and its suicidal doctrine of Bantustans," Smuts nonetheless wrote that "we shall have to tread an ever more lonely path, for our faith in what is right and proper will force us to diverge ever more steeply from our overseas friends. We have no alternative choice."[4] Smuts concluded with a remark of basic relevance to this study of the effect of external pressures: Macmillan's speech, he said, will "harden Native opinion . . . and spur on agitators," a point to which we will return later.

Among the letters to the *Transvaler*[5] a considerable number were bitterly emotional and dangerously negative. For example, "Boer" of Potchesfstroom wrote: "The West hates us with a venomous hate. . . . To the devil with the opinion of the outside world. . . . God

[3] *Die Transvaler,* February 27, 1960.
[4] *The Star* (Johannesburg), February 10, 1960.
[5] The letters quoted below appeared in the issues of February 13 and 27, 1960.

is still with us"; C. J. Bernard of Graskop said: ". . . we will fight till our last drop of blood"; P. J. Engelbrecht of Durban: "We believe that the Lord is still on our side"; "Afrikaner" of Witbank: "We are ready to give our last drop of blood for our existence"; and Paul Eloff of Mondeor: "We trust in God and do our duty." Macmillan was also attacked from the pulpit by Afrikaner preachers, notably Dominee G. J. J. Boshoff in Johannesburg, who likened the situation to the tale of Herod and John the Baptist: the white man, who brought the Gospel to Africa, is John the Baptist; the black man is the innocent daughter of Herod who is incited by agitators (her mother Herodias) to demand the head of John the Baptist. The weak Herod, in the person of Macmillan, representing poisonous world opinion, gives in to the evil demand!

While these emotional reactions were artifically stimulated by the press, their basic cause must lie deeper. Even if there was little new in Macmillan's speech, it was quite startling that a British prime minister, while a guest of a Nationalist government, should speak bluntly on delicate issues. To add insult to injury, the heresy came from a distinguished Conservative rather than a "hopeless" Labor leader. The Cabinet members must have been aware of the rapid pace of change in Africa, but they evidently expected their guest to be circumspect in speaking about it while in the Union. As for the Afrikaner rank and file as well as many English-speaking whites, it is perhaps true that they were so out of touch with African trends that they were really surprised to find the "wind of change" so near.

Finally, the increasingly sharp reactions of Afrikaner leaders may have resulted from a growing concern over the possible repercussions of the Macmillan episode on the position of the Nationalist Party. Would it strengthen the hands of the Bassons and Fagans in their moderate Afrikaner attack on government rigidity? How would it affect the campaign for a republic, which was already under way? On February 17, *Die Transvaler* suggested the need to establish the republic now in order to "save the situation for white civilization."

After seven weeks of controversy over Macmillan's views, the shooting of African demonstrators at Sharpeville on March 21 and the angry world-wide reaction shook South Africa to the core. It seemed to confirm that the wind of change had at last reached the Union.

The Sharpeville tragedy was the most disastrous of a number of out-bursts organized by the Pan-Africanist Congress under the leadership of Robert Mangaliso Sobukwe, a university language instructor who was sentenced to three years in prison after the March rioting. His new radical organization had grown swiftly in the past year at the expense of the more moderate African National Congress, the major organ of African nationalism since 1912.

REAFFIRMATION OF THE WHITE WILL TO RULE

The world soon learned, however, that white South Africans still had the power and the will to rule. The government's reaction to nationwide reports of African ferment and to rumors of imminent pressures from overseas was to proclaim a state of emergency on March 30. Swiftly the police rounded up and imprisoned nearly 2000 political suspects, including about 100 whites, an action shrouded in secrecy because the emergency regulations made it an offense pun-ishable by up to a £500 fine and five years' imprisonment even to mention the name of anyone detained under the emergency regula-tions. The opponents of the government were at a psychological dis-advantage after Sharpeville and the declaration of the emergency. Many liberals privately condemned the government for employing more force than necessary, but the overwhelming majority of white South Africans breathed a sigh of relief that the government had used enough force to prevent an explosion.

The emergency measures broke the back of African resistance for the time being. With the leaders in jail, even passive resistance could not be organized effectively. It should be noted, moreover, that only a limited amount of South Africa's white power was used. In addi-tion to a mobile police force, South Africa has a small Permanent Force of army commando units, air and naval forces, a large Citizen Force of white citizens who undergo periodic training, and *Skiet Kommandos* of relatively untrained Afrikaner farmers and towns-men who, like members of the Citizen Force, are subject to call by the minister of defense. Not all of these units were called into serv-ice, but their success on this occasion will make it easier for the gov-ernment to call them up in the future.

The government's position was also strengthened by the attempt to kill the Prime Minister, for it had the psychological effect of elevating Dr. Verwoerd in Afrikaner esteem at a critical moment when his policy was under heavy fire. Although he was admired by many Afrikaners as a strong leader, he had been considered an intellectual rather than a man of the people. When he "shed his blood" for them, he somehow became one of the people for the first time. As the *Transvaler* expressed it, "BLOOD BRINGS UNITY." This turned out to be politically significant in numerous ways. Shortly before the shooting, the *Rand Daily Mail* had headlined an appeal, "VERWOERD MUST GO," which led one of the extremist Nationalist M.P.'s to attack the paper in Parliament for inciting the assassin. This and other attacks, along with the stringent emergency regulations, forced the English press to pull in its horns.

Another important result of the shooting was its influence on the political strategists of the Nationalist high command. They had calculated, before the attempt on Dr. Verwoerd's life, that they would win a referendum to establish a republic by only a bare majority, not more than 52 percent at the most. They now came to the conclusion that Afrikaner voters would turn out in far greater numbers to give Dr. Verwoerd the republic he wanted, and that their majority had shot up to 60 percent. Although this estimate proved to be too high, they determined to push the republic through while they had a good majority.

HOPES FOR A "NEW DEAL"

With the iron hand of the government in firm control, the time came for thoughts of a velvet glove. On April 19, during the incapacity of the Prime Minister, Minister of Lands, Forestry, and Public Works Paul O. Sauer, made a widely publicized speech at Humansdorp.[6] The "old book" of South African history had been closed a month ago at Sharpeville, he said, and South Africa must reconsider her whole approach to the native question. He qualified this sweeping statement, however, by adding that although there must be an important change in the practical application of government policy, "it will not mean a deviation from the set policy."

[6] *Rand Daily Mail*, April 20, 1960.

When the *Rand Daily Mail* blew the "new deal" up into a party split, the glare of this exaggerated and ill-timed publicity naturally forced the Nationalists to close ranks. Minister of External Affairs Eric Louw told Parliament the next day that "Basically the Government's policy remains unchanged . . . [and] if any statement is to be made in regard to basic policy that statement will be made by the Prime Minister."[7] Several ministers, including the Minister of Bantu Administration and Development, Daan de Wet Nel, seemed unable to resist the temptation to make other statements, however, which enabled the English press to keep the "Nationalist rift" alive. The "kite-flying" of the *Rand Daily Mail* on April 21, for example, linked Mr. Louw with "extremist" Ministers de Wet Nel, Maree, and Hertzog, while the *Star* on April 20 opined that Louw was in the new deal camp with Ministers Sauer, Donges, Naude, Diedrichs, and Fouché. The *Sunday Times* contended on May 15 that nearly 50 Nationalist M.P.'s and senators had joined the new dealers.

There was clearly a difference of opinion in Nationalist ranks, but to call it a split was wishful thinking. Part of the explanation of the furor was the hope, as the *Rand Daily Mail* expressed it on April 23, that Mr. Sauer was a key political figure who "could form the basis of a political realignment involving the United Party, the National Union of Mr. Japie Basson, and an important section of the National Party." Mr. Sauer remained discreetly silent, however, and soon left the scene for an official visit to Argentina.

On May 20, Dr. Verwoerd put an end to the speculation by having Dr. Donges, the Minister of Finance, announce a "reform" program to Parliament. The Prime Minister made it clear that the government would not depart from the policy of separate development, which was the only way to eliminate "points of friction" between racial groups. The government had decided "to concentrate immediately on the development of industries on the borders of the reserves" in order to enable the Bantu homelands "to provide for both their increase in population and the returning flow of Bantu." Having thus reassured his conservative following, the Prime Minister then went on to make minor concessions to urban Africans, thereby making a gesture toward the new dealers. These reforms included the estab-

[7] *Die Burger*, April 20, 1960.

lishment of urban Bantu authorities with limited powers, reform of the liquor laws to end the necessity for liquor raids, improvement of the pass system, and encouragement to employers to pay higher wages by rationalization of their trades and by improving the productivity of their workers.[8]

Needless to say, the Prime Minister's compromise disappointed the Afrikaner reformers, to say nothing of the English-speaking South Africans who wanted the government to accept the principle that urban Africans are a permanent part of the population in the "white" areas. During the month of May the chambers of commerce and industries came forth with a variety of reform plans centered around this principle. Strong arguments, including a plea for the restoration of pass exemptions for many permanently settled urban natives, were put forward by important business spokesmen representing powerful economic interests. In the most forceful of these appeals, Mr. Harry F. Oppenheimer, chairman of the powerful Anglo-American Corporation, attacked the "entirely unrealistic assumption that the Africans in the towns are there only temporarily." He advocated not only reform of the pass laws but a new policy based on the fact that "these urban Africans are absolutely indispensable to the industrial life of the country." To those who fight change with the contention that only complete white surrender would satisfy extreme African nationalists, Mr. Oppenheimer gave the pragmatic reply, "You never know till you try."[9]

By mid-1960, nonetheless, it was clear that the new deal had gone with the wind of change. For a time, the hope persisted that concessions by the government would bring the Colored community toward integration with the whites, partly because of what Afrikaners referred to as the "loyalty" of the Coloreds during the Sharpeville crisis. This hope proved vain when Dr. Verwoerd informed the Council for Colored Affairs in December, 1961, that the Colored people would have their own parliament and cabinet within 10 years.

Since this combination of external and internal pressures thus proved unavailing, it is useful to pause and inquire why the new deal

---

[8] *The Star*, May 21, 1960.

[9] The complete text of Oppenheimer's review of the corporation's affairs was reprinted in the *Rand Daily Mail* on June 2, 1960.

failed. One of its most important obstacles was the power of *volkseen-heid*, the concept of the unity of the Afrikaner folk. Although per-haps 15 percent of the Afrikaner voters belong to the opposition United Party and a few have even joined the Liberal and Progressive Parties, most Afrikaners feel the need for loyalty to their own cul-tural group, a compelling force which is carefully nurtured in the country's now predominant and still growing Afrikaans primary and secondary schools as well as in the Afrikaans universities, the Dutch Reformed Churches, and the influential secret society called the Broederbond. Many well-educated Nationalists are highly critical of "Verwoerdism," particularly in Cape centers like Stellenbosch, where one can hear private attacks on the Prime Minister expressed in strong terms. But when it comes to public action rather than pri-vate talk, *volkseenheid* comes into play. However much the reform-minded Nationalist may deplore government policy, loyalty to his own cultural group usually keeps him from bolting the Party. He will probably rationalize his behavior by contending that he can be more useful by fighting from within. This group loyalty was a major handicap to one exception to the rule, Japie Basson, an Afrikaner M.P. who tried to organize the National Union Party in 1960.

A second weakness of the new dealers was inherent in their tactical position. Their criticism was not directed at *apartheid* but only at the government's methods of implementing the policy. This was re-emphasized at the 1960 annual meeting of SABRA, the South African Bureau of Racial Affairs, in Stellenbosch. The meeting of this group of *apartheid* theorists happened to occur at the time of Mr. Sauer's new deal speech at Humansdorp, and the English press widely pub-licized SABRA as a supporter of the Sauer approach. When the meeting concluded, however, SABRA not only advocated reforms to help urban Africans but strongly re-endorsed the basic policy of sep-arate development of the races. And the limitations on the reforms advocated by the Cape Nationalist organ, *Die Burger*, were indicated by the new names it coined for the old policy—*aparte vryheid* (sep-arate freedom) and *naasbestaan* (coexistence). The trend of the times was further revealed when Professor N. J. J. Olivier and other courageous Afrikaner reformers were purged from the SABRA ex-ecutive in 1961, despite their basic support for *apartheid*.

The progovernment propaganda in the Afrikaans press was a third handicap to the new dealers. Afrikaans newspapers soft-pedaled several warnings from the chairmen of large corporations, and played up the confidence expressed by these businessmen in the country's long-range economic future. This was also true of radio reports of the South African Broadcasting Corporation, which began to disseminate partisan Nationalist propaganda after the emergency was declared. *Die Transvaler* reassured its readers on May 30 that even if the value of shares on the Johannesburg stock exchange had declined by £600,000,000, the only people who lost anything were the very small percentage who panicked and sold.

Another Afrikaans press technique during the emergency was to play up Congo tribal riots, the Mau Mau revival in Kenya, the Rhodesia-Nyasaland troubles, and white emigration from the Congo and Kenya to the Union. Considerable publicity was also given to support for South Africa from the United States in the form of numerous letters from white racists in the Deep South. On June 5, *Dagbreek en Sondagnuus,* under the three-column headline "WHITES SHUDDER OVER LUMUMBA'S DEMANDS," reported that "fat white women together with their houses" were being sold to Africans for £7 for delivery on June 30, independence day! Immediately after Sharpeville, *Die Transvaler* published on its front page, three times within a single week, a photograph of the blood-spattered face of a white nurse whose car had been stoned near Cape Town. The object of these efforts was to convince Afrikaners that *apartheid* was their only salvation. It should be pointed out, however, that many Afrikaners must also have been reading the English press during this period because the main government-supporting Afrikaans newspapers have a circulation of only 352,000, in contrast to 1,626,000 for the English papers.

Finally, the efforts of the reformers were sidetracked in June by the rise of the republic issue as the main controversy. There was a quaint air of unreality in the fight of white South Africans over the republic, as if Queen Elizabeth were the real problem rather than Robert Sobukwe. Since Afrikaners have a history, culture, tradition, and language of their own, they are more of a nation than many of the new states in Africa. When Afrikaans-speaking whites became a majority, their leaders felt impelled to complete their nationhood by creating their own political institutions. As the late Governor General E. G. Jansen said in 1944: "In all our present state institutions there is actually nothing to which the Afrikaner can refer and say, 'This is what my people brought into existence.'" This bit of romanticism was built up into such a powerful social myth that nothing could stop the Afrikaners from getting their republic.

Many English-speaking South Africans reluctantly conceded the point; but, for tactical reasons, the opposition parties decided to wage a vigorous fight to reject a republic in the October 5, 1960, referendum, partly on the grounds that a vote for a republic was a vote for Verwoerd. After the return of Eric Louw from the Commonwealth Prime Ministers Conference in May, the United and Progressive Parties, supported by the English press, also argued that a South African republic would not be readmitted to the Commonwealth and that it therefore would suffer economically through the loss of Commonwealth preferences. These arguments perhaps reduced the Nationalist majority, but the republic still won by a majority of 52 percent.

APARTHEID: THEORY AND PRACTICE

Although the future of *apartheid* is complicated by many imponderables, the basic element at the moment is the apparent power and will of the whites to continue to rule, at least in the "white" areas. The problem would be simpler if *apartheid* were only a slogan to win votes. But it is far more than that. It has been built up into an emotional ideology. Dr. Verwoerd and his ministers continually tell Afrikaners that "You can't keep the black man down," but their alternative is a policy of separate development to enable Africans to rise to the top in their own sphere. To Afrikaner Nationalists such a policy is not only possible and moral but, most important of all, is the only way to save the whites from being swamped by the four to one nonwhite majority.

The theory of *apartheid* has a number of basic flaws. It is economically impracticable because, as many South Africans say, "You can't unscramble eggs." It is politically unrealistic because, in an age when self-determination is sweeping Africa, only a miracle could persuade black men to accept permanently a white man's plan for black destiny, no matter what its merits. It is constructive to the extent that it leads to the development of the rural reserves, but its failure to meet the needs of urban Africans is the heart of the problem. Even if *apartheid* succeeded in moving many Africans into the reserves, the white areas would still have a black majority. *Apartheid* theorists attempt to meet this dilemma by suggesting that Africans remaining in the white areas would be given political rights in the reserves or self-governing "Bantustans." The most far-sighted Nationalists realize that this fanciful idea is only a politician's dream, and a few have already conceded that the blacks remaining in the white areas must ultimately be given full and equal rights. In their view, the South Africa of the future might become a federation of several autonomous black Bantustans and one racially integrated state, in which the ratio of black to white would be less unequal. This scheme has advocates in several circles, including a small group at the Potchefstroom University for Christian Higher Education, the "dopper" Bible belt of Afrikanerdom.

Far-sighted supporters of the government concede the possibility that the policy may fail. In that case, they say, the government will have to "rethink" the whole situation. They contend, however, that *apartheid* has thus far been largely a theory, and they want to put it into practice with a program to develop the reserves even further than contemplated in the 10-year plan of £110,000,000 recommended by the Tomlinson Commission in 1955. Privately, a few go further and say that the present policy is only a transitional one to get the country over a difficult period until white attitudes change. On rare occasions it is even said that *apartheid* may in one sense be preparing the way for integration. The argument behind this heresy is that if *apartheid* is successful there will be many able African judges, administrators, doctors, businessmen, and others capable of holding their own in white company; in that event, South Africans might realize for the first time that blacks are not so different from whites.

Although the Nationalist government shelved the Tomlinson plan, it announced seven years later that it would spend R 114,400,000 (the new rand is worth one-half the old pound sterling) on the de-

velopment of the "Bantu homelands" during the five-year period
from 1961 to 1966—this was more than half the sum recommended
by Tomlinson for a 10-year period. Moreover, Dr. Verwoerd informed
Parliament on January 23, 1962, that the Transkei was to become
South Africa's first self-governing Bantustan.

The high price of *apartheid* is meanwhile becoming increasingly
apparent to South Africans. Thus far it has cost them so little that
they have never been able to weigh it realistically against the price
of integration. During the parliamentary debate on the budget for
1960-1961, opposition speakers stressed the expense of *apartheid* to
the taxpayers. But this is only part of the cost: it also exposes South
Africans to world-wide contempt; it causes a boycott of South African exports and discourages capital investment from overseas; it produces dangerous friction with the new states of Africa when South
Africa needs their friendship; it fosters conflict with India at a time
when India is becoming a great power in the Indian Ocean. It includes not only residential *apartheid* and marriage *apartheid*, but
inconveniences which annoy many South Africans—taxi *apartheid*,
bus *apartheid*, train *apartheid*, post office *apartheid*, bank *apartheid*,
university *apartheid*, and the sexual *apartheid* of the widely condemned Group Immorality Act.

To an observer like I. D. MacCrone, professor of psychology at the
University of Witwatersrand, its less tangible costs are even higher:

I think . . . of the growing intolerance in public and private life, of
the growing isolation due to the breaking down of communication not
only between White and Black but also between White and White, of
the uncharitableness towards and cynicism about our fellowmen which
may be on the increase, particularly in the younger generation, of the decline in the practices of democracy, of the growing authoritarianism and
demands for conformity, of the creeping fear and insecurity in so much
of our social life, of the stifling of honest thought and sincere opinion for
fear of the consequences, of the gradual erosion of the traditional spiritual
and moral values of our civilization in ourselves. If these things are so,
then I say the price we Whites have to pay for race domination is far
too high.[10]

[10] I. D. MacCrone, "Human Relations in a Multi-Racial Society," *Race
Relations Journal*, Jan.-June, 1958, p. 43.

As Professor MacCrone says, however, he is "an old-fashioned Cape Liberal." His reactions are not shared by enough whites to have much influence.

THE EFFECT OF EXTERNAL PRESSURES

With these reactions in mind, what can be concluded regarding the impact of world opinion on South Africa? Are external pressures like Macmillan's speech, the boycotts, and more than a decade of United Nations resolutions on South Africa effective in forcing changes of policy, or does foreign intervention only stiffen backs and give the conservatives an additional war cry in their local battles against reformers? In the short run, foreign intervention does stiffen resistance, as shown in the deeply emotional Afrikaner response to Macmillan. Yet one still wonders whether this rigidity may not reach a breaking point over a period of time and in face of continuously mounting pressure. Many influential Afrikaners share the worry expressed by *Die Burger*, which warned on April 7, 1960, that unless South Africa can produce a more positive race policy it must look forward to a permanent status as "the skunk of the world," with all the "catastrophic" political and economic implications of such a position.

A slowly growing number of reform-minded whites are reluctantly coming to the conclusion that continued external pressures are not only inevitable but essential. In an ambivalent spirit of hope mixed with regret they feel that economic difficulties might ultimately force a modification of government policy by hitting the pocketbook of the ordinary Afrikaner.

In assessing the boycott movement, one must distinguish between its effectiveness as an economic weapon and as a propaganda device. When the British Labor Party declared its support for a boycott of South African goods, Party Secretary Morgan Phillips declared on January 12, 1960, that the boycott would not bring the South African government to its knees, but it was a "symbolic act which, because it would hurt, cannot be ignored by the ruling classes in the Union, and will bring comfort to their victims."[11]

[11] *The Star*, January 13, 1960.

Boycotts are extraordinarily difficult to impose effectively even against countries which commit acts of aggression across international frontiers. Moreover, new world crises elsewhere will continually divert attention from South Africa. In any case, the Nationalist government appears disposed to "trek into laager," if necessary, in the attempt to withstand any long economic siege. However, the Johannesburg *Star*, which advocated an "attitude of calm contempt for the whole silly business of the boycott" on February 3, later changed its tune to stress the crippling potentialities of foreign economic pressure. In the view of some observers the quiet drying up of capital investment from overseas could ultimately prove more damaging than an incomplete boycott of exports. Although South Africa now has large internal capital resources, the loss of capital from overseas might, within a year or two, cause economic stagnation. In 1961 South Africans expressed frequent concern that the United Nations might use its foothold in South-West Africa to institute economic sanctions against their new republic.

We have seen that the impact of world opinion has not persuaded South Africa's whites to change their views. But what about its impact on nonwhites, whose feelings are unconsciously ignored by most whites in this oddly segmented society? To scare its white readers, the Afrikaans and occasionally the English press publicize the inaccurate and dangerous theme that the West has decided to "sacrifice the white man on the altar of black nationalism," a cliché hardly calculated to keep Africans quiescent. The angry Afrikaner reaction to Macmillan naturally aroused much black interest and pleasure. Newspaper clippings of his speech are said to have been widely circulated, translated, and frequently discussed in native townships. As one African told a reporter of the Johannesburg *Star*, "My people respect wisdom, courage and the words of a poet. Mr. Macmillan gave us all these things. This is one time when the powerful man from somewhere else in the world has come and gone and left us something tangible, something which means hope."[12] *This is the heart of the matter*. Foreign criticism may not force a change in policies, but it has a powerful impact by encouraging Africans to fight for change.

[12] *The Star*, February 24, 1960.

The Nationalists believe that foreign criticism is unfair, which it often is. As Afrikaners put it, *"Alles sal regkom"* (everything will come out all right) if only the outside world will let South Africans work out their own problems. This wishful thinking is useless since foreign criticism is inevitable. Even if *apartheid* were as moral and possible as Afrikaners contend, it would be doomed to ultimate failure by the fact that the outside world is certain to continue encouraging nonwhites in their fight against it. Unfortunately, most Nationalists are unable to accept this major premise and are therefore unwilling to change the policy. Some of the more cynical do accept it, but to them *apartheid* is only a slogan which will enable whites to remain supreme somewhat longer.

The new and uncompromising tone of Sobukwe's Pan-Africanists, who now outnumber the membership of the old African National Congress, reflects their growing confidence that time is on the side of the Africans. The reappearance of open Communist activity in 1960 for the first time in a decade is another significant fact. In April, despite the drastic emergency police ban, I was handed in Johannesburg an incendiary four-page mimeographed leaflet called "The Spark." I got rid of it quickly because it was a criminal offense even to hold it. Issued by the Socialist League of Africa, one of a number of Trotskyite Fourth International splinter groups in the Union, it summoned Africans to avenge the dead of Sharpeville and destroy the Capitalist rulers. And in July, the Communist Party of South Africa, which dissolved itself in 1950 shortly before the Suppression of Communism Act went into effect, came out into the open again with a manifesto of support for the "freedom struggle."

South Africa is a beautiful country, and its white inhabitants, Afrikaners included, are as warm-hearted, congenial, and hospitable as any people when their minds are not obsessed by racial fears. A small but significant minority has long engaged in serious thought and strenuous effort to improve race relations, a most impressive fact of which outsiders are insufficiently aware. Many South Africans consider the present Nationalist version of *apartheid* a pipe dream, but the overwhelming majority of both Afrikaans- and English-speaking voters in the two major parties still favor some form of separate development of the races. The fear of being swamped by the 4–1 nonwhite majority has mesmerized their minds into such rigid patterns that they seem incapable of restructuring changing facts into new configurations. They draw the wrong lesson from the chaos in the Congo and the bloody holocaust in Algeria.

This was confirmed by the general election of October 18, 1961, called two years early by Prime Minister Verwoerd in order to strengthen the position of his Nationalist Party:

Party	House of Assembly Seats	Popular vote
Nationalist Party	105	370,431
United Party	49	302,875
Progressive Party	1	69,042
National Union Party	1	35,903
Conservative Workers Party	0	6,229
Liberal Party	0	2,461
Independents	0	10,704

After this victory Dr. Verwoerd declared that the ever-increasing majorities of the government "follow attacks from within and without, such as few Governments experience, and belie all suggestions of internal weakness or dissension."[13] The forward-looking Progressive Party, which advocates a qualified franchise for people of all races, has won many followers since its birth in 1959 but it elected only one candidate. The "one man, one vote" Liberal Party of Alan Paton and others is much weaker. In 1962, therefore, it seemed most unlikely that South Africa would abandon racial segregation before it is too late.

White power can hold the fort for a time, but in the end South Africa will have to produce a policy more acceptable to leaders of all races. The whites are relatively well armed, determined to rule, and more or less trained for fighting, while the nonwhites who outnumber them are largely unarmed and undisciplined. Preparing for trouble, the Government has more than doubled its "defense" expenditures, jumping from $69,000,000 in 1960–1961 to $111,000,000 in 1961–1962 and to $168,000,000 (proposed) in 1962–1963. In the face of these odds, many non-European leaders are still willing to nego-

[13] *Digest of South African Affairs*, October 30, 1961, p. 2.

tiate. Radical elements, however, have already begun sabotage, prompting the Government to introduce a draconic sabotage bill which became law on June 27, 1962. The underground may ultimately resort to terrorism, recognizing that blacks will pay a devastating cost for such crimes but hoping that ruthless white retaliation will provoke the outside world to intervene. If this happens, South Africans may yet prove that one of their own professors was right in his fanciful 1947 prophecy that a United Nations military government will take over the Union in 1977.[14] In January, 1962, the Bow group of younger members of the British Conservative Party concluded its pamphlet on *The New Africa* with this warning:

We should make every effort to involve the United Nations in South Africa. Disgust with the policy of *apartheid* aside, we cannot afford to have in the Western camp the kind of divisions which South Africa's policies promote. It will probably take another Sharpeville before the right climate for actual military intervention is created.[15]

---

[14] Arthur Keppel-Jones, *When Smuts Goes: A History of South Africa from 1952–2010, First Published in 2015*, Pietermaritzburg, 1953 edition.
[15] The Bow Group, *The New Africa*, London, 1962. p. 66.

Part II

Pan-African, Afro-Asian and Eurafrican Movements

6

Concepts of Pan-Africanism: 1900–1958

PAN-AFRICANISM is a powerful ideal. It has cultural, economic, and political aspects, and a complex and varied historical evolution. It is related to the concepts of the "brotherhood of Negro blood," the "African personality," and *négritude*. At times it has fostered in the minds of some of its advocates the racist concepts of "Black Zionism," "black power," and "blackism." As a unifying idea to inspire the faith, confidence, and energy to transform Africa, it has great potentiality for good. If its racist aspects were to grow, it could produce evil. Whatever its future, Pan-Africanism in the past was a natural Negro reaction to centuries of domination and humiliation by whites. In the imagery of the South African Colored novelist Peter Abrahams,

Africa? She is a little like a heart. You've seen the shape of her. It's like a heart. Africa is my heart, the heart of all of us who are black. Without her we are nothing; while she is not free we are not men. That is why we must free her, or die. That is how it is.[1]

The enthusiasm of African leaders for the general principle of Pan-African unity was eloquently voiced at the two precedent-setting

[1] Peter Abrahams, A Wreath for Udomo, London, 1956, p. 57.

93

international conferences held by Africans in Ghana in 1958, the official Conference of Independent African States in April and the unofficial All-African Peoples Conference in December. In the words of George Padmore, one of its major interpreters, "Pan-Africanism offers an ideological alternative to Communism on the one hand, and Tribalism on the other. It rejects both white racialism and black chauvinism. It stands for racial co-existence on the basis of absolute equality and respect for human personality."[2]

This is indeed a high ideal which merits sympathetic but careful examination. The essential elements of Pan-Africanism as defined at Accra in 1958 will first be examined. We can then look back into the history of the movement, dividing it into four phases: the 1900 to 1945 period when it was dominated by American and West Indian Negroes; the 1945 to 1958 period when African nationalists still under colonial rule took it over and used it in the fight for freedom; the short period in 1958 and 1959 when President Nkrumah of Ghana emerged as the ideological leader of a movement for a united Pan-African state; and the period since 1960 when the establishment of many new states and leaders ended Nkrumah's primacy, led to the creation of rival Pan-African blocs, and turned the movement away from the idea of immediate political amalgamation and to the idea of economic and other kinds of cooperation or association.

THE ELEMENTS OF PAN-AFRICANISM

The essential elements of Pan-Africanism in 1958 are elaborated in the collection of loosely worded omnibus resolutions adopted by the 200 delegates from 28 states and territories at the All-African Peoples Conference in Accra in December. It is important to note, however, that the main political parties in French Africa—RDA and PRA—were on the whole unrepresented.

The ultimate goal of Pan-Africanism is the establishment of what is variously termed a Pan-African Commonwealth or a United States of Africa. As interim targets, the December Conference called for the amalgamation of independent African states into regional federations

[2] George Padmore, *Pan-Africanism or Communism? The Coming Struggle for Africa*, New York, 1956, p. 379.

or groupings on the basis of geographical contiguity, economic inter-dependence, and linguistic and cultural affinity, with the caveat, how-ever, that the establishment of such regional federations should not be prejudicial to the ultimate objective of a Pan-African Common-wealth. The Conference committee which drafted this resolution is said to have had in mind five regional groupings—northern Africa and western Africa at an early date, and eastern Africa, central Africa, and southern Africa later, when these areas are controlled by Afri-cans. The delegates drew little distinction between black Africa and the multiracial areas in the south. Tom Mboya from Kenya, chair-man of the Conference, told the delegates that even in central and south Africa it is not a question of whether Africans will win: It is "how and when."[3] Another Kenyan, Dr. Gikonyo Kiano, declared that "Bogus theories of multi-racialism, partnership or Bantustanism are essentially devices to deflect the African from his rightful goal of governing his country." White and Asian residents, he added, "will have to accept African citizenship first if they want to live there as citizens."[4]

Numerous observers at the Conference, however, reported that it was not antiwhite in tone. Mboya, they point out, declared that Africans will not practice "racism in reverse." And Prime Minister Kwame Nkrumah said at the opening session, ". . . we are not racialists or chauvinists. We welcome into our midst peoples of all other races, other nations, other communities, who desire to live among us in peace and equality. But they must respect us and our rights, our right as the majority to rule. That, as our Western friends have taught us to understand it, is the essence of democracy."[5] In the view of St. Clair Drake, an American observer at the Conference, it gave birth to a new concept of "residential Pan-Africanism," that is to say, contrary to racialism, the idea that all persons born or nat-uralized in African states, irrespective of race, creed, or color, are "Africans" provided they believe in absolute economic and social equality and the principle of one-man–one-vote. In the actual reso-lutions adopted, this rational approach occasionally disappeared in

[3] "Peoples Conference Plans Permanent Body," *Africa Special Report*, Febru-ary, 1959, p. 6.
[4] *Ibid.*, p. 6.
[5] All-African Peoples Conference, *News Bulletin*, Vol. 1, No. 1, p. 7.

favor of sweeping condemnations of such things as the "pernicious system of racialism and discriminating laws, especially as expressed in its extreme and most brutal forms"[6] in South Africa, Rhodesia, and Portuguese territories. Whether the nonracial ideal of residential Pan-Africanism will thrive is not yet clear.

A second element in this 1958 version of the Pan-Africanist ideal was its rejection of violence as a systematic and deliberate revolutionary weapon in favor of nonviolent positive action—strikes, boycotts, and civil disobedience. When the Egyptians and Algerians at the Accra Conference objected to this view, they obtained a clarification from Chairman Mboya to the effect that, although he believed in nonviolent methods, "this does not mean that if Africans are struck, they will not hit back."[7] This interpretation of the nonviolence principle was incorporated in the Conference resolution on imperialism and colonialism which promised "full support to all fighters for freedom in Africa, to all those who resort to peaceful means of non-violence and civil disobedience as well as to all those who are compelled to retaliate against violence. . . ."[8] In later conferences, moreover, the ideal of nonviolence no longer appeared to be an essential element of Pan-Africanism. It received little mention at the third All-African Peoples Conference in Cairo in March, 1961. As President Habib Bourguiba of Tunisia once said, the objective is freedom and the means to get it vary with the situation, and may include violence. This change of emphasis was no doubt attributable in part to the continuation of the Algerian war, the shooting of Africans at Sharpeville in South Africa in March, 1960, and the harsh Portuguese suppression of the Angola uprising in 1961.

A third aspect of the Pan-African spirit is that it is modernist rather than traditionalist: it condemns those aspects of tribalism, especially chieftaincy, which obstruct the African march to freedom and unity. There is a certain ambivalence in this attitude, however, for African leaders also stress the values of their traditional cultures and glorify the golden ages of their past.

[6] All-African Peoples Conference, *News Bulletin–Conference Resolutions*, Vol. 1, No. 4.
[7] "Peoples Conference Plans Permanent Body," *Africa Special Report, op. cit.,* p. 7.
[8] All-African Peoples Conference, *News Bulletin–Conference Resolutions, ibid.*

In the fourth place, although the Accra Conference adopted no resolution on the subject, it is clear that Pan-Africanism is socialist in its economic outlook. It welcomes the assistance of private enterprise and capital but believes that a high degree of government enterprise and ownership is essential to regenerate African society. There is considerable divergence, however, in the approach of various African states to the question of private versus public enterprise.

Finally, Pan-Africanism is neutralist, not in the negative sense of only refraining from taking sides in the cold war, but in the "positive nonalignment" sense of developing the "African personality" as a kind of countervailing force in world affairs. In its "keep the cold war out of Africa" cry, Pan-Africanism seeks a kind of Monroe doctrine for Africa to enable Africans to settle the problems of their own continent, a reaction that was intensified by foreign intervention in the Congo crisis.

In summary, the spirit or ideal of Pan-Africanism at Accra was federationist, anticolonial, nonracial, nonviolent, modernist, socialist, and neutralist. The Accra Conferences helped to give the movement status and to clarify its ideology. But we should note that this was the Pan-Africanism of 1958, for its ideology has changed in the past and could do so again. Among recent developments of interest was the organization of a Pan-Africanist Congress in South Africa, founded in 1959 by a group of Africans both younger and more uncompromising than the leaders of the old African National Congress. Although there was initially no organizational link between Pan-Africanist organizations of tropical Africa and South Africa, President Nkrumah of Ghana was in correspondence with the Pan-Africanist leader, Robert Mangaliso Sobukwe, until his imprisonment after the Sharpeville shooting.

THE HISTORY OF THE MOVEMENT

To deepen our understanding of Pan-Africanism, it is now essential to look back at its 60 years of history. The first striking fact is that it originated and found its earliest support and leadership not in Africa but among Negroes in the West Indies and the United States. A West Indian barrister named Henry Sylvester-Williams organized a Pan-African Conference in London in 1900. It was attended by about 30 Negro intellectuals, mostly from England and the West Indies, along with several American Negroes. The purpose of the Conference was to arouse British reformers to protect natives in African areas from abuses, but it did not advocate independence for Africans. However, William E. Burghardt Du Bois, an American Negro who was present, suggested that the British give, "as soon as practicable, the rights of responsible government to the Black Colonies of Africa and the West Indies."[9] The idea of Pan-Africanism thus first arose as an effort to bring peoples of African descent throughout the world closer together. Sylvester-Williams also sought to promote the rights of all peoples of African origin in "civilized" countries. He died soon afterward, however, and little was heard of the movement until the idealism aroused by World War I enabled Du Bois to launch a new movement.

Du Bois was a prolific writer who helped to found the National Association for the Advancement of Colored People and edited its organ, Crisis, from 1910 to 1933. In his 1903 book, The Souls of Black Folk, he challenged the submissive doctrine of the Negro leader Booker T. Washington, and urged American Negroes to fight for their rights instead. Embittered by his long uphill fight for racial equality, Du Bois turned to communism and retired to live in Russia at the age of 90. Unable to attend the Accra Conference in December, 1958, he sent his wife to read a speech recounting the history of Pan-Africanism and exhorting the delegates to awake and "put on the beautiful robes of Pan-African Socialism," and to realize that their bond with the white world is closest to the Communists, not to the West.[10]

Du Bois had attended the 1900 Conference and also a Races Congress in London in 1911. In 1919 he seized the opportunity presented by the Paris Peace Conference to organize the first Pan-African Congress. When Clemenceau was persuaded by Senegalese leader Blaise Diagne to approve such a meeting, 57 persons met in Paris to voice

[9] Quoted by Rayford Logan, "The Historical Aspects of Pan-Africanism," address to American Society of African Culture Conference, June, 1960, p. 2.
[10] W. E. B. DuBois, "Pan Africa, 1919–1958," All-African Peoples Conference, News Bulletin, Vol. 1, No. 3.

African complaints during the Peace Conference and to petition the Allied Powers to place the former German colonies in Africa under international supervision.

Two years later a second Pan-African Congress held three sessions in London, Brussels, and Paris in August and September, 1921. It adopted a moderate Declaration to the World, drafted by Du Bois, which demanded, among other things, the recognition of civilized men as civilized, despite their race or color. It also elected a delegation headed by Du Bois to present a petition to the Permanent Mandates Commission of the League of Nations asking that a Negro be appointed to the Commission as soon as a vacancy occurred.

In 1923 a third Pan-African Congress met in two sessions in London and Lisbon, and four years later, in 1927, 208 delegates from 11 countries, predominantly Americans, attended a fourth Pan-African Congress in New York. Du Bois planned to hold a fifth congress, in the continent of Africa for the first time, but the depression which struck the United States in 1929 killed his chances for financial support and put a damper on the Pan-African movement for 16 years until the end of World War II. The NAACP, concentrating on American Negro rights, gave only limited support to Du Bois's Pan-African Congresses, and the Communists dismissed them as petty bourgeois black nationalism.

Du Bois's efforts during the 1920s had also suffered from the meteoric rise and fall of a rival Negro leader whose inflammatory "Black Zionism" enabled him to build up a mass following of perhaps 2,000,000 Negroes in 30 branches of an organization called the Universal Negro Improvement Association. Of West Indian origin, Marcus Garvey was a spectacular showman who was named "Provisional President of the African Republic" at an international convention of the Association in Harlem in 1920. Garvey's "back to Africa" movement called for the establishment of a great Negro state in Africa as the homeland for all black people. He also campaigned for the establishment of Negro-owned and -run commercial and industrial enterprises throughout the world. However, when he attempted to establish the Black Star Line—a steamship line to be owned and operated by Negroes—he got himself into financial difficulties which jailed him in 1923 and undermined his movement.

Nkrumah, incidentally, named his new steamship company the Black Star Line, and in his autobiography wrote: "I think that of all the literature I studied [in the United States], the book that did more than any other to fire my enthusiasm was *Philosophy and Opinions of Marcus Garvey*."[11]

The failure of Garvey's scheme for a Black Star Line was accompanied by another blow when the Liberian government refused to support his plan for a Negro state in Africa to which any black could return. Long under attack by Du Bois and other American Negro leaders, the Garvey movement split apart in 1929, and had withered away by the time of Garvey's death in 1940.

The essential difference between Du Bois and Garvey has been summarized as follows by George Padmore:

> Where Du Bois differed from Garvey was in his conception of the Pan-African movement as an aid *to the promotion of national self-determination among Africans under African leadership, for the benefit of Africans themselves.* Marcus Garvey, on the other hand, looked upon Africa as a place for colonizing Western Negroes under his personal domination.[12]

If Garveyism is considered something of an aberration, it may be said that the second phase of Pan-Africanism did not begin until 1945 when a fifth Pan-African Congress was held in England. For 20 years students from West Africa had been meeting together in London in the West African Students' Union (WASU) which, in 1925, had combined four smaller unions under the leadership of a Nigerian student, Ladigo Solanke. The dozen Africans who started WASU were all law students who later had prominent careers in West Africa. They were keen on cooperation among the educated leaders of Nigeria, the Gold Coast, Sierra Leone, and Gambia, and they regarded WASU as a training ground for the future leaders of West Africa. They also established a number of WASU branches and societies in West Africa which enabled students to keep in touch with each other after they returned home. WASU grew into an organization of several hundred members and gradually widened its horizon to African affairs beyond West Africa. Kwame Nkrumah, mean-

[11] *The Autobiography of Kwame Nkrumah*, Edinburgh, 1957, p. 45.
[12] George Padmore, *Pan-Africanism or Communism? The Coming Struggle for Africa*, New York, 1956, p. 128.

while, was studying in the United States where he helped to organize the African Students' Association of America and Canada. In 1944 several colored organizations in England formed a Pan-African Federation, and in February, 1945, when the World Federation of Trade Unions was established by trade unionists, it included African delegates from British West Africa and the West Indies. These two groups, the colored organizations in England and the colonial trade unionists, with the encouragement of Du Bois, made preparations for the fifth Pan-African Congress which met in Manchester in October, 1945, with more than 200 delegates and observers present.

The fifth Congress was a milestone in the movement. Although Du Bois was in the chair, the initiative and leadership for the first time actually lay with Africans rather than American and West Indian Negroes. Kwame Nkrumah, Jomo Kenyatta, Peter Abrahams, and other future African leaders played prominent roles. Reports on African areas were presented to the delegates by Africans themselves rather than by others.

Another important change was the more radical and militant approach adopted by this younger and more African generation of political, labor, farmer, and student leaders, in contrast to the moderate approach of the small intellectual elite which had guided the movement in the past. By 1945, the demand for positive political action to obtain self-government had risen to the top of Pan-African aims. The new militancy is evident in the Declaration to the Colonial Peoples adopted at the 1945 Congress:

> We affirm the right of all colonial peoples to control their own destiny. All colonies must be free from foreign imperialist control whether political or economic. The peoples of the colonies must have the right to elect their own governments, without restrictions from foreign powers. We say to the peoples of the colonies that they must fight for these ends by all the means at their disposal. . . . the struggle for political power by colonial and subject peoples is the first step towards, and the necessary prerequisite to, complete social, economic, and political emancipation. . . . Your weapons—the strike and the boycott—are invincible. . . . Today there is only one road to effective action—the organization of the masses. And in that organization the educated colonials must join. Colonial and subject peoples of the world, unite![13]

[13] *Ibid.*, pp. 171–172.

Nkrumah, having come to England from the United States in 1945, went to Paris after the Congress to talk with the African members of the French National Assembly—including Sourou Apithy, Léopold Sédar Senghor, Lamine Guèye and Félix Houphouet-Boigny —about forming a movement for a Union of French West African Socialist Republics. At this time, however, French African leaders were not receptive to Nkrumah's ideas because they were committed to the concept of political evolution within a French Union. Back in England for two years before he returned to the Gold Coast, Nkrumah took advantage of the fifth Pan-African Congress to organize from among its delegates a West African National Secretariat. He also became chairman of the Circle, one of the student groups participating in the Secretariat which advocated a Union of African Socialist Republics and vowed personal allegiance to Nkrumah and the goal of West African unity.

Many of these ideas expressed at the fifth Pan-African Congress were similar to those emanating from the December, 1958, Conference in Accra, which was sometimes referred to as the sixth Pan-African Congress. However, the concept of an African personality, which Nkrumah was later to popularize, had only begun to take shape by 1945. The objective of the movement was more nationalist than Pan-African, that is to say, its major emphasis was on the fight for independence in each colony rather than on interterritorial association. Cooperation among colonial peoples the world over was called for as a method of obtaining this objective. This nationalist emphasis was quite natural since it was difficult to arouse any enthusiasm for federation when there were no independent states to federate. Consequently, for more then a decade after World War II, the nationalist aspect continued to dominate the movement, while its broader Pan-African goal remained as an ideal in the background.

AFRO-ASIAN RELATIONS

During this period, moreover, the interest of many Africans was focused on a new and notable Afro-Asian solidarity movement. It began with the formation of the African-Asian group in the United

Nations, and was followed by the Bandung conference of 1955 and the Afro-Asian Peoples Solidarity Conferences in Cairo at the end of 1957 and in Conakry in April, 1960.

The African-Asian group developed in the United Nations in December, 1950, during the Korean crisis. It continued to meet thereafter to discuss problems of common interest, and 13 of its 16 members (excluding Liberia, Ethiopia, and Thailand) joined in a successful endeavor to get the Moroccan question, the Tunisian question, and the item on race conflict in South Africa onto the agenda of the General Assembly. In addition to their hostility to colonialism, these states shared a common and related interest in fighting racial discrimination against peoples of color and in seeking ways and means for the economic development of their underdeveloped countries. Through bloc politics in the United Nations, they found that they gained additional strength, influence, and prestige, and were able to win membership for a larger number of their members in various United Nations organs and offices. They thus found that the advantages of maintaining this solidarity outweighed the differences and rivalries which sometimes divided them.

The advantages in this new relationship were one of the factors which induced the African-Asian countries to hold the historic conference in Bandung, Indonesia, in April, 1955. Twenty-nine states were represented by top officials at Bandung, including six African countries—Egypt, Ethiopia, the Gold Coast, Liberia, Libya, and the Sudan. Like the Pan-African Congresses, Bandung created no specific political organization, but it was psychologically important as an assertion of Asian and African personality in world affairs. As Indonesian President Sukarno said at Bandung, "The peoples of Asia and Africa wield little physical power," but they are 1,400,000,-000 strong and "can mobilize all the spiritual, all the moral, all the political strength of Asia and Africa on the side of peace."[14] In his closing speech, Prime Minister Nehru of India made a special appeal to Africans: "I think there is nothing more terrible, there is nothing more horrible than the infinite tragedy of Africa in the past few

[14] George McTurnan Kahin, *The Asian-African Conference*, New York, 1956, pp. 45–46.

hundred years. . . . it is up to Asia to help Africa to the best of her ability because we are sister continents."[15]

This Afro-Asian movement took a new turn during the last week in 1957 at the first Afro-Asian Peoples Solidarity Conference held in Cairo, where President Nasser assumed the leadership Nehru had held at Bandung. This was an unofficial conference of peoples rather an official conference of governments, which explains why its pronouncements were more emotional and unrestrained. A second important fact about it was the presence of a 27-man Soviet delegation, in contrast to Bandung where the Russians had been deliberately kept out. These two facts explain why the Cairo Conference adopted not only a battery of anticolonial resolutions but also numerous anti-Western resolutions condemning NATO, the Eisenhower Doctrine, the Baghdad Pact, and nuclear weapons. At the second Afro-Asian Peoples Solidarity Conference in Conakry, Guinea, in April, 1960, Africans played a far more important role than at Bandung or Cairo. President Sékou Touré sought to minimize Egyptian influence in the movement. It was decided that the Egyptian Secretary General would be re-elected for only one year, although the Secretariat was not moved from Cairo to Conakry as Touré had wanted, and the new steering committee reportedly contained 9 Communists among its 12 members. Early in 1961, President Sukarno of Indonesia sought to muster support for the holding of a third conference at Bandung. It is interesting to observe that the stimulus for many of these conferences appeared to come from a leader who sought to strengthen his own influence—Nehru, Sukarno, Nasser, Nkrumah, Sékou Touré, and, in September, 1961, Tito at Belgrade.

In addition to these meetings of political leaders, several other African-Asian efforts have been launched to organize student, cultural, and economic activities. In July, 1956, an unsuccessful attempt was made at an Afro-Asian student conference in Bandung to organize an Afro-Asian student federation. Two years later, in October, 1958, nearly 200 African and Asian writers assembled at Tashkent, capital of Soviet Uzbekistan, and decided to establish a permanent bureau at Colombo, Ceylon. In December of the same year the Afro-Asian Economic Conference was attended in Cairo by chamber of

[15] Ibid., p. 75.

commerce representatives of 13 Arab, 16 Asian, and 8 African states, and the U.S.S.R. Concerned over possible repercussions of the EEC Common Market on their economies, they decided to form an Organization for Economic Cooperation at the chamber of commerce level, which happened to meet simultaneously with the first All-African Peoples Conference in Accra.

What relationship does this Afro-Asian solidarity movement have to the development of Pan-Africanism? In one sense a diversion, it could be regarded in another sense as a stage on the road to the conceptualization of an African personality. When the new states of Africa were not yet numerous enough to give adequate voice to their own desire for self-expression, they found psychological satisfaction in unity with Asia. As they gained numbers and experience, however, the desire to emphasize their own uniqueness grew stronger. They found that the voices of Bandung and even Cairo were predominantly Asian. The need for Asia's help in support of African aims in world politics will no doubt induce African states to maintain solidarity with Asia whenever it is advantageous to do so. At the same time Africa, particularly south of the Sahara, has its own unique qualities, and differs from Asia in many ways. African leaders have therefore begun to look for better ways of asserting a distinctively African personality in world affairs.

A second reason for the new emphasis may have been African uneasiness at Communist influence. Communist China had played an influential role at Bandung, and the Soviet Union had scored a propaganda coup at Cairo. African delegates at Bandung were impressed by the sharp attack on Soviet colonialism made by Ceylonese and other Asian delegates. At Cairo, delegates from Ghana, Tunisia, Ethiopia, and the Sudan had tried to moderate the anti-Western tone of the Conference. Even President Nasser is said to have cautioned Egyptian delegates about the maneuvers of the Soviet delegation. Meanwhile, Soviet brutality in suppressing Hungarian nationalists in 1956 had startled African leaders. Anxious for Western aid, the new states of Africa perhaps also foresaw a practical value in developing an independent international posture.

Finally, the ambitious designs of President Nasser helped to crystallize the rival aims of Prime Minister Nkrumah for Pan-African leadership. Nasserism was also becoming increasingly irritating to the chiefs of state in Ethiopia, Libya, the Sudan, Morocco, and Tunisia. The latter three states, it should be recalled, had become independent only in 1956, while Ghana did not attain its independence until March 6, 1957.

PAN-ARAB AND PAN-ISLAMIC MOVEMENTS

Egypt's significance is enhanced by its special position not only in the Pan-African and Afro-Asian movements, but also in the related Pan-Arab and Pan-Islamic movements. However, its multiple interests in these four movements sometimes conflict.

For many centuries, Egypt has had links with the North African coastal area through Islam and the Arabic language. It also has a long-standing geographical interest in northeastern Africa because of its lifeline in the waters of the Nile. It is only in the past decade that President Nasser has brought the area south of the Sudan to Egypt's attention. In his 1955 book, *Egypt's Liberation: The Philosophy of the Revolution,* he wrote that Egypt cannot "remain aloof from the terrible and sanguinary conflict" between 5,000,000 whites and 200,-000,000 Africans:

> We cannot do so for an important and obvious reason: we are *in* Africa. The peoples of Africa will continue to look to us, who guard their northern gate, and who constitute their link with the outside world.[16]

In an odd note reminiscent of Rudyard Kipling, he added that "we will never in any circumstances be able to relinquish our responsibility to support, with all our might, the spread of enlightenment and civilization to the remotest depths of the jungle."

Although Egypt could never lead a united Africa, it has taken many steps to show that it is an African as well as a Middle Eastern state. In addition to its active role in the Casablanca and the Afro-Asian solidarity movements, it has (1) increased its diplomatic posts in Africa; (2) granted scholarships to several thousand African students for study in Cairo; (3) established an Institute of African Studies at Cairo University; (4) sent many Egyptian teachers, technicians, and

[16] Gamal Abdel Nasser, *Egypt's Liberation: The Philosophy of the Revolution,* Washington, D.C., 1955, pp. 109–110.

officials to Libya, the Sudan, Somalia and other countries; (5) employed Radio Cairo not only for broadcasts in Arabic, English and French but for a *Voice of Africa* program in at least 9 African languages which totaled 8¾ hours a week in 1962; and (6) used a clandestine Cairo Radio program, *The Voice of Free Africa*, for inflammatory broadcasts to the south since 1958, which exhort Africans to drive out the "white dogs" of the Western oppressors, and brand the United States as the banker of the sterling bloc and therefore another of Africa's masters. Nasser has also subsidized numerous exiled rebels from sub-Saharan Africa who make Cairo the headquarters for their revolutionary planning. Louis E. Lomax, an American Negro reporter, has published an interesting account of his encounter with some of these African nationalists in Cairo in 1960.[17]

In addition to this Pan-Arabism, Egypt is involved in the wider Pan-Islamic movement. More than 80 million Africans are Moslems, half of whom are Negroid peoples south of the Sahara. Since its penetration of the Sudan, more than a thousand years ago, Islam has successfully adapted itself to African customs, and is still expanding. Africans from the Sudanic belt have attended Islamic institutions in Fez and Tunis for centuries, but Al-Azhar University in Cairo is the main attraction. Its graduates have helped to develop numerous African Moslem religious brotherhoods, both traditional and reformist, as well as a number of modern Moslem clubs, centers, leagues, associations, and congresses which foster Islamic cultural, economic and political activities. In 1958–59 Al-Azhar's enrollment included 859 students from the Sudan, 184 from Eritrea, 146 from Senegal, 87 from Ethiopia, 64 from Lake Chad, 36 from Somaliland, 13 from Nigeria, 11 from Ghana, and 24 from 4 other African territories.[18]

The annual pilgrimage of thousands of Africans to Mecca is another unifying force. It not only renews the African's sense of Islamic solidarity and his pride in belonging to a universal religion, but it often exposes him to the anti-Western fervor of many an Arab propagandist. In the Republic of the Sudan, the last census included about half a million Nigerians, many of whom were stranded and poverty-

[17] Louis E. Lomax, *The Reluctant African*, New York, 1960, pp. 17–43.
[18] Bayard Dodge, *Al-Azhar, A Millennium of Muslim Learning*, Washington, 1961, pp. 209–210.

stricken pilgrims—a situation which led the Nigerian Government, in January, 1962, to refuse pilgrimage passports to applicants without the £286 deemed necessary to cover the cost of a round trip to Mecca.

The idea of Islamic solidarity propounded by the Pan-Islamic movement of the nineteenth century led to the organization in 1954 of the Islamic Congress, proposed by Saudi-Arabia and supported by Pakistan, Egypt, Syria, Yemen, Indonesia, Iran, Afghanistan, and Morocco. The Islamic Congress grants scholarships, mostly for study in Egypt, and contributes to Moslem cultural centers and Koranic schools in Africa and Asia. In January, 1956, it also established an Islamic Health Organization. Egypt tends to use the Pan-Islamic idea for political purposes, but the differences within the Moslem world are too great for Moslem political unity. Pan-Arabism remains Nasser's prime concern, and Egypt's Pan-African, Afro-Asian, and Pan-Islamic activities help to strengthen its prestige in the Arab world.

7

Pan-Africanism Since 1958

A THIRD phase of Pan-Africanism began in 1958 when Ghana's primacy as the first of the new sub-Saharan states enhanced Prime Minister Nkrumah's dominant role in the movement. During that year a remarkable series of precedent-setting international conferences were held *in* Africa *by* Africans for the first time. All of them were in one way or another Pan-African in spirit, indicating possible new combinations of African states. Many ideas for regional combinations varying from political unions to loose economic organizations grew out of these meetings.

PAN-AFRICAN CONFERENCES

The most significant of the African conferences of 1958 were those already described—the April and December meetings in Accra. Like those in Bandung and Cairo, the Accra Conferences differed in that the first was a meeting of governments and the second a meeting of peoples. The limited aim of the April Conference of Independent African States, as described by Nkrumah at the inaugural session, was to forge "closer links of friendship, brotherhood, co-operation and solidarity"[1] among the eight participating countries. The resolutions adopted by the Conference were naturally anticolonial, but

[1] Conference of Independent African States, *Speeches Delivered at the Inaugural Session*, April 15, 1958, Accra, 1958, p. 1.

their tone and substance were far more moderate than either the Afro-Asian resolutions at Cairo or those of the later All-African Peoples Conference. No mention was made of any form of Pan-African commonwealth. Instead, the Conference developed the concept of a distinctive "African personality" which will "speak with a concerted voice. . . ."[2] To give meaning to this concept, the eight states agreed to constitute their permanent representatives at the United Nations in New York as an informal but permanent body for consultation and cooperation. In addition, it was agreed that the Conference of Independent African States should meet every two years, and that interim meetings of ministers or experts should be held from time to time.

The idea of using the African permanent representatives to the United Nations as the machinery of Pan-Africanism was a notable development in international relations, and further illustrates the impact of the United Nations on Africa. The eight representatives met in New York soon after the Accra Conference and set up a coordinating body, chaired by each African state in turn, to meet once a month or at the request of any member. Four of the members were elected to a secretariat to meet every two weeks, and the representative of Ghana was made executive secretary. One of the group's first steps was a quite unique bit of all-African diplomatic technique. It appointed three delegations, each composed of three African diplomats, to visit Europe, South America, and Central America to win support for Algerian independence. Their efforts probably had some effect because in the U.N. Assembly debate on the Algerian question in December, 1958, a resolution favoring Algeria's right to independence and calling for negotiations failed by only one vote to gain the required two-thirds majority. After 1958 there were indications that this Pan-African diplomatic technique might be further employed, particularly against the *apartheid* policy of South Africa.

Meanwhile, the exuberant All-African Peoples Conference held its first meeting in Accra in December, 1958. As already pointed out, its resolutions were more ambitious in substance and more extreme in tone than those of the April conference of governments. Prime

[2] Conference of Independent African States, *Speeches Delivered at the Close of the Conference*, April 22, 1958, 2nd ed., Accra, 1958, p. 25.

Minister Nkrumah appeared in a brilliant Ashanti cloth robe instead of the Western dress he wore at the earlier conference of official delegates. Addressing the opening session, however, he said, "Do not let us forget that colonialism and imperialism may come to us yet in a different guise, not necessarily from Europe. We must alert ourselves to be able to recognize this when it rears its head and pre-. pare ourselves to fight against it."[3] In this ambiguous declaration, Nkrumah apparently had in mind Communist and possibly Egyptian intrigues as manifested at the Cairo Conference. He is reported to have said in private that he omitted any reference to Bandung because Nasser had corrupted its principles of noninterference by intruding Asian and Communist influences into African affairs.

Nkrumah's foreign affairs adviser at the time was George Padmore, the leading theorist of Pan-Africanism, who served in Ghana from 1951 until his death in 1959. A Negro journalist of West Indian origin, Padmore was educated in the United States at Fisk and Howard Universities and joined the American Communist Party in the late 1920s. He said that he quit the Party in 1934, when he finally realized that "Russia wanted to use Africa for her own purposes."[4] After 1934 he repeatedly attacked the Communists and called for a dynamic concept of Pan-Africanism, combined with democratic socialism, as "the only force capable of containing Communism in Asia and Africa. . . ."[5] His ideology of Pan-Africanism is set forth in his valuable book published in 1956 called *Pan-Africanism or Communism? The Coming Struggle for Africa*. Nkrumah and Padmore had been the joint secretaries of the organizing committee of the fifth Pan-African Congress at Manchester in 1945. Their Pan-Africanist efforts and successes at the two Accra Conferences of 1958 were thus the partial realization of a long-standing dream.

THE MOVEMENT GAINS STRENGTH

To win support for his own concept of Pan-Africanism, President Nkrumah created the Kwame Nkrumah Ideological Institute at

[3] All-African Peoples Conference, *News Bulletin*, Vol. 1, No. 1, p. 8.
[4] Smith Hempstone, *The New Africa*, London, 1961, p. 629.
[5] St. Clair Drake, "Rise of Pan-Africanism," *Africa Special Report*, February, 1958, p. 6.

Winneba where African nationalists are taught "positive action." As reported in the February 14, 1962, issue of *Ghana Today*, Nkrumah told 120 nationalists from "dependent African States" at the closing session of a three-month course that the future united Africa should establish a parliament with lower and upper houses, members of the two houses being elected from all independent African states regardless of size and population. He urged his listeners to prepare to resist violence where the colonial powers resorted to force. Nationalists from Angola, Mozambique, Portuguese Guinea, Cape Verde Islands, Southern and Northern Rhodesia, Zanzibar, Basutoland, Bechuanaland, and Swaziland attended the course.

This zealous African spirit soon led to friction within the African-Asian group in the United Nations, which had never been a solid bloc. This was particularly evident in a French Cameroons issue in the U.N. early in 1959, when India and other Asian members joined the Western powers to defeat an African proposal for new elections in the French Cameroons before it became independent on January 1, 1960. There was also disagreement between Africans and Asians over tactics to be used in the U.N. on the South-West Africa problem and on French nuclear testing in the Sahara. On November 8, 1959, Thomas L. Hamilton reported in *The New York Times* that the African delegates had failed to appear at an Afro-Asian group meeting. In general it seemed that the Asians were viewing controversial issues more dispassionately than the Africans. Possibly to show their displeasure, the Africans failed to support India in the 1959 elections for the Economic and Social Council, which enabled Japan to win a post.

The quick achievement of independence by Nigeria and 15 French-speaking states in 1960 brought other African leaders to the fore and ended Nkrumah's dominating position. A fourth phase of Pan-Africanism emerged, marked by a kaleidoscopic picture of shifting regional arrangements and groupings. A brief explanation of the evolution of French territories during the preceding decade is necessary in order to explain the background of this new Pan-African rivalry.

FRENCH AFRICAN FEDERATIONS

During the colonial period, French African territories had already been formed into two federations—the eight-territory Federation of West Africa and the four-territory Federation of Equatorial Africa. These twelve territories were regarded as integral parts of the "indivisible" French Republic which was established under the 1946 constitution. Ten years later the *loi cadre* of 1956, an enabling act, prepared the way for internal autonomy in each of the above 12 territories, thus undermining the two Federations. In September, 1958, under the new constitution of the Fifth Republic established by Charles de Gaulle, a referendum enabled each French colony to choose between independence and internal autonomy within a French-African Community. While 11 territories opted for membership within the Community, the vote of Sékou Touré's Guinea for independence set a precedent too strong for the others to resist for any appreciable length of time.

The ensuing Ghana-Guinea Union, formed in November, 1958, was more in the nature of an alliance than a political union. Nkrumah and Sékou Touré then met with President Tubman in Liberia in 1959 at Sanequellie to discuss the formation of a Community of Independent African States. Meanwhile, events in the remaining French territories were breaking down the French-African Community. Prime Minister Houphouet-Boigny of the Ivory Coast, who contended that political unity would have to be left to the next generation, succeeded in keeping Upper Volta and Dahomey out of the Mali Federation, composed of Senegal and the Sudan, which began to function in April, 1959. As a counterweight, he brought Upper Volta, Niger, and Dahomey into a loose economic arrangement with the Ivory Coast called the Conseil de l'Entente in mid-1959, which provided for a joint development fund and other forms of technical, economic, and diplomatic cooperation. The relatively wealthy Ivory Coast was strongly opposed to federations which would force it to subsidize poorer territories. The Entente development fund nonetheless involved a mild form of Ivory Coast subsidy. The formation of the Entente enabled Houphouet-Boigny to regain the initiative without really abandoning his opposition to federation.

In this rivalry of French African leaders, all except Houphouet favored federations in a Pan-African spirit and opposed Balkanization. It was this view which brought Senghor of Senegal and Modeiba Keita of the former French Sudan together in the Mali Federation. It also explains why the constitution of Sékou Touré's Guinea as well as that of Nkrumah's Ghana permitted the surrender of sovereignty in whole or in part to a larger political entity. Similar provisions are found in the constitutions of Egypt, Mali, and Tunisia.

In spite of the desire for federation, the rivalry of leaders and parties with differing concepts of political unity broke up the Mali Federation on the night of August 19, 1960, and chastened President Senghor's enthusiasm for federation. In the January, 1961, issue of *Foreign Affairs*, Senghor wrote that in its new role Senegal would "exemplify not so much a pan-African as an inter-African policy." His Prime Minister, Mamadou Dia, explained that "we were defenders of federalism, but we need not be fanatics, since obviously its time has not yet come and since we are faced with micronationalisms that need to be tamed, micronations that will have to be organized."[6]

In the meantime, General de Gaulle had taken an important step before the Mali Federation collapsed. He granted it independence within the French Community. Irritated by this action, Houphouet-Boigny and the other Entente leaders turned and demanded independence *outside* the Community. As a result the world witnessed the unexpected sight of all the remaining sub-Saharan French African territories (except French Somaliland) receiving independence by the fall of 1960.

RIVAL GROUPS

After the break-up of the Mali Federation, the Sudan retained the name Mali and, four months later, joined Ghana and Guinea in a new Union of African States, proclaimed on December 24, 1960, another loose arrangement with little institutional framework other than quarterly meetings of the three heads of state, rotating among

[6] Mamadou Dia, *The African Nations and World Solidarity*, New York, 1961, p. 145.

their respective capitals. The emphasis of the three governments on the need for a common ideology is reflected in Article 5 of the Union's Charter, published on July 1, 1961, which provides for a Co-ordinating Committee to impart to political organizations, trade union organizations, women's movements, and youth movements of the Union states "a common ideological orientation, which is absolutely necessary for the development of the Union."

Another significant step was taken on June 27, 1961, at the tiny border village of Paga, where Presidents Maurice Yaméogo of Upper Volta and Kwame Nkrumah of Ghana knocked down a symbolic wall to mark the suppression of customs barriers and the legalization of free transit between the two countries. The potential political importance of this agreement lies in the fact that Upper Volta is the only territory separating Ghana from Mali.

By October 1, 1960, when Nigeria became independent, Africa contained 26 independent states and no really substantial Pan-African political unions. The states of former French West Africa except Guinea were linked in a customs union and, with Togo included, a monetary union. In June, 1961, it was announced that the Republic of Cameroon would join a customs union of the four states of former French Equatorial Africa.

The year 1961 marked a further cleavage of African states into rival camps. After two preparatory meetings in October and November, 1960, at Abidjan and Brazzaville, 12 former French countries, not including Guinea, Mali, and Togo, met at Yaoundé in March, 1961. These "Brazzaville powers" formed an Afro-Malagasy Union to develop cooperation in defense, diplomacy, and other fields, and an Afro-Malagasy Economic Cooperation Organization (AMECO) which envisaged a full-scale common market working toward a common scale of taxes, common fiscal policies, identical prices for important primary products, the coordination of communications, and other forms of technical cooperation. At this meeting they also agreed to set up a joint airline to be known as Air Afrique.

Meanwhile, the heightening Congo crisis was sharpening differences of opinion between African states by bringing them into the open during United Nations debates. At their conferences in Abidjan and Brazzaville toward the end of 1960, the French territories adopted certain positions on major African problems; they supported the government of Kasavubu and the U.N. mission in the Congo; they favored De Gaulle's idea for a referendum in Algeria; and they resolved to set up a joint military command. It was partly in reaction to this unified approach of the Brazzaville powers that Ghana, Guinea, Mali, Morocco, and Egypt, along with delegations from Libya and the FLN rebels in Algeria, met in Casablanca in January, 1961. The Casablanca group passed resolutions almost diametrically opposed to those of Brazzaville: support for Lumumba and criticism of U.N. actions in the Congo, a U.N.-supervised referendum in Algeria, and their own military high command. They also agreed to establish an African Consultative Assembly and committees for political, economic, military, and cultural Pan-Africanism. Six months later, on July 17, 1961, the Casablanca five met at Conakry to establish their economic arrangements. They decided on a progressive reduction of customs duties and trade quotas among themselves over a five-year period beginning January 1, 1962. Also considered were a wide range of other economic activities, including the possibility of establishing an airline, a shipping company, a bank for African development, a payments union, and a Permanent Council of African Economic Unity.

While the lines between the Brazzaville and Casablanca powers were evolving, the background was being prepared for a third and overlapping group which came to be known as the Monrovia powers because the initiative for it came from Liberia. It proved attractive to nearly all African states except the Casablanca group. As early as January, 1959, President Tubman of Liberia had circulated a proposal for an all-inclusive Organization of African States, evidently modeled on the Organization of American States. He followed this by an overture to Ghana and Guinea, which led to a "summit" at Sanequellie in July, 1959, with President Sékou Touré and Prime Minister Nkrumah. At Sanequellie the three agreed to call a conference in 1960 to prepare for the formation of a Community of Independent African States in which each member would retain its own national identity and constitutional structure, and all would work together to help the people still under colonial rule to achieve independence. The formation of the Casablanca five in January, 1961, however, marked the end of this tripartite effort. When Tubman held the Monrovia conference in May, 1961, the Brazzaville and most other states were represented, but the Casablanca five were conspicuously absent. It was at this meeting that Sir Abubakar Tafawa Balewa, federal Prime Minister of Nigeria, demonstrated his leadership qualities. An economic group from the Monrovia powers met two months later to discuss a possible customs union, a development fund, the amalgamation of existing airlines, and other economic matters.

Twenty Monrovia powers met again in Lagos from January 25 to January 30, 1962, in an African summit attended by 17 chiefs of state or governments. The Casablanca five were still absent, and Libya, Tunisia, and the Sudan refused to participate, reportedly because the Brazzaville 12 would not agree to Algerian participation on the grounds that Algeria was not yet an independent state. The future of a continental Pan-African organization was further jeopardized by this beginning of a possible rift between North Africa and sub-Saharan Africa.

The split with the Casablanca five also seemed to widen when Nigerian Governor General Nnamdi Azikiwe criticized "those who would rather pay lip service to the Charter of the United Nations whilst secretly they nurse expansionist ambitions against their smaller and perhaps weaker neighbors." Azikiwe was apparently referring to Nkrumah's alleged designs on Togo and Morocco's designs on Mauritania. At any rate, President Sylvanus Olympio of Togo and President Mokhtar Ould Daddah of Mauritania greeted his declaration "with enthusiastic applause."

It should be added, however, that Emperor Haile Selassie of Ethiopia declared that no "fundamental and irreparable rift" exists, and that Azikiwe declared at the end of the conference that the 20 states would "welcome with open arms" those missing at Lagos.[7]

The 20 were not prepared to give final approval to a Liberian draft charter for an organization of African states, but they did agree to the idea in principle. At a subsequent meeting in June, a charter for the proposed organization of African and Malagasy States was approved by the foreign ministers, for final adoption at a chief-of-gov-

---

[7] J. R. L. Sterne, "The Lagos Conference," *Africa Report*, February, 1962, p. 4.

ernment conference late in 1962 or early in 1963. Not to be outdone, the Casablanca powers agreed two weeks later, on June 16, 1962, to set up the headquarters of an African Military High Command in Ghana, and to inaugurate an African Common Market the following January.

By 1962, therefore, Pan-Africanism had not produced any real political amalgamations of independent states. However, it had in spired a number of loose political and economic arrangements. These are listed in Table 5, along with several groupings of Eurafrican and Afro-Asian origin.

Other Pan-African ideas still in circulation included a Maghrebian Confederation of Morocco, Tunisia, and Algeria; a Greater Somalia composed of the three Somalis, the Ogaden province of Ethiopia and the northern province of Kenya; and a Greater Morocco, in cluding Mauritania, Rio de Oro, and part of Mali.

Of special interest in 1962 was the Pan-African Freedom Move ment for East and Central Africa. Sponsored by Julius Nyerere, the idea of an East African Federation of Tanganyika, Uganda, and Kenya was soon broadened to encompass Zanzibar, Ruanda-Urundi, and the three central African territories of Nyasaland, Northern Rhodesia, and Southern Rhodesia. At their fourth annual meeting in February, 1962, leaders from these territories broadened their scope still further by including Ethiopia and Somalia, as well as cer tain nationalist groups in South Africa, South-West Africa, Basuto land, Bechuanaland, and Swaziland. They renamed their organiza tion the Pan-African Freedom Movement of East, Central, and South Africa (PAFMECSA). Also as a result of Nyerere's initiative the East Africa High Commission created in 1947 by the British to provide certain common services for Kenya, Uganda, and Tangan yika is continuing as an East African Common Services Organiza tion. The February, 1962, PAFMECSA conference called for im mediate discussions to extend the Common Services Organization to include Ethiopia and Somalia.

A number of impracticable unification plans originated by Euro peans living in Africa were totally defunct. These varied from the wartime fantasy of South African Captain Desmond-Smith for a 24-state United States of Africa with mostly South African white

TABLE 9. Participation of African States in Major Conferences and Organizations, as of February, 1962

	Political Groups													Labor Groups		Economic Groups						
	Arab League	British Commonwealth	French Community	Afro-Asian Solidarity Conference (Cairo)[a]	Conference of Independent African States	All-African Peoples' Conference (Cairo)[b]	Belgrade Conference	Guinea-Ghana-Mali Union	Union Afro-Malgache	Casablanca Conference	Monrovia Conference	Lagos Conference	PAFMECSA[c]	All-African Trade Union Federation	African Trade Union Confederation[d]	Conseil d'Entente	Equatorial African Customs Union	West African Customs Union	West African Monetary Zone	European Economic Community	CCTA	U.N. Economic Commission for Africa
Casablanca powers																						
Algeria Provisional Government							X															
Egypt	X			X	X	X	X			X				X								X
Ghana		X		X	X	X	X	X		X				X							X[e]	X
Guinea					X	X	X	X		X				X							X	X
Mali				X	X	X	X	X		X				X				X	X		X	X
Morocco	X			X	X	X	X			X				X							X	X
Brazzaville group																						
Cameroon				X[f]	X				X		X				X		X			X	X	X
Central African Republic			X						X		X	X					X			X	X	X
Chad			X		X				X		X	X			X		X			X	X	X

Table 5 (Continued).

	Political Groups													Labor Groups		Economic Groups						
	Arab League	British Commonwealth	French Community	Afro-Asian Solidarity[a] Conference (Cairo)	Conference of Independent African States	All-African Peoples[b] Conference (Cairo)	Belgrade Conference	Guinea-Ghana-Mali Union	Union Afro-Malgache	Casablanca Conference	Monrovia Conference	Lagos Conference	PAFMECSA[e]	All-African Trade Union Federation	African Trade Union[d] Confederation	Conseil d'Entente	Equatorial African Customs Union	West African Customs Union	West African Monetary Zone	European Economic Community	CCTA	U.N. Economic Commission for Africa
Congo (Brazzaville)			X						X		X	X			X		X			X	X	X
Dahomey			X						X		X	X			X	X		X	X	X	X	X
Gabon									X		X	X			X		X			X	X	X
Ivory Coast			X	X					X		X	X			X	X		X	X	X	X	X
Malagasy									X		X	X			X					X	X	X
Mauritania			X						X		X	X			X			X	X	X	X	X
Niger						X			X		X	X			X	X		X	X	X	X	X
Senegal			X			X			X		X	X			X			X	X	X	X	X
Upper Volta						X		g			X	X			X	X		X	X	X	X	X
Independents																						
Congo (Leopoldville)					X	X	X				X	X								X	X	X
Ethiopia				X	X	X	X				X	X	X								X	X
Liberia				X	X						X	X			X							X
Libya	X			X	X						X				X							X

120

Nigeria		X	X	X				X	X				X X
Sierra Leone		X						X	X				X X
Somalia	X		X X	X X X		X		X X	X				X X
Sudan			X X	X X X							X		X X
Tanganyika	X							X					X
Togo		X	X	X X				X	X			X	X X
Tunisia		X	X	X X X				X	X				X X
Dependent areas													
Angola			X					X	X				
Kenya		X	X	X		X		X	X				
Mozambique			X					X	X				
Nyasaland			X			X		X	X				
Rhodesia, Northern			X			X		X	X				
Rhodesia, Southern				X		X		X	X				
Ruanda-Urundi													
Uganda		X	X			X		X	X				
Zanzibar		X	X			X		X	X				
South Africa			X			X^i							

a Five additional representatives from French West Africa; French Somaliland also represented.

b South West Africa also represented.

c Pan-African Freedom Movement for East, Central, and Southern Africa.

d Mauritius and Gambia also represented.

e Ghana withdrew from CCTA in February, 1961.

f Represented by the outlawed Union des Populations du Cameroun.

g Ghana and Upper Volta have formed a customs union.

h Libya attended the first meeting of the Casablanca powers, but declined to join the organization.

i Represented by the African National Congress.

121

governors, to the Capricorn Africa Society's less unrealistic but equally unrealizable postwar plan for a Dominion of British East and Central African Territories. The 1953 Federation of Rhodesia and Nyasaland was also in jeopardy in 1962, primarily because it was a European rather than an African creation.

The above summary of regional arrangements inspired by varying concepts of Pan-Africanism deals only with cooperation between governments. Pan-Africanism has also entered the world of nongovernmental organizations, where workers, students, journalists, artists, and writers have created their own associations to foster African unity. The most important of these is the struggle for workers' unity in the trade union movement, which closely reflects the power politics of African blocs. The potential strength of trade unions had induced several heads of African states to attempt centralization and strict control of the labor movement in their countries.

RIVAL TRADE UNION FEDERATIONS

In 1949, the International Confederation of Free Trade Unions (ICFTU) had been formed by free world unions after they withdrew from the World Federation of Trade Unions (WFTU), which came under Communist control. In the ensuing trade union competition, the national labor federations in British territories joined the Western-sponsored ICFTU. In French Africa the ICFTU also won the majority of workers in Morocco, Algeria, and Tunisia, along with most European workers. In French West Africa, however, almost all African unionists belonged to the French Confédération Générale du Travail (CGT), a WFTU affiliate, although the railroad workers formed an autonomous union and certain other unions affiliated with the international Catholic labor federation.

As the Pan-African spirit mounted, the desire for independence from both sides in the cold war naturally affected the labor movement. The earliest manifestation of it was the Union Générale des Travailleurs d'Afrique Noire (UGTAN), formed in 1957 under the leadership of French Guinea's Sékou Touré. UGTAN had the initial advantage of being the first labor unity movement with a neutralist, Pan-African ideology. Its aim of uniting all trade unions in West

Africa and even throughout the continent received a major boost when Ghana joined in 1959 after disaffiliating from the ICFTU.

For a number of reasons, however, UGTAN failed to establish its hegemony. Nigeria, Sierra Leone, and Gambia labor leaders resented Guinea's attempt to gain control of their unions. Nkrumah was apparently uneasy about a movement he could not control in view of Sékou Touré's leadership. And Sékou Touré weakened his own effort by insisting, against the wishes of other African leaders, that trade unionists campaign for a no vote in the De Gaulle referendum of 1958 on association with the French Community. In response to Touré's tactics, several unions stopped effective participation in UGTAN and others withdrew altogether.

Meanwhile, the ICFTU continued its efforts to unite all African trade unions under its banner. At its first regional conference in January, 1957, at Accra, it decided to form an African Regional Organization (AFRO). After considerable delay, AFRO was inaugurated at the end of 1960, with greater autonomy than any other ICFTU regional organization. The continued growth of African neutralism made it seem unlikely, however, that any organization under Western influence could produce Pan-African labor unity.

A new effort at workers' unity was launched at the All-African Peoples Conference in December, 1958, which recommended unanimously that an All-African Trade Union Federation (AATUF) be established. When AATUF was inaugurated in May, 1961, it stipulated that all member unions must break their international affiliations within 10 months—a provision directed specifically at members of the ICFTU. Ghanaians were prominent in the organization of the movement, which attracted unions in the Casablanca group, along with one faction of the Nigerian labor movement.

Many union leaders, however, reacted against the attempt of the Casablanca group to dominate the African labor movement. This led Tunisian, Senegalese, and Kenya trade union leaders to launch a countermovement which culminated in Dakar on January 14, 1962, when an African Trade Union Confederation (ATUC) was formed by the labor unions of 27 states and territories. ATUC avoided AATUF's stringent rule that all unions must break their ties with international confederations, and went on record as opposing state control of unions. African workers thus remained divided along the lines of the two main political blocs.

NEGRITUDE

To complete the analysis of Pan-Africanism, let us turn from its political and economic to its cultural aspects, particularly the related concept of *négritude*. As a political ideology, Pan-Africanism was developed primarily by English-speaking Africans. As an intellectual and cultural trend, its foremost exponents are French-speaking Negro apostles of *négritude* from Africa and the West Indies.

An American Negro, Samuel Allen, in a perceptive analysis of African poetry has contrasted the rich, confident, zestful, and humorous oral folk tales of the old Africa with the modern African poetry of *négritude*. Reminding us that the poet is the soul of the people, Allen concludes that there is no more telling indictment of the impact of the West on Africa than "the tension, anguish, and despair that pervade so much of the poetry of the contemporary Negro throughout the two hemispheres." In this respect, *négritude*[8] is an "antiracial racism"—a negative reaction to white racism and its heartless treatment of Africa as a dark continent of ignorant and inferior savages.

At the same time *négritude* has a much more affirmative aspect. As portrayed in African poetry it is a kind of innate and unique emotional quality common to blacks the world over—a kind of empathy with both the earth and the cosmos, acquired through the Negro's long exposure to tropical existence. The poem *"Cahier d'un Retour au Pays natal"* by Aimé Césaire, a Negro poet from Martinique who conceived the idea of *négritude*, reflects this quality:

> Hurrah for those who have never invented anything
> Hurrah for those who have never explored anything
> Hurrah for those who have never conquered anything
> But who, in awe, give themselves up to the essence
>   of things. . . .[9]

[8] Samuel W. Allen, "Tendencies in African Poetry," *Africa Seen by American Negroes*, John A. Davis, ed., Dijon, 1958, p. 192.
[9] Ulli Beier, "In Search of an African Personality," *The Twentieth Century*, April, 1959, pp. 346–347.

To the poets of *négritude*, Western culture does not possess this emotional quality of empathy and understanding. Léopold Sédar Senghor, who later became the first President of Senegal, is the best-known exponent of *négritude*. In his poem "New York," Senghor finds in the American metropolis only "artificial hearts paid for in hard cash," except in Harlem. Western culture is a "world that has died of machines and cannons," and can be saved only by the natural vitality and life force of the black peoples.[10] Interestingly, Senghor has more recently added the idea of "Africanity" to his vocabulary in order to take into account the non-Negro peoples of North Africa. Africanity is "a synthesis or rather a symbiosis of Negro-African, Berber and European contributions."[11]

The idea of the distinctive qualities of the Negro, it must be added, does not come exclusively from French-speaking Africans. Back in the 1920s, it was set forth by the Gold Coast educator J. E. K. Aggrey, who declared that "the Negro has a great gift for the world: the gift of the idea of meeting injustice and ostracism and oppression by sunny light-hearted love and work. . . . I am proud of my colour; whoever is not proud of his colour, is not fit to live."[12] Aggrey also prophesied that "there is a Youth Movement coming in Africa that some day may startle the world. This restlessness all over Africa stands for self-discovery and self-realisation. It tells of power just breaking through."[13]

The nature of self-discovery in Africa is evident in the cultural renaissance which accompanied the rise of the concept of *négritude*. The myth of white superiority is being broken down by revisions of African history by such writers as K. O. Dike and S. O. Biobaku in Nigeria, K. A. Busia and Nana Kobina Nketsia IV in Ghana, Cheikh Anta Diop and Abdoulaye Ly in Senegal, and Joseph Kizerbo in Upper Volta. In Diop's version of history, the Egyptians were Negroes; he interprets this to mean that European civilization is only an extension of the African genius since Western culture has Egyptian origins.

Reacting against the bias of the white man which leads him to use

[10] *Ibid.*, pp. 347–349.
[11] John Reed, "Is Négritude Relevant?", *Current*, September, 1961.
[12] Edwin W. Smith, *Aggrey of Africa*, London, 1929, p. 135.
[13] *Ibid.*, p. 118.

the word *black* to describe evil and ugliness, the poets of *négritude* glorify everything black:[14]

> Our god is black
> Black of eternal blackness. . . .   (R. G. Armattoe)

> And angels black as India ink
> And dark saints blacker still did sing.   (R. G. Armattoe)

> Woman nude, woman black
> Clad in your color which is life. . . .
> Your beauty strikes me to the heart
> As lightning strikes the eagle.   (Léopold Sédar Senghor)

> Give me back my black dolls
> to disperse
> the image of pallid wenches, vendors of love
> going and coming
> on the boulevard of my boredom.   (Léon Damas)

> Give me black souls
> Let them be black
> Or chocolate brown. . . .
> But if you can
> Please keep them black
> Black.[15]   (F. E. K. Parkes)

This glorification of *négritude* was occasionally accompanied by outspoken antiwhite sentiments. In the poetry of Jacques Roumain,

> . . . And the white man who made you mulatto
> Is nothing but foam, like spittle
> cast up on the shore.

David Diop writes,

> With his white hands red with black blood
> The white man turned to me
> And in the Conqueror's voice said
> Hey boy! a chair, a napkin, a drink!

[14] Unless otherwise noted, the following renditions of African poetry are taken from Samuel W. Allen, *op. cit.*, pp. 180–186. Poems by Aimé Césaire (quoted above), David Diop, Jacques Roumain, and Léopold Sédar Senghor appeared in *La Nouvelle Poésie Nègre et Malgache*, Léopold Senghor, ed., Paris, Presses Universitaires de France, 1948.

[15] *Voices of Ghana*, Accra, Ministry of Education and Broadcasting, 1958, p. 217.

One feels that Diop is even angrier at the arrogant "Hey, boy!" of the Conqueror than he is at the "white hands red with black blood."

The cult of *négritude* does not appeal to many Africans, and notably not to those in South Africa whose long and close contacts with large numbers of whites, coloreds, and Indians have deeply influenced their thinking. In the words of Ezekiel Mphahlele,

Négritude to us is just so much airy intellectual talk either in terms of artistic activity or a fighting faith. . . . I take my negro-ness for granted, and it is no matter for slogans. Imagine a Chinaman waking up one morning and shouting in the streets that he has discovered something Chinese in his sculpture or painting or music![16]

Although they should not be identified with the poets of *négritude*, a few Negroes have gone beyond glorifying blacks and condemning whites to the exaltation of "black power." In his book *Black Power*, Richard Wright admonishes Prime Minister Nkrumah to be hard, to enforce social discipline and militarize the Ghanaian masses in order to force them to make the sacrifices necessary to project Ghana immediately into the twentieth century. In a volatile attack on French atomic testing in the Sahara made in the Nigerian House of Representatives on August 11, 1959, Mr. R. A. Fani-Kayode of Ife declared: "This is the opportunity we have been looking for to show that black men all over Africa must stand or fall together. I have said it often and often in this House that *blackism* is the answer to our problems."[17] The most chauvinistic voicing of the concept of "black power" has come from another American Negro who joined Du Bois as a Communist sympathizer, Paul Robeson. Calling American Negroes "a segment of the power of Bandung," Robeson said to the Negro journalist Carl Rowan:

Yes, this black power moves me. Look at Jamaica. In a few years the white minority will be there on the sufferance of black men. If they're nice decent fellows they can stay. Yes, I look at Senator Eastland and say, "So you think you are powerful here. If only I could get *you* across the border." Although I may stay here the rest of my life, spiritually I'll

[16] Ezekiel Mphahlele, "The Cult of Négritude," *Encounter*, March, 1961, p. 52.
[17] *Debates of the House of Representatives*, vol. 5, no. 27, August 11, 1959, Lagos, 1959, p. 14.

always be part of that world where the black man can say to these crackers, "Get the hell out of here by morning." If I could get a passport, I'd just like to go to Ghana or Jamaica just to sit there for a few days and observe this black power.[18]

Limited to a few extremists, the element of chauvinism in the concept of black power has fortunately been repudiated by Africa's leaders. The spirit of modern Africa suggests, however, that the concepts of Pan-Africanism, the brotherhood of Negro blood, the African personality, blackism, black power, and *négritude* have a significant common denominator in their latent emotional content. The West cannot afford to ignore the possibility that further racial violence between black and white in South Africa, Portugal, and the Rhodesias might turn Pan-Africanism from a constructive political, economic, and cultural movement into an antiwhite trend with disastrous consequences.

OBSTACLES TO PAN-AFRICANISM

Let us now analyze the reasons why Pan-Africanists have made little progress toward the major goal of a united Africa. The barriers in the way of a successful United States of Africa are indeed so numerous and so high that some of them are even obstacles to nationhood, let alone Pan-Africanism. They may be summarized as follows, although not all of them are necessarily a barrier to unity in every instance.

First is the simple geographic fact that the area of Africa is larger than the combined areas of the continental United States, all of Western and Eastern Europe, and all the vast land mass of China. The lack of adequate transportation and communications facilities over Africa's 11,500,000 square miles is a major obstacle to unity.

Second is the historical fact that Africa has developed over many centuries a tremendous diversity of languages, cultures, and traditions. More than 800 vernacular languages are spoken in Africa. Along with their linguistic differences, Africans have developed different historical traditions, different religious beliefs—including

[18] Carl T. Rowan, "Has Paul Robeson Betrayed the Negro?", *Ebony*, October, 1957, p. 41.

animism, Islam, and Christianity—and varied social customs and institutions. Although African leaders were saying by 1960 that "the Sahara unites rather than divides us," it will take more than a slogan to overcome the differing historical and cultural evolutions of the Arab world north of the Sahara and the Negro world to the south. The multiplicity of vernacular languages, however, might be less of a barrier than appears at first glance. If Africa had only a few highly developed languages the situation might be even less conducive to Pan-Africanism.

Third is the more recent historical heritage of the colonial system. European powers divided Africa into arbitrary and artificial political units which largely ignored tribal boundaries. They carried into Africa their different political and governmental traditions and systems. They implanted differing cultural traditions in the modernized elites. The educated minority today learns one or more of at least seven foreign languages—Arabic, Afrikaans, and five European languages. West Africans, when confronted with this hurdle, often cite the example of Canada to indicate that the problem is not insurmountable for English- and French-speaking Africans. The December, 1958, Accra Conference adopted a resolution calling upon all states and countries in Africa which are in a position to do so to teach both English and French in their secondary schools.

In addition, Europeans established differing economic ties and trade and investment patterns which today, for example, link the former French territories with the French economy and the franc area and the former British territories with Britain and the sterling area. In those colonies where white settlers made their homes in substantial numbers, still another divisive factor was injected. It should be noted that these European influences were not necessarily divisive factors in every case; boundaries dividing tribes, for example, sometimes weakened tribal affiliations, thus preparing the way for the acceptance of larger political entities.

Potential economic rivalries of the new states are a fourth difficulty. They want to industrialize, which leads to tariffs to protect and encourage infant industries. Wealthier countries like the Ivory Coast and Gabon and areas like the Katanga province are reluctant to be drawn into political unions which, in effect, would force them to subsidize poorer areas. They compete with each other for foreign aid. The competition for markets for agricultural commodities is growing. Ghanaian and Nigerian cocoa, for example, compete with the expanding production of Ivory Coast and Cameroon. Ghana wants to become an important producer of aluminum, which is also produced in Guinea.

Personal rivalries of ambitious African leaders are a fifth factor which have caused trouble. Nkrumah, Nasser, Tubman, Sékou Touré, Houphouet-Boigny, Olympio, Haile Selassie, and many others are all strong men whose leadership roles do not lend themselves easily to self-sacrifice. It is perhaps unfair, at least in some cases, to attribute their attitudes to personal ambition, for the very nature of their new positions forces them to be strong national leaders in order to mobilize the strength and determination of their people to advance.

Finally, African nationalism itself is an important barrier. As Thomas Hodgkin has commented in his perceptive book, *Nationalism in Colonial Africa*, African nationalism tries to operate at a variety of levels: first, at the level of a particular language group or greater tribe, like the Yoruba or Ewe; second, at the level of a particular territory, like Ubangui-Shari or Nigeria; third, at the regional level of West Africa or the French *Afrique Noire*; and finally at the Pan-African level. The nationalisms of the first three levels all tend to conflict with Pan-Africanism in its widest meaning.

David Apter and James Coleman have described the ways in which African political leaders were forced by circumstances to emphasize "national" rather than Pan-African goals and symbols during both the period of agitation for independence and the period of nation-building after independence. The social revolution they sought to achieve after attaining the "political kingdom" of independence required "national unity, respect for authority, positive loyalty, and a sense of shared purpose," all of which made it "absolutely essential for leaders to create national symbols, national institutions, and a sense of national identity." Apter and Coleman also show how both the Socialist and the democratic ideals of the new states tended to reinforce nationalism and maintain the nation-state as a separate entity. When socialism becomes official state policy, the government becomes deeply committed to preserving the state and using it to achieve socialist goals. When democracy is practiced, the people tend to organize, campaign, and vote on *national* issues and symbols to which voters become attached through habit and tradition.[19]

THE "FEELING" OF UNITY

In conclusion, it is evident that African leaders have invented numerous concepts of Pan-Africanism. One key to understanding it lies perhaps in the "feelings" it inspires. One of Ghana's intellectuals believes that the common people of British and French West African territories "feel" a sense of unity despite the personal rivalries of some of their leaders. A variation of this idea has been expressed by James Baldwin, a peripatetic American Negro who was an observer at the first International Congress of Negro Writers and Artists in Paris in September, 1956. As the Congress debate wore on, he wrote, it became clear

. . . that there *was* something which all black men held in common, something which cut across opposing points of view, and placed in the same context their widely dissimilar experience. What they held in common . . . was the necessity to remake the world in their own image, to impose this image on the world, and no longer be controlled by the vision of the world, and of themselves, held by other people. What, in sum, black men held in common was their ache to come into the world as men. And this ache united people who might otherwise have been divided as to what a man should be.[20]

The Congress which Baldwin described was a cultural conference at which declarations of political views were supposedly out of order. But Alioune Diop, the opening speaker, referred to it as a kind of second Bandung; Diop is a Senegalese who edits the stimulating Parisian journal *Présence Africaine* which has been the chief literary outlet for the disciples of *négritude* since its founding in 1947.

[19] David Apter and James Coleman, "Pan-Africanism or Nationalism," mss. prepared for American Society of African Culture Conference, Philadelphia, June, 1960.
[20] James Baldwin, "Princes and Powers," *Encounter*, January, 1957, p. 55.

The questions discussed at the Paris Congress revealed some of the political undertones of cultural Pan-Africanism: "What are the essential qualities and enduring values of our Negro-African inheritance? How can it best be developed and renewed? How can we be ourselves? How can we make use of European ideas, institutions, and techniques, without becoming their prisoner—without ceasing to be African?" The conference ended with a resolution to engage "all black men in the defense, the illustration, and the dissemination throughout the world of the national values of their people." As Diop expressed it in his final remarks, black men must define themselves "instead of always being defined by others."[21]

This kind of cultural Pan-Africanism is a constructive psychological force which helps Africans to fulfill cultural needs. As for political Pan-Africanism, it lacks the common language and pan-national characteristics of Pan-Germanism and Pan-Arabism, but it has pan-continental possibilities somewhat similar to those of Pan-Americanism and Pan-Europeanism. Its ultimate goal of a single United States of Africa faces too many obstacles for realization in the foreseeable future. In its more limited regional aims, however, Pan-Africanism has already led to the formation of one loose political union and several promising economic organizations. The sudden appearance of many new African states at a peak in the cold war injected abnormal confusion into Africa's international relations. As the turmoil subsides, other and stronger political and economic organizations may develop along regional lines. If the sharp antagonism between the Casablanca and Monrovia powers diminishes with time, the two might still combine to put out "feelers" to each other. The independence of Algeria has eliminated one source of friction. Numerous African states have from time to time suggested meetings to negotiate the fusion of the two blocs. Tanganyika and Sierra Leone may have helped this movement along by their initial refusal to join either group. It should also be noted that several bilateral talks have been held to discuss customs unions and other forms of economic cooperation which would bridge the rival alignments.

Only one thing seemed clear in 1962. The existing combinations of states were marriages of convenience and subject to change. In the

[21] *Ibid.*, p. 60.

prophetic words of Richard Wright, "Above all, Africans must be regimentalized for the 'long pull,' for what will happen in Africa will spread itself out over decades of time and a continent of space . . . and there will be much marching to and fro; there will be many sunderings and amalgamations of people; there will be many shiftings and changes of aims, perspectives, and ideologies. . . ."[22]

[22] Richard Wright, *Black Power*, New York, 1954, p. 347.

8

Concepts of Eurafrica

THE idea of Eurafrica has a shorter and less volatile history than that of Pan-Africanism. Its origins as well as the aims and motives of its advocates were also quite different. It did not become front-page news until February and March, 1957, when the Rome Treaty was negotiated to establish a Common Market for France, West Germany, Italy, Belgium, the Netherlands, Luxembourg, and their overseas territories.

During the debate on Algeria in the United Nations General Assembly on February 4, 1957, French Foreign Minister Christian Pineau made a dramatic announcement that France was ready to lay the foundations of Eurafrica by erecting, within its own territories, a large Franco-African community based on common cultural, economic, and strategic interests. He declared to the Assembly that "Europe in its entirety, bringing to Africa its capital and techniques, should enable the immense African continent to become an essential factor in world politics."[1] Soon afterward, a group of Belgian, Italian, Dutch, West German, and French parliamentarians made a trip through French Africa to survey Eurafrican possibilities. They were reportedly much impressed by the discovery that Eurafrica, with a population of 220,000,000 Africans and 200,000,000 Europeans, was potentially the most powerful single bloc in the world. If

[1] *New York Times*, February 5, 1957.

Africans could be given sufficient freedom to make them feel equal, and if they were helped to build themselves up into modern nations, the Mediterranean might no longer be the dividing line between Europe and Africa, but only a great inland sea in a stretch of mutually complementary territory running from northern Norway down to southern Africa! Such was the Eurafrican dream!

THE HISTORY OF THE CONCEPT

Let us now review the history of this idea, looking first at its origins, then at the motives of its advocates, and finally, at the various organizations thus far created along Eurafrica lines. The origins of the concept of Eurafrica are obscure, but one possible embryo of it is found in a 1925 report by the General Electric Company regarding hydroelectric possibilities in European-owned Africa. In this view, the rainfall of tropical Africa, its high plateaus for European living, and its many rapids and waterfalls made possible the building of "an all-electric continent with a standard of living potentially higher than that of the United States—provided it was operated as a single unit."[2]

According to Eugène Guernier, a French writer, the term *Eurafrica* was first formulated by him in 1927. His ideas were elaborated six years later in his book *L'Afrique—Champ d'expansion de l'Europe*. Albert Sarraut, then French Minister of Colonies, had already aroused the interest of numerous readers with a 1923 book entitled *La mise en valeur des colonies françaises*, appealing for French action to develop the French colonial empire. Guernier broadened this appeal by advocating the integration of Africa into the economy of Europe as a whole. Along with the immigration of 15,000,000 to 20,000,000 Europeans into Africa, he wrote, it would "assure Europe 30 to 50 years of calm, prosperity and peace." With an ingenious geopolitical argument Guernier divided the world into three intercontinental *fuseaux* (longitudinal sections of the globe's surface)—Eurafrica, Asia-Australia, and the Americas. "Latitudinal" exchanges of agricultural products, he wrote, are a "nonsense" because there is no need to

---

[2] This report is cited by Volney D. Hurd, "Eurafrican Reechoes," *The Christian Science Monitor*, March 21, 1957.

exchange Danubian wheat for the wheat produced in the same latitude in Canada, or Louisiana cotton for Sudanese cotton. Conversely,
"longitudinal" exchanges appear to be *la loi fatale de la vie humaine*.
The black continent is thus incorporated in the white continent.
The resulting "Eurafrica" forms a "universal cycle"—a terrestrial
fuseau with a self-sufficient economy.[3]

The devastation of Europe during World War II attracted renewed interest in Africa's potential for strengthening Europe. The
concept of the Eurafrican *fuseau* was further publicized by Jean
Delorme in the June 6, 1941, issue of *La vie industrielle*, and by René
Viard in a 1942 book, *L'Eurafrique pour une nouvelle économie
européenne*. Delorme, who wrote that "men have always wanted their
garden near their house and their granary under their roof," limited
his vision to a Eurafrican *demi-fuseau* including only Africa north
of the equator. Viard, however, finding Delorme's idea "too conventional and, in reality, foreign to the natural conditions of the African
center," wanted the whole of the two continents in his Eurafrican
ensemble. Guernier, speaking on the subject again at a conference
on Eurafrica and the Common Market, held by the French Académie
des Sciences d'Outre-Mer in May, 1958, suggested that perhaps even
the Soviet Union, when China takes Siberia as its first colony, will
turn toward the West and join Eurafrica![4] The concept of a geographic union of Europe and Africa for economic purposes was also
supported in 1959 by François Perroux, whose economic theory
stressed the need for a "motor-cell" or axis around which auxiliary
industries could develop. The increasing economic interdependence
between producers and consumers made Europe and Africa complementary to each other and a free trade zone advantageous to both.

German interest in Eurafrica ideas dates back to the period not
long after the Treaty of Versailles, when the loss of its colonies
stimulated it to foster the development of trade with Africa. Franz
Ansprenger in his *Politik im Schwarzen Afrika* says that the word
Eurafrica was coined in Germany around 1933, which conflicts with

---

[3] Eugène Guernier, *L'Afrique—Champ d'expansion de l'Europe*, Paris, 1933,
pp. 271–278.
[4] Eugène Guernier, "L'Eurafrique et la communauté Européene," *Comptes
rendus mensuels des seances de l'Académie d'Outre-mer, L'Eurafrique et le
marché commun*, vol. 28, 1958, pp. 187–205.

Guernier's claim to have invented it in 1927. The idea was beclouded by the fulminations of Nazi leaders demanding the return of German colonies, but after World War II Eurafrica ideas revived and acquired a larger following. In 1952 Anton Zischka published his popular *Afrika, Gemeinschaftsaufgabe*, a book which attracted sufficient attention to be translated into French as *L'Afrique; Complément de l'Europe*. Calling the Schuman-inspired European Coal and Steel Community the first Eurafrican organism, Zischka appealed for a strong Franco-German nucleus of a European community, without Britain, for the common exploitation of African resources.

Although the concept of Eurafrica has a French and German aura, it also aroused interest in Italy and the Netherlands, two countries which, like Germany, had lost or were losing their colonies. They too were motivated in part by the desire to recoup their economic position without the burdens of the colonial relationship. Postwar German publicists, anxious to avoid the stigma of colonialism, were evidently unhappy to have the Eurafrica idea put forward during a debate on the Algerian question in the United Nations General Assembly. As Ernest Friedlaender wrote in February, 1957, in the *Hamburger Abendblatt*:

It is impossible to let the policies of the whole world revolve around one million French people in Algeria who want to remain masters of their house. Algeria will not stay French, any more than Indochina stayed French. The question is, how many more sacrifices will have to be made before this fact dawns on them? It should be said quite frankly: As long as Algeria remains an "internal French" affair, Eurafrica holds no attraction for us. Eurafrica as a cloak for a national and colonial policy of some European states would be no remedy for the difficulties of today. There is no remedy as long as the old status quo is to be maintained. The common economic power of Europe ought to be put forth only under the sign of the future, i.e., under the sign of freedom and friendship. The economic development of Africa with European assistance under this sign would be a fine and great task.[5]

Although Britain was not a partner in the Eurafrica ideology of the French and Germans, economic reasons for linking Europe and Africa were also in the mind of British Foreign Secretary Ernest Bevin. In his notable January 22, 1948, speech on British foreign

[5] Quoted in *Toward Freedom*, February, 1957, p. 3.

policy, he stressed the importance of finding economic support for his proposed Western European Union. "In the first place," he said, "we turn our eyes to Africa. . . . [We need] the closest possible collaboration with the Commonwealth and overseas territories, not only British, but French, Dutch, Belgian and Portuguese."[6]

In the United States, while the Marshall Plan for aid to war-torn Western Europe was getting under way, those who were particularly interested in Africa sought ways and means of helping it as well. In the State Department, consideration was given in 1948 to a proposal for an African development authority which, with U.S. financial support, would have attempted to expand and coordinate the economic development of Africa more effectively. It aroused little support, however, partly because the United States had no geographic basis for participation (that is to say, no territory of its own in Africa), partly because the European colonial powers were at that time unsympathetic to U.S. participation in such an organization, and partly because the United States was confronted by higher-priority needs in other areas.

In these early postwar years, another person interested in the idea of Eurafrica was Volney Hurd, Chief of the Paris News Bureau of the *Christian Science Monitor*. Hurd has related how he approached Jean Monnet, then in charge of French economic planning, to discuss the idea. They considered the possibility of an African development corporation in which Europe would hold the ownership through bonds and half-interest in the stock, while the United States would be given the other half of the stock in return for Marshall Plan aid and any other sums invested in Africa. With Monnet's encouragement, Hurd put this suggestion into the form of a report which he sent to European foreign ministers and to Marshal Jan Christian Smuts in South Africa. According to Hurd, he received personal replies from many foreign ministers, including Bevin in England and Count Carlo Sforza in Italy, as well as from Marshal Smuts. They all approved the idea in principle but most of them indicated that the Marshall Plan was about all they could handle at the moment. Smuts "sent a particularly warm letter, saying the idea paralleled much of his own thinking and sincerely hoping it would come about.

[6] *New York Times*, January 23, 1948.

He questioned whether the minds of Europe were advanced enough in their thinking at the moment, however, and so it would probably have to be left to the future."

Soon afterward, following a Marshall Plan meeting, Hurd again met Monnet, who told him: "A wonderful idea, Mr. Hurd! But my French colleagues are finding it difficult to think even about uniting Europe, let alone thinking about Africa! But what a shame, for it is still a very great idea—and I'm terribly sorry!"[7] Hurd does not mention, however, a basic weakness in Monnet's concept of Eurafrica. Monnet evidently shared the motivation of those who desired to help France first, Europe second, and Africa last. It was he who reportedly coined the myopic phrase that France could bring Africa as a "dowry to Europe," which Foreign Minister Robert Schuman used in announcing his plan for a European Coal and Steel Community. It is also said that while Monnet was enthusiastic about Eurafrica ideas in the abstract, he failed to give the necessary support to specific economic cooperation projects advocated by certain other French officials.

POLITICAL AND MILITARY ASPECTS

Thus far, economic motives in the thinking of advocates of Eurafrica has been stressed. They were also motivated by political and military factors. On the political side, certain leaders in weakened European countries began to conceive of a Eurafrica formula as a means of maintaining European political influence and prestige in African territories attaining independence. Another political motive was the belief that Eurafrica might save Africa from the Soviet threat. This was the theme of French Premier Guy Mollet in a speech to the Foreign Policy Association in New York on February 28, 1957. The Eurafrica plan, he said, would provide European help to enable African people to achieve real independence. "In the face of the Communist offensive in Africa," he added, "the democracies must offer more than a futile attempt to outbid the Communists.

[7] Volney D. Hurd's account of the Eurafrican idea is found in three of his articles in the *Christian Science Monitor*, February 21, March 21, and April 22, 1957.

The democracies should seek their solution not in support for in flamed nationalism but in the realm of international cooperation."[8]

A third motive of certain Eurafricanists was their hope for a better system of military defense for a Western Europe weakened by World War II. In the view of Adriano Moreira, a Portuguese specialist on Africa, the concept of Eurafrica is only a detail of the older move ment for European unity, which has usually been strongest during security crises in Europe. The postwar emphasis on Africa's strategic importance was a new departure in geopolitical theory. Early geo politicians, who stressed the role of geography in determining the politics of nations, paid little attention to Africa. Although German General Ludendorff rightly predicted that North Africa would play a decisive role in a second world war, most of the noted geopoliticians did not regard Africa as a power center. From the little they knew of Africa they concluded that its potentialities were too limited by its tropical climate, its lack of industrialization, and the fact that dur ing its history it had exerted little pressure on Europe. According to Sir Halford Mackinder's celebrated "Heartland theory" of geopoli tics, "Who rules Eastern Europe commands the Heartland; who rules the Heartland commands the world-island; who rules the world island commands the world." In this conception, Africa was of rela tively little strategic significance because it fell between the "inner or marginal crescent," and the lands of "outer or insular crescent."[9]

The experience of World War II, however, led to a new apprecia tion of Africa's strategic importance, partly because North Africa served as one of the springboards for the defeat of Germany. It is sometimes contended that Hitler made a major blunder by ignoring the advice of his geopoliticians and moving into Africa too late; in this view he might have won the war if he had overrun Spain and crossed the Straits of Gibraltar. The military importance of North Africa was particularly stressed by French writers. General de Montsa bert, a French officer, contended in April, 1953, that in current military concepts Eurasia and Eurafrica had replaced the separate continents of Europe, Asia, and Africa. He added:

[8] New York Times, March 1, 1957.

[9] Charles Kruszewski, "The Pivot of History," Foreign Affairs, April, 1954, pp. 388–401, analyzes Mackinder's theories.

It should be remembered that the European coal and iron are dangerously situated on the northern plain which has always been a favorite route of invaders from the East. In opposition to the laws of economics, military imperatives demand that there be iron and steel plants far from the great concentrations on the Rhine and not directly vulnerable to enemy attack. . . . In developing a heavy industry [in Africa] we would be following the example of the Russians, creating a "Urals" in the Atlas Mountains of Morocco and a "Siberia" in Central Africa.[10]

Despite the subsequent loss of Morocco and Tunisia, and the threat to the French position in Algeria, the same idea appears in the writing of another Frenchman, Maurice Moyal, in 1957. "Africa," he wrote, "is the natural complement of, and is vital to the defense, life and subsistence" of Europe. If Russian armies should use their crushing manpower superiority to sweep through Western Europe, only Africa could give NATO forces space to trade for time for America and the rest of the free world to mobilize their manpower and tremendous industrial potential before starting on the reconquest of Europe. Moreover, taking into account the new discoveries in the Sahara, he opines that Africa could offer the West an alternative heavy armament industry centered around the tremendous Tinduf iron-ore deposits and Ahnet natural gas resources in the heart of the Sahara.[11] The Belgians, it might be added, were interested in similar possibilities at their Congo base at Kamina in Katanga.

These military considerations prompted a number of postwar efforts to develop Eurafrican defensive arrangements. The first notable African Defense Facilities Conference met at Nairobi in August of 1951 to review ways and means of facilitating communications and the movement of troops and military supplies in eastern and central Africa. Britain, France, Belgium, Italy, Portugal, Southern Rhodesia, and South Africa were the main participants, with Ethiopia also represented and the United States having an observer present. Among the ideas emanating from the Conference is said to have been an agreement to construct a railway from Kamina to Kabalo, thereby linking Lobito with Dar-es-Salaam.

[10] General de Montsabert, "North Africa in Atlantic Strategy," *Foreign Affairs*, April, 1953, pp. 424–425.
[11] Maurice Moyal, "What Prospect for Eurafrica?" *New Commonwealth*, August 5, 1957, pp. 112–115.

Three years later, from March 11 to 18, 1954, a follow-up Confer
ence for West African Defense Facilities was held at Dakar by
Britain, France, Belgium, Portugal, the Federation of Rhodesia and
Nyasaland, South Africa, and Liberia, with the United States again
represented by an observer. The Dakar Conference was reported to
have signed secret recommendations for the use of West African
communications in case of war.

In 1955, when Britain transferred the Simonstown naval base to
South Africa, the Union agreed to make the base facilities available
to Britain and to all of Britain's allies in time of war whether or not
South Africa was at war. The 1955 and 1957 defense conferences between Britain and South Africa also produced an agreement to sponsor a future Southern Africa Defense Conference, to be held in the
Union. South Africa's Minister of Defense François Erasmus sought
to play a leading role in developing a Western alliance linking South
Africa with Britain, France, Belgium, and Portugal in common defense of the African continent. Belgian, French, Portuguese, Rhodesian, and American military officers visited the Union during the
1950s to confer on military coordination. No formal Eurafrican defense organization emerged, however, the British government being
reportedly cool toward the idea.

Meanwhile, South Africa strengthened its own defense forces considerably, and in 1955 the Minister of Defense said that an armored
task force for continental service beyond South Africa's borders was
being trained and equipped. A tropical warfare school, it was reported in August, 1959, was to be established in the Caprivi Strip.
According to the progovernment *Die Burger*, the Caprivi Strip was
probably chosen as the site of the school because it is "the Union's
farthest outpost if an attack comes out of the north. . . ."

Prospects for any formal plan or organization for the defense of
Africa by the colonial powers and South Africa were soon outdated
by the emergence of new African states. This fact was evident in the
striking communiqué released by the NATO powers after their December, 1957, meeting, the tone of which recognized that the West
had less and less of its past power to dispose of Africa's problems
and more and more necessity to deal with Africans. Implicitly ac-
knowledging the right of Africans to manage their own future, the

communiqué expressed the hope that the African countries and peoples who are disposed to do so "will cooperate with the free world in efforts to promote . . . the development of conditions of stability and economic and political well-being in the vitally important continent of Africa. . . . We affirm the readiness of our peoples to cooperate for our part with the countries and peoples of Africa to further these ends."[12] This was indeed a new tone, one that the Western powers could not have agreed upon a few years earlier.

EURAFRICAN ECONOMIC COOPERATION

Although the emergence of independent African states killed any prospects of a Eurafrican defense organization, it did not entirely destroy the possibility of some kind of a Eurafrican economic organization. Despite similar psychological obstacles, economic cooperation and organization were more promising because of the intense aspirations of African leaders for economic development of their new countries. In the beginning, at least, many of the new states were willing to participate in the Common Market of the European Economic Community (EEC) which went into effect on January 1, 1959.

The movement to unite Western Europe produced so many overlapping councils, assemblies, organizations, and communities that they are as difficult to unravel as the variety of Pan-African organizations described in the last chapter. Perhaps the most successful of the many postwar experiments in international association was the Organization for European Economic Cooperation (OEEC), established on April 16, 1948, as an outgrowth of an earlier Committee of European Economic Cooperation formed in July, 1947. The OEEC became a vital organization with a precise task because of the American request that it take the responsibility of recommending the division of American aid, totaling about $11,000,000,000, among its member countries.

In October, 1949, an active American campaign for more rapid and far-reaching measures of European economic integration was

[12] For complete text of communiqué, see *Washington Post and Times Herald,* December 20, 1957.

launched. The OEEC countries responded with several important steps. By an agreement of September 19, 1950, a European Payments Union (EPU) was established, and on August 25, 1952, the Schuman Plan came into effect with the establishment of the European Coal and Steel Community (ECSC). The latter was composed only of the six nations of Little Europe—France, the Federal Republic of Germany, Italy, and the three Benelux countries (Belgium, the Netherlands, and Luxembourg). It pooled coal and steel resources of member states and eliminated trade barriers like customs duties in these commodities, thereby creating a common or free market for coal and steel.

The basis for linking the overseas territories to the Common Market, which came about six years later, is found in Article 79 of the ECSC Treaty, extending to all members the preferential measures with respect to coal and steel enjoyed by any member in its own overseas territories. At the time, German and Italian steel producers were anxious to compete in the French African market, while Italian and Dutch interests wished to have access to the iron of Mauritania and Gabon. A further step toward European integration, the European Defense Community (EDC) Treaty signed on May 27, 1952, unfortunately failed to win ratification by the French parliament because it provided for the merging of the French army with some form of European army under a joint command. The creation of a European army seemed to depend on the prior establishment of a European political community.

Meanwhile, at its forty-ninth meeting on October 4, 1948, the Executive Committee of the OEEC had created an Overseas Territories Working Group consisting of Belgium, France, the Netherlands, Portugal, and the United Kingdom. The Eurafrican idea of bringing African territories into a common market soon took another step forward. From its first session in 1949, the Consultative Assembly of the Council of Europe, composed of 132 delegates chosen by the national parliaments of 15 countries, studied proposals for closer collaboration between European member countries and the territories with which they had special links. Out of these deliberations, it adopted on September 25, 1952, a notable resolution which came to be known as the Strasbourg Plan. Going beyond the field of technical cooperation it called for the coordination of the economies of the "zone formed by the countries of Western Europe, together with the overseas countries, territories and dominions, having constitutional ties with them." The Strasbourg Plan also provided for the creation of a European bank for the development of overseas territories, for long-term international price agreements to encourage production, and for preferential tariffs within the zone and on the basis of reciprocity with the dominions of the British Commonwealth.

It was to take more than six years, however, before a beginning was made in bringing such a Eurafrican economic zone into existence. In May, 1953, the Committee of Ministers of the Council of Europe transmitted the Strasbourg Plan to the OEEC for study, and in 1954 the Committee of Ministers approved the principle "that the policy of European integration entails, as a corollary, cooperation, in the interests of their common prosperity, between metropolitan powers, the overseas countries which have constitutional links with them, and the other member countries of the Council of Europe." To carry this principle forward, the Standing Committee of the Consultative Assembly adopted Order No. 77 on July 9, 1955, instructing the Secretary General to set up a group of independent experts to "submit any new proposals likely to encourage the economic and social development of Africa through cooperation on an equal footing within a Eurafrican Community."[13]

The history of the words *Eurafrican community* in Order No. 77 illustrates a basic flaw in the Eurafrican dream. Seven of the experts (four Europeans and three Africans), after a preliminary meeting at Strasbourg from November 20 to 22, 1956, took the unusual step of recommending unanimously that their own terms of reference be changed. They objected to Order No. 77 because it barred the appointment of experts from independent African countries to the group, and because the expression, "a Eurafrican Community," had acquired a special political significance. Complying with the request of the experts, the Standing Committee then adopted Order No. 105 on January 11, 1957, to replace Order No. 77. The new terms of ref-

---

[13] Report of the Group of Experts Presented to the Consultative Assembly of the Council of Europe, *The Development of Africa*, Strasbourg, September, 1957, p. 1.

erence deleted the objectionable words *Eurafrican community* and called for cooperation on an equal footing between the African countries and the member countries of the Council of Europe. The importance of psychological and political factors in international economic problems was again indicated by this incident.

With its new terms of reference, the committee of experts produced in September, 1957, a valuable report on "The Development of Africa" which was presented to the Consultative Assembly of the Council of Europe. It recommends not a Eurafrican community but a system of cooperation among member countries of the Council of Europe and the African countries which would also be open to other countries desirous of contributing to the economic and social development of Africa. Likening their proposal to the Colombo Plan, the experts suggested five additional bodies of international machinery for different economic development functions.

AFRICAN PARTICIPATION IN THE COMMON MARKET

Meanwhile, six months before this report was completed, the Eurafrica movement had culminated in the Rome Treaty of March 25, 1957, under which the six nations of Little Europe "established among themselves a European Economic Community" (EEC), based on a Common Market to be gradually implemented over the next 12 to 17 years. The possibility of linking the overseas territories to the Community was raised at an early point in the Treaty negotiations, and eventually became a condition of French agreement. Articles 131 to 136 relate to the association of "non-European countries and territories which have special relations with Belgium, France, Italy and the Netherlands."[14] Specific arrangements for this association are spelled out in an accompanying five-year Implementing Convention.

Article 133 of the Treaty provides for the progressive but total abolition of customs duties on imports from the overseas territories into the six member states. Customs duties on imports from the six, as well as duties of the overseas countries and territories on each

[14] The full text of Articles 131–136 is available in *Current History*, February, 1958, pp. 111–115.

other's products, are also to be progressively abolished, except that the overseas countries and territories may collect nondiscriminatory duties "to meet the needs of their development and the requirements of their industrialization, or duties of a fiscal nature the purpose of which is to contribute to their budget." The Implementing Convention deals also with quotas, which are usually more of an obstacle to trade than tariffs are.

A second important objective of the Treaty is found in Article 132, which provides that "Member States shall contribute to the investments required for the progressive development of these countries and territories." The size, sources, and allocations of this development fund are described precisely in two annexes to the Implementing Convention. A total of $581,250,000 was to be contributed over a five-year period, $200,000,000 each from France and the Federal Republic of Germany, $70,000,000 each from Belgium and the Netherlands, $40,000,000 from Italy, and $1,250,000 from Luxembourg. The entire fund was to be allocated within five years as follows: French territories were to receive the lion's share, a total of $511,250,000; Netherlands territories, $35,000,000; Belgian territories, $30,000,000; Italian Somaliland, $5,000,000. The territories of France were thus in effect subsidized by the other five member states. Numerous political and economic aspects of this arrangement were unsatisfactory to the five, but they agreed to it in order to please France. Germany evidently decided to pay the price and risk the possible taint of "collective colonialism" in the hope of successful bargaining with France for benefits on other matters.

The Common Market, it will be noted, covered French, Belgian, Italian, and Dutch territories, but did not include British, Portuguese, and Spanish territories or the independent states. The early hostility of Africa's independent states to the Common Market again revealed a conflict between psychological and economic factors. In the United Nations General Assembly in the fall of 1957, a heated discussion arose over the possible effects of the European Economic Community on non–self-governing territories. A controversial resolution on the subject was opposed by Western Europe and the United States. The American Delegation contended that (1) it would be premature to attempt to deal intelligently with possible future effects of the Common Market, (2) the Common Market would "prove to be a contribution to the economic development of the African territories concerned, on a basis of equality and mutuality of interest," and (3) the details of the operation of the Common Market still remained to be worked out and the GATT (General Agreement on Tariffs and Trade) organization was the only proper forum for the discussion of these details.[15]

The anticolonial group, however, would accept none of these arguments. They contended, among other things, that (1) the Common Market might have an adverse effect on infant industries in Africa, (2) links with the metropole might make African territories suffer during economic declines in Europe, (3) the Common Market would hurt the trade of non–self-governing territories outside the European Economic Community, (4) it might have an adverse effect on the economies of African states bordering the Common Market territories, (5) the reduction of tariffs in African countries might jeopardize African fiscal structures, and (6) the Common Market would discourage investment from countries outside the European Economic Community. In addition to these economic contentions, the anticolonials placed heavy stress on certain political arguments, namely, that (1) the Common Market was a violation of the right of self-determination in that the non–self-governing territories were not consulted regarding their association with the European Economic Community, (2) the absence of any provision regarding freedom of movement in the associated countries and territories of workers from member states might bring a flood of Europeans into Africa, and (3) it was incompatible with the principle of paramountcy of indigenous interests set forth in Article 73 of the U.N. Charter.

In a vain attempt to refute these arguments, the administering authorities asserted that (1) the arrangement would open up a market of 180,000,000 people, (2) African countries could establish their own tariffs, (3) the investment fund would bring new capital, (4) Africans were consulted about the establishment of the Treaty and would be regularly consulted in the future, (5) it was untrue to say that the association of non–self-governing territories in the European

[15] United States Delegation to the General Assembly, "Statement . . . in Committee IV," *Press Release No. 2788*, October 28, 1957.

conomic Community would keep them from attaining independ-
nce, (6) it was a violation of Article 2(7) of the Charter to discuss
he matter, (7) it was a bad precedent for the U.N. to discuss treaties
efore they were ratified, and (8) the anticolonial attitude in this
ase was a threat to the principle of regional cooperation. Needless
o say, the arguments on both sides contained an ample proportion
f red herrings.[16]

Soviet writers, incidentally, have picked up and elaborated many
f these themes for several years. *The Mizan Newsletter* for Septem-
er, 1961, summarizes the attacks on Eurafrica as a vehicle for "re-
enge-seeking schemes of resurgent West German imperialism," a
cheme for "the perpetuation of the dependence of the African peo-
les on the colonial powers," and a brand of "collective colonialism
gainst which the African peoples are waging a brave fight."[17]

---

[16] These arguments are summarized from statements in the United Nations
General Assembly, A/C.4/S.R. 672, 673, 674, 675, 676, 677, 678, 682, 683, and
684, October 19–31, 1957.
[17] "Soviet Views of Eurafrica," *The Mizan Newsletter*, September, 1961, pp.
15, 17.

9

African Cooperation with Europe

I_N the early years of implementation, the direct benefits of the Common Market to the associated African countries were below expectations. For reasons of international politics, the first tariff reduction applied by the six European members on January 1, 1959, was extended to all GATT countries, thereby denying preferential treatment to the associated African states. Although the second and third tariff reductions in 1960 and 1961 applied only to the six and the associated territories, pressures are again being generated to force further concessions to GATT countries. Each time such concessions involve African primary products, the advantage of association with the EEC is proportionately reduced.

Various measures taken by individual members of the Common Market have further nullified the beneficial effects of a common outside tariff. Cases in point are exemptions on the importation of tropical woods, the fact that Italy buys bananas only from Somalia, and special arrangements between France and its former colonies. Africans also complained that Germany's internal purchase taxes on coffee and cocoa prevented the expansion of domestic consumption. Philippe Yacé, President of the Ivory Coast National Assembly, once calculated that the consumer purchase taxes on coffee and other tropical products in the six raised more money than the total spent in Africa through the development fund.[1]

SLOW PROGRESS

Allocations from the development fund to the associated countries and territories were also disappointingly slow. The EEC Council decided in July, 1959, to allocate 70 to 75 percent of the fund to "economic" projects in such fields as transportation and agriculture rather than "social" projects in health, education, and welfare, although many African leaders would like to see a more even proportion between these two categories of aid. By the end of May, 1961, financing had been approved for only 152 projects involving $155,734,000. Part of the reason for the delay was a conflict between France and Germany over the relations between the associated countries and the EEC Commission which managed the fund. During the first two years France wanted all projects from the associated countries to be submitted through Paris, thereby preventing direct contacts between African leaders and the Commission. In response to German opposition, France relaxed its policy and insisted only that it be informed directly when an agreement had been reached, in order that it might coordinate its bilateral aid program with that of the EEC.

The major early beneficiaries of the development fund were the Ivory Coast, which received $17,500,000 through May 31, 1961; the Malagasy Republic, which received $15,700,000; and Senegal, which received $13,600,000. The Malagasy Republic received numerous grants for reconstruction after a typhoon struck the island in 1958. Senegal benefited because it was one of the first states to produce a comprehensive development plan, a fact which the EEC found appealing. The Ivory Coast was attractive because it has a good economic base for further development.

The future of African participation in the Common Market has been highly speculative ever since the Rome Treaty was signed in 1957. At that time, even though it was not expected that so many

[1] Sally H. Willcox, "Africa and the EEC: Prospects for 1962," *Africa Report*, August, 1961, p. 7.

African states would be independent by 1960, it was clear that the political map of Africa would be profoundly altered by 1973 when the Common Market was due to be fully implemented. Such political changes were bound to have economic repercussions. One hurdle was surmounted on June 20, 1960, when the EEC Council resolved a legal controversy over the issue of whether independence had voided the Rome Treaty provisions for associated countries and territories. The Council decided that the Treaty provisions continued to apply until revised, and that the independent associated states could send representatives to EEC headquarters in Brussels. Members of the EEC Commission staff traveled widely in the associated countries and territories in the summer of 1960 to build good will.

The admission of Greece as an associated member of the EEC opened up the possibility that other states might join. In 1961 it was even suggested that a Mediterranean common market attached to the EEC might be formed of Greece, Turkey, Israel, Spain, and Morocco, Algeria, and Tunisia. Because of Commonwealth preferences and other problems, Britain originally had kept out of the Common Market and had formed instead the European Free Trade Association (EFTA) or "outer seven" along with Denmark, Sweden, Norway, Switzerland, Austria, and Portugal. However, on July 28, 1961, Britain informed its partners in the EFTA that it would apply for full membership in the Common Market. Denmark and Norway also initiated action to become full members, while Sweden, Switzerland, Austria, and Ireland announced their intention to seek a looser form of association with the EEC under Article 238 of the Treaty.

Still another major development was the decision of the older Organization for European Economic Cooperation to change its form to keep pace with the times. It was replaced in October, 1961 by a 20-power Organization for Economic Cooperation and Development, composed of 18 Western European countries plus the United States and Canada. Its objectives are not only to promote the economic growth and trade of the industrialized West, but to expand aid to underdeveloped countries from capital-exporting nations. In early 1960, 10 states (including Japan, which is not a member of the OECD) plus the EEC Commission formed a Development Assistance Group to foster discussion while the OECD came into being. It has been replaced by a Development Assistance Committee which functions within the framework of the OECD.

By 1960, African attitudes toward the EEC showed signs of change. In December, 1958, at the first meeting of the U.N. Economic Commission for Africa, African delegates had taken the position that association with the Common Market was an obstacle rather than a help toward the achievement of economic independence. Some of them even seemed to believe that it was part of a British and French intrigue to divide West Africa permanently into two camps. Ghana and Nigeria were particularly concerned over the effect of Common Market tariffs on their large cocoa exports.

Two years later the Economic Commission for Africa took a more balanced position: "Although . . . no form of association with a group of industrial countries . . . would be in itself sufficient to solve the long term economic problems of any African country, some of them may legitimately consider such association necessary in order to alleviate their difficulties resulting from the breaking up of their sheltered markets." The Commission went on to state that the African territories could also hope to obtain some financial assistance and markets for their semiprocessed goods. However, it warned that if these benefits were not used to decrease the economic dependence of an Associated Country—"mainly by reducing its imports prices and internal costs, by diversifying the geographical pattern and commodity composition of its trade and by channeling as much investment as possible toward productive purposes— . . . association with EEC could easily . . . turn out to be a long term disadvantage to the country concerned."[2]

In June, 1961, representatives of the 16 associated African states met with delegates of the six Common Market countries in a Eurafrican parliamentary conference at Strasbourg to consider modifications in their present convention of association, which expires on December 31, 1962. The Strasbourg Conference proposed the establishment of a Council of Association composed of the representatives of each African associate and of the Council of the EEC Commission. It

[2] United Nations, Economic Commission for Africa, *Report on the Effects of Economic Groupings in Europe on African Economics*, E/CN.14/72, New York, 1960.

also recommended that a parliamentary conference be established to meet at least once a year alternatively in Europe and Africa; that African ambassadors be accredited to EEC headquarters and EEC representatives to each African government; and that a court of arbitration be established to settle litigation relative to the interpretation and application of the convention of association. A number of economic recommendations were also agreed upon, and a new Common Market Development Fund was planned for inauguration on January 1, 1963, on a partnership basis with more flexibility in operations and with larger capitalization. In a subsequent conference in Paris on the ministerial level, it was also decided that the African states would be permitted to levy special tariffs as necessary to promote their economic development and industrialization.

The Strasbourg recommendations of 1961 are far removed from the Guernier concept of Eurafrica in 1927, and indicate that economic ideas are being adapted to political necessities in an independent Africa. However, even though the links between the EEC and its associated African countries are evolving toward partnership, these changes may not be enough to sustain the present relationship. What, for example, will be the effect of the numerous overlapping Pan-African political and economic associations discussed in Chapter 7? Which of them will survive and what will be their ultimate effect on African-European trade?

REACTIONS OF PARTICIPANTS AND NONPARTICIPANTS

As a condition of its entry into the Common Market, Britain is now demanding the same trade advantages for its former colonies as those now enjoyed by former French, Belgian, and Italian possessions. Pushed to their logical conclusion, such arrangements would tend to foster two large economic groupings, with Africa and Europe in one and Latin America and the United States in the other. In theory this would isolate Liberia and Ethiopia, but special arrangements could presumably be made to incorporate them into a greater Eurafrican unit.

Any such plan is vigorously opposed by Latin American producers, who have a large stake in the European market—supplying, for example, 80 percent of the coffee imported by the EEC. In this the Latin states are backed by the United States, which does not want to see any contraction in the economies of its neighbors to the south. Opposition to a broadened concept of the Common Market has also come from the two most important African producers of tropical products belonging to the Commonwealth—Ghana and Nigeria. At the September, 1961, conference of neutralists at Belgrade, Nkrumah asked the rhetorical question: "What is this Common Market if it is not a new design for reimposing Europe's domination and exploitation on Africa?"[3] Three months later at a GATT ministerial meeting Nigeria proposed the free entry of five important tropical products into all industrialized countries, including those belonging to the Common Market. Much the same proposal has been made by the United States.

The reaction of the French-speaking African states to any break-up of their sheltered markets has been universally negative. The Finance Minister of the Ivory Coast said that the organization of Eurafrican markets was as defensible as the system of inter-American preferences on sugar. Gabon's Finance Minister, speaking in the name of the Afro-Malagasy Economic Cooperation Organization, stated that associated countries could not renounce tariff protection even partially unless they received equal if not greater advantages than those obtained from present trade arrangements.

In conclusion, it is clear that the concept of Eurafrica, as originally conceived, evoked no enthusiasm comparable to the Pan-African dream. Pan-Africanism became a powerful symbol of the aspirations of peoples with a common past seeking a common destiny. "Eurafrica" was a more limited intellectual effort by certain Europeans to devise a method of maintaining some form of mutually beneficial influence over their emerging dependencies. It was an effort to organize a system for the common military defense, political future, and economic development of Europe and Africa.

The present tenor of African nationalism, with its emphasis on neutralism and positive nonalignment, has largely vitiated the mili-

[3] Full text of speech printed as supplement by *Ghana Today*, September 13, 1961.

tary aspects of Eurafrica. Events have also demonstrated that political influence—a slippery concept that is difficult to measure in any case—is not necessarily linked to institutional arrangements. Many states have withdrawn from the Community but still remain friendly to France. If Tanganyika and Nigeria decide they want republican status within the Commonwealth, it will have little effect on their political links with the United Kingdom and other members.

On the other hand, the economic aspects of European-African relationships have a more clearly discernible impact. The existing economic arrangements earn foreign exchange for African states, guarantee markets for and affect prices of their products, and channel development loans and grants to them. Although far short of constituting a Eurafrican community, these arrangements have a value which cannot be ignored by African leaders. Moreover, they provide a defensive shield against Latin American competition. For these reasons, the former French territories in particular seemed unlikely in 1962 to abandon the present system, unless a better alternative becomes available. On June 21, 1962, the European Common Market's council of ministers agreed in principle to offer another $780,000,000 in aid to 16 African associated states and Madagascar for the five years beginning January 1, 1963.

TECHNICAL COOPERATION

In its original conception, we have seen, the idea of Eurafrica was largely a Franco-German product which implicitly excluded Britain. The British, meanwhile, had gone ahead to promote another and more limited kind of joint effort for technical assistance to Africa, steering clear of controversial political issues as far as possible. This was the Commission for Technical Cooperation in Africa South of the Sahara (CCTA), an important organ for aid to Africa by technicians and scientists. The CCTA is quite different from either the original idea of Eurafrica or from the Common Market, but it is nonetheless worthy of study as another attempt at regional cooperation between Europe and Africa.

In the economic development and social welfare programs launched by the colonial powers after World War II, several billion dollars were provided by taxpayers in the metropoles to promote African economic, social, and educational advancement. In an effort of this magnitude, high priority was inevitably given to research in the form of general surveys of resources and development possibilities along with detailed study of specific technical problems. The scholars and technicians who were drawn into this type of activity soon began to feel the need for a cooperative approach. They were troubled not only by the shortage of available information but also by the lack of comparable data in different colonial areas and by the diversity of methods of analysis applied in identical situations. As a result, they repeatedly began to call the attention of their respective governments to the basic need for cooperative efforts to deepen existing knowledge and make value judgments of broader application possible.

This was not a new idea. A similar appeal made by General Smuts in 1929 had led to Lord Hailey's renowned *Africa Survey*, an attempt to synthesize the work of many scholars in various fields and different countries, which was made possible by a grant from the Carnegie Corporation in the United States. Before World War II cooperative efforts had also been launched for the geological mapping of Africa (1937) and for locust control (1936–1939). The postwar effort was therefore new only in its magnitude and in the urgent need to prepare economic and educational foundations for the rapidly emerging states of Africa. For the period from 1946 to 1960, for example, the British Colonial Development and Welfare fund alone made £17,000,000 available for research and surveys.

In laying the groundwork for the CCTA, the British were initially motivated by the desire for good relations with France in the economic development of West Africa pursuant to the prewar plan of Lord Hailey, who headed the British delegation at an initial meeting in November, 1945. As Belgium, Portugal, and South Africa were drawn into the plan, another motive became evident. These powers were also concerned about the potential significance of the expansion of United Nations activities in Africa. By 1948, not only were the main specialized agencies of the United Nations interested in finding ways to help Africa, but the U.N. had set a precedent for Africa by creating an Economic Commission for Asia and the Far East. The time was ripe, therefore, for the colonial powers to take steps of their own to fill the void in Africa, partly as a means of curtailing possible

U.N. activities. This situation perhaps quickened the decision of the six governments responsible for African territories—Belgium, France, Portugal, Southern Rhodesia, the United Kingdom, and the Union of South Africa—to launch in 1948 a long-term program of technical and scientific conferences and exchange of technicians and research workers. Out of this movement the CCTA later developed as a permanent organization.

In the meantime, British initiative had stimulated cooperation through a number of bilateral meetings with French, Belgian, and Portuguese officials and technicians. The French were invited to London in February, 1947, to an economic conference on price, marketing, and commodity production policies in Africa, which was followed by a second conference in Paris in February, 1948, covering a wider range of economic problems. Agreement was reached to establish direct contacts between the British and French colonial offices for as complete and regular an exchange of information as possible on development programs and on general economic questions. Periodic economic conferences between the two governments were also recommended. A third conference was held in London in June, 1948, which, among other things, set up a cooperative system for research as well as a system for the automatic exchange of information and documentation. It recommended that Belgium be invited to join in further discussions in full meetings to be held two or three times a year, and that in addition to these arrangements a monthly exchange of visits take place alternately in Paris and London.

Meanwhile, to supplement these conferences in London and Paris on general economic questions, contacts were established between the administrations in the African territories as well. Two important Anglo-French conferences met in Dakar in May, 1947, one on the improvement of communications between British and French territories in West Africa and the other to plan a joint attack on animal diseases. The Dakar communications conference appointed a number of subcommittees to tackle the basic problem of communications barriers. These led to the development of plans to construct an inland road across Gambia to provide a link between the two French territories of Senegal and Guinea; to the study of the possibility of extending the Sierra Leone railway into French Guinea to provide an outlet to the sea for African produce; to the planning of an international coastal highway through the Ivory Coast, the Gold Coast, French Togoland, Dahomey, Nigeria, and the two Cameroons; the improvement of telephone and postal communications; and the establishment of a better system of transport regulations on the Niger River, which flows through both British and French territory.

At the same time the British were also initiating bilateral contacts with Belgium and Portugal. African economic matters were discussed in London with the Belgians at two conferences in June, 1946, and June, 1948, while in July of 1948 France joined the other two governments in Brussels to discuss policy on development loans from the International Bank for Reconstruction and Development. The three governments agreed to submit proposed requests for loans by individual countries to each other for examination.

Meanwhile, Portuguese representatives had come to London in December, 1947, to discuss means of establishing liaison and collaboration on similar problems. The Portuguese also met with the French in Lisbon in August, 1947, and with the Belgians in Brussels in April, 1948.

As British, French, Belgian, and Portuguese policy makers, administrators, and technicians thus got to know each other and each other's problems better through bilateral contacts, the beginnings were being made in the broader field of multilateral cooperation. A trypanosomiasis or sleeping sickness conference was held at Lourenço Marques in 1946 by representatives of the Belgian Congo, British East Africa, Portuguese Africa, and South Africa. This was followed in February, 1948, by a second conference on the same subject in Brazzaville at which the United Kingdom, France, and Southern Rhodesia joined Belgium, Portugal, and South Africa. The year 1948 was also marked by four other multilateral conferences—a labor conference at Jos, Nigeria, in February, a phytosanitary conference on parasitic and plant diseases in London in August, a rinderpest conference on cattle disease in Nairobi in October, and a soil conference at Goma in the Belgian Congo in November.

By 1948, plans for cooperation were so well developed and involved so many joint administrative and financial matters that the six main participants—Belgium, France, Portugal, South Africa, Southern

Rhodesia, and the United Kingdom—agreed to the previously mentioned long-range program of scientific and technical conferences for the future. In January, 1950, this movement culminated in the permanent organization known as the Commission for Technical Cooperation in Africa South of the Sahara, which was to review all joint administrative and financial problems in the technical and scientific fields. A secretariat for CCTA was set up in 1952, and the formal Agreement giving the Commission the necessary legal status for the work it was already doing was signed in London on January 18, 1954, the Federation of Rhodesia and Nyasaland having then replaced Southern Rhodesia as one of the six signatories.

THE ACTIVITIES OF THE CCTA

The definition of the CCTA's powers and functions in Article VI of the Agreement reveals that it is an advisory body limited to making recommendations to member governments. It meets at least once a year, and its recommendations and conclusions, including the admission of new members, must be unanimous. Article IV of the Agreement restricted its territorial scope in the early years to Africa south of the Sahara.

Meanwhile, an important regional scientific conference in Johannesburg in October, 1949, had drawn up a list of priorities for research and recommended the establishment of a Scientific Council for Africa (CSA). This research council came into existence in November, 1950, as an independent body of experts to act as the scientific adviser of the CCTA. The Council was established by the same six governments, but its members, according to Article 4 of its Constitution, are "eminent scientists able as far as possible between them to speak with authority on all the main branches of the sciences of direct interest to Africa South of the Sahara." In setting up the Council, due regard was also paid to equitable representation of the geographical divisions of Africa, and its first members were selected to represent the various scientific disciplines as well as the main research organizations in Africa. Members of the Council are eligible for reappointment, and the Council fills its own vacancies subject to confirmation of its nominations by the participating governments.

On January 1, 1955, the secretariats of the CCTA and the CSA were amalgamated, with one office in London and another in Bukavu in the Belgian Congo. In addition to its other duties, this joint secretariat administers an Inter-African Research Fund and an Inter-African Foundation for the Exchange of Scientists and Technicians. The cost of the secretariat and of CCTA publications and conferences totaled about $500,000 in 1958. Among the first projects of the Research Fund was the preparation of a valuable climatological atlas of Africa, financed in part by a special contribution of £12,500 from the six member governments. A bibliography of economic studies pertinent to Africa has also been published. Current projects include an educational map of the continent, an atlas of vectors of disease, and a basic work summarizing scientific studies of Africa.

The scope and variety of the CCTA's early work is well outlined in a 300-page CCTA report of 1955 on *Inter-African Scientific and Technical Co-operation, 1948–1955*, which summarizes the conclusions and recommendations of 32 technical conferences held under the aegis of the CCTA during these years. It also mentions 27 additional technical bureaus and committees then operating under the auspices of the CCTA which help to ensure continuity of effort between conferences by acting as information centers and liaison organizations.

Now, how does this complex organizational structure function? At the outset, it should be remembered that the CCTA and CSA are only advisory bodies which make recommendations. Therefore, as in the case of most international organizations, it is difficult to cite precise and tangible contributions made by the CCTA itself. During its formative years, the CCTA had the good fortune to have as its secretary general an enterprising and personable French official, Paul-Marc Henry, who was well aware of the outmoded aspects of the Eurafrica ideology. Because of the differing colonial policies of member governments, the possibility of friction was always in the background. Under Henry's guidance, however, the organization concentrated at first on the physical sciences. When it turned to the less exact and more controversial social sciences at its first Inter-African Social Science Conference in Bukavu in 1955, it sought to eliminate contentious subjects such as differing colonial policies from the discussion. As a result of such tactics, CCTA conferences were generally successful, during the first decade, in maintaining a harmonious spirit.

Henry also endeavored to broaden the contacts of the organization by establishing working relations with the World Health Organization and its African Regional Bureau, the Food and Agricultural Organization, UNESCO, the International Labor Organization, and the World Meteorological Organization. Moreover, he won the interest and cooperation of government departments and universities in the United States and other nonmember countries, many of whom have sent observers to CCTA conferences.

The CCTA also began to consider the possibility of expanding its membership at an early date. Liberia, Ethiopia, the Sudan, and Spain were regularly invited through diplomatic channels to take part in all meetings. In a valuable December, 1955, report on CCTA and CSA progress, Henry wrote:

> . . . technical and scientific cooperation must be adapted to the changing political structure of the continent. There is no reason, a priori, why territories achieving their independence should not in turn accept the very principles adopted by the Member Governments previously responsible for their interests at international level. The technical and scientific problems which call for solution are in no way affected by political changes. It would be a serious mistake to believe that scientific and technical contacts must cease to be achieved at regional level merely because representatives of certain independent African territories might be taking part in international gatherings with world-wide competency. . . . the Commission should have no major difficulty in adapting itself to new conditions prevailing in Africa.[4]

Henry's approach bore fruit when Liberia and Ghana became the first African states to join the CCTA in 1957.

THE BUKAVU CONFERENCE

To explain more precisely how the CCTA operates, let us review its first Inter-African Conference on the Social Sciences held at Bukavu from August 23 to September 3, 1955, which Melville J.

---

[4] CCTA/CSA, *Inter-African Scientific and Technical Cooperation 1948–1955,* London, n.d., p. 73.

Herskovits and I attended as American observers. Approximately 100 delegates and observers participated, including scholars, administrators, and diplomatic advisors from the six member countries and several others. The Conference divided itself into six sections, each dealing with research problems in a different group of social sciences. When the 12-day session was over, it had produced 72 recommendations, even more than some United Nations meetings, including a number of overlapping, repetitious, and impracticable suggestions. For example, one recommendation asked governments to finance the translation into other languages of social science works of major importance in order to assist (1) research workers and (2) African students. At the final plenary session, Secretary General Henry turned down a request to eliminate repetitive recommendations, saying that governments might be impressed to find that scientists of different disciplines in different committees had independently arrived at the same conclusions. Although this was a specious argument, Henry was right in refusing, because a last-minute discussion of changes would have caused an inordinate amount of trouble and delay. As it was, the 72 resolutions were quickly voted through in six blocks, one from each section. Too numerous for summary here, the recommendations identified the major gaps in social science research, and left the assessment of priorities to a small Inter-African Committee for Social Sciences meeting after the Conference.

The Conference was reminiscent of the United Nations not only in the large number of repetitious resolutions adopted but also in the politics behind the scenes. The Portuguese, for example, wanted the Conference to create a permanent CCTA social science secretariat as a means of counteracting and forestalling the "pernicious" influence of UNESCO in Africa, which would also have helped the Portuguese to say that they were practicing international cooperation and were not isolated from the rest of the world. The idea elicited little support, however, and it never came to light in formal discussions at the Conference.

In summary, the value of the Bukavu Conference, as of most international gatherings of this sort, lay not only in its recommendations but in its usefulness in bringing new and old acquaintances together for an exchange and clarification of ideas. In a more tangible sense, it helped influential delegates muster additional support for their own ideas at home. Steps were later taken to carry out quite a few Bukavu recommendations.

THE FOUNDATION FOR MUTUAL ASSISTANCE

In 1958, after Ghana and Liberia joined the CCTA, it took a further step of potential importance. On January 17, it was announced in London that a Foundation for Mutual Assistance (FAMA) had been organized to act as a clearing house for aid to underdeveloped areas south of the Sahara. In considering ways of expanding its services, the CCTA had studied the operations of the better-known Colombo Plan for the economic development of Southeast Asia. FAMA was an outgrowth of this study, although much more modest in scope than Colombo. In explaining the organization, Secretary General Claude Cheysson of France, Henry's able successor who was appointed in 1957, called it an international group to arrange bilateral aid agreements between states. He said that FAMA would have no funds of its own, would not allocate aid, and would not supersede or replace any existing agreements for cooperation. A state which wanted to make aid available to Africa, he added, might not know just how much aid might be effectively granted. The Foundation would know where such aid might be applied, and would bring requests for aid and offers of aid together. At its third meeting in 1961, FAMA approved its first five joint regional action programs: two for cattle diseases, one for tsetse fly control, one for primary education, and one for fishing research. During that year technical aid included the sending of 51 experts on missions, the award of 154 scholarships, and the training of 95 students, either in special FAMA courses or in cooperation with U.N. specialized agencies. The 1962 program includes courses on nutrition, agriculture, artificial insemination of cattle, and soil conservation.

AFRICANIZING THE CCTA AND FAMA

Although the CCTA, the CSA, and FAMA do not have the Eurafrican connotations of the Common Market, they suffer from a similar psychological disability—that of being European creations in an era when Africans feel the need to create their own institutions. In recognition of this fact, CCTA headquarters was moved from London to Lagos in 1958, and Secretary General Cheysson has been working hard to adapt the organization to the imperatives of independent Africa.

The February, 1962, annual meeting at Abidjan marked the end of European control of the CCTA and its transformation into a truly African organization. By that time, the Commission had acquired 22 African members, and Belgium, France, and the United Kingdom had stepped down to the status of associate members. The African delegates made it clear that there would be no further cooperation with South Africa or Portugal. A decision was also reached to delete "south of the Sahara" from all texts concerning the CCTA, opening up the possibility of the admission of North African states.

Africanization of the CCTA's personnel has been promoted by Cheysson for the past few years, and many of the higher administrative positions are already held by Africans. At Abidjan it was also decided to replace the Secretary General with an African, although no appointment was made at the time. There appears to be a general understanding, however, that the more technical posts must remain in the hands of Europeans, at least for the next few years.

Many observers have been concerned that inter-African rivalries will impair the effectiveness of CCTA. Ghana withdrew in March, 1961, because the organization did not conform with the "unitary aspirations" of African states. This did not mean that the other Casablanca powers would follow suit. For example, at the Abidjan meeting Maurice Camera of Guinea stated bluntly that "We are ready to accept all assistance given without strings attached from anywhere."[5] It is interesting to note that at the 1961 annual meeting, when "moderate" Nigeria led the move to expel South Africa, President Sékou Touré of "radical" Guinea was reportedly willing to leave South Africa in. Thus, while taking a radical position in the U.N. and other public forums, Guinea was adopting a more detached and pragmatic view on the same or similar problems when they arose in small and private technical organs like the CCTA.

[5] "The CCTA Session," *Africa South of the Sahara*, February 15, 1962, p. 5.

Claude Cheysson has hoped for some time that the CCTA could actually help to bridge the gap between the Casablanca and Monrovia groups. For example, in January, 1961, before the Casablanca states had withdrawn from the Lagos conference, Cheysson stated: "Now that it is confirmed that the Casablanca group will participate in the Lagos conference, the Abidjan assembly will follow the implementation of the technical resolutions adopted. . . . ." He seems to have had in mind a working relationship between the CCTA and an enlarged African political grouping. Although this hope was doomed by the Casablanca boycott of the Lagos meeting, African leaders on numerous occasions have stressed the positive results of Guinea's and Mali's participation in the CCTA.

At the close of the Abidjan conference, an appeal was launched for financial aid from "all friendly countries." It was not clear at the time whether this was intended to include the Soviet bloc, or even if those countries would wish to cooperate with an organization so closely associated with European leadership. In any event, the fact that the major suppliers of funds and technicians are no longer in control makes the future effectiveness of the organization something of a question mark.

The varying concepts of Eurafrica and of other forms of regional cooperation between Europe and Africa illustrate the combination of psychological and economic factors which impede such efforts. Europe is not the only continent, however, to encounter difficulties in evolving new relationships with Africa. In the following chapters, the problems of India, the Soviet Union and the United States in dealing with the new Africa will be analyzed.

Part III

---

*Africa's Relations with India
and the Soviet Union*

10

Africa and India

THE attitude of Africans toward India and Indians has varied from time to time and place to place. During the colonial era, West African leaders found inspiration in India's successful struggle for its own independence and in the Gandhian tactics of nonviolence. As Obafemi Awolowo wrote, "India is the hero of subject countries. Her struggles for self-government are keenly and sympathetically watched by the colonial peoples; the more so because they are marked by untold sufferings."[1] After 1947, the vigorous efforts of India in the United Nations to help others toward independence were deeply appreciated by many African leaders. However, in those areas where large numbers of Indians lived in daily contact with Africans, notably in South Africa and East Africa, economic and cultural conflicts frequently produced racial friction.

AFRICAN ATTITUDES TOWARD INDIA AND INDIANS

Indian traders in Africa were often accused of sharp commercial practices, including profiteering and black-market operations during the war years. This hostility sparked a disastrous Zulu riot against Indians in Durban in January, 1949, which caused 142 deaths, 1087 injuries, and severe property damage. Other racial incidents occurred

[1] Obafemi Awolowo, *Path to Nigerian Freedom*, London, 1947, p. 25.

in East Africa during the 1950s. In March, 1961, a group of anti-Lumumba Congolese leaders issued a communiqué demanding that Indian troops be kept out of the United Nations force in the Congo because they must not be allowed to enter "under cover of the United Nations . . . and continue their country's national policies in the heart of Africa." With the influx of new African states into the United Nations in 1960, a new source of friction arose. As described earlier, African leaders were angered by India's unwillingness to support some of their more extreme proposals in the U.N.

The most vociferous critics of India and Indians are found among the whites of South Africa, Southern Rhodesia, and Kenya. W. Van Heerden, editor of *Dagbeek en Sondagnuus*, a South African newspaper, has contended that the Indians in Africa are "a wooden horse within the walls of Troy."[2] In an address presented in January, 1956, at a conference on the Asian in Africa held by the South African Bureau of Racial Affairs, Van Heerden sought to prove that India has imperialistic ambitions in Africa which go beyond ideological support for African nationalist movements. American visitors in South Africa are sometimes asked whether the United States would help South Africa if it were invaded by armed forces from India. The question is intriguing not for its substance, which is full of imponderables, but because South Africans occasionally worry about such a possibility.

In Southern Rhodesia, it was once argued that India would go Communist after the death of Nehru, and would then seek to take over all of Africa as a southern springboard for the conquest of Western Europe. In East Africa similar fears have been expressed, including stories in the Kenya and Tanganyika press in January, 1951, to the effect that Tanganyika might be made an Indian state under United Nations trusteeship. This fantasy attained such proportions that both the Indian commissioner and the American consul general in Nairobi felt impelled to take the unusual step of issuing press releases to deny it. Since the United States was allegedly a party to the plot, the American press release stated that no support has been given by the United States to any plan for the con-

[2] W. Van Heerden, "Africa's Role between East and West," *Digest of South African Affairs, Fact Paper 5*, February, 1956, p. 10.

version of Tanganyika into an Indian state, and that "the American Delegation to the United Nations will not sponsor such a proposal."[3] The Indian statement declared that "no such 'plan' has been put forward by or on behalf of the Government of India or any other responsible organization or person, and the Government of India never did nor does contemplate making use of other peoples' territories for colonization."[4]

EUROPEAN HOSTILITY TOWARD INDIANS IN AFRICA

Political controversy between Europeans and Indians in Kenya dates back to 1920 when Indians were first given representation in the Legislative Council. At that time Indians outnumbered Europeans 23,000 to 10,000, and the East African Indian National Congress claimed Kenya as an Indian colony which should be attached to India until it was ready for self-government. Excited Kenya whites petitioned the Queen against the "terrible Asiatic menace," and sent a delegation to South Africa to enlist support against rumors of possible adverse action by London.

Rational denials of such rumors were ineffective because the hostility toward India and Indians was basically an emotional reflection of the insecurity felt by European minorities engulfed by peoples of color. Europeans who contended that white withdrawal from Africa would leave a vacuum that India would fill seemed oblivious of the determination of emerging African leaders to be free from all foreign domination. To make matters worse, white politicians in Kenya, Southern Rhodesia, and South Africa continually exploited white fears in order to win votes. The result was a collection of offensive clichés about Indians who can "live on the smell of an oily rag."

This kind of folly led the Southern Rhodesian legislature in 1953 to adopt a bill to prevent Asians in Southern Rhodesia, Northern Rhodesia, and Nyasaland from moving from one territory to another except in transit. An unnecessary irritant to race relations, the bill

[3] American Consulate General, Nairobi, "Rumored Proposal for Conversion of Tanganyika into an Indian State," press release, January 11, 1951.
[4] *Kenya Daily Mail*, January 11, 1951.

was passed unanimously despite the fact that the total number of Asians in the three territories was then less than 19,000. It was occasioned by the widespread but erroneous rumor that Indians were moving into Nyasaland and Northern Rhodesia in great numbers just before the establishment of the Federation in 1953 in order to beat an expected federal law banning Asian immigration entirely.

TABLE 6.   Indians in Africa

Country	Indians	Total Population	Date
East Africa			
Kenya	147,300	6,551,000	1961 estimate
Tanganyika	87,300	9,238,000	1961 estimate
Uganda	76,200	6,682,000	1961 estimate
Zanzibar	18,334	299,111	1958 census
	329,134	22,770,111	
Federation of Rhodesia and Nyasaland			
Nyasaland	8,504	2,590,000	1959 census
Northern Rhodesia	5,450	2,170,000	1959 census
Southern Rhodesia	5,127	2,730,000	1959 census
	19,081	7,490,000	
Union of South Africa			
Cape	20,243	5,308,839	1960 census
Natal	394,237	2,933,447	1960 census
Transvaal	62,918	6,225,052	1960 census
Orange Free State	16	1,373,790	1960 census
	477,414	15,841,128	
Mozambique	15,235		1955 census
Others			
Congo (Leopoldville)	1,227		
Ethiopia and Eritrea	1,645		
Nigeria	300		1960 estimate
Ruanda-Urundi	2,471		
Sierra Leone	76		
Somalia	2,209		
	7,928		

The Southern Rhodesian law was designed to prevent the supposed influx of Indians into the two northern territories from later moving on to the south. Local European politicians promised the voters they would pass such a bill if elected. Some of the liberals later regretted their action when they discovered the falsity of the rumor, but it was then too late. As one of them remarked, their purpose could have been achieved less pointedly by a law placing economic rather than racial restrictions on immigration into Southern Rhodesia.

India is a target of European antagonism partly because of the presence of about 850,000 Indians in Africa, partly because of India's policy of championing the fight of colonial peoples for freedom, and partly because of the widespread belief that India has imperialistic ambitions of its own in Africa. Nearly half a million of Africa's Indians live in South Africa, while most of the remainder live in the three East African countries of Kenya, Tanganyika, and Uganda. Their territorial distribution is summarized in Table 6.

THE INDIAN COMMUNITY IN AFRICA

Contact between India and Africa is quite ancient. When the Portuguese arrived in East Africa at the end of the fifteenth century, they found that Indian traders were already established as money lenders and middlemen along the coast. However, Africa's present Indian population dates mainly from the last hundred years. In the 1860s, Natal began to import Indian labor for its sugar plantations, a practice already under way for a generation in the British territories of Mauritius, Trinidad, Jamaica, and Guiana. It has been estimated that about 143,000 Indians came to South Africa before this immigration ended in 1911. Only 27,000 returned to India. The largest group were poor indentured laborers, although a considerable number of well-to-do Indians entered the field of commerce.

In British East Africa, aside from those who came earlier to Zanzibar, Indian immigration did not begin until 1896, when the first group of 350 laborers was brought in from the Punjab region to work on the construction of the Kenya-Uganda railway line. Altogether, about 32,000 workers were imported, 6700 of whom decided to remain in East Africa when their contracts were terminated. Many others arrived in the years following and built up a strong position in the commercial life of East Africa. By 1960, nearly 80 percent of East Africa's 330,000 Indians were concentrated in less than 20 towns.

Many observers have pointed out the positive contribution the Indians made to African economic development both as laborers and as traders. In South Africa they planted sugar, mined coal, laid the railways, raised fruit and vegetables, brought trade goods to remote rural areas, and helped build South African industry. In British East Africa, in Winston Churchill's often quoted words, it was the Indian trader who, "penetrating and maintaining himself in all sorts of places to which no white man would go, or in which no white man could earn a living, has more than anyone else developed the early beginnings of trade and opened up the first slender means of communication."[5] Sir Harry Johnston also had a friendly regard for Indian achievements. He once called East Africa the "America of the Hindu," although he later said that he did not want to encourage the "riff raff of India."[6]

In East Africa, Indians also provided a cheap source of good labor for government departments and public services. Moreover, they did not become farmers, which enabled Kenya to avoid future friction between Indians and Africans over land ownership. Finally, the achievements of Indians demonstrated to Africans that it was not only Europeans who could achieve success and distinction. By hard work, Indians not only proved their talents as skilled craftsmen, but became doctors, dentists, lawyers, plantation managers, businessmen, and government officials. At the same time, it should be added, Indian successes aroused the antipathy of Africans who wanted their jobs.

This background helps to explain the special interest of the government of India in Africa. During a foreign affairs debate in the lower house of the Indian Parliament on August 17, 1961, Prime Minister Nehru declared that India was opening new missions in Africa and was extending the domain of activity of existing missions.

[5] Winston S. Churchill, *My African Journey*, London, 1908, p. 49.
[6] Roland Oliver, *Sir Harry Johnston and the Scramble for Africa*, New York, 1958, p. 258.

India would be represented in all the new states of Africa, he said, and would give them all possible help, chiefly technical help.

Indians are interested in Africa not only because of its large population of Indian origin, but also because of the career of Mahatma Gandhi. Gandhi lived for many years in South Africa, where he founded the Natal Indian Congress in 1894 and inspired the early passive resistance movements between 1906 and 1914. Gandhi's son, Manilal, editor of the Natal newspaper *Indian Opinion* when he died in 1959, was a leader in the passive resistance movement against *apartheid* in 1952.

Prime Minister Nehru has consistently maintained that the Indians in Africa must recognize the paramountcy of African interests. As far back as 1938, he said:

I think the Indians in Africa have done a great deal of work. Some of them have also derived a great deal of profit. I think the Indians in Africa or elsewhere can be useful members of the community. But only on this basis do we welcome their remaining there, that the interests of the people of Africa are always placed first.[7]

After India attained its independence, Nehru reiterated in 1950:

It has been our deliberate policy to develop Indian-African cooperation; and we have declared often enough that we do not want any Indians in Africa to claim any privileges at the cost of the African. . . . Our definite instructions to them and to our agents in Africa is that they must always put the interests of the indigenous population first.

And in a foreign policy debate in the House of the People on September 15, 1953, Nehru described the official policy of India as follows:

We have been accused of interfering in the affairs of other countries in Africa. We have also been accused of some kind of imperialistic tendency which wants to spread out in Africa and take possession of those delectable lands which now the European settlers occupy. As a matter of fact, this House knows very well that all along, for these many years, we have been laying the greatest stress on something which is rather unique . . . we have rather gone out of our way to tell our own people in Africa . . . that they can expect no help from us, no protection from us, if they

[7] This and the following quotations from Nehru are found in Current Affairs Publications, *Nehru on Africa*, New Delhi, 1954.

seek any special rights in Africa which are not in the interests of Africa
. . . . we have told them: "We shall help you naturally, we are interested in protecting you, your dignity or interests, but not if you go at all
against the people of Africa, because you are their guests, and if they do
not want you, out you will have to go, bag, and baggage."

When Nehru tells the Indians they must put the interests of the
people of Africa first, he does not, of course, have the whites in mind.
"In South Africa," he has said, "the question of the Indian, though
important to us, we have deliberately allowed to become a secondary
issue to the larger question . . . of racial discrimination. . . . the
opposition resistance movement there is far more African than it is
Indian. The leadership is African. We want it to be so." U. N.
Dehbar, President of the Indian National Congress, urged the South
African Indian Congress in October, 1956, to resist "with all your
might" the "racial tyranny" of the South African government. The
weapon, he added, "should always be the weapon of non-violence,"
and the watchword should always be "unity not only among your-
selves but also with your African brethren and all others who are
your co-sufferers and comrades."[8]

Nehru angered Africa's whites in 1953 by tacitly sympathizing with
the Mau Mau and by attacking Britain's plan to establish a Central
African Federation. Later, however, he seems to have had second
thoughts about the rebellion in Kenya. The anti-Indian feeling in
Uganda may also have troubled him. In a mild message to the annual General Conference of African Students held at Bombay from
May 9 to 12, 1956, he said, "We live in a world of violence and
yet it is wisely recognized that violence is bad and does not yield
results. I hope earnestly that the problems of Africa will be solved
peacefully." Another moderate view was expressed on December 1,
1955, by P. D. Saggi, general secretary of the All India Convention
of Race Relations, during a Rhodesian visit:

I have been most agreeably surprised to discover that there is not
nearly so much racial discrimination in the Federation as I had been led
to believe. Had I not come here I should have had a completely different
opinion. In India I had been told that whatever happens in South Africa

[8] *India News*, October 20, 1956, quoted in *Africa Digest*, January–February,
1957, pp. 143–144.

by legislation automatically happens in Rhodesia by convention. I know now that this is not true.[9]

This moderate tone is also evident in the Trusteeship Council discussion of Tanganyika in March, 1956, where Krishna Menon, India's most volatile representative, expressed appreciation of the fact that "in all these answers and in the statements that we have heard [from the administering authority] there is an absence of the desire to perpetuate racial discrimination."[10]

The Indian community in East Africa is divided by sectarian rivalries, which are perpetuated in schools set up by each group to educate its own children. About two-thirds are Hindu who tend to keep themselves separate. Since the split which created India and Pakistan in 1947, the gulf between Hindus and Moslems in East Africa has tended to widen. Many Hindus take considerable interest in the affairs of India, and some of those who have earned enough money in East Africa return to India.

In general, the Moslems are more inclined than the Hindus to regard East Africa as their home. The best-organized and most progressive of several Moslem groups in East Africa is the Ismaili Khoja sect, which in 1960 numbered about 50,000. The long reign of its most famous leader, the third Aga Khan, lasted from 1886, when he became the forty-eighth Imam at the age of 8, down to his death in July, 1957. Known to the West as a rich Indian prince whose race horses won the Derby in England five times and who was President of the League of Nations Assembly in 1937, the Aga Khan first visited East Africa in 1890. The gold and diamonds and platinum in which his devoted followers weighed him on various ceremonial occasions was paid into a central fund which supported good Ismaili schools, clinics, libraries, dispensaries, and charitable institutions in East Africa and central Asia. L. W. Hollingsworth likens the Ismailis to "a vast co-operative society having more than a million subscribers and presided over by an irremovable head who is under no obligation to render any account of the sums he receives and disburses."[11]

[9] *East Africa and Rhodesia*, December 1, 1955, p. 464.
[10] United Nations Trusteeship Council, *Official Records*, T/PV/618, March 8, 1956.
[11] L. W. Hollingsworth, *The Asians in East Africa*, London, 1960, p. 143.

The present Aga Khan, who succeeded his celebrated father in 1957, expressed his views on African-Indian relations during a three-week visit to East Africa in May, 1961. When asked if the Ismaili community was apprehensive about the rising power of African nationalism, he replied that "they are conscious of it but 'apprehension' is a strong word" which "implies a lack of confidence in the country." In Kenya, he thought, the ultimate political authority in any truly democratic system was bound to be African. "This is the real meaning of *Uhuru* and the sooner we accept this fact . . . the better it will be for Kenya. . . . On the other hand," he added, "I do think and believe that a multi-racial society can be created—a society in which the rights of every individual will be observed and respected."[12]

AFRICANS IN INDIA

During the 1950s, the government of India took a number of steps similar to those of the United States and the Soviet Union, although on a smaller scale, to improve its knowledge of and contacts with Africans. With a staff recruited from Africa and Britain as well as India and including a director, five readers, and two African-language lecturers, the University of Delhi opened a School of African Studies in August, 1955, to give a two-year postgraduate diploma course. Planned for 30 students, it had 17 in its first year. In the same month, an Africa and Asia Study Group in Bombay organized a visual exposition on Africa, and a similar study group was later formed in Delhi. An African Society of India was also formed along the lines of the learned societies in Europe and America.

India also took steps to bring more and more African students to India. By 1956, about 250 Africans were studying in India, 122 of them under the Government of India Cultural Scholarships Scheme which paid a monthly stipend of 200 rupees, sufficient for all expenses including study tours of India. Those studying Hindi were eligible for an additional 30 rupees a month for six months. In 1956, of the 122 Africans under this Scheme, 69 were from British East Africa, 18 from Rhodesia and Nyasaland, and 13 from British West

[12] "Aga Khan," *Reporter—East Africa's Fortnightly Magazine* (Nairobi), May 13, 1961.

Africa. The majority were students at universities in Bombay, Delhi, Madras, West Bengal, and the state of Uttar Pradesh; the remainder were distributed among 10 other Indian states. About 25 additional Africans were in various Indian universities on scholarships offered by private donors, state governments, and Indian universities, while 13 others were receiving training in various Indian vocational institutes under a Cottage Industries Scheme. Their subjects of study covered a broad field: 25 were in medicine, 25 in arts and humanities, 14 in law, 12 in teacher training, 12 in commerce, 11 in engineering, 8 in agriculture, and 3 in veterinary science. By the end of 1959, it was estimated that the number of African students in India had risen to 350, mostly from East Africa, about 90 of whom were attending the University of Delhi.[13]

The effectiveness of India's program to build contacts with Africans is not entirely clear. In a stimulating commentary on the problems it creates, Taya Zinkin, Bombay correspondent of the *Manchester Guardian*, concluded on June 16, 1956 that the Indians are "singularly unsuccessful" in their efforts to please Africans. Like Americans, Indians appear to be interested in the more exotic aspects of traditional primitive life, a fact which usually irks educated Africans. After protests by African students, the Indian Board of Film Censors in March, 1956, at the instance of Prime Minister Nehru, banned the showing of eight films allegedly disparaging African nationalism or portraying "primitive aspects of life in a way likely to wound African sensibilities." The banned films were *African Queen*, *Snows of Kilimanjaro*, *West of Zanzibar*, *Untamed*, *Mogambo*, *Below the Sahara*, *African Adventure*, and *Tanganyika*.

A second difficulty appears to be the trouble Africans have in entering Indian homes to see how Indians live. There is no color bar as such, but there are caste prejudice, social snobbery, and other barriers to easy social intercourse. Many upper-class Indians are said to feel that "Africans . . . are Christianized savages, people without real indigenous culture; they look down on them much as they look on their own Nagas: primitive people who have to be educated."[14]

[13] Wayne Fredericks, "The Department of African Studies—University of Delhi," *African Studies Bulletin*, May, 1960, pp. 16–18.
[14] Taya Zinkin, "Africans in India," *Kenya Weekly News*, July 13, 1956, p. 32.

Taya Zinkin's observations are seconded by Khushwant Singh, in an October, 1960, article recording the complaints of an African student. According to Singh, it will be a long time before the color complex is erased from Indian minds because the caste system, which the Indian government is trying to wipe out, was "essentially based on color complexes." The Sanskrit word for caste is *Varna*, which literally means color, and the "Untouchables" are "dark and negroid."[15]

These African reactions to life in India, however, are similar to African reactions to life in the United States. They are only short-range, partial reactions. In the long run, the personal contacts and friendships now being developed may prove of real value.

INDIAN POLICY ON AFRICA IN THE U.N.

Indian policy on African issues is particularly interesting in the United Nations. In this forum, the attitudes of Indian delegates have varied all the way from the moderate and reserved approach of Shiva Rao, an early Indian representative on the Committee on Information from Non–Self-Governing Territories, to the eloquence and showmanship of Krishna Menon. When India was first elected to the Trusteeship Council, Menon enlivened its prosaic proceedings with his colorful oratory and gestures as he warmed to his themes. As he once told the Council, "Our responsibility is to criticize, make suggestions and probably to make noise—we are conscious of the last factor."[16] Another Indian representative with deep antipathy toward the colonial powers was Mrs. Lakshmi Menon, no relation to Krishna. When Puerto Rico chose to become self-governing in a new form of association with the United States, Mrs. Menon fought the United States's decision to cease transmitting information to the United Nations on Puerto Rico. And it was she who precipitated the crisis at the 1953 General Assembly over the Central African Federation by unsuccessfully seeking, against Britain's adamant opposition, to stimulate an Assembly discussion of the matter. On another occasion she opposed the integration of British Togoland to

[15] Khushwant Singh, "Frank Conversation at an Empty Table," *UNESCO Courier*, October, 1960, p. 28.

[16] United Nations Trusteeship Council, *Official Records*, Thirteenth Session, T/PV/518, March 17, 1954.

the Gold Coast until, possibly after an appeal by Nkrumah to Nehru, India changed its position.

First and foremost of India's early policies toward Africa as reflected in the United Nations was its constant pressure for rapid advance of colonial peoples to self-government. In one of his interventions in the Trusteeship Council, Krishna Menon quoted British Prime Minister Gladstone's phrase: "There can be no good government without self-government. Good government is no substitute for self-government." With this general theme as a guiding star, well-prepared Indian delegations questioned the reports of the administering authorities on the trust territories with minute care. No device to cloak colonial authority escaped them. If there was a legislative or executive council in the territory, they wanted to know how many Africans were on it. If there were Africans, were they nominated or elected? If elected, how and by whom? On what matters could they vote? On what matters did the Council have competence? Could its decisions be vetoed? Was African representation proportional or communal? If not proportional, why not, and when would it be changed? If there were Africans in the civil service, how many were in senior posts? What were they paid? Could they disagree with official policy? Such questions were year after year addressed to the special representatives who were sent to the Trusteeship Council from each trust territory to answer its questions.

In its campaign for African liberation, India played an able role in building up United Nations pressure for the establishment of final time limits for independence of trust territories and of intermediate target dates for political advancement. The able India representative on the 1954 U.N. visiting mission to East Africa helped influence the United States representative to support a suggestion for time limits for the attainment of self-government or independence for Ruanda-Urundi and Tanganyika. Later, after the United States government in effect reversed the position of its representative, the Indian Delegation collaborated with the United States Delegation in the Trusteeship Council on a modified proposal for the establishment of intermediate target dates for the political advancement of trust territories on the road to self-government.

Indian delegations also expressed a consistently strong dislike of administrative unions, arrangements which provided for certain common administrative services between a trust territory and an adjacent colony under the administration of the same metropole. India was particularly concerned over the East Africa High Commission, an administrative union of Kenya, Tanganyika, and Uganda. In India's view, this attempt to provide common and more efficient administrative services was a potential threat to the political integrity of the trust territory, which might bring Tanganyika under the domination of Kenya's white settlers.

Indian delegates also asked a host of questions on educational, health, economic development, and other matters, but it was clear that their fundamental aim was to get the colonial powers out of Africa as soon as possible. They occasionally paid tribute to British policy, particularly in West Africa, but were sometimes quite scathing toward the French, especially in North Africa. India played a leading role in the successful effort of 13 Arab-Asian states to bring U.N. pressure on France to free Tunisia and Morocco, and it urged the granting of as many oral hearings as possible to African petitioners.

Another basic Indian policy, consistently pursued from session to session, was to bring steady pressure for the continual expansion of U.N. activities affecting Africa. India not only pressed the administering authorities to make more use of the World Health Organization, UNESCO, and other specialized agencies of the U.N., but it favored the creation of additional machinery and the extension of the terms of reference of existing organs.

India played a prominent role in all United Nations efforts on the three South African agenda items—South-West Africa, *apartheid*, and the treatment of peoples of Indian origin in South Africa. The last problem, the item of most direct interest to India, naturally aroused bitter Indian feeling long before the United Nations was born. After a series of discriminatory ordinances adopted by South Africa since 1913, round-table discussions between the two governments produced the Cape Town Agreement in 1927:

1. Both governments reaffirm their recognition of the right of South Africa to use all just and legitimate means for the maintenance of Western standards of life.

2. The Union Government recognizes that Indians domiciled in the Union, who are prepared to conform to Western standards of life, should be enabled to do so.

3. For those Indians who may desire to avail themselves of it, the Union Government shall organize a scheme of assisted repatriation to India or other countries where Western standards are not required.[17]

Few Indians took advantage of the assisted repatriation scheme, and in 1943 the South African government passed a law providing that Europeans could sell land to Asians only with the permission of the Ministry of the Interior. Meanwhile, European agitation against Indians had mounted, and Indians had become more embittered. In the Indian parliament on November 6, 1944, Dr. N. B. Khare is reported to have said, "I wish India was in a position to declare war on South Africa now."

In response to an Indian plea, the General Assembly of the United Nations took up the problem in 1946 at its first session. India charged that South Africa's discriminatory laws were a violation of fundamental human rights and a contravention of the 1927 and 1932 agreements between the two governments, and that this discrimination impaired friendly relations between nations. South Africa's reply was presented by its Prime Minister, Field Marshal Jan Smuts, who contended that the question concerned not Indian nationals but nationals of the Union of South Africa, and that under Article 2(7) of the Charter, the question was therefore a matter of domestic jurisdiction over which the General Assembly had no competence. Smuts pleaded that there was no question of treaty obligations because the instruments referred to were declarations of proposed government policy rather than international agreements; moreover, since these agreements had never been registered with the League of Nations, they were not of an internationally binding character. South Africa argued further that the concept of fundamental human rights was very nebulous and had never been defined in international law; in any case, South Africa's laws did not violate such rights as the right to exist, nor the rights of freedom of conscience, speech, and access to the courts. To settle the dispute over whether South Africa did or

[17] Full text quoted by G. H. Calpin, *Indians in South Africa*, Pietermaritzburg, 1949, p. 64.

did not have the legal right to enact the legislation in question and
whether the treatment of her citizens of Indian origin was or was
not a matter of domestic jurisdiction, the Union representative urged
the Assembly to submit the matter to the International Court of
Justice for its opinion.

To South Africa's contention that the issue was a matter of domestic jurisdiction outside the competence of the United Nations,
the Indians responded that (1) it was an international problem in
view of the history of the agreements between the two governments,
(2) it was within the scope of the Charter since it concerned human
rights as provided in Articles 13, 55, 62, and 76 and the Preamble of
the Charter, and (3) Articles 10 and 14 authorized the U.N. to take
up the problem.

When it became clear that there was not enough support for either
an Indian resolution condemning the Union or a proposal by the
United Kingdom and Sweden to refer the legal issues to the International Court of Justice, the Assembly adopted a compromise proposal by France and Mexico. It declared that friendly relations between India and South Africa had been impaired, and that the
treatment of people of Indian origin in South Africa should conform
to the relevant provisions of the Charter and to South Africa's international obligations under the bilateral agreements. The two governments were requested to report at the next session of the Assembly
on the progress made toward alleviating the problem.

This resolution was a defeat for South Africa, but it only produced
a long stalemate over the problem because the Union refused to accept the U.N. resolution as a basis for the proposed discussions. Almost every year thereafter, the General Assembly rehearsed the same
arguments with the same inconclusive result. Meanwhile, in 1946
India had withdrawn its high commissioner in Pretoria and instituted
economic sanctions against South Africa.

By 1960, more than 90 percent of the Indians in the Union were
South African born, and showed no interest in repatriation to India
where their standard of living would be lower. Financial bonuses offered by South Africa to those who would leave were raised from £20
to £40 for an adult and from £10 to £20 for a child after the anti-
Indian riots in Durban in 1949. From 1945 to 1961, however, only

about 750 Indians left, 290 of them after the Durban riots. Two Indian writers in a paper presented in 1956 at an Institute of Race Relations meeting in Durban contend that in order to reduce tension at both the domestic and international levels, the European will have to face up to the fact that South Africa is the fatherland of the Indians too. To their pleas they add this interesting reminder:

It is not beyond the bounds of possibility that events in Africa may bring the same intense pressure to bear upon the white minority to return to Europe. Perhaps, the Indian's present reluctance to migrate will then be appreciated. But with a little kindling of our sympathetic imagination now, one need not wait for that unfortunate and distressing day in the future. One may even succeed in forestalling it. It is little realized that the repatriation slogan is easily learnt and is possible of extension from the Indian to the European. Let us drop it: it is a dangerous game! Eventually the European stands to lose more than the Indian.[18]

Moreover, in view of the growing strength of India as a world power, particularly in the environs of the Indian Ocean, it is in South Africa's interests to cultivate better relations with India.

Other African discussions in the United Nations in which Indian delegates took an active part are well described by Ross N. Berkes and Mohinder S. Bedi in their book *The Diplomacy of India—Indian Foreign Policy in the United Nations,* particularly in the chapter on "The Advancement of Cardinal Principles."

AN ANALYSIS OF INDIA'S AFRICA POLICY

The Africa policy of India is difficult to evaluate because its motivations were sometimes contradictory. One stimulus was certainly the Indian urge to play a leading role in world affairs. To Nehru, Africa was for a time a valuable component of the "third force" with which he sought to moderate the cold war. In the United Nations, where Indian delegates endeavored to identify themselves with African aspirations, India found a forum for exercising this leadership and winning the friendship of Africans, at least until the new African states in the U.N. took over their own causes. A second motive was

[18] South Africa Institute of Race Relations, *The Indian as a South African,* Johannesburg, 1956, p. 57.

the intense personal feeling of many Indian leaders about the racial humiliations of the colonial relationship as they knew it in their own experience. One of the favorite remarks of Indian representatives in their early U.N. attacks on colonialism was to remind their listeners that "we are fresh from colonial rule ourselves." A third factor influencing Indian policy was certainly the Gandhian tradition of non-violence and Nehru's sincere desire for peaceful change. There is no evidence of Indian imperialism in Africa in any of these factors.

The surplus population argument, often used as evidence of an Indian threat to Africa, is highly speculative at best. All Indian immigration to South Africa has been banned for 50 years, and Indian immigration to East and Central Africa has been severely restricted for a decade. India had about 400,000,000 people in 1960, and population experts believe it could reach 800,000,000 in 1986 if the high birth rate continues. Alarmists contend that these teeming millions will spill over into the vast empty spaces of Africa. This view seems to ignore the fact that India has been preoccupied with its internal development needs and with difficulties on its own borders. By 1986 the population of Africa will also have grown tremendously. It is also worthy of note that the Indian government, after a decade of halfhearted effort, has begun to give real support to a major family planning campaign which, by publicizing several methods of birth control, aims at stabilizing the Indian population. Meanwhile, India's development plans are strengthening its capacity to maintain a large population within its own borders.

India's economic stake in Africa is small but significant. It has embargoed trade with South Africa since 1946, but it was the largest importer of East Africa products in 1959 and the fifth largest exporter to East Africa. India took 17.4 percent of Uganda exports in 1959, which placed it second on the list of countries importing from Uganda. African countries with significant trade with India are indicated in Table 7.

As these figures reveal, India has an adverse trade balance with Africa. The main item in Indian imports from Africa is cotton. Indian trade missions sought to expand Indian trade with Africa by negotiating trade agreements with all the new states of Africa. As for Indian capital investment in Africa, it is negligible; while wealthy

Indians who live in Africa have invested considerable amounts, the only investment from India, according to the *Economist* of November 12, 1960, is in a cotton mill in Ethiopia.

TABLE 7.   Indian Trade with Africa in 1960 (in Millions of Dollars)

Country	Indian Exports to Africa	Indian Imports from Africa
Egypt	$28.2	$ 34.1
Kenya	9.4	28.2
Southern Rhodesia	2.4	29.0
Sudan	12.2	19.1
Tanganyika	4.4	11.5
Mozambique	1.8	11.4
Uganda	1.2	2.6
Total	$59.6	$135.9

SOURCE: Data provided by the Indian Embassy in Washington, D.C.

The decline of British sea power in the Indian Ocean and the potential of India sea power in helping to fill the vacuum has been cited as a factor conducive to Indian expansion. Professor Frank L. Schoell, who was called in as a consultant by the United Nations Commission on the racial situation in South Africa, believes that Nehru is "a sincere lover and seeker after peace," but that present conditions favor a continuation of Indian expansion and that "it will take a great deal of diplomacy and first rate statesmanship to stop it from becoming imperialism." In Schoell's view, "The British Empire paved the way for Indian expansion by Indian immigration, with the consent of the Indian Government, to solve the labor problems of the colonies. The question now is whether New Delhi will be moderate and resist the temptation of using their natural outposts all round the Indian Ocean for political purposes."[19]

No matter what the government of India tries to do, however, the extent of its influence in Africa will be curtailed by other factors. In the first place, the Asians in Africa are not at all single-minded. In addition to religious differences between Hindus and Moslems, there are political differences between leftist Indians and such moderate

[19] "India's Policy," *Kenya Weekly News*, February 10, 1956, p. 3.

groups as the Ismaili followers of the Aga Khan, and economic differences between prosperous Indian traders and poor Indian agricultural and industrial workers. In a letter published in the *East African Standard* on March 21, 1951, the Moslem politician and journalist Allah Ditta Quereshi attacked the political views of the East African Indian Congress: "To talk of all Asians of the sub-continent as Indians is sheer lunacy. We repeat that we do not desire to be known as Indians. We Muslims mean to live here . . . as East Africans."

The increasing concern of Indians over their impending fate in an independent Kenya was reflected in the intemperate remarks of the Kenya Hindu leader, R. B. Pandya, in the Indian magazine *Seminar* in June, 1960:

. . . we should not be placed in a situation by which we may have to exchange the domination of white racialism for that of black racialism with the significant difference that while the former is benevolent, satisfied, contented, civilized, experienced in the art of human justice and fairness, the latter is narrow-minded, greedy, hungry, frustrated, grasping, suffering from a supposed sense of grievance, violent in heart and capable of slipping back to tribal savagehood.[20]

Pandya's provocative language was no help to Kenya Indians seeking to build better relations with Africans, especially since the latter were on the eve of attaining power. Resentment of Indian traders continues from Kampala and Nairobi to Durban and beyond, and there is widespread fear of a recurrence of the 1959-1960 Uganda boycott of Indian shopkeepers. The rapid Africanization of government posts is also of mounting concern because it reduces employment opportunities for Indians. It would be a real loss, particularly in East Africa, if Indian skills and experience were not fully utilized as new states launch development programs. A hopeful note was sounded in Nyasaland, however, when Hastings Banda assured Indians in an August, 1961, election speech that they had nothing to fear because "ninety per cent of your business is done with Africans over whom I have complete control." No doubt the attitude of such African leaders as Banda will play a large part in shaping future relations between Africans and Indians.

[20] Quoted by Dev Murarka, "Indians in Africa," *African Trade and Development*, February, 1961, p. 9.

When so many African states attained independence in 1960, India became more conscious that anticolonialism was not enough to sustain its foreign policy. The leading role of Indians in the Afro-Asian movement, which Nehru held at the Bandung conference of 1955, had already declined by 1957 when Nasser welcomed the first Afro-Asian Peoples Solidarity Conference in Cairo. The many all-African conferences since 1958 bypassed India altogether. Within the U.N., Africans not only took over the leadership of the anticolonial struggle but even came into conflict with India over certain African issues. The moderate position of India on such items as the French Cameroons elections in 1960 and the attempt to impose strong U.N. sanctions on South Africa irritated African leaders. Furthermore, India has been placed in the unwelcome position of having to choose between different factions in the Congo and to support one side or the other in the Morocco-Mauritania dispute.

Its prestige among Africans received a sudden boost, however, when India invaded Goa and two other Portuguese territories in December of 1961. African opposition to the use of force to settle international disputes was far outweighed by a long-smoldering resentment against Portugal, not only for its obdurate resistance to change but because of its brutal suppression of the rebellion in northern Angola.

The Afro-Asian Organization for Economic Cooperation which was meeting in New Delhi during the invasion of Goa received little publicity, but its economic program suggests a basis for an Indian policy toward Africa in the future. Nehru urged African and Asian delegates to build economic groupings themselves. He pointed out that the gap between technologically advanced countries and under-developed countries was increasing, and that it would be an answer to the problem for the latter to tie themselves only to the more developed countries. As the London *Times* noted, the conference promoted "a lowered political temperature" and a more businesslike approach to foreign aid. Although India needs technicians for its own development program, it has a valuable opportunity to provide Africa with skilled technicians who are familiar with the problems of under-developed countries and who do not cost as much as Western experts. It has already made a small beginning through bilateral agreements to provide technical experts for air force training in Ethiopia and Ghana, and it has supplied teachers, doctors, and administrative and technical personnel to other African countries. As a country which maintains democratic freedoms along with a high degree of government economic planning, India could serve as a useful example for Africans.

11

Soviet Ideas About Africa

BECAUSE the turmoil in postwar Africa proved ideal for Communist exploitation, many observers jumped to the false and dangerous conclusion that it was caused by Communists. It was a false conclusion because Africa's protest movements were primarily a natural reaction to foreign domination. It was dangerous because confusion over the causes of political agitation handicapped the West's ability to develop an effective policy. In fact, by over-emphasizing Communist penetration of Africa in the first 10 years after the war, Westerners only helped it with free and unnecessary publicity. As one of Africa's friendliest new prime ministers told a visiting American congressman in 1961, his people would have had little knowledge or interest in communism if Americans had not so greatly exaggerated its influence.

Under a front-page banner headline, "SHOCKING INFORMATION—RUSSIA'S SECRET PLAN FOR AFRICA UNVEILED," South Africa's tabloid *Die Landstem* on August 1, 1959, published an article by its editor, Piet Beukes, reporting that the Russians take 3000 native leaders out of Africa annually and give them a thorough Communist indoctrination in administrative and organizational methods; that 1750 Russians every year learn all the Bantu languages of Africa at a special institution in Czechoslovakia; and that, in sharp contrast, there is no single institution in the whole of the West where African leaders are trained or where whites study the Bantu languages of Africa.

This journalistic extravaganza is mentioned not because of its substance but because editor Beukes at least cited his source of information. He says that first Khrushchev told it to an Indian diplomat in Moscow; second, the Indian diplomat told it to a Western diplomat at a cocktail party in New York; third, the New York diplomat evidently passed it on to another Western diplomat in Washington; and fourth, the latter reported it to Mr. Beukes when he visited Washington. When he published it for his readers in *Die Landstem*, therefore, they could at least know they were getting fifth-hand information!

RUSSIAN INTEREST IN AFRICA

This anecdote is not intended to belittle Soviet activities, but only to emphasize that many of the alleged facts about communism in Africa are fifth-hand information that come to us via the world of rumor or cocktail party gossip. The truth, however, is grave enough. Although communism made relatively little progress in Africa before 1958, the facts indicate that after a generation of misapplied ideological efforts, Soviet policy shifted into higher gear. By 1960 it had become much more effective, partly because of new tactics and partly because of a notable extension of its diplomatic, economic, and cultural missions in Africa. Meanwhile, the sudden emergence of new states in Africa rapidly expanded Soviet opportunities.

It therefore becomes more important than ever to understand the nature of Soviet activities. At the outset, let us distinguish between the expansion of communism in Africa on the one hand and the rising influence of the Soviet Union as a great power in Africa on the other. Although these two are closely related, they are not the same. In 1961, it seemed certain that the influence of the Soviet Union as a great power would rise in Africa in the next decade. Whether this would turn Africans more and more to communism was another question. In this chapter and the next, we will discuss Soviet ideas about Africa and Communist penetration through nongovernmental organizations. In a third chapter attention will be given to Soviet policy toward Africa, at first through the United Nations and later through the expansion of diplomatic, economic, and cultural missions in Africa.

It should not be forgotten that the Russians were interested in Africa, particularly Egypt and Ethiopia, long before the Communists seized power. During the scramble for Africa in the late nineteenth century, Russia also participated in the Moroccan settlement in Madrid in 1880 and in the Congo arrangements at Berlin in 1885. With the advent of communism, Russian ideas about Africa had to be fitted into the Communist ideological pattern. Soviet journals like *World Economy and World Politics, The New East, The War and the Working Class, New Times, Soviet Ethnography,* and *Problems of Economics* have been publishing occasional articles about Africa since the 1920s. One student of Soviet writings has also counted 113 publications on Africa printed in the Soviet Union between 1917 and 1945, and an additional 100 issued between 1945 and 1956. These were mostly pamphlets, however, and included translations from English and French works.

Soviet scholars have had to twist the facts to fit Soviet ideology, and even to reverse themselves when the ideology shifted. This "Agony of Soviet Historians," as Bertram Wolfe called it,[1] is well illustrated in their treatment of Russia's own colonialism. In the April, 1952, issue of *Foreign Affairs,* S. M. Schwarz pointed out that in the previous 15 years, the Communist Party had completely reversed its line on Russian colonial policy. Until August, 1934, the annexationist-colonialist role of Russian tsarism was still under official attack, but later Soviet historians had to portray Russian colonial expansion even under the tsars as a "liberation" movement.

THE IDEOLOGY BEHIND SOVIET POLICY

The basic tenet of Communist ideology on Africa is the familiar thesis of Lenin that imperialism is the highest stage of capitalism,

[1] Bertram D. Wolfe, "Operation Rewrite: The Agony of Soviet Historians," *Foreign Affairs,* October, 1952, pp. 39–57.

which carries the implication that the destruction of capitalism and colonialism are but two aspects of one and the same task. This proved to be a powerful idea among Africans anxious to rid themselves of colonialism, and it still handicaps the West today. A second important Soviet theme is the systematically distorted portrayal of Africa as a land of oppressed peoples suffering under colonial slavery. And a third is the contention that a new step in the imperialist struggle for Africa is a greedy American drive for the economic, political, and military expansion of United States interests. The flavor of this propaganda is conveyed in the following examples.

In an article on "The Colonial Policy of the Labour Party and the Position of the Workers in Africa" published in *Problems of Economics* in 1949 (No. 2), I. Lemin wrote that the aim of the British Labor Party was "to maintain and strengthen the system of colonial slavery in its most horrible and cruel form." Ignoring statistics of population growth, he warned of danger that the African working population would die out because of monstrous exploitation and low wages. S. R. Smirnov, writing in *Soviet Ethnography*, No. 3, in 1950 on "The British Policy of 'Indirect Rule' in Southeast Nigeria," branded Lugard's well-known technique of administration as Britain's "desperate attempt to hamper the birth of a Nigerian society, an attempt to restrain the headlong development of the national-liberation movement." Quoting Lenin's remark that the British imperialists "beat the record not only for the number of their stolen colonies but also for the refinement of their repulsive hypocrisy," M. Csipov wrote in the December 5, 1948, issue of *Trud*, "In the majority of British colonies in Africa, the native population is being driven from the land by violence, and this land is being handed over to European settlers or to big capitalist planners." S. Datlin, in a radio broadcast in Moscow on August 8, 1952, declared that

. . . the United States and South African fascist-racialists do not recognize human dignity for the colored, who are regarded merely as slaves. . . . The Wall Street sharks, scared out of their wits by the unprecedented growth of liberation movements in the colonies, and particularly in Africa, are demanding that their satellites tame the blacks. . . . Transforming the country into a hotbed of inhuman exploitation, the South African authorities are acting on the direct orders of the U.S. and

British imperialists who have vested interests, both economic and strategic, in South Africa.[2]

As for American imperialism, I. Lemin contended in the article cited above that "the American military authorities direct all the military measures adopted in Africa," while "American monopolists" try to grab African trade and investment from the British. The aim of all this, he wrote, was to transform Africa "into a base of military operations for the aggressive war which the Anglo-American bloc is preparing." M. Batlin, in *The Peoples of Tunisia, Algeria and Morocco, and Their Struggle for Independence*, wrote that "the imperialists want to turn North Africa into a springboard for aggression against the U.S.S.R. . . . It is creating for North Africa's large population a second front after that of Korea. . . . Thus bloody United States imperialism has become the most dangerous enemy. . . ." D. F. Federof, reviewing V. M. Shurshakov's 1951 book on *The Regime of International Trusteeship* in *Soviet Book* in September, 1952, contended that "reality shows that, ready to unleash a new world war, the imperialist plunderers, headed by the U.S.A., are trying to transform the trust territories into military strategic bases, assigning them no small importance in their criminal plans." Not only does this apply to the Mariana, Caroline, and Marshall Islands under U.S. trusteeship, Federof wrote, but "the same prospect awaits Tanganyika in the near future, which is already being covered at present with a network of military air fields, naval ports and other installations of a strategic character."

The above three Soviet propaganda themes have been relatively consistent. A fourth doctrine merits special attention because new Soviet tactics led to its modification in 1955. This was the ironical and contradictory picture of the "national bourgeoisie" of Africa. Committed by doctrine to the principle that revolutionary leadership must be in the hands of the working class, the Communists found in Africa as in other colonial areas that the workers and peasants had not developed to the point of being able to assume such leadership. The Communist appeal, therefore, had to be directed at

---

[2] S. Datlin, "The Struggle of the South African Peoples for Peace and Liberty," USSR Home Service (mimeo. trans.), August 8, 1952.

the nationalist-minded bourgeois intelligentsia. This troublesome problem was discussed in a 1950 article in *Soviet Ethnography*, No. 1, by the leading Soviet Africanist, I. I. Potekhin, entitled "The Stalinist Theory of Colonial Revolution and the National Liberation Movement in Tropical and South Africa." Potekhin warned that the African bourgeoisie "supports the revolutionary movement of the masses of the people only with a view to taking advantage of the fruits of the revolution and seizing political power for the suppression and enslavement of the masses of the people of its own country." He cynically argued, however, that these reactionary nationalistic elements could be used in "the special strategic stage of the colonial revolution, the stage of the nation-wide anti-imperialist front when the national bourgeoisie still supports the revolutionary movement."

The sardonic implication was clear that African nationalist leaders would be due for liquidation after the Communists were through using them. Potekhin even went on to name some individuals he had in mind. He branded Gold Coast Paramount Chief Ofori Atta and Bamangwato Chief Seretse Khama as "feudal or semi-feudal lords," and said that the Nigerian nationalist leader, Nnamdi Azikiwe, followed "the ideology and policy of petty bourgeois national reformism," a "colonial edition of the reactionary American philosophy of pragmatism" (evidently a reference to Azikiwe's American education). Zik's fellow nationalist, Nwafor Orizu, was also labeled a national bourgeois leader who attacked British colonial policy but "at the same time advocates the preservation of the bases of capitalism."

Egypt's President Nasser was referred to in the 1952 *Large Soviet Encyclopedia* as one of "a reactionary group of officers connected with the United States." When Prime Minister Nkrumah was turning a cold shoulder to Communist influence in the Gold Coast before independence, his administration was attacked for representing "the interests of the reactionary section of the bourgeoisie and not the workers."[3] President Tubman of Liberia was described in the 1954 *Large Soviet Encyclopedia* as "an agent of American monopolies" heading a government of "landlords and capitalists." King Idris of

[3] Derek Kartan, *Africa, Africa: A Continent Rises to Its Feet*, London, 1954, p. 57.

Libya was branded "the stooge of the English."[4] Ethiopia was called a feudal society under the domination of American imperialism. And in a 1955 book, Potekhin declared that the African National Congress started as a "feudal summit, the tribal chiefs . . . a feudal comprador organization collaborating with imperialism. . . ."[5]

IDEOLOGICAL SHIFTS SINCE 1955

By 1955, however, the Communists evidently felt the need to reverse or at least to modify the party line in order to facilitate their efforts in Africa and elsewhere. The resulting shift was more than a temporary tactical maneuver. In the view of Robert C. Tucker, a specialist on Soviet affairs, Stalin was really unable to recognize African and Asian nationalism as a "third force" which he could usefully work with and exploit, while Khrushchev is willing to do business with Nehru and others. Soviet collaboration with Nasser began in July, 1955, when D. P. Shepilov, then Editor-in-Chief of *Pravda*, was sent to Egypt where he apparently arranged an arms deal with Nasser while Khrushchev was in Geneva at a Big Four summit meeting on disarmament.

In May, 1955, the Party's theoretical organ, *Kommunist*, declared that "serious mistakes have occasionally been committed in appraising the role of the national bourgeoisie of the countries of the East in the anti-imperialist movement." After the Twentieth Party Congress in February, 1956, Potekhin and other Soviet scholars and theorists therefore began to reverse themselves. African leaders were praised rather than reviled, and it was contended that colonial peoples may find more than one road to socialism. In October, 1956, Potekhin wrote in *Moscow News*, No. 20, that "a great popular independence movement has surged up throughout the continent," and "a national bourgeoisie . . . has made its appearance and is claiming its place in the sun. . . . In every colony there are political

---

[4] Academy of Sciences of the USSR, Institute of Economics, *The Imperialist Struggle for Africa and the Liberation Movement of Its Peoples: A Collection of Articles*, Moscow, 1953, p. 298.

[5] *The Growth and Formation of a National Community of the Southern African Bantu* (mimeo trans. of Ch. 12), Moscow, 1955.

leaders of ability and energy: Nkrumah, Azikiwe, Jomo Kenyatta and others. . . ." A related item of propaganda guidance issued by the Central Committee of the Party warned against the indiscriminate branding of certain small states at the United Nations as U.S. satellites only because their official representatives sometimes are "compelled to vote contrary to their own conviction under the pressure of American diplomacy. . . ."[6]

However, when African states moved quickly toward independence at the end of the 1950s and the Chinese Communists became a significant force in world politics, the opportunist "soft" line swung back toward the earlier position. The Soviet attitude toward the "national bourgeoisie" hardened. This was evident in the declaration issued by the 1960 Moscow Conference of 81 Communist Parties, and was re-emphasized in the program adopted at the Twenty-Second Soviet Communist Party Congress in October, 1961. The latter document brands national bourgeoisie leaders as "the reactionary circles of the local exploiting classes," who serve as "allies of imperialism." Although the 1961 program retains the line that the choice between capitalism and socialism is "the internal affair of the peoples themselves," it expresses a vigorous confidence that the national liberation movement will not end with the gaining of political independence, but will, with Soviet aid, move onward to complete the "anti-imperialist, anti-feudal, democratic revolution" by establishing a "national democracy." As class differences between the workers and the propertied classes become more acute, the new program declares, the national bourgeoisie is increasingly disposed toward rapprochement with imperialism and internal reaction.[7] Nonetheless, this 1961 doctrine symbolizes a real difference between the Stalinist and Khrushchev regimes because the "national democracy" appears to be a new concept—a kind of way station on the road to the "people's democracy."

This emphasis on the growing class struggle is evidently designed to combat the view of those African leaders, including Guinea's

---

[6] E. Zhukov, "Disintegration of the Colonial System of Imperialism," *Party Affairs*, August, 1956.

[7] "The 22nd CSPU Congress," *The Mizan Newsletter*, November, 1961, pp. 5–7.

Sékou Touré, who have asserted that classes do not exist in Africa. Potekhin challenges this trend in a 1960 booklet, *Africa Looks Ahead*, an abridged English translation of which has been published as a *Supplement to Mizan Newsletter No. 4*, April, 1961. He attacks the theory of an "African socialism" which denies the existence of classes in Africa. He acknowledges that "the process of class formation" is still unfinished, but contends that Marxist-Leninist theory is nonetheless applicable to African conditions, where one does find "feudalism of the patriarchal type" and "an African petty bourgeoisie" which now has new opportunities for development in independent African states. The peasant communes of Africa can nonetheless, if power is in the right hands, "serve as the connecting link for a direct transition to socialism," enabling Africa to bypass the capitalist stage of development.

These propaganda shifts during the African revolution illustrate the difference between long-range Soviet ideology and short-range propaganda tactics. The renewed emphasis on the role of the working class indicates that the old line was reversed only while nationalist leaders were in the actual process of winning their revolutions. When the new states began to resist Communist penetration, however, Soviet theory regarding the inevitable betrayal of the revolution by the national bourgeoisie seemed to be confirmed.

This partial reversion to the pre-1955 line might also result from a renewed conviction that the African revolution is moving toward the left. In any event, in those countries where Soviet ability to influence the leaders is most limited, a growing restiveness is evident among the more radically inclined—especially among youth and trade union leaders. The Russians may also feel under pressure from Peking's more militant brand of orthodoxy which favors the immediate formation of Communist cadres and direct support to extremist elements.

AFRICAN STUDY PROGRAMS IN RUSSIA

In the foregoing analysis, the emphasis has been on the ideology of Soviet writers. Meanwhile, efforts to improve the serious study of Africa were under way. In anticipation of new problems and opportunities in Africa, Russian scholars took steps, comparable in certain respects to those taken a little earlier in the United States, to stimulate African studies in the academic world as a means of broadening the nation's knowledge of Africa and of training personnel for Africa work. Russian publications about Africa had increased since 1953, but at the Twentieth Party Congress in Moscow in February, 1956, Mikoyan declared that "whereas the whole East has roused itself, the Institute of Eastern Studies continues to doze even today." Two months later the Oriental Institute of the Academy of Sciences decided to shift its emphasis to "southeast Asia and Africa" and to train more personnel in Oriental and African studies. A further step was announced in September when Moscow Radio reported that a separate section on Africa would be created in the Oriental Institute, and that Soviet scholars would be sent to their areas "for scientific work and to raise their qualifications." In 1957, the Institute's journal, *Soviet Eastern Studies,* turned more of its attention to contemporary problems, and a new popular monthly, *The Contemporary East,* was founded. In the same year, Potekhin spent a short period in Ghana, his first visit to Africa aside from a short trip to Egypt the year before. In earlier years, Soviet writers had to rely heavily on the works of Western scholars, who had been doing research in Africa for many decades.

In September, 1957, the *Herald* of the U.S.S.R. Academy of Science published an article describing a five-year research plan, including a large number of new studies on the general theme of "the role and significance of Africa in the colonial system of imperialism." A list of these studies was published in *Soviet Ethnography* (No. 3, 1957). The first title in the list, "The Economic Development and Struggle of the Peoples of Nigeria Against Imperialist Enslavement after World War II," indicates the continuing ideological orientation of these efforts by Soviet scholars. Potekhin, then Assistant Director of the Institute of Ethnography, declared that "the studies should serve to assist the peoples of Africa in their struggle against colonialism." In October, 1959, it was announced that various Africanist activities would be concentrated in a single Africa institute under Potekhin's direction.

It should be noted, however, that our knowledge of the extent and particularly of the quality of Soviet Africanist teaching, research, and other activities is still inadequate. A thorough analysis, based on personal investigation on the spot, is much needed, although considerable information is being culled from press, radio, and other announcements and reports, and from the writings of Soviet authors about Africa. The bimonthly *Mizan Newsletter*, issued by the Central Asian Research Centre at Oxford University, is the most useful review of this kind of information. Another informative survey is G. A. von Stackelberg's "Soviet African Studies as a Weapon of Soviet Policy" in the September, 1960, *Bulletin* of the Institute for the Study of the U.S.S.R. in Munich, an organization composed chiefly of émigré scholars from the Soviet Union.

According to a tentative appraisal of Soviet African studies in *The Mizan Newsletters* of February and April, 1961, the Africa Institute has a staff of three or four senior research associates and a large number of junior research associates. The Institute tries to be interdisciplinary, with ethnography as its base, but it is weak in political science and economics. Organizationally, it is not linked with a university in the manner of American programs of African studies. Most of its research associates have had no opportunity to do field work in Africa, and they feel compelled to produce timely political and educational studies quickly. The result is often a kind of "generalized specialist journalism" rather than academic study in depth. The Institute performs a valuable service to the Soviet Union, however, by making the public more aware of the importance of Africa and by training personnel for government service, including research associates attached to Soviet diplomatic and other posts in Africa.

At Leningrad the leading Africanist is D. A. Ol'derogge, who studied African languages in Germany in 1927–1928 and began to teach Swahili in 1929 in a new Africa section of the Oriental Institute. In 1934, Leningrad University took over the teaching of African languages, with Ol'derogge teaching Swahili and Zulu and N. V. Yashmanov, who died in 1946, teaching Hausa and Amharic. A number of philologists trained by them are now teaching these four African languages, plus Luganda and Ge'ez, and plans are under way to begin the teaching of Luba, Kongo, Mandingo, and Yoruba. According to Kenneth W. Mildenberger, "African language schools, each staffed with twenty senior scholars," were operating in 1960 i Leningrad, Moscow, and Kiev.[8] Courses given at Leningrad Unive: sity in recent years have included seminars on the reading of th contemporary Swahili and Hausa press.

In August, 1960, at the twenty-fifth International Congress c Orientalists in Moscow, the Africa Section, which Potekhin chairec initiated a resolution to establish a separate International Congres of Africanists to hold its first meeting at one of the African universit centers in 1962. The extent to which this Soviet proposal will injec extraneous political considerations into international academic ci: cles remains to be seen. A small committee to organize the Congres met in Nigeria in September, 1961, under the chairmanship of K. C Dike, Principal of the University College, Ibadan. Professor Dike' pointed remarks revealed once again that Africanism is far more tha a superficial phenomenon monopolized by politicians. In openin, the committee meeting, he paid tribute to the work of foreign schol ars but emphasized that an International Congress of Africanist would

. . . afford African scholars from all over this continent a chance t work together. . . . We Africans feel the time has now come for us t speak for ourselves and to take to ourselves the obligation to study witl thoroughness and depth our own past and our own present and our ow prospects. Particularly, too, we feel that in the history, literature and art of Africa it is time for an African interpretation to be given prominence This means that an International Congress of Africanists must be inits ated in a particular spirit and with a particular purpose. I visualize sucl a Congress as an attempt to channel all the endeavors of the Africa: studies movement into one broad stream, and as providing above all th focus for the endeavors of African scholars . . . mobilized as one hug team devoted to the study of our continent. . . . We hope for a Con gress in which African Africanists for the first time can take the lead anc make the decisions. . . .[9]

The committee decided to invite about 150 delegates, including si: each from France, the United Kingdom, the United States, and th

---

[8] Kenneth W. Mildenberger, "African Studies and the National Defense Education Act," *African Studies Bulletin*, December, 1960, p. 20.

[9] Opening speech by Dr. K. O. Dike (mimeo.), International Congress of Africanists, Organizing Committee Meeting at University College, Ibadan, September 8–11, 1961, pp. 4–7.

Soviet Union, to the first International Congress of Africanists to be held for one week in December, 1962, at the University of Ghana. In another decision, somewhat odd in the light of this aura of Africanism, the committee asked Potekhin and Professor Melville J. Herskovits of the United States to draw up a draft constitution for the Congress, to be considered at the 1962 meeting.

12

Communist Channels
in Africa

LET us now turn to the many and varied nongovernmental channels through which Communist ideas penetrate Africa. The most obvious of these channels, the Communist Party, had little success either in the old colonial Africa, where European administrators took the necessary steps to keep Communists out and hold Communist propaganda to a minimum, or in newly independent states where strong African leaders were willing to deal with Moscow but not to permit the growth of local Communist opposition. Counting Communists in Africa is largely guesswork. L. N. Chernov, a Soviet writer, contends that the combined strength of Communist Parties in black Africa has increased from 5000 to 50,000 during 1960 and 1961. My own guess is much lower. Local Communists are concentrated mainly at the northern and southern ends of the continent, where the European impact has been strongest. The present status of communism in more than 40 African countries is summarized below. The data is taken mostly from *World Strength of Communist Organizations*, published by the Department of State's Bureau of Intelligence and Research in January, 1962.

COMMUNIST PARTIES IN AFRICA

Country	Communist Strength
Algeria	5000 membership, estimated in 1958; Party outlawed since September 12, 1955.
Angola	No known Communist Party; the Conakry-based Movimenta Popular de Libertacao de Angola (MPLA) is subject to considerable Communist influence.
British High Commission Territories of Basutoland, Bechuanaland, and Swaziland	Party nonexistent in Bechuanaland and Swaziland; existence of a Basutoland Communist Party first publicized in November, 1961.
Cameroon	One faction of Communist-supported Union des Populations du Cameroun (UPC) is conducting terrorist activities in southwestern Cameroon. Chinese Communists have trained certain UPC members in guerrilla warfare techniques. The two largest Cameroonian trade unions are affiliated with the Communist-front WFTU. The Union Nationale des Étudiants Kamerunais in France gives evidence of considerable Communist indoctrination.
Congo (Leopoldville)	No real party apparatus exists, although there are several self-styled Communist Party members and Communist sympathizers.
Egypt	Estimated membership 1000. Illegal Party comprises one primary organization and at least two splinter groups.
Entente states Dahomey Ivory Coast Niger Upper Volta	No organized party. Communist sympathizers mainly among trade unionists and students.
Equatorial African States Chad Central African Republic Congo (Brazzaville) Gabon	No organized party. Central African Republic has a Communist-influenced party of little consequence.

Country	Communist Strength
Ethiopia	No political parties permitted. Communist propaganda disseminated through Soviet supported hospital and information center in Addis Ababa.
Federation of Rhodesia and Nyasaland	No organized Communist Party and little evidence of Communist activity.
Gambia	No known Communist activity.
Ghana	No organized party, although pro-Communist sentiment is evident among certain Convention Peoples Party members, youth organizations, the press, and Ghana Trade Union Congress.
Guinea	No Communist Party in Guinea, but there are Communist sympathizers in the ruling Parti Démocratique de Guinée and its affiliated trade union and youth organizations. Had 1000 Soviet bloc technicians in 1961 and bloc credits of more than $110,000,000.
Kenya	No organized party. A few politicians with pro-Communist attitudes.
Liberia	No organized party. Several Liberians were recently arrested for an alleged Communist plot, which included the organization at a youth movement, to overthrow the government.
Libya	No organized party.
Malagasy Republic	The Madagascar Communist Party, a "Titoist" group, claims 1500 but may be less than 100. The main target of Communist penetration is AKFM, an alliance of radical nationalist movements.
Mali	No organized party. Mali's ruling party, the Union Soudanaise, contains a number of Communist sympathizers, some of whom have positions of considerable influence.
Mauritania	No known Communist movement.
Morocco	The Communist Party of Morocco has an estimated membership of 1000-1500, but was outlawed in 1952 by the French and again in 1959 by the present government.
Mozambique	No known Communist Party. A few individual Communists, and Communist sympathizers.

Country	Communist Strength
Nigeria	500 estimated Communists. A Nigerian Communist Party was formed in February, 1961, but most Nigerian Communists did not affiliate. Nigerian-Soviet Friendship Society has little following.
Ruanda-Urundi	No organized party. Dominant UPRONA Party in Urundi has sought and received Soviet bloc and radical African support.
Sierra Leone	No organized Communist Party.
Somali Republic	No organized party. Some infiltration of political, labor, and student organizations by pro-Communist elements.
South Africa	South African Communist Party illegal. Has estimated 800 members and perhaps 6500 sympathizers. Communists also influential in African National Congress and other organizations.
Sudan	Sudan Communist Party illegal since mid-1940s. Estimated 1500 members and 4000 sympathizers.
Tanganyika	No organized party. Small Tanganyika African National Congress is pro-Communist in orientation.
Togo	No organized party. Certain Togolese youths who were educated in France have been influenced by Marxist doctrine.
Tunisia	Tunisia Communist Party illegal. Estimated membership of 1000.
Uganda	No organized party. A few Communist sympathizers among Africans and Asians who have studied abroad.
Zanzibar	No organized party. A segment of the Zanzibar Nationalist Party is pro-Communist. Communist China active in Zanzibar.

Algeria is the main Communist stronghold north of the Sahara. The Party members, however, are mostly European workers, artisans, and lower civil servants. The Soviet Union had little success in exploiting the Algerian rebellion partly because of the uncertainty of French Communist policy. Khrushchev may have been cautious in the hope of helping to wean President de Gaulle away from NATO.

The illegal Algerian Communist Party, moreover, did not join th
nationalist FLN in its fight for independence.

South of the Sahara the most interesting case study of communis
is provided by South Africa, where the first Communist Party in th
whole continent was founded in Cape Town in 1921 by white Sout
Africans. During the 30 years before it was outlawed in 1950, i
checkered career had little success. Although South African delegate
at the Sixth Comintern Congress in 1928 advocated black and whit
unity, the Congress went on record in favor of a "black republic,"
line which was not abandoned until 1935 after it had done consi
erable damage to the Party. Communist candidates polled 6806 vote
in the national elections of 1943 but only 1783 votes in the 194
elections, and the Party dissolved itself on June 20, 1950, just b
fore the Suppression of Communism Act went into effect. Afte
Sam Kahn was ousted from Parliament in 1952 on the charge of con
munism, a by-election was held in which natives of Cape Provinc
overwhelmingly elected Brian Bunting, editor of the Communist-lin
weekly *Advance*, to Kahn's seat. When Bunting was kept out c
Parliament on the same charge, a third Communist sympathizer wa
elected by Africans.

A number of Communists have become leaders in the Africa
National Congress, particularly since the outlawing of communisr
in 1950. Communists also attained a strong position in the Congres
Alliance made up of the black African National Congress, the Whit
Congress of Democrats, the multiracial South African Congress o
Trade Unions, the South African Colored People's Organization, an
the Indian National Congress. At the end of May, 1961, when thes
and other groups formed a National Action Committee to organiz
protest demonstrations against the establishment of a republic, bot
the Liberal Party and the Pan-Africanist Congress withdrew from i
charging that it was Communist-dominated.

The Communist Party did not come out into the open again unt
July, 1960, four months after the Sharpeville shooting, when it pub
lished a manifesto of support for the "freedom struggle." By 196C
however, younger Africans were increasingly attracted by the "Afric
for the Africans" slogan of the new Pan-Africanist Congress. Th
Communists remained relatively restrained in tactics, the most mil

tant being Indians and Coloreds. Even after Sharpeville, they appeared not to want immediate change but to hold the lid on while continuing their organizing work. Possibly these tactics were employed partly because violent action would have little success, and partly because the Communists were not strong enough to dominate a revolution.

Because of the Nationalist government's rigid refusal to make concessions to African, Colored, and Indian demands, it nonetheless appeared likely after Sharpeville that the underground resistance would resort increasingly to extremist tactics, beginning with sabotage and turning sooner or later to bloodshed. By the end of 1961, in fact, several attempts at sabotage had occurred. In an article published in the January, 1949, issue of *Foreign Affairs*, Max Beloff suggested that the Soviet slogan of "popular democracy" is largely fraudulent in its implications, but the Communist belief in the equality of races as against the assumption of race superiority is genuine, which "makes Communism in the long run a much greater danger in Asia and Africa than in Europe." If he is right, the relentless policy of *apartheid*, by unintentionally embittering more and more nonwhites against whites, might turn out to be doing more for communism than any other single factor. In this context, incidentally, one of the reasons why the Nationalist government compelled the Soviet Union to close its consular offices in Pretoria and Cape Town in February, 1956, is worthy of note: Soviet officials were ignoring the color bar by inviting nonwhites to social functions at the Soviet Consulate General in Pretoria, a step never taken by the American Embassy at its large Fourth of July or other parties.

INFILTRATION OF AFRICAN POLITICAL MOVEMENTS

A second channel exploited by Communists is the African political parties and protest movements which grew rapidly after World War II. In fact, from the limited evidence available, it may be surmised that the Russians preferred not to organize and develop Communist Parties but to work through other channels, at least through the 1940s and 1950s.

The new political movements in British territories were predominantly nationalist efforts little influenced by Communists, despite the wooing of African students in England by British Communists. The neighboring French territories, however, offer several instructive examples of Communist efforts to penetrate African parties. It should be recalled that the Communist Party was strong in France after World War II. In the French Cameroons, Ruben Um Nyobe is reported to have been advised by French Communist friends that he would serve their mutual interests best not by forming a Communist Party but by leading an African mass movement. Félix Moumié, Nyobe's successor as head of the resulting Union des Populations du Cameroun, once said that he was influenced by Chinese Communist leader Mao to employ the strategy and tactics of guerrilla warfare in the Cameroons. The deaths of Nyobe in 1958 and Moumié in 1960 hurt the movement. Its members exiled because of the violence it precipitated in May, 1955, the UPC split. The less radical faction was amnestied, and won one-fourth of the seats in the Cameroon National Assembly in April, 1960. The extremists continue to operate in southwestern Cameroon.

The Ivory Coast provides another striking example of Communist efforts to penetrate French territories. In 1945 a wealthy African landowner and physician named Félix Houphouet-Boigny, supported by a Union of African Planters, was elected from the Ivory Coast to the French National Assembly. In Paris he came into contact, like Nyobe, with Communists who encouraged him to form a large African party, an aim which was apparently furthered by certain Communists or Communist sympathizers who were then officials in the government of the Ivory Coast. Along with other African representatives in the French parliament, he issued the manifesto of a new political organization, the Rassemblement Démocratique Africain (RDA), which assembled a Congress of 800 delegates at Bamako in October of 1946. On a platform which called for political and social equality, democratic local assemblies, and freely consented union with France, the RDA had a phenomenal growth. By 1949 it claimed a membership of 700,000 in the Ivory Coast, and another 300,000 in other French territories. Whether or not this claim was exaggerated, the RDA held 25 of the 27 seats in the Ivory Coast Representative Assembly after the May elections of 1948.

The RDA was never a Communist Party, which enabled the Communists to bring influence from the outside on a new party of the masses which could be regarded, in the Comintern tradition, as a single national front against imperialism. French Communists, including Raymond Barbé, a member of the Central Committee of the Communist Party who attended the 1946 Congress in Bamako, went to the Ivory Coast to help Houphouet-Boigny organize public meetings with the theme, "The people of Africa will never fight against the U.S.S.R.," along with denunciations of the Marshall Plan and American imperialism. Communist study groups were organized in Paris and West Africa to indoctrinate RDA leaders, and in the French National Assembly the RDA and other African deputies formed a voting bloc with the French Communists.

Communist influence over the RDA began to dwindle by 1949, however. It was evident from the beginning that a number of important African political leaders outside the Ivory Coast disliked the Communist ties of the RDA. Possibly they were also annoyed by the idea of an African organization's being directed by Frenchmen. As these and other rising leaders reshaped and strengthened their own political organizations, they began to make such inroads in RDA voting strength that RDA politicians gradually came to the decision to drop their Communist ties as a political liability. The French government was meanwhile moving to the right and removing Communist sympathizers in French officialdom in Africa.

An Ivory Coast clash between supporters and opponents of the RDA in February, 1949, led to the arrest of RDA leaders, which was followed by a series of demonstrations, arrests, boycotts, and shootings. French officials attempted to suppress RDA excesses and to persuade its leaders to break with the Communists. The deaths and injuries resulting from the 1949 and 1950 riots, incited partly by Communist-inclined agitators, may also have hurt the RDA. At any rate, RDA representatives in the Ivory Coast Assembly declined, RDA representation in Paris dropped, and RDA deputies stopped voting with the Communists in the French Parliament. On October 6, 1951, Houphouet-Boigny announced to a large assemblage of his followers in the Ivory Coast that he had broken with the Communists because "there should be no class struggle in Africa."

A third and still different example of Communist penetration of former French territories is the better-known case of Guinea. President Sékou Touré, once an RDA leader, founded his own Part Démocratique de Guinée on a Socialist platform of democratic centralism. Although Guinea in 1960 was closer to communism than any other African country, Sékou Touré disturbed Moscow because in Aimé Césaire's words, he wanted to "Africanize Marx" rather than "make Africa Marxist," and he refused to adhere to Communist ideology. As Walter Z. Laqueur suggested in the July, 1961, issue of *Foreign Affairs*, in this period of transition from the age of proletarian internationalism to the era of Communist schisms "we will do well to encourage independence of mind and to avoid confusing radical nationalism or Afro-Communism with orthodox Marxism-Leninism."

Sékou Touré's determined Africanism was again exhibited on January 7, 1962. Speaking at the opening of a Russian commercial exposition in Guinea, with Soviet Deputy Premier Anastas I. Mikoyan present, Touré declared that while Guinea would accept aid from any country, it "refuses to be drawn into choosing sides in a power struggle between world blocs."[1] His statement followed the withdrawal of the Soviet ambassador in December after an alleged anti-government plot stimulated by an "Eastern bloc" embassy and the French Embassy. Whatever the facts about the plot, it is worthy of note that Mikoyan, upon his departure after a brief visit to improve relations, asserted that "in supporting the Guinean people in the struggle for consolidation of the independence of their country, the Soviet Union does not seek profit for itself, does not set political or other conditions, and does not harbor any intention of meddling in your country's internal affairs or imposing its ideology."[2]

COMMUNIST INFILTRATION OF LABOR MOVEMENTS

A third channel the Communists sought to exploit was the trade union movement, especially through the World Federation of Trade Unions (WFTU). The major labor federations of Europe and the American CIO had formed the World Federation of Trade Unions in 1945. As the cold war intensified, however, the WFTU began to

[1] *New York Times*, January 8, 1962.
[2] *Ibid.*, January 14, 1962.

split apart until, in December, 1949, the Western unions formed a separate International Confederation of Free Trade Unions (ICFTU).

Although under Communist leadership, the WFTU differed from its predecessor, the Red International of Labor Unions (1923–1935), which was outspokenly Communist and acted as the trade union arm of the Third International. The WFTU had no direct connections with the Soviet government and therefore posed as the legitimate spokesman for the social and economic demands of world labor. In 1959 it had 95,000,000 members, but only 5 percent of them came from countries outside the Soviet bloc. Its headquarters were in Prague, since it had been expelled from Paris in 1951 and asked to leave Vienna in 1955. The WFTU has ample funds at its disposal because, unlike the ICFTU and the International Federation of Christian Trade Unions, it accepts direct government subsidies.

After the Western unions split away, the WFTU turned its attention to Africa and Asia. An ICFTU mission which visited West Africa in 1951 was forcefully struck by the extent of WFTU activity, especially in the distribution of literature and funds for organizing purposes. For the next five years, the WFTU concentrated its efforts upon Nigeria, the Sudan, South Africa, and the French territories. Opposition from British, Portuguese, and Belgian administrations virtually excluded it from other areas.

Attempts to form a single labor federation in Nigeria, where the trade union movement is one of the most highly fragmented in all of Africa, have never been successful. The Nigerian Trades Union Congress, formed in 1943, split apart because of pressure from its more militant elements. A radical Ibo named Nduka Eze had organized the United Africa Company workers into the second-largest union in the country, and in 1947 succeeded in affiliating the Trades Union Congress with the leading nationalist party, a controversial issue which split the TUC a year later. In 1950 Eze succeeded in organizing a new Nigerian Labor Congress which sought to unite all labor. Early in 1951, however, he was reported to have returned from Prague with a Communist donation of £2000 of WFTU funds. As a result of this and other factors, his influence collapsed and the Nigerian Labor Congress disintegrated. Additional splits and realignments followed, and a new Trades Union Congress of Nigeria (TUCN) contended that the old Nigerian Trades Union Congress (NTUC) was still receiving WFTU funds. The NTUC has supported the All-African Trade Union Federation, sponsored by the Casablanca powers, which predicates membership upon disaffiliation from all international labor organizations. The TUCN backs the rival African Trade Union Confederation.

The Sudan possessed one of the most advanced and highly organized labor movements in all of Africa until the Abboud government adopted a severely restrictive policy toward unions. Soon after the creation of a Sudan Workers Trade Union Federation in 1949, Communists had gained control of about half of the organized labor movement. In the summer of 1957 negotiations to merge the two labor federations collapsed when the Communists gained control of the executive body of the merger group.

By 1958, the Communist-led SWFTU reportedly controlled 70 percent of the workers. Although it never joined the WFTU, it sent an unofficial delegation to the 1957 WFTU conference in Leipzig. In March, 1958, its non-Communist rival joined ICFTU. After General Abboud took over the government in November, 1958, however, affiliations with international labor organizations were no longer permitted.

In South Africa the Communists have for many years penetrated the trade union movement. They control the South African Congress of Trade Unions (SACTU) formed in 1955 of nonwhite unions and racially mixed unions. Its officers and executive committee members were prosecuted by the government in the long South African treason trials which ended in 1961. The relationship between SACTU and the WFTU is obscure. By 1961 it had not affiliated with the WFTU possibly to avoid repressive action by the government.

The main strength of the WFTU lay in French-speaking Africa where concentrated efforts by the Communist-led Confédération Générale des Travailleurs (CGT) enabled it to claim 90 percent of the trade unions in French West Africa by 1955. The CGT was composed almost entirely of Africans, while the Force Ouvrière, which affiliated with the ICFTU, was principally a European organization.

Even Frenchmen who were formerly CGT tended to join the FO when they came to Africa. The FO incurred the hostility of many African trade unionists by using its officers for strikebreaking activities and by accusing Africans of being Communists. At the same time, CGT leaders aroused resentment by keeping Africans in subordinate positions and by being hostile to African nationalism, adopting the line that true liberation from colonialism must wait for a Communist takeover in France.

As a result, a CGT Africaine was formed in 1956 under the leadership of Sékou Touré, who broke away from both the CGT and the WFTU. A CGT loyalist faction led by Diallo Abdoulay of Senegal, Vice-President of the WFTU, lost a bitter fight for control of the French African labor movement, and later entered into wholehearted participation in the Union Générale des Travailleurs d'Afrique Noire (UGTAN) formed by Touré at Cotonou in January, 1957. UGTAN maintains no affiliations with international labor organizations, but has cordial relations with the WFTU, which has heavily subsidized its trade union college at Conakry (East Germany also contributes). UGTAN has been referred to in the Soviet press as "a great victory for African workers."

Since the dissolution of the African CGT unions, the numerical strength of the WFTU has dwindled to negligible proportions. By 1961, half of the remaining WFTU affiliates had been outlawed. Given this situation and the aggressive tone of African nationalism, the Communists did not concentrate on recouping their losses, but rather on undermining the position of the ICFTU. They have therefore welcomed and even promoted the Casablanca-sponsored All-African Trade Union Federation. This effort was countered, however, by the formation of the rival African Trade Union Confederation, which has a much wider following and includes many ICFTU unions. The Communists would have preferred a genuine neutralist labor federation embracing the whole of the trade union movement.

Meanwhile, Communists have continued to train labor leaders in bloc countries. In August, 1959, the Soviets organized a trade union school in Budapest, the first four-week course being attended by 30

216 AFRICA IN WORLD POLITICS

African students. In May, 1961, it was reported that 48 trade unionist from Nigeria, Morocco, Tunisia, and East Africa had recently com pleted a year of training in East Germany, with 38 more to follow in August. In addition, the new university in Moscow will cater t African trade unionists.

OTHER COMMUNIST FRONT ORGANIZATIONS

The "front" organization is a fourth type of Communist instru ment. About 40 "friendship associations" and other identifiable from organizations were operating in Africa in 1961. A Soviet Associatio for Friendship with the Peoples of Africa was born in April, 195⁹ and a year later a Chinese African People's Friendship Associatior sponsored by 17 Chinese organizations, was created. These and othe bodies give financial assistance to enable Africans to attend meeting of such Communist front groups as the World Federation of Deme cratic Youth, the International Union of Students, the World Peac Council, the World Federation of Teachers, the Women's Interna tional Democratic Federation, and several others.

The Congress of Democrats in South Africa is a good example c a local front organization. According to Edwin S. Munger, it grew out of a 1952 meeting in Johannesburg of peoples from all parts c the country, including numerous liberal Europeans with no Commu nist associations. The group divided broadly into two camps, thos favoring immediate universal suffrage and those supporting a qual fied franchise. The former, including leaders with Communist tie established the Congress of Democrats, while the latter formed Liberal Association and later the Liberal Party. The Liberal Part contained certain persons who supported immediate universal fran chise but refused to join a Communist-led group. The Congress c Democrats never had many more than 500 members, and it suffere from the involvement of several leaders in the treason trial, whic cost time, money, and adverse publicity.

A different and more significant type of nongovernmental organ zation for the dissemination of Communist propaganda is the Afrc Asian Peoples Solidarity Conference described in the chapters o Pan-Africanism, which held its first meeting in Cairo at the end c

1957. Although there was something of an air of unreality about the flamboyant propaganda of the Soviet Delegation, its successes were nonetheless significant.

Headed by a "beaming, Oriental-looking" Uzbek official, it brought the Soviet Union into Asian-African councils, thus fulfilling a Soviet aim thwarted at Bandung. The fact that this was a conference of peoples rather than governments enabled Soviet representatives to be even more unrestrained than usual. They not only promised to support independence movements and approved the confiscation of Western investments, but they made a lavish offer of economic aid without strings to all Asians and Africans—which, incidentally, was not mentioned in *Pravda*'s account of the Conference. In the first Soviet public statement, a spokesman said, "We are ready to help you as brother helps brother. Tell us what you need, and we will help you and send, to the best of our capabilities, money needed in the form of loans or aid."

Despite words of caution from Nasser to Egyptian delegates and despite efforts of delegates from Ghana, Tunisia, Ethiopia, the Sudan, and India to moderate its anti-Western tone, the Conference adopted a battery of resolutions condemning NATO, the Eisenhower Doctrine, the Baghdad Pact, nuclear weapons, and other Western innovations.

Perhaps the major Soviet gain was the foothold the Russians obtained to carry on their activities. The Conference voted to create an Afro-Asian Peoples Solidarity Council to meet at least once a year and to have a permanent secretariat in Cairo with an Egyptian secretary general and members from the Soviet Union, Communist China, French Cameroons, Ghana, India, Indonesia, Iraq, Japan, Sudan, and Syria. At the second Conference in Conakry, Guinea, in 1960, the Communist influence in the leadership of the movement increased. Even at Conakry, however, the Soviet Delegation did not entirely succeed in its objections. Partly because of this, the Soviet Committee for Afro-Asian Solidarity, which backstops Soviet participation in the movement, held a separate Soviet Afro-Asian Solidarity Conference in October, 1960, in Stalinabad, capital of the Tadzhik S.S.R. In the Communist atmosphere of Stalinabad, with many African and Asian students in the Soviet Union present, the Conference resolutions were quite anti-Western:

Imperialist monopolies, above all those of the U.S.A., are striving to retain colonial exploitation, at whatever price and in whatever form. They are attempting to impose a puppet government . . . . They are binding young independent states with the chains of unjust agreements, they are fighting to preserve the old and create new military bases on others' territory. . . . The U.S.A. and the powers belonging to the aggressive blocs NATO, SEATO, and CENTO still look upon the peoples of Asia and Africa as cannon fodder and upon their territory as a strategic bridgehead.[3]

The Stalinabad Conference thus provided the Communists with an additional instrument of persuasion, uninhibited by the neutralists in the Cairo secretariat of the Afro-Asian solidarity movement. The Soviet Afro-Asian Solidarity Committee also sent observers to the second All-African Peoples Conference in Tunis in 1960, but was not represented at its third Conference in Cairo in 1961.

AFRICAN STUDENTS

At the Sixth Congress of the Communist International in 1928 it was affirmed that "an important if not predominant part of the Party ranks in the first stage of the movement is recruited from the petty bourgeoisie, very frequently students." In ensuing years the Communist-controlled World Federation of Democratic Youth (WFDY) in Budapest and the International Union of Students (IUS) in Prague have become significant channels for Communist propaganda. The WFDY has a Department for Cooperation with Colonial Countries which has developed links with numerous Africa youth organizations since 1953, including the Union of Sudanese Youth, the Rural Youth League of Togo, the Working Youth of Ubangui-Chari, the Association of Moroccan Students in France, the Democratic Youth of Madagascar, the African Youth League of the Ivory Coast, the Togoland Youth Movement, the Maabang Youth Association (Ghana), the Congo Youth Union, the Niger Youth Union, and the Union of South Africa Indian Youth Congress. The IUS

[3] George A. von Stackelberg, "Soviet Afro-Asian Policy Enters a New Stage," Bulletin—Institute for the Study of the USSR, November, 1960, pp. 22–23.

has a Bureau for Problems of Colonial Students which acts as a kind of clearing house for aid, especially in the form of scholarships for study in Soviet bloc countries.

In the early postwar years only a small number of African students studied behind the iron curtain. Many thousands, however, attended universities in Britain and France where they were more or less systematically cultivated by British and French Communists. Many of these potential African leaders were contacted by young members of "cultural associations" with innocuous names, who arranged sightseeing tours for them, invited them to meals, and sometimes paid their expenses to student conferences in Prague, Warsaw, or Moscow. In London, when the inroads the Communists were making by such tactics were discovered not long after the war, members of the Fabian Bureau attempted to counter them by developing their own program of help for colonial students.

According to a Soviet report (*Komsomolskaya Pravda*, November 11, 1955), 22 African youth delegations visited the U.S.S.R. between 1951 and 1955. Approximately 550 African students (Egyptians not included) attended the sixth World Youth Festival in Moscow from July 28 to August 11, 1957. This number probably doubled at the seventh Festival in Vienna in 1959.

Although the Soviet effort to indoctrinate African students is one of the most significant Communist methods, it was not entirely successful. George Padmore once remarked that West African students "shed their Marxist garments on returning home and revert to what they have always been at heart—bourgeois nationalists. . . . The British Communist Party will be sadly disappointed if it is relying upon these opportunistic intellectuals to lead the proletarian revolution in Africa!"[4] In Ghana the National Union of Students seceded from the IUS in February, 1957, declaring that the "IUS subordinated the welfare of the students to the dictates of political regime. . . ."

Within the Soviet Union, the Russians appear to be having occasional difficulties with African students, just as the United States, India, and other countries do. T. C. Okonkwo, a Nigerian student

---

[4] George Padmore, *Pan-Africanism or Communism? The Coming Struggle for Africa*, New York, 1956, pp. 329–330.

who contended that he had encountered racial bias in Moscow State University and that the Soviet Union tried to brainwash African, Asian, and Latin-American students, was attacked as a Pentagon agent who was trying with American money to woo African students away from Soviet schools. According to Osgood Caruthers in the *New York Times* for October 30, 1960, the official trade-union journal *Trud* reported that Okonkwo was expelled after two years of study in which he failed to pass a single examination. Okonkwo, along with Andrew R. Amar of Uganda and Michael Ayih of Togo, replied to Soviet attacks by issuing a long "Open Letter to All African Governments" from Frankfurt, Germany, on September 20, 1960, which was reprinted in the December 17, 1960, *America*. Claiming to represent the views of the Executive Committee of the African Students Union in Moscow, the three Africans "stress the great danger Communism is to true Africanism," and cite numerous examples of alleged indoctrination, suppression of freedom, and racial discrimination against Africans. In April, 1962, it was reported that two Kenya students had been arrested as Western agents and 15 others placed under restriction.

Nonetheless, the Soviet Union, like the United States, is expanding its facilities for African students. The People's Friendship University (now renamed Patrice Lumumba University) was established in February, 1960, in Moscow for students from underdeveloped areas, with plans for 500 students in 1960–1961 and an ultimate capacity of between 3000 and 4000 students. In March, 1960, it was reported that East Germany, offering "Red Fulbrights" on a large scale to Africans and Asians, was financing 2000 students from 40 countries in its universities; new students were required to attend a six-month course in special schools for foreigners in Leipzig to learn the German language as well as the principles of Marxism-Leninism.

The number of African students in Soviet bloc universities appears to have doubled in the academic year 1960–1961, reaching an estimated total of nearly 1200. This figure does not include industrial trainees, but covers those enrolled in institutions of higher education for at least one semester. About 440 were studying in the Soviet Union, 320 in East Germany, 200 in Czechoslovakia, and 200 in other bloc countries. They came from about 30 African countries, including 366 students from Guinea, 225 from Algeria, 174 from the Sudan, 50 from Somalia, and lesser numbers from 25 other African states and territories. These figures do not include Egyptians, about 150 of whom were studying in the Soviet Union and approximately the same number in other bloc countries.

This is a large and significant increase, but it should be noted for purposes of perspective that a far greater number of African students were attending universities in the Western bloc during the same period, including 2831 enrolled in the colleges and universities of the United States. According to a French estimate there were somewhere between 7000 and 9000 African students in France during the academic year 1960–1961, about 40 percent of whom were in secondary schools. The greatest number of Africans are studying in the United Kingdom, including 6800 from Nigeria alone and 3800 from Ghana in 1960–1961. At that time, out of a total of 17,000 African students, 11,000 were working for advanced degrees. In Belgium early in 1962 there were about 1000 Congolese students and 850 technical trainees.

SUMMARY

To summarize the evidence thus far presented, after 40 years of world communism (1) there were relatively few Communists in Africa, (2) Communists had failed in most of their efforts to gain control of African political movements, (3) the number of Communists in the trade unions had declined by the end of the 1950s, (4) Communist influence in front organizations had often been exposed, (5) Communist efforts with African students had not been altogether successful, and (6) the opportunist and cynical tactics of communism had been unintentionally revealed by ideological shifts and by such actions as the suppression of Hungarian nationalists in 1959, the Chinese invasion of Tibet in 1956, Khrushchev's callous attack on Secretary General Hammarskjold at the U.N. General Assembly in 1960, and his deliberate resumption of nuclear testing during the conference of neutralists at Belgrade in September, 1961. Before drawing any conclusions about Communist prospects in the future, however, we must examine other aspects of Soviet policy.

13

Soviet Policy in Africa

THE duality of Soviet policy must not be forgotten. On the one hand the Soviet Union attempts to foster communism in Africa, while on the other it seeks to promote its interests and influence as a great power. The nongovernmental channels through which Communist ideas are spread in Africa have already been analyzed. The efforts of the Soviet government to expand its influence through diplomatic, trade, aid, and cultural missions will now be reviewed.

SOVIET ACTIVITIES IN THE U.N.

During the first 15 years after World War II, while Soviet penetration of Africa was curtailed by colonial governments, Russian diplomats found the United Nations a particularly valuable forum for spreading anticolonial propaganda and subverting the Western alliance. In fact, the United Nations was more useful to the Soviet Union in the colonial field than in any other. How the Soviet bloc exploited the U.N. is therefore well worth describing.

When the Trusteeship Council began its first examination of African trust territories at its third session in the summer of 1948, the Soviet representative obviously set out to make the most of a valuable opportunity. His preparations had clearly been made with care and detail. His speeches, damning colonialism in the lurid language appreciated by African nationalists, cover approximately 1000 inches of the 7700 inches of printed summary records of the third session, in contrast to 450 inches for the United States representative, who took quite an active part in Council discussions. The double-barreled technique of Soviet delegates is (1) to exaggerate, oversimplify, and distort African problems, and (2) constantly and deliberately to repeat the same themes, sometimes even with cynical humor. For example, when the British, answering questions on the penal system in the Cameroons, reported that Africans in jail usually gain weight, the Soviet delegate called it "a very striking example . . . of how the indigenous inhabitants live," and declared that "although prison life is not particularly sweet, nevertheless we see that an indigenous inhabitant who is imprisoned is fed better than he can feed himself when he is on his own." Repeating this technique a few days later when British Togoland was under discussion, he contended that the diet of Togolanders in jail "includes more protein than the diet of people outside jail. . . . This is eloquent indeed." Although the tears of the bear often looked like those of the crocodile, even to anticolonial delegates who shared some of the Russian views of Africa, the general effect of Russian extremism was indirectly to encourage other anticolonial members to move toward a more extreme or at least a less reserved attitude toward the colonial representatives. This tended over a period of time to embitter and confuse Council issues and debates.

When the time came to propose resolutions regarding each trust territory, Soviet delegates in the early years had another standard technique. For each territory, no matter what its stage of development, they would introduce a series of similar recommendations, calling for (1) participation of the people in the government, (2) replacing the tribal system with democratic government, (3) return of alienated land, (4) replacing the head tax with an income tax, and (5) increasing the budget for educational, cultural, and health purposes. These were voted down one by one. When taken out of the context of the arguments used in supporting them, however, they seemed so harmless that the unwary reader might wonder why other delegations opposed the U.S.S.R.'s apparent effort to help colonial peoples. Over the long run these persistent tactics helped to build up the image of the Soviet Union as a friend who always fought for colonial peoples. Conversely, the more conscientious though not necessarily correct position of the United States led it into numerous negative votes and abstentions which were often insignificant in individual cases, but over the long run built up an opposite image of the United States as a defender of the colonial powers if not of colonialism.

Another successful tactic of the Soviet Delegation was its use and abuse of what the Trusteeship Council termed "individual observation" in the Council's Annual Report to the General Assembly, which is perhaps the most important and most studied Council document. Although the observations and recommendations of each delegation are recorded in the official record of the Council's meetings, the Soviet Union, in this case supported by all the other nonadministering powers, wanted them also included in the Council Report to the Assembly. Since the administering members wanted the Report to contain only the conclusions and recommendations adopted by the Council as a whole, a long procedural wrangle ensued which split the Council six to six. In the end the Soviet view prevailed because the other nonadministering members attached so much importance to having their individual observations reported to the Assembly.

The Soviet Delegation was also active in the discussions of an item which was usually billed on the agenda of the U.N. meetings under the innocuous title of "dissemination of information about the United Nations," an admirable cause generally supported by all members. In debate on this item, Soviet delegates joined those of other nonadministering members in bringing constant pressure on the British, French, Dutch, and Italians to increase the flow of information about the United Nations in trust territories, primarily in the form of these official records. To the Soviet Union this was a useful channel for disseminating Soviet views under a United Nations format, as well as a further opportunity to put Western delegates on the defensive. The visiting missions to trust territories often checked up on the administering authorities by asking in schools and libraries and other appropriate places to see what United Nations material was available.

The extent to which U.N. documents in libraries and schools are used is of course uncertain. There was one group of Africans, however, to whom many of these documents were sent directly: the thousands who sent written petitions to the Trusteeship Council. Since petitioners were at the outset dissatisfied persons, most of whom did not understand the constitutional limitations of what the U.N. could do for them, they were very likely to be even more dissatisfied when they read the decisions on their petitions. Soviet delegations made a special effort to capitalize on the opportunity for Soviet propaganda presented by this situation. The colonial powers managed to keep them off the visiting missions to Africa, but the Russians served for many years on the Petitions Committee, which became a permanent body and met between as well as during Council sessions in order to deal with the mounting accumulation of petitions.

The Soviet tactic in this Committee was systematically and deliberately to accept allegations of petitioners as true and imply that explanations by administering authorities were false. Although his proposals were usually voted down, the Soviet representative nonetheless managed to get them printed as individual proposals in the Committee's Report to the Council. Africans who read the summary records of the meetings at which their petitions were discussed, which were sent to them along with the final report adopted by the Trusteeship Council, often found that the only country whose representative recommended what they wanted was the U.S.S.R. This unqualified Russian support naturally appealed to them more than the disappointing moderation of United States representatives.

Another opportunity for false propaganda came when the Petitions Committee, in order to expedite its work, decided to adopt individual resolutions only on those petitions containing specific complaints. This is how *Izvestia* reported the decision on June 10, 1952: "The Anglo-American bloc acting in violation of the demands of the United Nations Charter, rejected the Soviet proposal to examine all petitions and to take a decision on the subject of each of them separately, and it imposed its anti-democratic decision on the Council."

As African issues spread throughout U.N. machinery, Russian tactics in the Trusteeship Council were carried over into other U.N.

organs, notably the General Assembly. In the image-building which portrayed the United States as a supporter of colonialism, the Assembly was most important of all because it exposed the American position to the most publicity. The Soviet Union scored a propaganda coup on February 16, 1957, at the eleventh session when the Assembly adopted, after extensive revisions, a Soviet proposal for timetables for independence of trust territories. This was the first time a Soviet draft resolution in the Fourth or Trusteeship Committee was ever adopted by the Assembly.

Another Soviet coup came when the fifteenth General Assembly adopted a 43-power Afro-Asian resolution calling for immediate steps to end colonialism. An earlier Khrushchev proposal had called for "complete independence forthwith," and had provided that "all strongholds of colonialism in the form of possessions and leased areas in the territory of others must be eliminated." The latter proviso was intended as an attack on U.S. bases abroad. This Soviet draft was rejected, but the 43-power alternative was adopted by 89 to 0 with 9 abstentions. The United States received a bad press because it abstained, along with Britain, France, Belgium, Portugal, Spain, South Africa, Australia, and the Dominican Republic. Added publicity was given the vote because of the behavior of the only Negro on the U.S. Delegation, a Cleveland social worker and educator named Mrs. Zelma Watson George, who stood up and joined in the applause for the Assembly decision. According to Murray Marder, writing in *The Washington Post* of December 22, 1960, the U.S. Delegation abstained only after the direct intervention of President Eisenhower in response to a personal plea from British Prime Minister Macmillan.

Premier Khrushchev, during a major speech at a meeting of Communist Party organizations of the U.S.S.R. on January 6, 1961, claimed that "the basic point in the Soviet Declaration—the need for abolishing colonialism in all its forms and manifestations rapidly and for good—was in the main reflected in the resolution adopted by the United Nations." In the Assembly debate, he stressed, the colonialists, including the United States, "were isolated by the socialist and neutral countries—countries which are also working for the abolition of colonialism."[1] This was the only reference to the United Nations in Khrushchev's speech, an indication of the importance the Russians attach to the colonial issue. A year later, at the sixteenth Assembly, the United States switched from an abstention to an affirmative vote on a follow-up resolution to establish a special committee of 17 members to make recommendations on the implementation of the 1960 declaration.

Whether the U.N. will be as useful to the Soviet Union in the future remains to be seen. Soviet opportunities for exploitation of the colonial issue may diminish as colonies disappear, although several thorny problems still remained in 1962, notably the Portuguese colonies and South Africa. Moreover, the strong African bloc in the U.N. has occasionally been irritated by Soviet tactics, and now wants to lead its own fights.

EXPANSION OF DIPLOMATIC AND TRADE RELATIONS

The year 1958 marked the beginning of an important expansion of Soviet government activities regarding Africa. In September, a new department to deal with African affairs was established in the Foreign Ministry. Within the next three years, the diplomatic, consular, and trade posts of not only the U.S.S.R. but the whole Soviet bloc were substantially increased throughout the continent, as is shown in Table 8.

These figures are somewhat tentative, however. Nonresident ambassadors—those accredited to one country but stationed in another—may leave behind a secretary or some other form of semipermanent representation. The distinction between trade and diplomatic representation is also somewhat blurred, for while certain of the trade missions have an independent existence of their own, others for all practical purposes have become merged with the embassies. Even given these qualifications, these 80-odd posts represent quite a jump from 1954 when there were only Soviet diplomatic missions in Ethiopia and Egypt and a Czech consular mission in Cape Town.

---

[1] C. B. Marshall, *Two Communist Manifestoes*, Washington Center of Foreign Policy Research, 1961, p. 78.

TABLE 8. Bloc Diplomatic or Consular (D) and Trade (T) Representation in Independent African Countries as of January 1, 1962.

	Albania	Bulgaria	Communist China	Cuba	Czechoslovakia	East Germany	Hungary	North Korea	North Vietnam	Outer Mongolia	Poland	Romania	U.S.S.R.
Congo (Leopoldville)					D						D		D
Egypt	D	D	D	D	D	T	D	T	T		D	D	D
Ethiopia	D[a]	D	D	D	DT		D[a]				D[a]	D[a]	D
Ghana			D	D	DT	T					DT		D
Guinea		D	D	D	DT	T	D	D	D	D	DT		D
Libya													D
Mali		D	D	D[a]	D		D[a]	D[a]	D	D[a]	D		D
Morocco			D	D	DT		D[b]		D[b]		D		D
Nigeria					D								D
Somali Republic		D	D		D								D
South Africa													
Sudan	D[a]	D[a]			D	T	D				D		D
Tanganyika			DT								D	D[a]	D[b]
Togo			D[b]		D								D
Tunisia		T			DT						DT		DT

[a] Nonresident.
[b] Agreement concluded, but no mission yet established.

Beginning about 1956 and mounting noticeably in 1958, Soviet bloc trade missions also entered Africa. By 1961 perhaps 85 or more trade delegations of one kind or another had negotiated numerous trade agreements between African and bloc countries. The case of Tunisia is an interesting example. Despite its "pro-Western" policy in the 1950s, Tunisia negotiated trade agreements in 1957 with Yugoslavia in June, the Soviet Union in July, and Czechoslovakia in September, and the Soviet Union established a permanent commercial mission in Tunis. In 1958, Tunisia signed trade agreements with Hungary in January, Poland in February, and Communist China in September; in 1959, trade missions arrived in Tunis from Poland in May, China in June, Bulgaria in July, and the Soviet Union in September; in 1960, Soviet delegations came in January and April, a two-week Polish exposition opened in April, and an East German trade delegation arrived in May. The year 1961 witnessed a general increase in these bloc activities in Tunisia, including a reported 2000 tourists from the Bloc, and a $2,800,000 Soviet loan for 12 years at 3 percent interest announced on August 31. Tunisia had sent a mission to Moscow after failing to get Western support in the Bizerte crisis of 1961; in view of the four-year build-up of trade relations with the Soviet bloc, however, Tunisia would presumably have asked for Soviet aid in any case.

In 1960 United States trade with Africa totaled $761,000,000 in U.S. exports and $535,000,000 in U.S. imports, while Russian trade amounted to only $148,000,000 in U.S.S.R. imports and $94,000,000 in U.S.S.R. exports. For the Russians, however, this was a notable increase over the 1956 figures when U.S.S.R. exports to Africa totaled only $24,000,000 and imports $29,000,000. U.S. trade, meanwhile, remained at about the same level. Soviet bloc trade, it should be noted, is almost entirely state trading under barter, credit, or payments agreements, while U.S. trade flows through private channels.

A breakdown of Soviet and bloc trade with Africa on a country-by-country basis in 1956 and 1960 is shown in Table 9, which has been prepared from preliminary statistics compiled in 1961 by the International Trade Analysis Division of the U.S. Department of Commerce.

TABLE 9. Soviet Bloc and U.S.S.R. Trade

Country	Exports to Africa			
	1956		1960	
	Soviet Bloc[a]	U.S.S.R. Alone	Soviet Bloc[a]	U.S.S.R. Alone
North Africa				
Algeria	$ 3,301,000	$ 162,000	$ 10,790,000	$ 1,909,000
Egypt	76,710,000	22,658,000	158,929,000	63,467,000
Libya			2,402,000	876,000
Morocco	24,506,000	63,000	22,740,000	6,474,000
Sudan	7,419,000	411,000	16,690,000	6,542,000
Tunisia	1,081,000	16,000	6,713,000	2,879,000
West Africa and the Congo				
Angola			405,000	
Cameroon[b]	993,000	14,000	871,000	24,000
Congo (Leopoldville)[c]	2,200,000	21,000	1,918,000	51,000
French West Africa	1,560,000	4,000		
Ghana	4,944,000	27,000	14,995,000	1,567,000
Guinea			22,025,000	5,242,000
Ivory Coast			53,000	
Nigeria	11,162,000	11,000	16,747,000	6,000
Senegal, Mali, and Mauretania			6,471,000	3,000
Togo			38,000	
East and Central Africa				
Ethiopia			969,000	635,000
Kenya	489,000			
Rhodesia-Nyasaland	907,000	[d]	1,984,000	18,000
Tanganyika	398,000			
Uganda	109,000		96,000	
South Africa and Malagasy Republic				
Malagasy	600,000			
South Africa	10,112,000	498,000	14,515,000	3,849,000
	$146,492,000	$23,885,000	$299,351,000	$ 93,542,000

[a] "Soviet Bloc" here includes U.S.S.R., Communist China, Poland, East Germany, Romania, Bulgaria, Hungary, and Czechoslovakia.
[b] January–November.
[c] January–June.
[d] Less than $500.

| Country | Imports from Africa | | | |
| | 1956 | | 1960 | |
	Soviet Bloc[a]	U.S.S.R. Alone	Soviet Bloc[a]	U.S.S.R. Alone
North Africa				
Algeria	$ 4,341,000	$ 3,483,000	$ 2,150,000	$ 1,634,000
Egypt	139,231,000	15,956,000	244,291,000	88,682,000
Libya			674,000	414,000
Morocco	4,665,000	178,000	16,001,000	3,480,000
Sudan	6,103,000	[d]	23,589,000	5,763,000
Tunisia	1,926,000		3,943,000	1,605,000
West Africa and the Congo				
Angola			2,617,000	356,000
Cameroon[b]	1,361,000	458,000	482,000	231,000
Congo (Leopoldville)[c]	70,000	[d]	580,000	
French West Africa	2,536,000	1,188,000		
Ghana	5,743,000	5,743,000	22,536,000	20,370,000
Guinea			12,603,000	3,905,000
Ivory Coast			2,904,000	2,848,000
Nigeria	1,311,000		9,605,000	5,519,000
Senegal, Mali, and Mauretania				
Togo			81,000	
East and Central Africa				
Ethiopia				
Kenya				
Rhodesia-Nyasaland	20,000	[d]	17,012,000	9,293,000
Tanganyika				
Uganda			5,102,000	
South Africa and Malagasy Republic				
Malagasy	200,000	100,000		
South Africa	5,633,000	2,122,000	18,909,000	4,293,000
	$173,140,000	$29,228,000	$383,079,000	$148,393,000

While Czechoslovakia led the bloc in exports to Africa in 1956, the value of U.S.S.R. exports was almost twice that of the Czechs in 1960. Egypt, which accounted for more than two-thirds of all bloc trade in 1956, accounted for slightly over half in 1960. By 1960 China's trade with Africa had reached sizable proportions, mounting to $78,000,000 in imports from Africa and $49,000,000 in exports in 1960. In both 1956 and 1960, Soviet and bloc imports exceeded exports.

The most striking example of Soviet economic penetration is Guinea, where bloc countries quickly filled the vacuum left by the sudden French withdrawal in October, 1958. By the end of 1960, bloc credits to Guinea totaled $102,000,000. Bloc trade with Guinea rose to $14,100,000 in 1959 and $40,000,000 (out of a total Guinea trade of $104,900,000) in 1960. In 1959 the bloc supplied $8,900,000 of Guinea's total imports of $61,900,000, while in 1960 the bloc's total rose sharply to $22,000,000 out of $49,800,000.

The expansion of Soviet bloc trade with Africa was accompanied by the gradual expansion of Soviet aid since 1958 in the form of loans or credits, as shown in Table 10, usually for 12 years at 2.5 to 3 percent interest.

TABLE 10.   Soviet Loans or Credits to Africa

Date of Loan	Recipient	Amount of Loan
1958	Egypt	$275,000,000
1959	Ethiopia	100,000,000
1959	Libya	28,000,000
1960	Guinea	35,000,000
1960	Ghana	40,000,000
1960	Congo (Leopoldville)	3,662,000
1961	Sudan	22,000,000
1961	Tunisia	28,000,000

In 1961 Soviet opportunities through aid programs therefore seemed plentiful because many other African countries were either negotiating for Soviet help or likely to do so in the future. Already in 1958, the United States government had drawn some significant conclusions from a study of the Soviet bloc's economic aid program.

According to this study, the Soviet bloc, in the five years since it began aid programs in 1953, had made $1,200,000,000 available, mostly to Asian countries. Although relatively small, this aid had made an impressive political impact because it was concentrated on a limited number of dramatic projects in key countries and, perhaps more important, because it was carried out efficiently by Soviet technicians who have skillfully avoided undue interference in local affairs. Finally, the evidence of the U.S. study indicated that Soviet bloc aid could be increased quite substantially without being a heavy burden on the bloc's economy. By 1961 there were 1250 Soviet technicians in Africa, about 450 of whom were in Egypt.

CULTURAL EXCHANGES

In addition to diplomatic and trade missions, the Soviet bloc has also stepped up the sending of a wide variety of cultural missions to Africa. Many cultural agreements have been signed providing for exchanges and cooperation in science, the arts, drama, sports, broadcasting, and cinematography. In 1960 the number of cultural delegations traveling through Africa increased, and about two dozen Soviet exhibitions were held in nine African countries between January, 1960, and May, 1961. Seven Soviet bloc athletic teams had visited Ethiopia, Morocco, and Tunisia between 1957 and 1959, and in 1960 they concentrated on West Africa, mostly soccer teams like the Moscow Dynamos, who played a return match against the Ghana Black Stars in Moscow in 1961. The years 1960 and 1961 also witnessed an increase in exchange visits by Soviet and African women's and youth organizations. It has been estimated that a total of about 500 delegations traveled to and from the Soviet bloc in 1960, a substantial increase over the total of 177 in 1957, 202 in 1958, and 389 in 1959.

The radio war in Africa mounted in 1958, although Soviet radio broadcasts had been heard as far south as South Africa for many years. In an amusing incident reported in Nigeria in May, 1952, a monitor at the Eastern Regional Headquarters of the Nigerian Broadcasting Service in Enugu inadvertently tuned Radio Moscow into the Eastern Nigerian radio rediffusion system for 35 minutes. Radio

Moscow, it seems, was broadcasting on every frequency used by the British Broadcasting Company, and even misleading the listeners by giving the six pips of the BBC station break signals! The expansion of broadcasting to Africa was slow until 1958 when, on April 19 Radio Moscow began 15-minute-a-day programs in both English and French on three different meter bands. By October, the time for broadcasts beamed to Africa was reportedly tripled.

By the end of 1961, bloc broadcasting to Africa reached a total of 200 hours per week—a rise of over 100 percent since the beginning of the year. To this figure must be added 10 hours per week partially beamed to Africa and 166 hours per week of Arabic language broadcasts. The significance of this expansion lies mainly in the fact that radio reaches more Africans than any other medium.

The U.S.S.R. increased its output by 75 percent, adding the Ethiopian language of Amharic for the first time, initiating Portuguese language broadcasts exclusively tailored for Portuguese Africa, and expanding its Swahili broadcasts fivefold. It is estimated that these Swahili programs could reach a theoretical maximum of 10,000,000 to 15,000,000 East Africans, including those to whom Swahili is a second language. At the end of the year, Radio Moscow began various experimental transmissions in the Somali language, and in early 1962 it announced that Hausa broadcasts to West Africa would begin soon. The Soviet Union has also extended its "Russian by Radio" broadcasts to Africa in both English and French, in response to "many of our listeners who have requested that we start 'Russian by Radio' lessons. . . . By listening regularly you will, with time, be able to read Russian magazines, newspapers, and books. . . . We will send you Russian textbooks, answer all your questions, and fulfill any other request which you might have. . . ."

The other bloc countries also stepped up their radio propaganda to Africa. Radio Peking, which is said by many Africans to provide the clearest reception, expanded its broadcasting 80 percent by increasing its English output and by initiating French and Swahili programs. The European satellites—excluding Albania and Hungary—more than tripled their output to Africa in English and French. A detailed breakdown of the weekly hours of broadcasting to Africa by Communist bloc radio stations is shown in Table 11.

TABLE 11. Weekly Hours of Broadcasting by Communist Bloc Radio Stations to Africa as of December 31, 1960, and December 31, 1961

	U.S.S.R.		European Satellites		Communist China		Total	
	1960	1961	1960	1961	1960	1961	1960	1961
Amharic		7:00						7:00
Arabic[a]	50:10	50:45	102:40	101:30	14:00	14:00	166:50	166:15
Swahili	3:30	17:30	8:45	28:35		7:00	3:30	24:30
English	19:15	21:00	8:10	32:05	28:00	35:00	56:00	84:35
French	19:15	21:00	2:55	2:55		14:00	27:25	67:05
Portuguese		7:00			7:00	7:00	9:55	16:55
	92:10	124:15	122:30	165:05	49:00	77:00	263:40[b]	366:20[c]

[a] Beamed to North Africa and the Middle East.
[b] An additional 66:30 hours per week, exclusive of Arabic, were beamed in part to Africa by the bloc.
[c] An additional 10:30 hours per week, exclusive of Arabic, were beamed in part to Africa by the bloc.

Other highlights of Communist radio activities included the af filiation of Mali and Cuba to the International Radio and Television Organization, a Soviet-sponsored association. Guinea, Mali, and So malia also received technical assistance from the bloc in constructing or improving radio facilities, while exchanges of technical personnel were arranged with Tunisia, Ghana, and Guinea.

Soviet themes are also widely disseminated through Communist o Communist-oriented newspapers and periodicals, about 20 of which are published in Africa and the Malagasy Republic. Other magazine and printed materials are brought in from bloc countries and sold cheaply in Africa. In South Africa, numerous Communist-oriented journals have been published from time to time, the most impor tant of which is the well-edited weekly *New Age* (formerly the *Clarion*, and then the *Guardian*) which may have a circulation ap proaching 30,000 and a readership of 100,000, mostly Africans. *The African Communist*, an orthodox Leninist periodical which had to move its headquarters from Cape Town to London, now gets back to South Africa by mail.

The attractive Soviet Information Center in Ethiopia has dis tributed Soviet journals and other materials to selected individuals and organizations for some time. The large increase in bloc diplomatic and consular posts in Africa in 1960 and 1961 opened the way for a much wider dissemination of Communist propaganda.

In October, 1960, the International Organization of Journalists, a Communist group in Prague, arranged a meeting of journalists near Vienna, where delegates from Mali, Guinea, and elsewhere formed a provisional committee for the cooperation of African journalists to set up an all-African organization of journalists. According to Stefan C. Stolte, the provisional committee was given for its work an initial installment of $250,000 by the head of the Soviet press department in Moscow. At Bamako the following May, delegates from Algeria, Ghana, Guinea, Upper Volta, Cameroon (UPC members), Mala-gasy, Mali, Togo, and the U.A.R. met to create a Pan-African Union of Journalists to "struggle against colonialism, imperialism and neo-colonialism and in favor of peace."

COMMUNIST CHINA'S AFRICA POLICY

The expansion of Communist China's interest and influence in Africa merits special mention. Chinese leaders made numerous contacts with Africans at the Bandung conference in 1955, and in 1958 official Chinese delegations began to visit black Africa. Chinese Embassies were opened in Khartoum in 1958, Conakry in 1959, and Accra in 1960. The first major Chinese effort was made in Somalia where an Embassy staff of about 40 was assembled in 1961. The Chinese encourage the Somali unification movement to incorporate Ethiopian and other Somalis into a Greater Somalia. The Russians, in contrast, are inhibited from encouraging this Somali irredentist movement because of their long contact with and interests in Ethiopia. Peking has also opened a diplomatic mission in Mali, and is planning embassies in Dar-es-Salaam and Lagos.

The Chinese Communists have been particularly active since the spring of 1960. As Kurt L. London pointed out in the July-August, 1962, issue of *Problems of Communism*, they attempt to stimulate constant exchange of visiting delegations. In 1960, for example, about 270 of the 800 delegations traveling to Peking were African. A Chinese-African Friendship Association and a Chinese Institute of African Affairs have been established, along with a National Afro-Asian Solidarity Committee and a Special Committee for Africa within the Chinese Communist Party.

The Chinese emphasize their kinship with Africans as nonwhite peoples who hate colonialism and neocolonialism and are in need of rapid development. Chinese propaganda continues to stress the old doctrinaire Communist call for proletarian revolution in contrast to the softer themes of peaceful coexistence and respect for neutralism which Khrushchev has tried in the hope of competing more successfully with Western propaganda.

These and other differences between Russian and Chinese Communists are symbolized by the current tendency to abandon the term *Soviet bloc* in favor of the usage *Sino-Soviet bloc*. Whether these differences of interest and outlook will ultimately outweigh the similarities of objectives is still a matter of speculation. In either case, they dovetail nicely by fostering further confusion, discord, and instability in Africa. In this sense, China's tactics might be considered an asset to the Russians because they confuse the West and indirectly enable Moscow to behave more correctly toward the new governments in Africa without abandoning the overall Communist objective of subversion.

THE EFFECTS OF SOVIET BLOC ACTIVITIES

What effect will the multifarious Communist activities described in these two chapters have on the geopolitical future of Africa? Their sheer weight of numbers tends to make Soviet prospects look promising. Moreover, the African revolution is still going on, and the sociology of revolutions suggests that leftward or radical change are likely to continue for some time. This tendency might be reinforced by the fact that the generation of Western-educated African leaders who won independence will sooner or later be replaced by leaders with a more African or at least less European educational background. The African revolution thus contributes inevitably to the Russian objective of detaching Africa from the West. In this limited sense, every Western loss might be considered a Soviet gain. By 1960, in any case, it had become clear that the influence of the Soviet Union as a great power would rise substantially in Africa during the next decade, if only through the expansion of Soviet bloc diplomatic, economic, and cultural activities in new states.

It must be re-emphasized, however, that the rising influence of the U.S.S.R. in Africa is not identical with the spread of communism. In 1962, African leaders were quite willing to accept aid from the Soviet bloc but quite unwilling to take orders from Moscow. Whether this situation will change depends on many imponderables. One of these uncertainties is the extent to which communism will succeed or fail outside Africa. For example, will India remain free of Communist domination? Would Africa move toward communism if India swung into the Communist camp? Was Senator John Sparkman, Democrat of Alabama, right when he warned, in his December 30, 1957, report to the Foreign Relations Committee, that if one free Asian country falls to communism "an irreversible trend may be started which in time might abridge the independence of all these states," ncluding the Middle East and Africa? Can communism conquer Africa south of the Sahara without first taking over the Islamic world of the Middle East and North Africa? Is the monolithic Communist empire of Stalin turning into an uneasy collection of quarreling dictators? No Sovietologist, Orientalist, Arabist, or Africanist scholar can know the answers to these questions.

Whatever happens in other continents, it is worthy of note that in Africa the U.S.S.R. does not have the geographical advantage it has in Asia, where it can send agitators, arms, and propaganda across its own borders directly into neighboring countries. This can be partly overcome in various ways, but the history of Soviet imperialism indicates that people don't just "go Communist." Force as well as ideology is essential for Communist success. A hard core of Communist intellectuals with efficient political machines backed by armed force seems to be needed. In Africa in 1962, this combination of requirements was unavailable, even in Guinea where Sékou Touré's Africanism still outshone his Marxism.

The ideology of communism, moreover, has flaws which limit its attractiveness as a commodity for export to Africa. In addition to its slippery attitude toward the "national bourgeoisie," it is handicapped because African leaders reject some of its basic tenets regarding the class struggle, the leadership role of the proletariat, and economic determinism with the implication that man is not yet master of his own destiny, and the doctrine that the Communist state is a stage in the historical process. Many African leaders have developed their neutralist or positive nonalignment attitudes into almost a counter-ideology. As a result, African Communists find that their "Africanism" is suspect, and they have difficulty retaining the confidence of their countrymen. That is why communism still had little influence as a political creed in the Africa of 1962.

The Soviet practice of setting up satellites or puppet states in Eastern Europe and Asia was therefore unsuitable for Africa, at least during the peak of the African revolution. It is quite interesting that African states, despite their lack of physical power, were able to discourage the Soviet Union from efforts to draw Africa into the Soviet camp, and thus to limit its objective to the detachment of African states from the West. At the same time, African attitudes forced the United States to abandon the idea that neutralism is "immoral," and to limit its major objective to keeping African states out of the Soviet bloc. The world thus witnessed a curious competition in which the two strongest powers in all its history were forced by weak African states to accept and even encourage something which neither of them really favored. How long the Communists would continue these tactics remained uncertain. Numerous Western observers were inclined to regard them as a kind of first stage in a two-stage process of subversion, a plausible theory in light of the new Communist doctrine of "national democracy." In this view, when the Communists have sufficiently weakened African links with the West, they will move on to the second stage of turning Africa from neutralism to communism. In this kind of cold war, the role of private or non-governmental organizations is particularly important because they promote person-to-person contacts and their propaganda can be more subtle.

In his book *African Nationalism*, Ndabaningi Sithole, a Southern Rhodesian who spent three and a half years in the United States, affirms that the "bitter lessons of history" have turned Africans permanently against "the humiliating experience of living under foreign rule."[2] With gentle irony, he suggests that Africans were perhaps fortunate that Western colonialism taught them to hate foreign rule because it inoculated them against the Communist virus.

There is no doubt about African hatred of foreign rule, but this kind of logic depends on the validity of its premises, which might be stated as follows:

> Major premise: Communism means foreign rule.
> Minor premise: Africans hate foreign rule.
> Conclusion: Therefore, Africans will never accept communism.

If communism is equivalent to foreign rule, the West might have less than it thinks to worry about. If the major premise is wrong, however, the logic collapses. If strong leaders are able to Africanize Marx, an indigenous communism based on independence from the Kremlin might still develop, without the stigma of foreign rule.

Africa has already proved that it can change quickly, and opin-

[2] Ndabaningi Sithole, *African Nationalism*, Cape Town, 1959, p. 137.

ions about its future should therefore be expressed with appropriate reserve. The widespread poverty and explosive racial tensions in Africa remain ripe for Communist exploitation. African leaders continue to be interested in the reputation of Russia and China for rapid material development of backward regions. They still wonder whether Africa cannot profit from Communist economic methods without succumbing to Soviet political domination. If Africa must be developed primarily by its own people, they ask, do not Russia and China offer more practical models than the Western nations for the use of planned societies to attain rapid development? This question may seem increasingly relevant to them if Western nations prove unwilling, unable, or reluctant to promote the large-scale aid needed to meet the development objectives of African leaders. Finally, the Communists have a significant advantage in the more effective posture of the Chinese and Russians on race relations between black and white. The Chinese are nonwhites and the Russians, who do not have a large Negro population, have been able to avoid the reputation of basing discrimination on color.

Part IV

American Policy in Africa

14

American Interests in Africa

W_{HY} is the United States meddling in Africa's affairs?" we are often asked. Those who word the question so tendentiously usually have their own answer. They are predisposed to believe that the real motive of the United States must be profit in the form of African trade, investments, and raw materials. This simple formula ignores the complex pluralism of American life. It not only presents a false version of the motives of the United States government, but it fails to take into account the multitude of special interests of American groups and individuals. And it shows little awareness that the interests and activities of private citizens and the press are one vital element in the foreign policy of the United States which cannot be controlled or coordinated by the government.

Until about 1950, American specialists on Africa were so few in number that they were able to keep in touch with each other's ideas and projects. During the 1950s, however, many Americans who became interested in Africa seemed to develop an irresistible urge to "do something about it." Proposals for Africa mushroomed to proportions which seemed fantastic to European observers, who were inclined to wonder whether we did not have too much money for our own good. In the long run, however, this interest and education of Americans in African affairs should nonetheless be helpful to all concerned.

THE SCOPE OF AMERICAN INTERESTS IN AFRICA

The interests of the United States in Africa are frequently elaborated in speeches and position papers prepared by State Department officers. The word *interests* is often used ambiguously along with such overlapping words as *aims, purposes, objectives, goals,* or *principles.* If one has an *interest* in Africa it could mean, according to Webster, either that he is participating in an enterprise for profit or advantage or that he has the "excitement of feeling accompanying special attention to some object." The first type, the search for profit or advantage, may be illustrated by the private investment of American businessmen in Africa or by the propaganda of the United States Information Agency to win an advantage in the cold war. The second type, the excitement of feeling, might cover the interest of American Negroes in Africa, the curiosity of American tourists, or the concern for the welfare of mankind which motivates certain philanthropic, religious, and civic groups. As these examples show, however, the two types of interest are not completely separable because a single person or organization may be motivated in varying degrees by both.

American interests in Africa are often divided into strategic, economic, and humanitarian categories. Although convenient, this classification tends to confuse the general or national interest with the special interests of particular individuals and groups; the words *public* and *private* interest are sometimes used to make the same distinction. The term *strategic interest* is often used in a loose manner that confuses political strategy and military strategy. The ambiguity in the phrase *economic interest* lies in its usage to cover the private investment of American businessmen, the public investment by the United States government through loans and technical assistance, and the advantage of economic expansion to the nation as a whole. The term *humanitarian interest* is a catch-all for a wide variety of private missionary, philanthropic, reformist, and other activities, and has even been loosely applied to describe the United States aid program in Africa.

To avoid the above ambiguities, this analysis of American interests will be divided into (1) the special interests of private citizens and groups which we will discuss in this chapter, and (2) the national interest, to be taken up in Chapter 15.

Because of its size and wealth and the character of its democracy, the United States has tens of thousands of private or nongovernmental organizations of every imaginable type. So many of them are interested in foreign affairs that the State Department has established a large Bureau of Public Affairs with many divisions to deal with them. This Bureau attempts to keep the State Department informed of the public's opinions and to keep the public informed of the government's views.

The American private organizations conducting activities in Africa are described in a State Department document entitled *International Educational, Cultural and Related Activities for African Countries South of the Sahara*, published in August, 1961. About 600 organizations are listed—223 business companies, 203 missionary agencies, and 173 educational, philanthropic, civic, and other private agencies. These groups participate in American policy toward Africa in two ways. Their behavior influences African opinion and therefore affects our relations with Africa; and their views influence policy makers in Washington. Although all specialized groups exert pressure of one type or another, they vary considerably in that some of them openly attempt to bring pressure on governments while others deny any attempt to influence policy. Their diversity makes them exceedingly difficult to classify, but most of them can be included within seven main groups: (1) business companies, (2) church and missionary organizations, (3) a wide variety of civic and foreign affairs associations, (4) philanthropic foundations, (5) universities, (6) labor unions, and (7) Negro groups. Two other categories of Americans whose Africa interests and activities have become significant are unorganized. They are the large number of tourists and the small but significant band of journalists.

AMERICAN BUSINESS IN AFRICA

One of the oldest of American interests in Africa is that of the business world. In 1961 about 220 American firms were doing business in Africa south of the Sahara through branches, subsidiaries affiliates, or investments. Our trade with Africa has always been rela tively small, but it is interesting to recall that in the heyday of sailing vessels, Yankee clippers were carrying about a million dollars' worth of Massachusetts cotton sheeting and shirting to East Africa every year. The Salem brig *Laurent* in 1825 opened American trade with Zanzibar, where an American became the first consul from the outside world. Until the eve of the Civil War, although our primacy de clined as other nations entered the Zanzibar trade, about half the vessels calling at Zanzibar were American, chiefly from Salem. The word *Amerikani* or *merikani* became a Swahili word for calico, and one of the clipper captains wrote that the trademark "Massachusett sheeting" was especially prized in the interior of Africa where it wa conspicuously displayed on cotton *dotis* or loincloths. Our total trade with Africa, just before the Civil War, was valued at about $7,000, 000. During the war, however, American trade suffered heavy losses and European steamships thereafter took over most of the trade o American sailers, particularly after the opening of the Suez canal in 1869. In Zanzibar, nonetheless, as Norman R. Bennett's research has shown, a number of enterprising American traders continued profita ble operations, mainly in kerosene and ivory, for another half century It was not until 1915 that the American consulate was finally closed and moved to Mombasa on the Kenya coast.

The conquest of Africa by Europe in the late nineteenth century further curtailed American commercial expansion, and it was not until World War I that the United States witnessed a notable rise in its trade with Africa—to a peak of about $150,000,000. Declining again during the Great Depression, it did not reattain this level until the outbreak of World War II. During the war years it jumped sharply to more than $1,000,000,000, and it has fluctuated above this level ever since.

In February, 1948, Juan T. Trippe, President of Pan-American Airways, took 16 newspaper and magazine editors and publishers on the first flight of a new direct air route from New York to Johannes burg via the Azores, Lisbon, Dakar, Monrovia, Accra, and Leopold ville. Africa, he said, will be a "continent bright with promise—a land of destiny beckoning to American trade and American travellers."[1] In October, 1949, a group of New York businessmen formed the Pan-African Society of America, later renamed the African Affairs Society of America. Its President, W. Emlen Roosevelt, said that it would aid in the development of cultural, economic and political relations between Africa and the United States. As the business community began to undertake new ventures in Africa, American investment rose rapidly from $104,000,000 in 1943 to $298,000,000 in 1950, $568,000,000 in 1954, and $834,000,000 in 1959. Despite this rapid growth, our investments in Africa, like our trade, remained quite a small percentage of our world total.

The attainment of independence by 19 African states in 1960–1961 opened more doors to American private investment. In the past, South Africa was most attractive because it was more highly developed than other parts of Africa and therefore presented the best opportunities for profitable investment. However, the rate of investment growth in South Africa and the Federation of Rhodesia and Nyasaland was slowed by political disturbances in 1960, while the rate of investment in West Africa was rising. Although the new states in this area have Socialist economic ideas, they nonetheless want to encourage the inflow of private capital. Many of their leaders realize that the economic progress they seek cannot be achieved unless the private sectors of their economies are developed along with the public sectors. Their desire for more business is highlighted by the early action of Ghana and Nigeria in opening trade and investment promotion offices in New York. The potentialities of these two countries for investors were enhanced by the elimination of import licensing controls and the lack of dollar exchange problems. On April 30, 1962, the Ivory Coast also announced the opening of a Resources and Development Agency in New York to join the Ivory Coast Trade Mission which was already operating.

In 1959, Nigeria imported goods valued at $535,000,000, but only $18,000,000 worth of these goods came from the United States. Investment opportunities in Nigeria, Ghana, and Liberia are being explored in a pioneer Rockefeller Brothers' Fund project which, by October, 1961, had completed 23 detailed studies of feasible investments. A further effort to improve commercial relations was launched

[1] *New York Herald Tribune*, February 26, 1948.

in 1961 by a group of American businessmen who organized an African American Trade and Development Association.

Africans are disappointed, however, by the slowness of American investors to respond to the inducements offered by their governments. In 1961 it seemed likely that political uncertainties in the new states would retard for some time the development of the mutual confidence required for sizable investment from private sources overseas.

A final point worthy of note is that American businessmen have also helped to stimulate interest in Africa in other ways. A considerable number of them have made donations to assist the development of African studies in American universities, have given financial aid to African students in the United States, and have made financial contributions to other worthy African projects. The extent to which the private interests of American businessmen are a part of the "national interest" in Africa will be discussed in the next chapter.

MISSIONARY ACTIVITIES

A second group with a major interest in Africa are the church organizations which support several thousand missionaries, the largest group of American civilians resident in Africa. In 1961, activities in Africa were conducted by at least 60 Catholic, 89 Protestant, and 54 interdenominational or nondenominational agencies. Missionary estimates assembled for the Senate Foreign Relations Committee's study of Africa in 1959 showed that in 1956, American Protestant denominations had 2652 workers south of the Sahara, while American Catholic missionaries numbered 785 in 1959. Protestant expenditures for this work in 1956 totaled about $24,000,000, and the expenditures of American Catholic organizations in 1958–1959 totaled about $6,500,000. Since European missionaries in Africa were far more numerous, Americans were only 18 percent of the combined Protestant mission force and less than 3 percent of the total number of Catholic missionaries. Catholic and Protestant estimates of the total number of African converts to Christianity vary widely; in 1957, the Catholic estimate was 37,000,000, while the Protestant calculation was 27,000,000.

In evaluating church interests in Africa, it would be a mistake to think only of the number of Africans converted to Christianity. In addition to these evangelical efforts, American and other missions gradually extended their work into the field of education, medicine, and even agricultural and other economic activities—a form of technical assistance. In early years, nearly all the formal Western education in Africa was in mission hands. The ideals of Christianity, including its emphasis on the equality and freedom of man and on improving the status of women, stimulated African aspirations for a better life. It thus proved to be a powerful force in laying the groundwork for revolutionary change, and might well have been given greater attention in this book as one of the principal external pressures on Africa.

It must be added, however, that the Christian record was marred by the behavior of whites in Africa. The narrow-minded sectarianism of Christian churches was confusing, and the inability of many early missionaries to understand and appreciate African customs and traditions hurt the Christian cause. Numerous American missionaries, upon their return home, have unwittingly given their countrymen a distortedly one-sided picture of African life, based largely on the rural areas in which missions often work. The habitual failure of the great majority of Western whites to practice the Christian ideal of racial equality produced startling results. In South Africa, by 1960, about 3000 separatist churches had been established by Africans after secession from the mission churches or splits among themselves. Some of them are antiwhite, with reverse color bars in Heaven where whites are turned away at the gate. In his book *Defeating Mau Mau*, L. S. B. Leakey has shown how the tunes of Christian hymns were exploited by the Mau Mau:

. . . these propaganda messages could safely be sung in the presence of all but a very few Europeans, since the vast majority could not understand a word of Kikuyu and if they heard a large, or a small, group singing to the tune of "Onward Christian Soldiers", "Abide with Me", or any other well-known hymn, they were hardly likely to suspect that propaganda against themselves was going on under their very noses.[2]

[2] L. S. B. Leakey, *Defeating Mau Mau*, London, 1954, p. 54.

Further north, in the black African area just south of the Sahara, Islam is progressing much faster than Christianity. By 1960, in fact, in addition to the 40,000,000 Moslems in the Arab world north of the Sahara, there appeared to be another 40,000,000 or more in black Africa. Part of the reason for the success of Islam is the fact that its missionaries south of the Sahara are usually dark-skinned. Islam knows no color barriers. Christians are now committed to developing African church leadership almost everywhere. In the future, the nature and functions of Christian activity will have to change considerably to meet the new situation, particularly in Africa's fast-growing towns.

The interest and influence of American churches in Africa is further revealed in still another important activity. Through nationwide programs of conferences, study groups, and publications, church leaders have not only had a major role in educating Americans about Africa, but they have helped to transform the latent anticolonial bias of Americans into an active political force. Churches have been interested not only in the difficulties sometimes encountered by American missionaries trying to operate in colonies controlled by European powers who preferred missionaries from their own countries, but in the much broader question of the political, economic, social, and educational advancement of Africans.

In 1940, the Federal Council of Churches created a Commission To Study the Basis of a Just and Durable Peace under the chairmanship of John Foster Dulles. The work of this Commission was discussed at a church conference in March, 1942, which published a statement calling for autonomy for all colonial peoples along with some form of international supervision until autonomy was achieved. Three months later, a Church Conference on African Affairs was held under the leadership of Emory Ross, Secretary of the North American Foreign Missions Conference, at Otterbein College in Ohio. Its recommendations included an appeal for international inspection of all European dependencies in Africa, and a plea that a separate section on Africa be established in the State Department. In September, 1943, delegates from Protestant churches of the allied powers met at Princeton to adopt six guiding principles for peace, one of which was "the goal of autonomy for subject peoples and

. . . international organizations to assure and supervise the realization of that end." In January, 1945, Ross submitted additional proposals for "eventual self-government . . . as the goal for all dependent peoples" to a second national church conference.[3] By going beyond educational functions to the adoption of political positions, the church group thus became an important factor in rekindling American sentiment against colonialism and in favor of international supervision of colonies.

After the war, church organizations broadened their educational efforts to improve American knowledge of Africa. Perhaps the most important projects were the extensive African study programs undertaken in 1952–1953 and again later under the auspices of the National Council of the Churches of Christ, an interdenominational group representing several million Protestants. Three books on Africa were specially written for the 1959–1960 program, and several thousand churchmen received special training in how to use these books as teachers. When the American image in Africa began to suffer from adverse publicity over Little Rock and other racial questions, the churches turned more attention to this issue. In February, 1960, for example, a conference of the United Presbyterian Church called on the United States government to put itself "emphatically and clearly" on record in favor of racial equality as well as self-determination for the peoples of Africa. One other fact worthy of note is that the churches reached a wider audience than any of the other special groups interested in Africa. Further research is needed on the details of their activities and the extent of their influence.

CIVIC GROUPS

A third group is composed of the multitude of civic associations, councils, commissions, committees, and clubs concerned with international relations, including educational and cultural as well as political and economic matters. During the 1950s the number of meetings, programs, and publications devoted to Africa mounted in the Council on Foreign Relations, the Foreign Policy Association, and

[3] Maurice Levallois, "Les tendances anti-colonialistes des Etats-Unis, de l'U.R.S.S. et de la Chine," *Renaissances*, October, 1945.

their many branches and affiliations. The same was true in organizations with national as well as international interests like the American Association of University Women. The phenomenal interest in Africa also made possible the birth of a considerable number of new organizations devoted exclusively to African affairs, several of which merit special mention.

The African American Institute, publisher of the illustrated monthly *Africa Report,* had by 1961 grown into a substantial organization with offices in New York and Washington and branches in Accra, Lagos, Leopoldville, and Dar-es-Salaam. In addition to a variety of efforts to educate Americans and Africans about each other, the Institute has developed scholarship, loan, and other assistance programs for African students in the United States, and has undertaken to place American teachers in African schools.

The African Studies Association, publisher of the quarterly *African Studies Bulletin,* was formed in 1957 by American scholars engaged in teaching and research about Africa. In addition to fostering teaching and research, the Association has helped to improve American library and archival resources on Africa, and its fellows have assisted the Africa programs of other organizations in many ways. By 1962 its membership had grown to more than 300 fellows and about 800 other members.

The American Society of African Culture, publisher of the monthly *AMSAC Newsletter* and occasional volumes, is a society of American Negro scholars, artists, and writers. It is affiliated with the Paris Society of African Culture which publishes the journal *Présence Africaine.* In December, 1960, AMSAC opened a West African Cultural Center in Lagos and launched an Exchange Program for African and American Negro Performing Artists.

An organization of a still different type is the American Committee on Africa, publisher of the monthly *Africa Today* and occasional pamphlets. It is a liberal pressure group which aids African petitioners who come to the United Nations; raises funds for the legal defense and family welfare of political prisoners, mainly in South Africa; and pleads for steps to end colonialism. Although its one-sided approach antagonizes many Europeans and arouses misgivings in certain American circles, it sometimes evokes a warm emotional response among Africans. When a white leader of the Liberal Party in South Africa once told me that members of the African National Congress were cheering the Soviet Union and hissing the United States at their meetings, I asked several Africans if this were true. One of them denied it with the interesting comment: "We don't judge the United States entirely by the State Department; after all, you also have the American Committee on Africa, which has kept some of us from starving while we were suffering from persecution by our own government."

In addition to the above organizations devoted exclusively to Africa, numerous smaller associations have recently been established, including the Africa League, the African Research Foundation, the African Service Institute, the African-American Students Foundation, and the Foundation for All Africa.

PHILANTHROPIC ACTIVITIES

The fourth of the main groups is the 11,000 private foundations or philanthropic organizations in the United States, a figure which does not include some 50,000 other tax-exempt organizations that call themselves foundations. In the single year 1958, the grand total of American philanthropic grants for all areas and purposes was $7,000,-000,000, an incredible figure to Africans whose combined national budgets for 27 independent states in 1960 totaled only half this amount. The Ford, Rockefeller, and Carnegie organizations and a few other giants are best known, but about 100 foundations are large general-purpose organizations with professional staffs and interests of a national and sometimes international character.

In the past Africa has enjoyed only a microscopic percentage of the grand total of American philanthropy. Nonetheless, the Rockefeller Foundation's International Health Division has made contributions to research on yellow fever since 1920, and the Carnegie Corporation has made an impact on African education since 1928. Recently both Carnegie and Rockefeller have broadened their African interests in the fields of education and research. In the single fiscal year 1959–1960, for example, the Carnegie program included eight grants totaling $1,189,500 for African projects, while the Rockefeller program included nine grants in 1960 totaling $1,152,600. The Rockefeller grants went to university and government institutions in Africa itself, except for an $80,000 grant to an American university to enable African scholars and government officials to study international law. In the Carnegie program for 1959–1960, five African universities or other institutions received small grants totaling $142,000, while American institutions received more than $1,000,000 for African projects or, in one case, for the study of new nations in both Africa and Asia. Other Carnegie and Rockefeller projects, not included in the above figures, were also beneficial to Africa.

Although the Ford Foundation did not begin active operations until 1951, its primacy in funds has enabled it to take the lead. Its International Training and Research Program has invested about $9,000,000 in establishing or strengthening African training and research in a dozen American universities, and has undertaken the pump-priming work of training young American scholars in Africa. Including the awards made in 1962, a total of 145 Americans have received Ford area-training fellowships for study in Africa. Many of these scholars, upon their return, began to teach courses about Africa in their universities and in other ways to help develop the interest and competence of their countrymen in African matters. From 1960 to 1962 Ford also made grants of more than $40,000,000 to American universities for broader study programs on non-Western or underdeveloped areas, about 10 percent of which applies to African Studies programs.

The Foundation's Overseas Development Program expanded its work in 1958 to include Africa. Its emphasis is on assistance to African development, especially through education and training. It attempts to work with African governments and institutions to help their programs, rather than to develop programs that are "identifiably 'Ford's' or American." For example, early grants were made to establish an institute of economic and social research at Lovanium University near Leopoldville and to strengthen the East African Institute of Social and Economic Research at Makerere College in Uganda. When the Congo crisis in 1960 jeopardized the future of Lovanium, Ford joined Rockefeller in grants to enable the university to continue. Other grants enabled several African countries to obtain valuable statistical assessments of their supply and demand for trained manpower. By 1962 Ford assistance for African development projects had risen to not less than $5,000,000 a year. Consequently there were few countries in Africa that had not received at least some help. Nigeria, where the Foundation has a resident representative, has received the most assistance.

Other foundations which have made grants relating to Africa include the Rockefeller Brothers Fund and several smaller organizations which give financial assistance to individual Americans for research and study in Africa or to Africans for research and study in the United States.

AMERICAN UNIVERSITIES AND AFRICA

A fifth group interested in Africa is to be found among the 2000 universities and other institutions of higher education in the United States. In 1960, Frederick R. Wickert classified 76 African programs of American universities into the nine types listed in Table 12.

These university programs have been uneven in quality, but their quantity is still on the rise. More and better programs were encouraged by the 1960 Report of the Committee on the University and World Affairs, a small group established in July, 1959, by the Ford Foundation at the request of the Department of State. Stressing the need for additional university efforts with greater financial aid from the government to meet the world responsibilities of the United States, the Committee called for more interdisciplinary area studies programs for Africa and other regions, more help from American universities to those overseas, and more exchange of students and faculty.

When a wartime African research and studies program at the University of Pennsylvania was discontinued after World War II, the United States was left with a glaring vacuum in African studies. We had area programs for all the other major regions of the world, but nothing on Africa. Efforts to fill the vacuum in the late 1940s were handicapped by a dearth of trained faculty and interested students. Several pump-priming efforts by the Carnegie and Ford Foundations, however, prepared the way for the launching of graduate programs of African studies at a number of universities.

TABLE 12. Categories of American University African Programs, with Numbers of Programs in Each Category

Name of Category	One American University Involved in the Program	Two or More American Universities Involved in the Program	Total
1. African studies	11	1	12
2. Research (and survey)	15	3	18
3. Professors to do teaching (one-way or exchange)	6	1	7
4. American students to study in Africa (including study tours)	5	3	8
5. African students to study in the United States	2	1	3
6. An American university or a teaching base in Africa (or Lebanon) to make American-type university education more readily available to students in Africa	8	0	8
7. Technical assistance	15	0	15
8. Presentations of American culture	3	0	3
9. "Sister" relationships	2	0	2
	67	9	76

SOURCE: Frederick R. Wickert, "American Universities and Africa," *African Studies Bulletin*, December, 1960, p. 25.

The first major program was developed at Northwestern University with grants from the Carnegie Corporation and the Ford Foundation. Beginning in 1953, Boston University developed an extensive program with Ford support; in the fall of 1959 Boston also began a special Africa training program for officials of the International Cooperation Administration. Howard University organized a graduate program in 1954, oriented partly toward its students from Africa and partly toward American students, who were mostly Negro. In 1957 the School of Advanced International Studies of the Johns Hopkins University inaugurated a program to train graduate students for careers devoted to Africa in government, business, or nongovernmental organizations. The University of California at Los Angeles in 1960 and Columbia University in 1961 launched programs of considerable promise. African area specializations have also been inaugurated at the Kennedy School of Missions (since 1929), Yale, Michigan State, and several other universities. By 1961, many students of these Africa programs had themselves become teachers or employees of United States government agencies.

Efforts to improve the quality of existing graduate programs are now more necessary than new programs themselves. At the undergraduate level, however, there is a real need for a larger number of courses on Africa. Meanwhile, several universities are developing their library facilities on Africa. Early in 1960 another important step was taken when the Library of Congress, with a grant from the Carnegie Corporation, established an African unit to systematize its Africana, already the nation's largest collection.

A British observer has raised some timely questions about the "career and consultant" orientation of African studies in the United States. In the October, 1961, issue of the *Journal of African Administration*, Anthony Kirk-Greene points out that American universities and foundations have justified their African studies efforts on grounds of national concern and historic urgency. He therefore asks whether we can any longer claim, as did the Northwestern program in 1953, that "it is precisely because the United States has no territorial possessions in Africa, and hence, because American scholarship can be carried on in terms of a psychic distance which permits a minimum of emotional involvement, that it can make a special kind of contribution to African Studies." Because of America's new "interests" in Africa, Kirk-Greene suggests, Africans are likely to suspect the objectivity of these programs which train their students for careers in government and business, and those professors who also serve as consultants to government and business. He concludes, however, with a sensible appeal for a proper balance between uncommitted, objective study and overcooperation with government and dependence on its funds.

In addition to African studies at home, several universities are undertaking projects in Africa. An outstanding example is the work of Oklahoma State University on agricultural education in Ethiopia. Under a contract signed with the International Cooperation Administration in 1952, Oklahoma State has provided as many as 60 professionals at a single time in Ethiopia to develop a four-year agricultural high school and a four-year agricultural college.

Finally, American universities are engaged in the training of African students in the United States. In 1960-1961, more than 2800 African students were in the United States. Although the total number of all foreign students rose rapidly after World War II, by 1960 it was still only 1.6 percent of total university enrollment in the United States. It was large enough, however, to alert a wider group of Americans to the need for better training, counseling, financial, and hospitality arrangements, particularly for Africans.

AMERICAN LABOR IN AFRICA

A sixth group involved in Africa is the organized labor movement in the United States. Although for many years American labor's interest in world affairs was a somewhat parochial concern with such matters as tariffs and immigration, this attitude has gradually broadened since the 1930s. In 1949 the AFL, the CIO, and the United Mine Workers played a significant part in the formation of the International Confederation of Free Trade Unions (ICFTU), which was inaugurated after a split with the Communists in the World Federation of Trade Unions (WFTU). In Africa, the ICFTU has organized indigenous workers into trade unions, countered Communist efforts to penetrate the African labor movement, and sought to speed the end of colonial rule. However, the aggressive manner in which the AFL-CIO pursues these aims within the ICFTU has antagonized European unions—especially the British Trades Union Congress (TUC)—which consider the tutelage of African trade unions to be the special preserve of the administering powers and which resent the militant anticolonialism of the AFL-CIO. The resulting family quarrels have reduced the effectiveness of the organization.

The constructive work of the ICFTU in Africa has nonetheless been largely due to the efforts of U.S. labor leaders, who have exhibited an egalitarian and less paternalistic approach to African problems as well as a better understanding of the significance of African nationalism. The trade union training college in Kampala, Uganda, which opened its first course in November, 1958, and which will one day be staffed entirely by Africans, owes its existence to both the initiative and the financial backing of the AFL-CIO. American labor leaders have pushed to expand the role of Africans in the executive bodies of the ICFTU beyond their proportionate numerical strength and financial contributions. When the ICFTU's African Regional Organization (AFRO) was inaugurated in November, 1960, it had more autonomy than other ICFTU regional organizations largely because Americans supported African insistence on control of their own affairs. These measures enabled Tom Mboya of Kenya and other African trade unionists who wish to retain their connections with the ICFTU to resist the encroachments of the All-African Trade Union Federation sponsored by the Casablanca powers.

In addition to their activities through the ICFTU, American trade unions have their own programs for Africa. After an initial focus on Egypt, Tunisia, Algeria, and Morocco, attention turned southward in the latter 1950s when numerous U.S. labor officials, including Walter Reuther, Irving Brown, Maida Springer and A. Philip Randolph, made trips to Africa. In 1958, several AFL-CIO representatives also attended the All-African Peoples Conference in Accra.

Since the organizing of workers by Americans was difficult if not impossible because of the hostile attitude of local European officials, U.S. trade unions concentrated on material aid. According to a U.S. Department of Labor report, the CIO sent organizing kits to unions in Ghana, Tunisia, and Morocco. After its merger with the AFL in December, 1955, aid was continued through CARE to Kenya, the Cameroons, Nigeria, Guinea, the French Congo, and other countries. Individual unions have also made contributions of money and equipment like hospital supplies, office equipment, motor transport, motor films, and books.

At an early stage, Tom Mboya was singled out as a favorite of American labor, which aroused bitterness among British officials in East Africa. In 1957 he was given $35,000 by the AFL-CIO and later an additional $21,000 to build a national headquarters for the Kenya Federation of Labor. It has often been alleged that much of this money was used by Mboya for political activities.

Another AFL-CIO effort was a scholarship program for trade union leaders inaugurated in 1957 with an appropriation of $50,000. Maida Springer, an American Negro, was sent to the Sudan, Tanganyika, Kenya, Uganda, Northern Rhodesia, Nyasaland, Nigeria, Ghana, Liberia, and Sierre Leone to recruit prospective trainees for study in the United States. The program was abandoned three months after its inception because of a strong negative reaction from the British government. In December, 1957, under pressure from the British Trades Union Congress, the AFL-CIO reluctantly agreed to transfer all its Africa activities to the ICFTU. An informal condition of this agreement, known as the Atlantic City compact, was the establishment of a trade union training center in Africa itself—which became the Kampala College.

This agreement has somewhat circumscribed the independent efforts of the AFL-CIO in Africa. Nonetheless, it takes pro-Africa policy positions on such important African issues as the Bizerte crisis, the Portuguese colonies, Algeria, and *apartheid* in South Africa. Moreover, certain of its component unions continue to give direct assistance to African unions. For example, the International Ladies Garment Workers Union has provided six-month scholarships to give six Africans on-the-spot training in this country in trade union activity, and the Utility Workers' Union of America, Local 1–2, has initiated a joint labor-management program to train workers from Algeria, Morocco, Tunisia, Nigeria, and Kenya in greater technical efficiency in the production and distribution of electricity. Another notable development occurred in February, 1960, when the AFL-CIO authorized $80,000 for the Afro-Asian Institute of Labor Studies in Israel. Finally, American unions have given financial support to the anticolonial American Committee on Africa.

In the summer of 1961 the AFL-CIO inaugurated a program to find summer jobs for African students attending American colleges.

About 250 students were placed in 1961 in union offices and industrial plants; the AFL-CIO paid up to 50 percent of a student's wages if asked to do so.

INTEREST AMONG AMERICAN NEGROES

The seventh group with a special interest in Africa is found among the 20,000,000 Negroes in the United States. The African revolution has aroused new and ambivalent interests and reactions among them. In earlier years Negro leaders had only occasional and limited success in arousing popular interest in Africa. The ups and downs of Negro attitudes are well described by several of the 22 Negro contributors to the 1958 volume, *Africa from the Point of View of American Negro Scholars*, edited by John A. Davis for the aforementioned American Society of African Culture. In the words of James W. Ivy, the "back to Africa" movement which has recurred periodically since the eighteenth century was repudiated by Negro intellectuals as a white stratagem to rid the country of free Negroes or as a dodge to keep them from fighting for full citizenship rights. The enthusiasm of the Negro masses was nonetheless excited in the 1920s by the demagoguery of Marcus Garvey, the most famous apostle of "back to Africa." Another contributor, Rayford W. Logan, believes that Carter G. Woodson, who founded the Association for the Study of Negro Life and History in 1915, did more than either Garvey or the NAACP leader, W. E. B. Du Bois, to popularize interest in Africa among Negroes. In Logan's words, "More than any other American, Woodson had made known the medieval kingdom of Ghana so that it evoked real meaning when the Gold Coast became self-governing on March 6, 1957 (the one hundredth anniversary of the Dred Scott decision)."[4]

Even before Ghana's independence day, many Americans were startled by the unusually emotional welcome Negroes gave Prime Minister Kwame Nkrumah, particularly in Harlem and Chicago,

[4] Rayford W. Logan, "The American Negro's View of Africa," *Africa from the Point of View of American Negro Scholars*, ed. John A. Davis, Dijon, 1958, p. 220.

when he visited the United States in 1956. Not long before, when the editor of *Ebony* magazine asked readers what subjects they wanted to read about, Africa was last on a list of 10. In a later poll, Africa reportedly jumped to first place.

The rise of Africa not only won more attention in the Negro press, but it attracted Negroes in other ways. Opportunities for employment in our new diplomatic consular and other posts in Africa stimulated numerous Negro demands that the United States government employ more Negroes in Africa. The successful fight of Africans for freedom was a psychological boost to American Negroes in their efforts to invigorate the fight against racial discrimination. And it helped to bring new followers to the Black Muslim extremist movement in the United States, which advocates racial separation with ultimate black supremacy.

TOURISTS AND JOURNALISTS IN AFRICA

In addition to the above seven groups, two others are worthy of mention because, even though they are unorganized, their response to Africa also affects African-American relations. They are the tourists and the journalists.

The behavior of American tourists in Africa affects African opinion of the United States, while the tourists themselves, upon their return, have helped interest other Americans in Africa. The dollars earned from tourism are also important, particularly to East Africa. Efforts to promote American tourism in Africa attained limited success during the decade before 1959, particularly in Egypt, South Africa, and the scenic highlands of East and Central Africa, home of Africa's great game reserves. The South African Tourist Corporation, which opened an office in New York, was particularly active in its appeals to American tourists. The violence in South Africa and the Congo in 1960, however, caused a sharp drop in visitors to these two countries.

Statistics compiled by the United States Immigration and Naturalization Service reveal that Africa is still far less visited than any other world area. These statistics do not separate tourists from other visitors. They show the number of American citizens departing from

he United States for major world areas during the year ending June
0, 1960, as follows:

Europe	797,211
North America	785,526
Cruise	136,375
Asia	112,065
South America	70,554
Oceania	22,351
Africa	10,871

Tourism is bound to increase as interest in Africa grows and as air
ransport improves.

The greatest attraction for the tourist in Africa is its rich variety
of wild animal life both inside and outside its great game reserves.
African independence has raised the question of whether the game
conservation policies of the colonial powers will be continued, an
issue of concern to a considerable number of Americans.

To put into effect an integrated program for the protection and
preservation of Africa's animals in their natural habitat, the New
York Zoological Society sponsored an initial survey of national parks
and game reserves throughout sub-Saharan Africa, the first such study
of its kind. Subsequently, the Society established an African Wildlife
Fund, which concentrates its efforts primarily on East and Central
Africa. In cooperation with other American foundations, the Fund
has channeled about $85,000 in assistance for educational and re-
search projects, direct aid to existing game reserves, and support to
organizations and individuals working on African wildlife problems.

More important than the tourists is the small number of journalists
whose growing interest in Africa had made the American public far
more aware of Africa's complexities by 1960. United Press International estimated early in 1962 that its treatment of Africa had reached
8000 cabled words a day, a tenfold increase in the last five years.
Unhappily, this expanded coverage did not promote better understanding between Africans and Americans, at least in the short run.
At the April, 1961, African Freedom Day rally in Washington, D.C.,
Kenya's Tom Mboya stated bluntly that "the American Press is
America's worst enemy in Africa."[5] This view was echoed in October

[5] "Two African Views of the U.S. Press," Africa Report, May, 1961, p. 16.

by many outspoken Africans at a large conference in Boston spon sored by the U.S. National Commission for UNESCO. A Nigeriar delegate contended that the distorted portrayals of Africa by Ameri can journalists were more damaging to the United States than its widely publicized incidents of racial discrimination. In a speech at the opening of a U.S. exhibition in Ghana on October 27, 1961, President Nkrumah complained of ". . . a constant barrage of mis representation from the foreign press, which invents false news about our actions and puts the worst possible construction upon every thing we do."[6] Even Ambassador George Padmore of Liberia, a con servative African state with a long tradition of friendship for the United States, recently complained that "the American press, more so than any other foreign news [medium], castigates the efforts of [Africa's] pioneers." The damage it does to the influence of the United States abroad, he said, "cannot be undone by foreign aid or by sending emissaries of the same racial or religious background to these foreign lands."[7]

Representatives of the American press counter with the charge that in most African states—where newspapers are often organs of government propaganda—the tradition of a free press is neither re spected nor understood. They complain that nationalist leaders are hypersensitive to criticism, and that they react with unnecessary vigor to every negative comment, however justified, which might affect them at home or abroad. Africans reply that this evades the issue, which is not the freedom of the press but the irresponsibility of jour nalists guilty of inaccurate and biased reporting. While both posi tions contain some measure of truth, the gulf between them has engendered much ill will.

Newspapermen have a difficult task. Their editors want lively "news" to attract readers, which forces journalists to take material out of context. When they report daily, they have neither the time to check facts thoroughly nor the perspective necessary for balanced judgments. Headline writers tend to make the situation worse by em phasizing only one aspect of a story. It is a most unusual journalist who understands the anthropologist's concept of cultural relativism

---

[6] Embassy of Ghana, Press Release No. 169, Washington, November 29, 1961.
[7] "Two African Views of the U.S. Press," *Africa Report*, May, 1961, p. 16.

and who has the perspectives of the historian and the insights of the behavioral scientist. Without this background, Western journalists have an inevitable bias which colors their interpretations of non-Western peoples and environments and leads some of them to an excessive preoccupation with what Africans consider the wrong subjects, among them communism, dictatorship, cannibalism, and the more primitive aspects of African life. As always in such situations, moreover, a few cases of bad reporting are seized upon while many instances of good reporting are ignored.

Biased reporting is dangerous not only because it angers Africans but because it misleads Americans. For example, some journalists use a double standard in evaluating African states, which they tend to divide into "good" and "bad." Many articles are written about authoritarian states in the "bad" Casablanca group, while one-party states in Liberia and other more conservative states are often glossed over or ignored. The Western tendency to classify Nigerian and Tanganyikan leaders as "good" moderates of pro-Western orientation not only may prove highly misleading to Americans but tends to force Africans to take unnecessary and artificial steps to establish their nonalignment and Africanism in order to avoid this Western "kiss of death." A colleague of Tanganyika leader Julius Nyerere has remarked that if the American and European press continue to call Nyerere moderate, pro-Western, and anti-Communist, they will undermine his political position.

Wide play was given in the United States press to a speech made on December 12, 1961, by Guinea's President Sékou Touré in which he stated that a certain "Eastern bloc" embassy was linked to a plot against the government. Early reports failed to mention that in the same speech Touré also denounced "Uncle de Gaulle," French neo-colonialists, and even the Freemasons. When the Soviet Ambassador was subsequently recalled from Guinea, Americans who had come to regard Touré as an African Castro tended to hail this move as a shift away from the Communist orbit. In reality, it was not a fundamental policy shift but part of a pre-existing pattern of action designed to preserve the posture of nonalignment.

Another illustration is a news report on October 21, 1961, which complained indignantly that Nkrumah's protest to Khrushchev

against the explosion of the "50-megaton" bomb, although distri
uted to the press and the various embassies in Washington, had n
found its way into Ghana's newspapers. The fact is that on the san
day Accra's *Daily Graphic* headlined: "Kwame Appeals to Mr. I
Stop This Giant Bomb Test—Alarm Over Radio-Active Fallo
Mounts." A later issue featured the unsubstantiated claim by Amer
can scientist Linus Pauling that the 50-megaton bomb would har
400,000 children. However, the American public's negative image c
Nkrumah was reinforced by this implication of "perfidy," while he
on the other hand, was given legitimate cause for complaint.

The oversimplified treatment of African issues in the press leads t
unsophisticated public reactions which can be harmful to our foreig
policy when they inspire such heated and ill-informed controversie
as the debate over American policy toward Katanga. While it woul
be unfair to focus blame on hard-working and conscientious journa
ists for this situation, the American press must nonetheless improv
its Africa reporting if American policy in Africa is to be effective
Heaven forbid that professors take over the duties of journalists, bu
it would be helpful if more journalists could obtain special trainin;
in African studies. The kind of reporting usually found in the *Time*
of London, the *Economist*, and the weekly *West Africa* shows tha
relatively impartial analysis rather than one-sided opinion is botl
feasible and desirable. If Americans must be patient, so must Afri
cans, who could help by improving their public relations program:
and by calling more press conferences to explain official policy.

THE BOSTON CONFERENCE, 1961

Although this survey of American interests is not all-inclusive, it
has highlighted the main private activities and pressures which directly affect our relations with Africans and indirectly influence the
foreign policy adopted by our government. The abundance and significance of these groups were well revealed at the noteworthy conference, Africa and the United States: Images and Realities, held in
Boston from October 22 to 26, 1961. The eighth in a series of biennial conferences sponsored by the U.S. National Commission for
UNESCO, this unusual gathering was made possible by the com-

ined financial support of the U.S. government and many private agencies and individuals. The 2000 delegates represented not only the special groups mentioned in this chapter, but many others which are developing an interest in Africa—secondary schoolteachers, musicians, museum directors, archivists, librarians, writers, doctors, and lawyers. The presence of more than 100 Africans helped the conference a long way toward its objectives of broadening and deepening American understanding of the achievements and aspirations of Africa's peoples; reassessing Africa's educational needs and the best ways of meeting them in the new states; appraising the African programs already undertaken by special groups in the United States; and exploring the false images and stereotypes which affect African-American relations. As a result of careful preparations, moreover, the work of the conference was followed up for many months through "echo" conferences, press, radio, and television.

The speakers on the conference program of more than 70 meetings included many African leaders. Their ability and their frank expression of African points of view helped the conference to avoid paternalistic American prescriptions for Africa. Mutual criticism was sometimes sharp but always friendly. In appraising the conference, one of the outstanding Nigerian participants, Stephen O. Awokoya, remarked that never before had he realized "what magnificent resources are at the disposal of the United States for international reconstruction and assistance." The United States, he added, "does not need to explode an atomic device in order to demonstrate its power, its capacity for good . . . . this country is triggered up for a real cultural explosion" to send its citizens around the world to "help in works of construction and not works of destruction."[8]

Conference discussions also developed a realistic perspective on the "Africa boom" in the United States. Was it only a temporary fad? Was it producing too many half-baked ideas? Weren't there too many right hands unaware of what the left hands were doing? Shouldn't all American projects on Africa be "coordinated"?

In the exchange of views on these questions, it became clear that

[8] From the tape recording of Awokoya's remarks at the 8th plenary meeting, 8th National Conference of the U.S. National Commission for UNESCO, October 26, 1961.

the dedication and determination of Americans interested in Africa was far more lasting and significant than a fad over something new. Half-baked ideas and projects were plentiful, but they tended to fall by the wayside.

The "coordination" issue was more troublesome, because the many voices of America are indeed confusing and uncoordinated. Why is it that efforts to coordinate overlapping and competing projects, both within the government and among private agencies, have little success? It is only in part the result of built-in bureaucratic resistance to "being coordinated" among the personnel of government, foundations, universities, and other institutions seeking to enhance their own programs. More important is the fact that the individualism fostered by our type of democracy results in a rich pluralism in private initiatives. When pushed to excess, this pluralism appears to incapacitate us. In the end, however, opposing groups neutralize each other, unsound programs collapse of their own weight, and our diversity proves to be a reservoir of strength.

It was clear at the Boston conference, nonetheless, that a great deal needs to be done to make American organizations interested in Africa more aware of each other's projects in order to minimize wasteful duplication. A number of cooperative efforts of this type were in fact already under way. As a final perspective on the coordination controversy, what do Africans think about it? When asked whether there is a need to coordinate American projects, they have sometimes responded that, as far as they can see, there is nothing to coordinate; in other words, there are not enough American projects, at least in Africa, to merit an effort at coordination!

15

Our "National Interest" in Africa

WHAT is the "national interest" in Africa? One thing is clear; it is not just the sum total of the special interests of private groups and individuals, because these interests sometimes conflict with each other. Nor can it be said that the national interest is necessarily that of the dominant groups, since these groups may act in a manner contrary to the interest of the nation as a whole. The same is true of the government, of course, since its decision makers may also take steps based on a mistaken conception of the national interest.

THE IDEA OF NATIONAL INTEREST

A broad perspective on the whole complex of our foreign policy problems is the first essential for understanding the national interest in Africa. Our foreign policy machinery has enormously expanded because of a fundamental change in the international position of the United States. Even after World War I, the American people and their government remained predominantly isolationist, hoping to avoid entangling commitments overseas. It was not until World War II that a widespread change in American attitudes occurred.

271

The isolationist spirit of the interwar years is partially reflected in Charles A. Beard's notable two volumes on the national interest published in 1934—although Beard considered himself not an isolationist but a "continentalist" who advocated an intelligent internationalism. After studying thousands of actions justified by "national interest," Beard wrote that he "was tempted to conclude that the conception was simply a telling formula which politicians and private interests employed whenever they wished to accomplish any particular designs in the field of foreign affairs." However, in his first book, *The Idea of National Interest*, he shows how national interest became the pivot of diplomacy, replacing such earlier concepts as the will of the prince, dynastic interest, reason of state, and national honor. Tracing the idea in American history, he found two conflicting conceptions of it. One was the Jeffersonian idea that it was in the national interest to have low tariffs and small military forces and to occupy contiguous territory for exploitation by American farmers. The other was the Hamiltonian conception which favored high tariffs, the vigorous expansion of foreign markets, and, ultimately, the acquisition of distant territories. Beard stressed economic factors, and his only mention of the national interest in Africa was a short description of 105 American private investments in Africa valued at $102,229,000 in 1929.[1]

In a second and more opinionated volume, *The Open Door at Home*, Beard elaborated his own idea of the national interest. In place of "pushing and holding doors open in all parts of the world with all engines of government, ranging from polite coercion to the use of arms," Beard urged the American nation to open doors at home and "to substitute an intensive cultivation of its own garden for a wasteful, quixotic, and ineffectual extension of interests beyond the reach of competent military and naval defense."[2] In his view the supreme national interest of the United States is "the creation and maintenance of a high standard of life and ways of industry conducive to the promotion of individual and social virtues . . . subject to the paramountcy of national security."

[1] Charles A. Beard, *The Idea of National Interest—An Analytical Study in American Foreign Policy*, New York, 1934, pp. 232–233.
[2] Charles A. Beard, *The Open Door at Home—A Trial Philosophy of National Interest*, New York, 1934, pp. v–vii.

Beard's hopes for a peaceful avoidance of overcommitments were exploded by World War II, although the idea of teaching other countries by the example of our own—a lesson without words—is being echoed a generation later by George Kennan and others. World War II led to a drastic change in the American position. Emerging from the war with great wealth and power, the United States inevitably became the leader of the Western world. At the same time, many old diplomatic needs and traditions were dealt mortal blows by the development of nuclear missiles and the rise of new states in Asia and Africa eager to exert a third force in world affairs.

To many Americans the national interest seemed to require more effective methods of using our wealth and power in peacetime. Influenced by the fact that they had been drawn unwillingly into both world wars, they came to believe that our security and freedom could be endangered not only by acts of military aggression but by political and economic maladjustment anywhere—from Timbuktoo to the Little Karoo. This led to a wider acceptance of the belief that the United States should no longer wait for crises to explode, but should help to prevent them. Fear of communism and the threat of Soviet expansion crystallized this feeling. That is why the American people were willing to support their government's unprecedented expansion of the three major arms of American foreign policy—economic, military, and propaganda activities. From July, 1945, through December, 1961, American taxpayers provided more than $57,000,000,000 for foreign economic aid and technical assistance, about $1,800,000,000 of which went to Africa. Another $29,600,000,000 was furnished for military aid. The people also supported the government's costly decisions to build a worldwide network of bases for the Strategic Air Command, to join Western Europe in the "entangling alliance" called the North Atlantic Treaty Organization, and to form military alliances with countries in other strategic areas. And finally, in the use of propaganda as an instrument of foreign policy, they are paying well over $100,000,000 a year for the United States Information Agency.

The national interest of the United States in Africa is an integral part of this broader interest in American security, prosperity, and freedom. It is more than an interest in economic gains or military bases. It is most of all a political interest in having the proper balance of freedom and stability in Africa. Let us examine these three elements in the national interest—the military, the economic and the political—in more detail.

THE MILITARY ELEMENT

The military potential of Africa in the event of a third world war is difficult to estimate. During the first decade after World War II, soldiers and statesmen often stressed Africa's military importance in four respects: its strategic bases; its critical raw materials; its military manpower; and, to a lesser extent, its potentialities as an industrial and military supply center. The evidence for this view was derived mostly from the experience of World War II.

The importance of African bases was demonstrated when North Africa was a battleground, and Middle Africa and the Cape provided vital Allied supply lines during World War II. In his final report as Chief of Staff, made public on February 15, 1948, General Dwight D. Eisenhower stressed the strategic importance of keeping the Mediterranean open to free communications and commerce. United States bases in Morocco and Libya, as well as postwar American aid to Italy, Greece, Turkey, Iran, Palestine, Libya, and France, were all designed in part to achieve the objective of either keeping the Mediterranean open or at least closing it to the Soviet Union which might keep us from controlling it, as the Axis did in World War II.

A French officer, General de Montsabert, described Africa's military significance in 1953 in these striking but soon outmoded words: "In terms of modern strategy there no longer are three separate and distinct continents—Europe, Asia and Africa. There are only *Eurasia* and *Eurafrica*." Europe, he thought, could not breathe without North Africa in the Atlantic theater of operations in a third world war; from Casablanca to Berlin, from Kiel to Gabes, "everything interlocks, and because it does, the whole area constitutes a single and indivisible theater of war . . . ." French North Africa, he said, is "The redoubt of Eurafrica . . . made almost impregnable by its situation between sea and desert," and containing an "unequalled grouping of

land, sea and air bases, all of them beyond the range of Russian medium bombers."[3]

Montsabert's view was partially echoed in 1958 by Rear Admiral
Charles Bergin when he testified before the House Committee on
Foreign Affairs during the 1958 hearings on foreign aid:

The size, population, untold wealth of natural resources, and geographic position flanking both the NATO area and the oil fields and communications of the Near East make Africa of vital strategic importance.
The loss of the northern region bordering on the Mediterranean would
result in the encirclement of Europe and pave the way for the extension
of communistic influence over the entire continent.

At the same time, so long as this area, which includes the newly independent countries of Morocco, Tunisia, and Libya and the ancient
kingdom of Ethiopia, remains oriented to the West, Soviet designs on
Africa can be largely blocked. On the positive side, a friendly north Africa
also makes it possible to maintain important defense bases in the area,
particularly the air and naval installations in Morocco and Libya and the
key communications setup in Ethiopia.[4]

South of the Sahara lie other important bases or potential bases,
including a multimillion-dollar airfield built by the United States at
Roberts Field in Liberia and also the Liberian port of Monrovia,
which was constructed with United States lend-lease funds and could
be converted into a submarine base on the strategic "bulge" of West
Africa, which lies along the vital South Atlantic sea lanes and is the
closest point to South America. Freetown in nearby Sierre Leone
proved of great value as a harbor for many ships of the British Navy
during World War II. The Allied positions in the Middle East,
India, and North Africa all received support from the chain of bases
stretched across West and Central Africa, as well as from the Cape
supply route which is protected by the South African naval bastion
at Simonstown.

In 1962, however, Western bases in Africa were increasingly threatened by nationalist pressures. Much of West Africa was up in arms
at French nuclear testing in the Sahara. The Belgians had lost their

[3] General de Montsabert, "North Africa in Atlantic Strategy," *Foreign Affairs*,
April, 1953, pp. 419–425.
[4] U.S. Congress, House Committee on Foreign Affairs, Mutual Security Act of
1958, Hearings . . . on HR 12181, February 18-March 13, 1958, Parts I-VIII,
Vol. 1, Washington, 1958, p. 583.

military installations at Kamina in the Congo. The Pan-African Freedom Movement for East and Central Africa was on record with unqualified condemnations of foreign bases, and Kenya Africans were demanding the removal from their country of the most important British base south of the Sahara. The government of Tunisia was striving to get the French out of their base at Bizerte. And the United States had agreed to abandon by the end of 1963 a chain of air bases in Morocco recently built at a cost of $400,000,000, leaving only the large air base at Wheelus Field in Tripoli under American control. Meanwhile, technological advance in nuclear missiles is increasing the vulnerability of African bases.

As for strategic raw materials, Africa's significance as a supplier is highlighted in Table 13.

TABLE 13.   African Percentages of World Production of Major Minerals in 1959

Mineral	Percentage
Diamonds, industrial	98.6
Lithium minerals	97.5
Columbium-tantalum	74.8
Cobalt	74.0
Gold	51.4
Beryl	47.7
Corundum	44.3
Platinum group metals	38.1
Chromite	30.9
Antimony	29.1
Phosphate rock	28.8
Copper, mine	25.6
Copper, smelter	23.4
Uranium oxide (U_3O_8)	20.4
Vermiculite	20.4
Manganese ore	20.3
Asbestos	14.8
Tin, mine	11.3

SOURCE: Adapted from Table II in U.S. Department of the Interior, Bureau of Mines, "World Mineral Production in 1959," *Mineral Industry Surveys*, January, 1961, p. 7.

In addition, in the period 1951-1959, Africa produced 95 percent of the world production of palm kernels, 85 percent of the palm oil, and 62 percent of the sisal (which was 45 percent of the hard fibers).

A word of caution is in order, however, about the tendency to exaggerate the vital need of the United States for these raw materials. In 1949 Edward S. Mason concluded that the United States could get along without Africa's resources. In his view, if the United States were alone and at war, the loss of any or all of the raw material supplies outside of North America, the Caribbean, and the northern half of South America would cause only a relatively small decline in the output of war materials. He based this contention partly on the lesson of war production in blockaded Germany in World War II, which demonstrated what could be done by using substitutes and by applying effective raw material controls. In addition, American stockpiling of critical materials and the development of many new sources of uranium improved our position after the war. Substitutes and raw materials would be costly, of course, but Mason believed that the United States had no raw material interests outside the Western Hemisphere important enough to merit the diversion of substantial military resources for their defense. As will be noted later, however, new discoveries of mineral deposits in Africa along with our growing need for raw materials may increase our dependence on African resources.

Turning to military manpower, one finds that Africa made a substantial contribution to World War II. British West Africa is said to have furnished 146,000 troops; British East Africa, 228,000; the Anglo-Egyptian Sudan, 25,000; and South Africa, 25,000 white troops, along with 40,000 colored and 85,000 natives in labor battalions. And the French territories, including North Africa, probably supplied more troops than the British. These were mainly colonial troops, however, and it seems unlikely that Africa would furnish many men to the West in another world war.

Finally, in the decade after the war, publicity was occasionally given to the continent's possibilities as an industrial and supply base, particularly in South Africa. The potential military significance of the remarkable growth of secondary industry in the Union during the 15 years after World War II attracted the attention of numerous observers. Until Morocco and Tunisia became independent, there was also occasional interest in the idea that the mineral and other resources of French North Africa might become a basis for industrialization of some importance if the West's access to European coal and iron were put off by Russian invasion. However, the African revolution is also eliminating the possibility of using the continent for this purpose.

In the light of the above evidence, it is clear that Africa in 1962 contained fewer Western military assets than Europeans had hoped for. It might also be noted that in Africa the United States does not have security arrangements like those of NATO in Europe, SEATO in Southeast Asia, CENTO in the Middle East, and the OAS in the Western Hemisphere. Neither the Soviet nor the Western bloc seemed likely to draw Africa into its camp, but it nonetheless remained important to each side to prevent the other from gaining control of the new states and their military resources.

ECONOMIC INTERESTS

The military aspect of the national interest in Africa has been treated in more detail than it perhaps deserves. Let us turn briefly to the economic element in the national interest. As described earlier, American trade and investments in Africa rose rapidly during the past two decades. It is important to note, however, that our African trade remained less than 5 percent of the total world trade of the United States, while our investments in Africa were little more than 2 percent of our total private investment overseas. The growth of direct American investments in Africa from 1950 to 1960 is shown in Table 14.

Although American trade and investments represented a considerable economic stake for the business interests concerned, they were not vital to our national economy. As economist Andrew M. Kamarck wrote in 1958, "We could get along without African commodities and African markets with an imperceptible ripple in our standard of living."[5]

[5] Andrew M. Kamarck, "The African Economy and International Trade," The United States and Africa, American Assembly, New York, 1958, p. 119.

TABLE 14. Total American Direct Private Investment in Africa
(in Millions of Dollars)[a]

Area or Country	1950	1957[b]	1958[b]	1959[b]	1960[c]
North Africa	56	106	121	145	195
East Africa	12	30	35	43	47
West Africa	42	147	183	228	290
Central and South Africa					
Rep. of South Africa	140	301	321	323	285
Rhodesia and Nyasaland	26	59	65	72	83
Other countries	12	21	22	21	26
Total	287	664	746	833	925

[a] Detail may not add to totals because of rounding.
[b] Revised.
[c] Preliminary.
SOURCE: Adapted from U.S. Department of Commerce, Office of Business Economics, Survey of Current Business, August, 1961, p. 22.

In the future, however, Africa's economic significance to the United States may further increase. Our most important direct economic interest is in Africa's raw materials which, as we have seen, also have a military significance. Not long ago it was estimated that our degree of dependence on outside raw materials might double by 1970, when we may have to import one-fifth of the raw materials needed for our expanding industrial economy. Africa's role as a supplier is meanwhile growing because of new discoveries and exploitation of oil, iron, bauxite, and other resources. Moreover, the increasing participation of U.S. government agencies in the economic development of Africa will stimulate further trade and investment.

The United States also has what might be called an indirect economic interest in Africa. To be more precise, it is an economic interest in Europe which is affected by Africa's economic relations with Europe. As Assistant Secretary of State George C. McGhee described it in his speech "United States Interests in Africa" on May 8, 1950, in Oklahoma City, the United States desires "to assure the development of mutually advantageous economic relations" between the metropolitan powers and the peoples of Africa "in the interests of contributing to restoration of a sound European economy and in the interests of furthering the aspirations of African peoples." Since the United States has provided many billions of dollars to strengthen the postwar economy and defenses of Western Europe, it has a natural interest in additional ways and means of accomplishing the same objective. European trade and investments in Africa are not only far larger than those of the United States, but they are a much higher percentage of total Western European trade and investments. African raw materials are vital to Europe.

Particularly in the postwar years, it might be added, the Gold Coast, Nigeria, and Northern Rhodesia earned hundreds of millions of much-needed dollars for the sterling area, while the Belgian and Portuguese territories earned dollars on a smaller scale. It should be noted, however, that the French territories were a liability in this respect. According to a calculation by Philip W. Bell, they used up $718,000,000 of the dollar reserves between 1946 and 1950 and were thus responsible for 15 percent of the total franc area deficit with the dollar area during those years. In addition, French colonial expenses in this period were roughly three or four times those of the British, and this did not include the high cost of the war in Indochina.[6]

If American private enterprise in Africa is to serve the national interest of the United States, a new kind of approach is needed. Many Africans tend to equate foreign investment with exploitation and neocolonialism. This is particularly true of the extractive industries because of the feeling that the subsoil wealth of Africa belongs to Africans and should not be exploited by outsiders. It raises the question of whether African governments will ultimately nationalize foreign mining operations. This is not a new idea, it should be noted, for the British Labor Government, as long ago as 1946, issued an abortive statement on colonial mining policy which foreshadowed eventual government operation of all mines in British dependencies.[7] One also wonders what will happen to American investment in the

[6] Philip W. Bell, "Colonialism as a Problem in American Foreign Policy," *World Politics*, October, 1952, pp. 96–102.
[7] Colonial Office, *Memorandum on Colonial Mining Policy*, Colonial No. 206. London, 1946.

Republic of South Africa, where our largest private investments in the whole continent are found, when the long expected political explosion finally comes. Another question, different but relevant, is whether it is in our national interest to expand American business in Africa by displacing European interests. Such questions as these are often ignored.

Africa's need for private enterprise by its own people has been well demonstrated by Stacy May of the Rockefeller Brothers Fund. To the "stew" of development, he writes,

government action can contribute the onions, carrots, salt and pepper that are essential to give it character and savor. But someone has to provide the *potatoes and the beef*—and I think this can only come from the private sector since it occupies an overwhelmingly dominant place in African economies of today.

May was not pleading for private enterprise *instead of* government activity, but pointing out that the ultimate support for government enterprises "must come from taxes levied upon the private economy." Foreign investment on a partnership basis can help to stimulate African entrepreneurship and capital formation, and "is about the most effective and cheapest way of importing the technical knowledge and managerial skills of which countries in the early stages of industrial development are so badly in need."[8]

To foster both American and African private initiative in West Africa, particularly in the industrial production and processing of goods, equipment, and materials, the Rockefeller Brothers Fund has prepared many detailed "feasibility studies" of possible business ventures. These studies provide specific data on market opportunities for each enterprise, its capital requirements, financing plan, operating cost prospects, labor and material requirements and availabilities, power, transport, and distribution facilities and their rates. A balance sheet and income account projection from the beginning through the expected showing at full operation is also prepared in order to appeal further to potential investors.

[8] Stacy May, "Private Enterprise and the Future of Africa," address to the U.S. National Commission for UNESCO biennial conference on Africa and the United States, *Images and Realities*, October 23, 1961 (mimeo.), pp. 9–13.

African leaders have frequently and forthrightly proclaimed their desire to attract foreign private investors. Moreover, they have protected the property rights of existing enterprises, and have offered numerous "pioneer status" inducements to attract others. Thus far, however, both African and American government leaders have been disappointed by the slow response from established firms in the American business community.

Speaking in Washington on "Africa's Challenge to American Enterprise" on December 1, 1961, Assistant Secretary of State for African Affairs G. Mennen Williams remarked that we must help Africans find a place for private enterprise, "but we would be remiss if we did not say very candidly that private enterprise itself must be prepared to make major adjustments." If the major emphasis is placed on management, rather than ownership, he added, many new possibilities are opened.

African leaders not only want foreign enterprises to train and employ African labor, but they want local resources used, and they expect foreign investors to give Africans an opportunity to participate with them. Fortunately a number of American firms have already won respect for their pioneering efforts in these directions. The Liberian Mining Company has split profits with the Liberian government, brought Liberians on to its board, made large donations to educational and other worthy enterprises, and made shares of its stock available to Liberians on an installment basis, to be paid for out of eventual earnings. Olin Mathieson supplied pharmaceuticals, fertilizers and technical assistance to Guinea when the French pulled out. American Metal Climax, which has a 43.5 percent interest in Rhodesian Selection Trust Limited, has supported the advancement of African mineworkers in the copper belt of Northern Rhodesia, and has given financial support to numerous African educational and other projects. American oil companies in West Africa have pioneered in developing African entrepreneurship in gasoline stations. The more foreign enterprise is Africanized, the less likely it is to be nationalized. Business initiative such as this operates in the national interest of the United States and in the private interests of the companies concerned, as well as in the interests of Africa.

POLITICAL ASPECT

Finally, the national interest in Africa has a political aspect which is related to but more important than the above military and economic considerations. It can be stated briefly. If democracy is to flourish in the United States, free institutions must also continue to exist in other fortunate parts of the world. That is why it is in our national interest for Africa to remain free of Communist dictatorship. This requires the kind of balance between freedom and stability which satisfies men's needs and enables them to work toward democratic ideals through some form of parliamentary institution. It does not require a complete imitation of Western democratic forms, but it does imply that the ultimate control of the government must be and must remain in the hands of the people rather than those of a ruler. This is the essence of democracy. The twin pillars of this kind of political freedom are economic growth and educational progress. It is therefore in our national interest to help Africa strengthen these pillars. The fact that we cannot be certain our efforts will succeed should not deter us from making the attempt.

Our success will depend in part on whether Americans are mature enough to avoid undue cynicism when African states fall short of their democratic ideals. In his *Modern Democracy*, Carl Becker pointed out that democracy has flourished for a relatively short period in history, and only in societies which (1) were either small in size or had means of communication sufficient to create the necessary solidarity of interest and similarity of information over large areas, (2) were economically secure, and (3) had a citizenry capable of understanding inevitable conflicts of interest and willing to reconcile divergent opinions. Such conditions are not likely to exist in most of Africa in the near future. While the system of tribal chiefs-in-council in the old Africa had its democratic aspects, the new political units are not small groups of tribesmen who know and understand each other. They are relatively large states made up of many peoples with differing customs, traditions, and languages.

Numerous observers have contended that Africa will be democratic if one does not insist on too strict a definition of democracy in the "Western style." Others hold that benevolent despotism will be necessary in the new democracies during a transition period while society is readjusting itself to cope with the problems of the new freedom. Whatever their purpose, single-party regimes are popular throughout Asia and Africa—Sukarno's "guided democracy" in Indonesia, Ayub Khan's "basic democracy" in Pakistan, Nasser's "presidential democracy" in Egypt, Bourguiba's "national front" in Tunisia, Nkrumah's "positive discipline" in Ghana, and many others. Immanuel Wallerstein pointed out in the November 25, 1961, issue of *West Africa* that of 12 new West African states, 7 have no legal opposition party at all and 4 have one party which is clearly dominant.

Tanganyika leader Julius Nyerere has maintained that united nationalist movements which win the struggle for independence cannot reasonably be expected to divide themselves in midstream "for the sake of conforming to a particular expression of 'democracy' which happens to be seen in terms of a government party and an opposition party." This does not mean, he adds, that "such a country is not democratic or does not intend to be democratic." In Nyerere's opinion, "the two basic essentials to democracy are freedom of the individual and insurance that the government of a country is freely chosen by the people."[9]

Nyerere's belief in African forms of democracy is stimulating, and the research of certain American scholars has confirmed that there is democratic freedom of discussion within Africa's single parties. This view is vigorously challenged, however, by the Nigerian leader, Obafemi Awolowo. In his autobiography, he condemns the "new-fangled theory now being propounded with erudition and gusto in the Western democracies" which holds "that it is inappropriate and hardly fair to expect a newly emergent African nation to practice democracy . . . ." Democracy and a one-party system of government, Awolowo argues, are "mutually exclusive":

Under a one-party system, the party in power arrogates to itself the right to be the only ruling party for all time. All other parties, therefore,

---

[9] Julius Nyerere, "Will Democracy Work in Africa?" *Africa Special Report*, February, 1960, pp. 3, 4.

which differ from or are in opposition to it are either suppressed or absorbed. At subsequent elections, if there are any, the consent of the people cannot be said to be genuinely sought and freely given, because there is only one choice open to the electorate. . . . The people are entitled as of right to be given the chance to examine all sides of the problems confronting them, before expressing their majority will at the polls. Such an examination, however, will be possible only where people who hold different shades of opinions are allowed to organize themselves into parties if they wish, and are also free to explain their respective points of view to the electorate. . . .

In acting as the apologists for those who destroy and discredit democracy, the spokesmen of the Western democracies do grievous harm to that noble ideal. . . .[10]

In Becker's definition of democracy, the essential test is that the source of political authority be and *remain* in the people and not in the ruler. Both Awolowo and Nyerere would presumably accept this premise. Their difference appears to lie in the question of whether the people can *remain* the source of political authority under a one-party system. The danger in single-party states headed by magnetic personalities is that "power tends to corrupt, and absolute power tends to corrupt absolutely," to recall Lord Acton's epigram. In governments of this type there is always danger that advisers will become sycophants who tell the ruler what they think he wants to hear. The ruler then comes to believe that his interests are the people's interests. At this stage the people may lose their role as the source of political authority, even though a majority may continue to support the ruler. The word *democracy* becomes meaningless when it is stretched to include any government supported by a majority of the people—a definition which would cover the dictatorships of Khrushchev, Hitler, Mussolini, Franco, and Salazar.

The thoughtful views of Awolowo and Nyerere reflect African awareness of the basic truths and values of democracy and the dignity of the individual man, which are not a Western monopoly but date back to the philosophy of Buddha and Confucius. The task of making democracy work in Africa is the task of Africans. Americans can help by a sympathetic attitude, by aiding African political, eco-

---

[10] Obafemi Awolowo, *Awo—The Autobiography of Chief Obafemi Awolowo*, Cambridge, England, 1960, pp. 304–305.

nomic, social, and educational development, and by setting a high standard of democracy in the United States.

ROLE OF THE PUBLIC

In the foregoing analysis of American interests, private interests have been discussed separately from the national interest in order to clarify certain terms which are often used ambiguously. Needless to say, these two kinds of interests are not entirely separable, and American policy in Africa is affected by both. While some private groups lobby for their own special interests, others attempt to impress their view of the national interest on policy makers in Washington. What effect does such pressure have? In the view of Paul H. Nitze, who once headed the State Department's planning staff, "the American people most effectively exercise their general control over foreign policy by choosing between alternative sets of leaders rather than by giving advice on day-by-day policy decisions."[11] Most of the Africa policy recommendations coming into the State Department from private groups receive only routine reading and acknowledgment. An original idea may be picked up and pursued by an officer whose thoughts incline him in the same general direction. Unless the government has the understanding and support of the American people, however, its policies will in the long run prove ineffective. That is why public opinion must be taken into account in policy decisions, even though policy makers have an obligation to do what seems to them to be in the national interest.

Policy on African problems is often decided in the context of a wide variety of other issues which may be under simultaneous consideration. Since some of these issues may have to remain confidential for diplomatic reasons, the public suffers from the disadvantage of not having all the facts available to it. Public discussion of the complex African issues confronting us is nonetheless vital to the successful functioning of our democratic system of government. Not only does it broaden and deepen our knowledge of Africa; it helps us clarify

[11] Quoted by Ernest Lefever, *Ethics and United States Foreign Policy*, New York, 1957, p. 162.

for ourselves as well as others our moral support for the basic values of freedom and justice. Its confusion of voices sharpens the debate over the national interest in Africa and prepares the way for a sound conception to emerge.

16

The Making of Africa Policy

THERE was no doubt a grain of truth in the popular story among foreign diplomats in Washington in 1961 that American policy was made by two men, the President and his brother, the Attorney General. The facts, however, were not so simple. In 1949 the Hoover Commission on the Organization of the Executive Branch found that more than 40 different departments and other executive agencies were directly concerned with aspects of our foreign policy. To complement the preceding analysis of nongovernmental organizations which influence American policy toward Africa, the Africa policy-making machinery of the United States government must now be examined.

THE ROLE OF THE STATE DEPARTMENT

One of the most striking facts about the Department of State, the President's principal arm in the conduct of foreign affairs, is its expansion since World War II. Although still one of the smaller departments, it grew from an agency of 4726 employees with a $15,-000,000 budget in 1930 to 26,449 employees with a budget of $331,-000,000 in 1950. Foreign Service officers and other persons employed abroad are included in these figures, which also cover the contributions of the United States to international organizations and other international activities.

Until 1950, however, Africa received little attention at top levels in the government. It is not much of an exaggeration to say that our few posts in Africa were still a dumping ground for senior Foreign Service officers who weren't good enough for promotion to Class 1 before retirement. The scanty information these officers dispatched to the inadequate and badly organized Africa office in the State Department often came from Europeans with understandably one-sided views. By 1950 efforts to remedy this deficiency were under way both inside and outside the government. The handful of Africanists found a valuable ally in a Rhodes scholar with a real appreciation of the need for university training programs on Africa, Assistant Secretary of State George C. McGhee.

In the United States's first major policy statement on Africa on May 8, 1950, Mr. McGhee pointed out that there was "no comprehensive program of African area studies in any American university." His appeal for help from "American private interests, teaching institutions, and foundations"[1] undoubtedly stimulated or strengthened university and foundation support for the study of Africa. A year later McGhee was able to address the first summer Institute on Contemporary Africa held for six weeks at Northwestern University. In 1954 a comparable summer session was held for eight weeks at the School of Advanced International Studies of the Johns Hopkins University. Graduate students from all over the United States, many of whom now hold important university or government posts dealing with Africa, attended these two summer sessions.

Mr. McGhee also assembled the country's Africanists at meetings in his office to get their views and encourage their efforts, a practice his successors largely neglected until late in 1960, when President-elect Kennedy asked for policy recommendations from a temporary Task Force on Africa—a group of about 40 specialists recruited from universities, philanthropic foundations, and business firms. New Assistant Secretary of State for African Affairs G. Mennen Williams carried the practice further when, early in 1962, he appointed a con-

[1] Speech, "United States Interests in Africa," Oklahoma City, May 8, 1950, issued as State Department Press Release No. 469.

tinuing advisory council of nongovernmental specialists on Africa to meet periodically with State Department officials. This 40-member Advisory Council on African Affairs held its first meeting on June 13–14, 1962.

Another "first" of George McGhee was the idea, later put into practice, of bringing Foreign Service officers in from the field for a year's academic training in one of the new graduate programs of African studies. And he also brought our diplomatic and consular officers in Africa together for the first time to study and compare their problems—at Lourenço Marques in March, 1950, for officers south of the Sahara, and at Tangier in October, 1950, for officers north of the Sahara. McGhee's pump-priming activities to increase our African competence were thus a basic contribution of lasting value.

For many years, officers working on European problems in the Department of State had handled the occasional African matters that required attention. In 1937, however, action responsibility for much of Africa was given to the Near Eastern division. During World War II, in 1943, a separate office for Africa was established within this division. By January, 1956, when South Africa and Madagascar were transferred to it, this Office of African Affairs was responsible for all of Africa except Algeria, Egypt, and the Sudan.

On September 10, 1956, the status of African affairs was raised by the establishment of a semiautonomous Africa unit of 34 officers headed by a deputy assistant secretary of state. The new Africa unit was divided into an Office of Northern African Affairs and an Office of Southern African Affairs (the latter was renamed the Office of Middle and Southern African Affairs in 1958). However, it remained structurally under the Bureau of Near Eastern, South Asian, and African Affairs for two years until the House, on July 10, 1958, finally adopted a bill passed a year earlier by the Senate to authorize a separate Bureau of African Affairs with its own assistant secretary. The number of officers in the Bureau rose to 44 in 1960, to more than 70 in 1961, and to 97 in 1962, when it was further reorganized.

By 1958 other substantial changes had also occurred. The quantity and quality of political and economic reporting from Africa had much improved. Not only was the Foreign Service sending better officers to senior posts in Africa, but promising young diplomats began

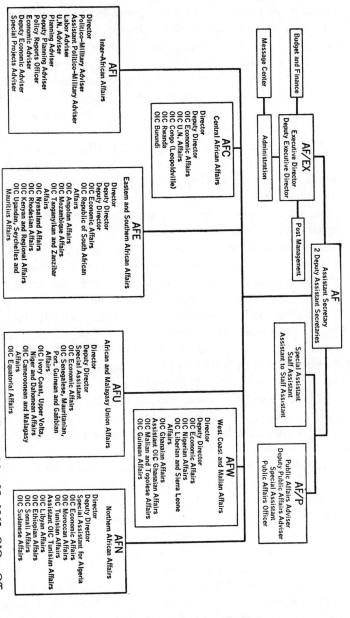

Fig. 2. Offices in the Bureau of African Affairs (AF), Department of State, effective May 25, 1962. OIC = Officer in Charge. Total personnel complement on July 9, 1962, was 163—97 professional and 66 clerical workers.
Source: Prepared by the author from data supplied by the Bureau of African Affairs.

AF
Assistant Secretary
2 Deputy Assistant Secretaries
Special Assistant
Staff Assistant
Assistant to Staff Assistant

Budget and Finance

Message Center

Administration

Post Management

AF/EX
Executive Director
Deputy Executive Director

AF/P
Public Affairs Adviser
Deputy Public Affairs Adviser
Special Assistant
Public Affairs Officer

AFI
Inter-African Affairs
Director
Politico-Military Adviser
Assistant Politico-Military Adviser
Labor Adviser
U.N. Adviser
Planning Adviser
Deputy Planning Adviser
Policy Reports Officer
Economic Adviser
Deputy Economic Adviser
Special Projects Adviser

AFC
Central African Affairs
Director
Deputy Director
OIC Economic Affairs
OIC U.N. Affairs
OIC Congo (Leopoldville)
OIC Rwanda
OIC Burundi

AFE
Eastern and Southern African Affairs
Director
Deputy Director
Deputy Director
OIC Economic Affairs
OIC Republic of South African
  Affairs
OIC Angolan Affairs
OIC Mozambique Affairs
OIC Tanganyikan and Zanzibar
  Affairs
OIC Nyasaland Affairs
OIC Rhodesian Affairs
OIC Kenyan and Regional Affairs
OIC Ugandan, Seychelles and
  Mauritius Affairs

AFU
African and Malagasy Union Affairs
Director
Deputy Director
Special Assistant
OIC Economic Affairs
OIC Senegalese, Mauritanian,
  Port. Guinean and Gambian
  Affairs
OIC Ivory Coast, Upper Volta,
  Niger and Dahomean Affairs
OIC Cameroonean and Malagasy
  Affairs
OIC Equatorial Affairs

AFW
West Coast and Malian Affairs
Director
Deputy Director
OIC Economic Affairs
OIC Nigerian Affairs
OIC Liberian and Sierra Leone
  Affairs
OIC Ghanaian Affairs
Assistant OIC Ghanaian Affairs
OIC Malian and Togolese Affairs
OIC Guinean Affairs

AFN
Northern African Affairs
Director
Deputy Director
Special Assistant for Algeria
OIC Economic Affairs
OIC Moroccan Affairs
OIC Tunisian Affairs
Assistant OIC Tunisian Affairs
OIC Libyan Affairs
OIC Ethiopian Affairs
OIC Somali Affairs
OIC Sudanese Affairs

to ask for African posts. A 1958 review of 2600 post preference forms indicated that 146 officers had a serious interest in and wished to spend at least part of their career in Africa. The need for higher-caliber and better-trained officers was still so great, however, that President Kennedy's Task Force on Africa urged him to give high priority to recruiting additional top-flight personnel.

If it seems strange that the State Department did not have a separate Bureau of African Affairs until 1958, it should be noted that the United States Foreign Service had 256 officers in the single country of West Germany in 1957 in contrast to only 248 officers in the whole of Africa. Since German affairs were combined with those of all other European countries in a single bureau, it was sometimes asked why a separate bureaucratic structure was needed to handle our small African operations. The main reason was clear. When African affairs were handled in the same bureau that dealt with Near Eastern and South Asian problems, they could not be given sufficient attention because top officials were too busy with other crises.

In 1939, the United States had 3 legations, 3 consulates general, 8 consulates, and 1 consular agency in Africa. By July, 1961, there were 28 embassies, 11 consulates general, 9 consulates, 1 embassy branch office, and 1 consular agency in 37 African countries. The number of Foreign Service and other officers manning African posts rose from 664 in October, 1957, to 1359 in July, 1961. In Washington, 27 African countries had established embassies by the end of 1961. United States diplomatic and consular posts in Africa are shown in Table 15, which indicates the number and type of officers at each post.

Within the Department of State, the responsibility for initiating action on most African problems rests with the Bureau of African Affairs, where the country "desk officer" is the main point of contact with the African country or countries of his office. He also maintains close relations with their embassies in Washington. He is primarily an operations officer who makes many decisions on routine matters. He also participates in policy making by drafting proposals for approval by the office director and the assistant secretary.

On matters of greatest importance, policy recommendations go to the National Security Council. Created in 1947 to advise the Presi-

TABLE 15. United States Diplomatic and Consular Posts in Africa

Offices	Foreign Service	ICA Officers	USIA Officers[a]	Army, Naval, and Air Attachés	Foreign Agricultural Service
Embassies					
Abidjan, Ivory Coast	8	7	1	2	
Accra, Ghana	24	34	6	1	
Addis Ababa, Ethiopia	18	121	3	6	
Bamako, Mali	8	5	2		
Bangui, Cent. Af. Rep.	4		1		
Brazzaville, Congo	7		1		
Cairo, Egypt	45	34	17	13	2
Conakry, Guinea	12	2	1		
Cotonou, Dahomey	4		1		
Dakar, Senegal	12	6	2		
Dar-es-Salaam, Tang.	7	2	3		
Fort Lamy, Chad	3		1		
Freetown, Sierra Leone	8	5	1		
Khartoum, Sudan	20	69	5	5	1
Kigali, Rwanda	2				
Lagos, Nigeria	20	49	7	1	1
Leopoldville, Congo	17	7	5	4	
Libreville, Gabon	4		1		
Lomé, Togo	6	3	1		
Mogadiscio, Somali Rep.	14	52	3		
Monrovia, Liberia	13	86	5		1
Niamey, Niger	5		1		
Nouakchott, Mauritania[b]	4				
Ouagadougou, Upp. Volta	4	2	1		
Pretoria, South Africa	16		2	7	1
Rabat, Morocco	27	30	4	4	1
Tananarive, Malagasy	7	5	1		
Tripoli, Libya	18	102	11		
Benghazi Office	6		2		
Tunis, Tunisia	17	54	8	1	
Usumbura, Burundi	5		2		
Yaoundé, Cameroon	10	3	2	1	
Consulates General					
Alexandria, Egypt	5		1		
Algiers, Algeria	9		2		
Cape Town, South Africa	4		2		

Offices	Foreign Service	ICA Officers	USIA Officers[a]	Army, Naval, and Air Attachés	Foreign Agricultural Service
Casablanca, Morocco	9		1		
Johannesburg, S. Af.	7		1		
Kampala, Uganda	5		2		
Lourenço Marques, Moz.	3				
Luanda, Angola	5				
Nairobi, Kenya	11	14	4		1
Salisbury, Rhod.-Nya.	13	9	5		1
Tangier, Morocco	9		14		
Consulates					
Asmara, Eritrea	5		1		
Constantine, Alg.	2				
Douala, Cameroon	4		1		
Durban, South Africa	3				
Elizabethville, Congo	3				
Enugu, Nigeria	3	6	1		
Ibadan, Nigeria	3	15	1		
Kaduna, Nigeria	4	1	2		
Oran, Algeria	1		1		
Port Elizabeth, S. Af.	2				
Port Said, Egypt	2				
Stanleyville, Congo	2				
Zanzibar, Zanzibar	2				
Consular Agency (Beira) and Resident Consuls					
Beira, Mozambique	1				
Blantyre, Nya.	1				
Lusaka, N. Rhodesia	1				
Total	494	723	140	45	9

[a] Of the 134 USIA officers, 13 are radio technicians assigned to the "Voice of America" relay base in Tangier.

[b] No office maintained.

SOURCE: Prepared from data in U.S. Department of State, *Foreign Service List*, Washington, July, 1961, and August, 1962 data on new posts.

dent on the integration of domestic, foreign and military policies involving national security, the National Security Council is composed of the President, Vice-President, Secretary of State, Secretary of Defense, and Director of the Office of Defense Mobilization. Others may participate by invitation of the President. The NSC has a Planning Board which prepares papers that ordinarily serve as the basis for its policy recommendations to the President, who makes the final decision.

Since 1947 the Department of State has also had a Policy Planning Staff to formulate long-term programs for the achievement of U.S. foreign policy objectives. The way in which it operates is interestingly portrayed by Robert Elder in his book *The Policy Machine*. Because of other priorities, however, both the National Security Council and the Policy Planning Staff were late in devoting adequate attention to Africa.

Officers in the Africa Bureau must clear important decisions with officers in other interested bureaus. Africa policy is thus seasoned by many cooks, some of whom have conflicting tastes. These may be geographical bureaus, like the European Affairs Bureau, or functional bureaus, like the Economic Affairs Bureau or the Legal Adviser's Office, all of whom have officers who keep an eye on Africa. In the 1950s, particularly, if an African issue was sufficiently controversial to arouse the British, French, or Belgian ambassador to call on the secretary of state, the Bureau of European Affairs was likely to have a powerful voice in the final decision.

A second Department of State office handling African matters is the Office of Research and Analysis on Africa in the Bureau of Intelligence and Research. In principle, research officers in this Bureau refrain from making policy recommendations, but their research is oriented to consider the possible consequences of various policy alternatives. In addition, the Africa Office receives many requests from policy-making officers for spot comments on current crises. In its early years the Bureau of Intelligence and Research operated on the principle that it should include only trained research workers. The amalgamation of the Department of State and the Foreign Service in the mid-1950s strained this rule by bringing in analysts who lacked research training, although many had had first-hand field experience in Africa. In 1961 the professional staff of the Africa Office declined from 23 to 15 when certain long-term African research activities of the Department of State were transferred to the Central Intelligence Agency.

THE STATE DEPARTMENT'S "POSITION PAPERS"

Still another bureau has initial action responsibility for the difficult African issues which arise in the United Nations. This is the Bureau of International Organization Affairs, which prepares the "position papers" that guide United States Delegations at United Nations meetings. Within this Bureau is an Office of Dependent Area Affairs which deals with problems of trust and non–self-governing territories. Because of the great decline in the number of dependencies, it went out of existence as a separate office on June 1, 1962, when it became a unit of the Office of U.N. Political, Security and Dependent Area Affairs.

A brief description of how position papers on the problems of African trust and non–self-governing territories were prepared in the Office of Dependent Area Affairs will help to explain how another part of the Africa policy machine operates. When the United Nations Secretariat circulates the provisional agenda for a future meeting, usually well in advance, individual officers are assigned the task of drafting position papers for each item on this agenda. These position papers take the form of (1) a concise statement of the problem confronting the U.S. Delegation, (2) a brief recommendation of the position to be taken by the Delegation, and (3) a longer background section explaining the problem in more detail, along with the reasons for the recommendation or recommendations. For example, if it were a position paper on the Trusteeship Council's examination of the annual report of the United Kingdom on its administration of the trust territory of Tanganyika, the drafting officer would have to study the report in detail, along with other relevant data. He would then single out the main problems on which the Trusteeship Council ought to focus; prepare a list of detailed questions which the United States representative might, if appropriate, ask the special representative of the administering authority when he appeared at the Council table; and perhaps draft a statement which might be made by the

United States representative, after modification in the light of Council discussion, on the general view of the United States regarding British administration of Tanganyika during the preceding year.

In the procedure of the Office of Dependent Area Affairs in the 1950s, the officer's draft was usually revised after criticism by his colleagues and sent out for clearance after approval by the Office director. Since it dealt with Tanganyika, it would have to be cleared with the Africa Bureau, and since the British then administered Tanganyika it would have to be cleared by the European Bureau. If recommendations were made on Tanganyika tariffs, they would have to be cleared by the Economic Affairs Bureau, and if the legality of Tanganyika's administrative union with the neighboring colonies of Kenya and Uganda was at issue, the American position would have to be cleared by a specialist on African matters in the Legal Adviser's Office.

In the early 1950s this clearance was undertaken first in a Departmental Committee on Dependent Area Affairs, and then in an Interdepartmental Committee on Non–Self-Governing Territories. In the latter Committee, the clearance of the Department of Commerce, for example, might be sought on the matter of Tanganyika tariffs; and the Department of the Interior, which is responsible for the administration of American "colonies," would clear recommendations for Tanganyika which might have a bearing on American administration in the trust territory of the Pacific Islands or in Samoa, Guam, or the Virgin Islands.

These two Committees served a valuable purpose in the beginning because they helped to educate many government officials who otherwise had little opportunity to become acquainted with African problems and because they helped to expedite the clearance process. As African issues became more numerous and more difficult, however, Committee members began to refer position papers back to their own superiors rather than clearing them on the spot. Having thus lost their clearance function, the two Committees fell into disuse.

When all the position papers for a Trusteeship Council or General Assembly session are thus completed, they are formally transmitted to the head of the American Delegation in a "position book," which constitutes his instructions from the Department of State. As a result, U.S. representatives at such meetings are relatively well prepared. If these classified position books are made available to scholars in the future, a comparison of them from year to year will provide interesting source material on the evolution of American positions on African issues.

Quite naturally, this elaborate machinery often has to be bypassed. Many of the most difficult problems arise unexpectedly during U.N. meetings, sending members of the American Delegation scurrying to one of the several direct telephone lines to Washington maintained by the State Department. A hasty call alerts the Department to the need for a position on a proposal that may be coming up for a vote within a few hours. In Washington, the officer concerned then has to attempt to clear a position in short order.

THE PERSONAL FACTOR IN POLICY MAKING

The elaboration of Africa policy-making machinery in this chapter should not be allowed to obscure the fact that much depends on the personal factor. Policy is sometimes made at top levels by strong personalities who disregard the machine either deliberately or subconsciously. In this context, Dean Acheson's remarks on the importance of the White House staff, including the President's speech writers, are particularly relevant. Acheson writes that "this is often where policy is made, regardless of where it is supposed to be made," and he cites the example of the Point Four proposal contained in the inaugural address of January 20, 1949, which was "vigorously opposed in the Department before its enunciation." The bureaucratic routine through which Foreign Service officers must go, he adds, produces capable men and excellent diplomatic operators but makes them "cautious rather than imaginative." That is why, he believes, big ideas like the Point Four program and the Fulbright education exchange program have not emanated from the State Department. And in the conception and development of the Marshall Plan, "the leading parts were, with few exceptions, played by men whose training and experience were broader than the State Department mill provided."[2]

[2] Dean Acheson, "The President and the Secretary of State," in American Assembly, *The Secretary of State*, Englewood Cliffs, 1960, pp. 44–49.

A good example of the bypassing of some of the Africa policy machine is the number of quick decisions which have had to be taken at top levels during the fast-moving Congo crisis since mid-1960. Another was the unusual March 22, 1960, decision regarding the Sharpeville shooting in South Africa. Lincoln White, the Department's press officer, was authorized to make the following statement if the question was raised at a press conference. In response to an Indian journalist, he said:

The United States deplores violence in all its forms and hopes that the African people of South Africa will be able to obtain redress for legitimate grievances by peaceful means. While the United States, as a matter of practice, does not ordinarily comment on the internal affairs of governments with which it enjoys normal relations, it cannot help but regret the tragic loss of life resulting from the measures taken against the demonstrators in South Africa.[3]

Since this extraordinary commentary on a domestic incident within another country was made the day after Sharpeville and before the facts were well established even in South Africa, it was obviously a quick decision which did not follow the normal pattern of the policy machine. Six days earlier, Assistant Secretary of State for African Affairs Joseph C. Satterthwaite, in testimony before the Senate Foreign Relations Committee, had remarked that a government was simply "not free to make gratuitous statements on the internal affairs of a foreign country."[4]

The impetus for the Sharpeville statement came from Assistant Secretary of State for Public Affairs Andrew H. Berding at the Secretary of State's regular staff meeting the morning after the shooting in South Africa. Berding felt that the Department's press officer would certainly be questioned, and that the situation would not permit a "no comment" reply. Certain officers opposed such "emotional diplomacy," but their views did not prevail. A phrase in the original

---

[3] Department of State, *Transcript of Press and Radio News Briefing*, Washington, March 22, 1960.

[4] As quoted in *West Africa*, No. 2234, March 26, 1960, p. 337, which differs in wording from the official record in U.S. Congress, Senate Committee on Foreign Relations, *United States Foreign Policy*, Hearings, 86th Cong., 2nd sess., January 28, February 11, and March 16, 1960, Part I, Washington, 1960, pp. 134–135.

draft which condemned the South African police was stricken out, however, on the grounds that the exact facts were unknown.

Since speed was essential for a favorable world reaction, the American ambassador in Pretoria, who presumably knew most about the facts of the case, was not even consulted. South African Foreign Minister Eric Louw called him in the next day to protest against the American declaration, an action which naturally won the United States favorable publicity in African and Asian circles. Interestingly, the Department's quick action beat Moscow and Peking to the punch by two days; it was not until March 24 that they issued statements condemning South Africa for Sharpeville. In Britain the official reaction was still slower; Foreign Minister Selwyn Lloyd denounced South African policy on April 2, and the House of Commons on April 8 adopted a resolution urging the government at the forthcoming Commonwealth Prime Minister's Conference "to bring home to the South African Government" the British position.

The statement released by Lincoln White was not cleared in the White House, which reportedly was uneasy about it, partly because of the military interests of the Department of Defense in South Africa and partly because of President Eisenhower's cautious approach toward intervention in the affairs of other countries. State Department officers in later explanations insisted that the statement did not depart from previous declarations of American policy toward South Africa. They had not expected the statement to be so widely publicized, but were pleased at the favorable press reactions both at home and abroad.

OTHER POLICY-MAKING BODIES

In addition to the aforementioned Bureaus dealing with Africa, the Department of State has a Bureau of Educational and Cultural Affairs which conducts an important exchange of persons program. It will be discussed, along with the African operations of the Agency for International Development (AID) and the United States Information Agency (USIA) in later chapters.

Outside the Department of State and its related autonomous agencies, the major departments which have officers working on

Africa are the Departments of the Army, the Navy, the Air Force, and Defense; the Departments of Agriculture, Commerce, and Labor; and the Department of Health, Education, and Welfare. A brief catalogue of their African activities will complete this analysis of the Africa policy machine. Comparable information is unavailable on the Central Intelligence Agency, which collects and analyzes information and conducts operations in the field to support American policy. In theory, all these offices serve in an advisory and supporting capacity to the secretary of state insofar as they deal with foreign policy matters. In practice they sometimes take steps which have the effect of policy decisions.

THE DEPARTMENT OF DEFENSE

Many officers in the Department of Defense and the Departments of the Army, the Navy, and the Air Force deal with African problems as a part of their general duties. These include both military and civilian specialists on such matters as military intelligence, military operations, military assistance, and technical services for transport and communications.

The responsibilities of the Department of Defense include the development and coordination of policies, plans, and procedures in international political-military affairs. The principal adviser and assistant to the Secretary of Defense on these matters is an Assistant Secretary for International Security Affairs, whose office established a Middle East-Africa unit in 1955 and a Regional Directorate for Near East, South Asia, and Africa in 1957. Since October, 1960, the number of officers in the Africa section of this Directorate has risen from one to four.

The Africa section has responsibilities for the two major bases of the United States in Africa, the Navy and Air Force base at Port Lyautey in Morocco and Wheelus Air Base in Libya. The United States Air Force is also permitted to use Moroccan bases at Nouasseur and Sidi Slimene, but has withdrawn from bases at Ben Guerir and Ben Slimene. It has agreed to withdraw all other military personnel, including those at Port Lyautey, by the end of 1963.

In addition to these bases in Libya and Morocco, the Defense Department supports two Military Assistance Advisory Groups of American military personnel in Africa, one in Ethiopia and the other in Libya, and four military missions in Liberia, Mali, Morocco, and Tunisia. It also has an important Army and Navy communications facility at Asmara in the Eritrean province of Ethiopia. Furthermore, the National Aeronautics and Space Administration maintains satellite tracking and space exploration facilities at Kano, Nigeria, near Johannesburg, South Africa, and in Zanzibar.

Increasing attention is also being devoted to Africa by the war colleges of the various armed services. The best-known of these, the National War College, was established in 1946 by the Joint Chiefs of Staff to train selected military personnel in the essentials of national security. A limited number of civilian officials from the State and other departments and agencies are invited to attend the college each year. In May, 1957, Africa was added for the first time to the areas annually selected for a visit of several weeks by a small study group; by 1961 about 200 War College participants had made such trips through Africa.

THE DEPARTMENT OF LABOR

In the Bureau of International Labor Affairs, headed by an assistant secretary of labor, one of the Bureau's five area specialists follows labor developments in Africa with the help of an assistant Africa area specialist. In the Bureau of Labor Statistics there is also a specialist on Africa in the Division of Foreign Labor Conditions who analyzes embassy reports and other sources of information and prepares research memoranda and country monographs on labor in Africa.

In 1962, seven Foreign Service officers were stationed in Africa as labor attachés in Ghana, Guinea, Kenya, Morocco, Nigeria, Senegal, and Tunisia. Other Foreign Service officers supplement the work of the labor attachés by occasional reporting on labor matters. In addition to reporting to Washington on African labor affairs, the labor attachés attempt to promote in Africa a better understanding of American labor policies and practices.

U.S. labor programs involving training and technical assistance projects in Africa are carried out by the Agency for International Development. When AID or the State Department brings African labor leaders to this country, their programs are arranged by the Department of Labor. The Department of Labor does special research and publishes training material tailored to the needs of the AID missions. It recruits or provides labor experts to give technical assistance to ministries of labor, trade unions, and other organizations and agencies. It also provides programming and training for exchange program visitors to the United States whose primary interests are in the labor field. In developing these activities, the Department has the advice of the secretary of labor's Trade Union Advisory Committee on International Affairs, which assures consultation between the United States government and the top American labor leaders.

Publications of the Department of Labor include the *Directory of Labor Organizations—Africa*, which was first published in 1958 and is presently undergoing a complete revision with anticipated publication in mid-1962; a biweekly summary of labor developments in Africa and elsewhere; and two monthlies, *Labor Developments Abroad* and *International Labor*. Monographs and summaries of the labor situation in specific African countries are also prepared.

THE DEPARTMENT OF COMMERCE

The Department of Commerce promotes U.S. foreign trade and private investment abroad through two bureaus—the Bureau of International Business Operations and the Bureau of International Programs—both under the supervision of the Assistant Secretary of Commerce for International Affairs. The international program provides specific services to business, and helps to formulate and support the foreign economic policies of the United States.

African affairs (excluding Egypt) are the responsibility of an African Division created in September, 1961, within the Bureau of International Programs. This Division has a professional staff of 14 officers and is organized in three regional sections covering North Africa and Horn, Middle Africa, and Southern Africa.

Most foreign service posts in Africa have staff officers who cover economic and commercial affairs. Separate attachés for commercial

affairs work in several American embassies in Africa, and their number will mount under a Department of Commerce export expansion
program. The reports of these officers are reviewed, interpreted, and
disseminated to the American business community by the Africa Division and other functional units within the Department of Commerce.

Since 1957, eight trade missions have been sent to Africa, covering
various countries in East and West Africa, the Rhodesias, South
Africa, and Tunisia. Additional trade missions are planned. The Department has also participated in international trade fairs and exhibitions in Tripoli, Tunis, Casablanca, and Addis Ababa. A Special
Trade Exhibit was held in Accra in January, 1962, and others are
planned for Lagos and elsewhere in Africa.

Material on Africa appears frequently in Commerce Department
publications, including the *Foreign Commerce Weekly* and various
country pamphlets in the World Trade Information Series. The Department has also published useful investment handbooks on Nigeria,
Rhodesia-Nyasaland, and South Africa.

THE DEPARTMENT OF HEALTH, EDUCATION, AND WELFARE

Within the Office of the Secretary of Health, Education, and Welfare (HEW) is an Office of International Affairs, under the direction of a deputy assistant secretary. This office, which assigns none
of its staff exclusively to African affairs, assists in and coordinates the
international activities of the Department's five component agencies
—the Office of Education, the Public Health Service, the Social Security Administration, the Office of Vocational Rehabilitation, and
the Food and Drug Administration. One of its major functions is to
provide professional backstopping for State, AID, and USIA. For
example, experts are supplied to serve on U.S. delegations, international advisory groups, and foreign technical assistance assignments;
and technical materials and advice are provided for USIA and other
information programs. The Office of International Affairs and the
component HEW agencies also participate in the preparation of
position papers and related documents for the United Nations and

its specialized agencies. During the fiscal year 1961 the Department and its agencies scheduled the itineraries of or gave other assistance to some 6000 foreign visitors from 91 countries, perhaps 300 of whom came from Africa north and south of the Sahara.

Of the five component agencies of Health, Education, and Welfare, the Office of Education and the Public Health Service are the most closely connected with Africa. The Food and Drug Administration has no international unit as such, and the Office of Vocational Rehabilitation and the Social Security Administration are involved in African affairs mainly through the scheduling of exchange visitors. In one case, however, a grant of $10,000 was made in the fiscal year 1962 by the Office of Vocational Rehabilitation to evaluate methods for rehabilitating individuals paralyzed by triorthocresyl phosphate. This was a study prompted by the incident in 1959 when a number of Moroccans were unintentionally poisoned by surplus U.S. Air Force fuel oil which was used for human consumption.

The National Institutes of Health of the Public Health Service sponsor grants and fellowships for foreign scientists to work in the medical and biological laboratories of this country and for American scientists to do research or obtain specialized training abroad. Thus far, this program has had little impact on Africa. Out of the 1185 awards for the fiscal year 1961, only 18 went to Africa, and 15 of these went to South Africa alone. On January 3, 1962, however, an agreement was signed with the government of Ghana to establish an NIH West African Research Unit in that country to collaborate with the National Institute of Health and Medical Research of Ghana on problems of mutual interest to the two governments. This project is the first of its kind to be undertaken in Africa.

The Office of Education acts as agent for the Department of State in the recruitment of American teachers for the teacher exchange program and in the administration of the training program for foreign visiting teachers. The Office also recruits and services American educators who go abroad under AID technical assistance programs. The Comparative Education Section provides advisory interpretations of foreign student credentials and replies to requests from both government agencies and private individuals for information on educational opportunities abroad. The teaching of 11 African languages

TABLE 16. United States Agricultural Exports to Africa under Specified Government Programs, July, 1960–June, 1961 (in Thousands of Dollars)

| Country | Public Law 480 | | | | P.L. 665, Sec. 402 Sales for Foreign Currency and Economic Aid | Total Agricultural Exports Under Specified Government Programs |
	Title I Sales for Foreign Currency	Title II Famine and Other Emergency Relief	Title III Foreign Donations	Title III Barter		
Algeria						
Angola			1,743			1,743
British East Africa		1,337	139			1,476
British West Africa			120	23		143
Cameroon			71			71
Canary Islands				4,653		4,653
Congo (Leopoldville)		4,696	373	573		5,642
Egypt	65,670		19,026a		1,245	85,941
Ethiopia		928	204	2		1,134
French Equatorial Africa			15			15
French Somaliland				35		35

						Total
French West Africa			934	110	1,000	2,044
Ghana			671	1,606		2,277
Liberia			303	76		379
Libya		8,049	1,011			9,060
Madeira Islands			6			6
Malagasy			54			54
Mauritius (and dependencies)						
Morocco		11,051	4,379	363	4,852	20,645
Mozambique				1,160		1,160
Nigeria			74	633		707
Federation of Rhodesia and Nyasaland			4			4
Seychelles (and dependencies)		280	2			282
Somalia			25	59		84
South Africa						
Spanish Africa						
Sudan		35,248	384			35,632
Tunisia				15		15
Western Portuguese Africa						
Total	65,670	61,589	29,538	9,308	7,097	173,202

[a] Includes donations under Title III to the Syria region of the U.A.R.; quantity reports show that most of the Title III donations went to the Egypt region.

SOURCE: Data supplied by U.S. Department of Agriculture, Foreign Agricultural Service.

was also being sponsored in the academic year 1962–1963 under Title VI of the National Defense Education Act.

THE DEPARTMENT OF AGRICULTURE

To help expand foreign trade, the Department of Agriculture established a Foreign Agricultural Service in 1933. The agricultural attachés it sends to our diplomatic and consular posts are responsible for promoting U.S. agricultural exports and reporting on local agriculture. This Service grew slowly, and did not enter Africa before World War II. In 1961, eight of its 52 officers with the rank of attaché were stationed in Africa—in Leopoldville, Nairobi, Monrovia, Lagos, Salisbury, Pretoria, Rabat, and Cairo. Each of the eight was responsible not only for the country in which he was stationed but also for a number of surrounding countries.

The Africa and Middle East Analysis Branch of the Economic Research Service in 1961 had two agricultural economists for northern Africa and three for southern Africa. This Branch was formerly a part of the Foreign Agricultural Service. Officers in the Foreign Agricultural Service, Commodity Divisions, also covered Africa as part of their wider duties.

Beginning in 1954, under the Agricultural Trade Development and Assistance Act (Public Law 480), the Foreign Agricultural Service has participated in worldwide agricultural development and assistance programs which cost $15,800,000,000 by the end of 1961. Exports under this program have amounted to about one-fourth of total U.S. agricultural exports in recent years. Public Law 480, which supplies surplus American agricultural products to underdeveloped countries, is the largest Food for Peace project. Africa's share of U.S. agricultural exports in 1961 is shown in Table 16, which lists a total of $173,-202,000 under government-financed programs. It should also be mentioned that agricultural commodities exported to Africa outside these government-financed programs totaled only $48,030,000 in 1961.

THE INFLUENCE OF CONGRESS

Finally, no account of the Africa policy machine would be complete without consideration of the powerful influence of Congress, which is exerted through the control of appropriations and in many other ways. The secretary of state finds that in addition to the House Foreign Affairs and Senate Foreign Relations Committees, almost every other congressional committee is concerned with some aspect of foreign policy—from the disposal of agricultural surpluses to visa and passport policy. In 1962, the support of Congress was vital for American aid to Africa, for American policy in the Congo, and for the Administration's proposal to purchase up to $100,000,000 worth of U.N. bonds to avert a U.N. financial crisis.

As the importance of Africa became more apparent during the 1950s, an increasing number of congressmen devoted attention to it. Each year two senators or two representatives served on U.S. Delegations to the U.N. General Assembly, where African issues occupied a major part of the agenda. Greater attention began to be given to Africa in congressional hearings and debates. In constituencies with an important Negro vote, the new interest of American Negroes in African affairs serves as a further stimulus to congressmen to inform themselves about Africa.

African and Near Eastern affairs were handled in the same congressional committees until 1959, when both the Senate Foreign Relations Committee and the House Foreign Affairs Committee established separate subcommittees for Africa. Congressional committees send about one hundred groups of congressmen (sometimes with only one member to the "group") annually on overseas visits. Among those who have gone to Africa since 1955 are:

1955	Representative Frances P. Bolton
1956	Senator Theodore F. Green
1957	Representatives Wayne L. Hayes, Barratt O'Hara, and Marguerite Stitt Church
1958	Senator Mike Mansfield
1960	Representatives Charles C. Diggs, Jr., William T. Murphy, and Barratt O'Hara
1960	Senators Frank Church, Gale W. McGhee, and Frank E. Moss
1961	Senators Albert Gore, Philip A. Hart, and Maurine B. Neuberger

1961   Representatives Robert H. Michel and Silvio O.
         Conte
1961   Senator Thomas J. Dodd

These visits are an excellent means of giving members of Congress a "feel" for the subject of Africa, which can be of real value when they have to form judgments on African issues. The reports of several congressional visitors to Africa have been printed as documents available to the public. A pioneering trip was made in 1955 by Congressman Frances P. Bolton, who has been a member of subcommittees dealing with Africa for the House Foreign Affairs Committee since 1947. Mrs. Bolton performed an outstanding public service by stimulating further congressional and public interest in Africa. She not only made an extensive report to Congress but delivered many public lectures illustrated by excellent color movies taken during her trip.

In 1959 and 1960 the Senate Foreign Relations Committee undertook a study of Africa as part of a larger study of United States foreign policy. The statements made to the Committee and the background study prepared for it by the Northwestern University Program of African Studies were widely read and therefore helped to broaden and deepen American interest in and knowledge of Africa.

Unlike its opposite number in the House, the Senate Foreign Relations Committee receives an annual appropriation of $5000 for entertainment, which has been used increasingly for visitors from Africa, including President Sylvanus Olympio of Togo, President Ahmadou Ahidjo of Cameroon, and Julius Nyerere of Tanganyika. Members of the House Foreign Affairs Committee are sometimes invited to these social occasions, which in effect supplement the consultative work of the Africa subcommittees. In the future, such joint meetings may be used increasingly as a means of avoiding too many joint sessions of Congress to hear visiting chiefs of state.

PROBLEMS OF COORDINATION

The foregoing survey of the overlapping African interests and operations of federal departments and agencies reveals a vast problem of organization and coordination in the Africa policy machine.

The committee system of policy making and policy coordination has been subjected to many caustic criticisms in recent years. Henry M. Wriston denounces the committee system as a "vicious and omnivorous time-consumer" which "tends to the kind of compromise that takes the shine off what once may have been a bright idea . . . ."[5] Robert R. Bowie, former head of the Policy Planning Staff, contends that it leads to "cautious hedging,"[6] and Henry A. Kissinger writes that when the advantages and disadvantages of alternative policies are discussed,

. . . the risks always seem more certain than the opportunities . . . . much of the committee procedure is designed to permit each participant or agency to register objections. . . . The impact on national policy is pernicious. Even our highest policy bodies, such as the National Security Council, are less concerned with developing over-all measures in terms of a well-understood national purpose than with adjusting the varying approaches of semi-autonomous departments. . . . The ideal "committee" man does not make his associates uncomfortable. He does not operate with ideas too far outside of what is generally accepted. Thus the thrust of committees is toward a standard of average performance. They therefore produce great pressure in favor of the status quo. . . . Committees are consumers and sometimes sterilizers of ideas, rarely creators of them. . . .[7]

In March and April, 1961, President Kennedy abolished 59 such committees. The best-known victim of the President's action was the Operations Coordinating Board (OCB), in which, since 1953, the heads of major government departments had met periodically to ensure coordination in implementing the recommendations of the National Security Council. The spade work for the OCB was done in "working groups," including one for Africa headed by a senior officer in the Bureau of African Affairs.

Another method of improving policy making and coordination which is tried from time to time is reorganization of the policy machine. Within the Department of State there is a continuing disagree-

[5] Henry M. Wriston, "The Secretary and the Management of the Department," in American Assembly, op cit., p. 106.
[6] R. R. Bowie, "Analysis of Our Policy Machine," New York Times Magazine, March 9, 1958, p. 16.
[7] Henry A. Kissenger, "The Policy-Maker and the Intellectual," The Reporter, March 5, 1959, pp. 31–32.

ment between those on the one hand who think that all the political, economic, educational, research, and other functions for an area like Africa should be under the authority of the geographical bureau for that area, and those on the other hand who believe that functional bureaus dealing with worldwide economic, educational, research, and other problems should predominate, each having geographical subdivisions. In the proliferation since World War II, the Department has added many functional bureaus to its old geographical bureaus. The geographical bureaus have gone on to employ functional "advisers" in addition to their country desk officers, while the functional bureaus have employed area specialists. In State's Bureau of African Affairs, these functional advisers perform some of the task of maintaining liaison and coordination with other bureaus.

Reorganizations solve some problems but always seem to create others. Almost all reorganizations upset morale and undermine the efficiency of workers during the uncertain transition period from one system to another. Criticizing reorganizational tinkering, Dean Acheson stresses the fact that "man hours spent in thinking and planning on future action, are by far the most profitable form of investment." This is a truth, he says, which "makes mincemeat of most of the plans for reorganization."[8] In the last analysis, effective coordination depends upon informal personal links between competent officers who understand mutual problems and have confidence in each other. This is true from the level of the President's cabinet down to the lowest working level in each department.

---

[8] Dean Acheson, *op. cit.*, p. 283.

17

Africa Policy in the Colonial Era

IT was not until May 8, 1950, that the first declaration of American policy toward Africa was made by an assistant secretary of state in charge of African affairs, George C. McGhee.[1] The only major statement made earlier was a largely historical account of "American Relations with Africa" on August 19, 1943, by Henry S. Villard, then an assistant chief in the Division of Near Eastern Affairs. This late recognition of African problems seems strange to observers confronted by the crises of the 1960s. It should be remembered, however, that the United States did not become deeply involved in Africa until World War II. In the immediate postwar years, moreover, the time of top officials was monopolized by crises in Europe, the Far East, and the Middle East which obscured the rapid changes under way in Africa. It is remarkable that Assistant Secretary McGhee found as much time as he did for Africa. As the head of the Bureau of Near Eastern, South Asian, and African Affairs, he was largely preoccupied with Arab-Israeli, Indian-Pakistani, Turkish-Syrian, and other crises.

---

[1] The policy statements referred to in Chapters 17 and 18 are listed in chronological order, with their dates and press release numbers, on pp. 443–448 of the List of Sources.

American policy toward Africa may be divided into three main periods: the two centuries from 1776 to 1950, during most of which the main concern of the United States was trade; the years between 1950 and 1958 when the major issue was the controversy over American policy on "the colonial question"; and the period since 1958 when the United States had to learn how to deal with the new states of Africa.

AMERICAN TRADE WITH AFRICA

During the long years from the Declaration of Independence in 1776 to World War II, American relations with Africa were seldom important. Several issues in which the United States became directly involved are nonetheless worthy of brief recall. When the republic was born, it lost the valuable protection of Britain. As a result, its Mediterranean trade was plundered by the piratical Barbary states of Morocco, Algiers, Tunis, and Tripoli. According to Thomas Jefferson, about 1200 American seamen and between 80 and 100 American ships engaged annually in this trade, which was valued at over £900,000 around 1770. Our first diplomatic emissary in Africa arrived in Morocco on June 19, 1786, to negotiate a treaty with the Emperor to protect American trade. The capricious unwillingness of the Barbary rulers to abide by their agreements, along with the fact that the United States still had to ransom captured seamen, soon led to the beginning of an American Navy which emerged victorious from the Barbary Wars after 1800.

Aside from the earlier slave trade described in Chapter 1, the first substantial link between the United States and Africa south of the Sahara was the settlement of Liberia by the American Colonization Society, which transported 6000 free Negroes from the United States between 1821 and 1867. Liberia became an independent republic in 1847. The United States government largely neglected it thereafter until World War II, when its strategic location on the West African coast stimulated the building of a harbor at Monrovia and the extension of other economic and technical assistance. Two American business companies became the most important exporters and revenue producers for Liberia: the Firestone Plantations Company after 1926 and the Liberia Mining Company after World War II.

A third area of United States interest was the Congo, which is interesting because of the different kind of American involvement in the Congo crisis of the 1960s. After he found Livingstone for the New York *Herald* in 1871, the versatile explorer and publicist Henry Morton Stanley aroused much attention with his stories of the 40,-000,000 Africans beyond the gateway of the Congo needing clothes and trinkets to adorn their "dusky bosoms." Soon the New York Chamber of Commerce and other business groups were petitioning their government to help American traders obtain an open door in Africa. In 1883 the secretary of state told the chairman of the Foreign Relations Committee that the government was interested in the trade of the Congo region. Through "a mixture of sentimentality and ignorance," as historian George F. Muller describes it,[2] the United States was the first country to recognize the flag of King Leopold's International African Association in 1884. An American delegation with Stanley as its scientific adviser gave further help to the King at the Berlin Conference of 1884.

A piquant detail of these early years was the behavior of Richard D. Mohun, who was appointed United States commercial agent to the Congo Free State on January 27, 1892. His letter to the State Department dated the following December 23 gives a graphic account of one of his trips to the Congo interior. The story is best told in his own words:

I desired to see the natives making cloth, and asked permission of the chief to visit the town, which was readily granted. I took only six men with me armed with revolvers under their shirts. When I had gotten about ten minutes distance from the town I was most foully attacked from the bush with spears and poisoned arrows. Fortunately none of my men were struck, and before they could throw their arrows again we had opened fire. We captured the village and I burned it to the ground to teach them a lesson. This is only one of five or six times I have been compelled to fight during the past six months.[3]

[2] George F. Muller, A *Diplomatic History of the Congo Free State*, unpublished doctoral dissertation, Johns Hopkins School of Advanced International Studies, 1948, p. 164.

[3] United States Archives, *Consular Letters*, No. 16, Boma, December 23, 1892.

Soon afterward Mohun accompanied a Belgian expeditionary force into the interior. When three of its officers became ill, Mohun accepted the commandant's invitation to act as officer in charge of two Krupp field cannons and 100 soldiers! "Of course," he reported to the Department of State, "it is quite understood that I shall not accept any remuneration from the Congo Free State."[4]

When the exploitation of African labor in the Congo Free State became an international scandal, the American public, along with government officials, gave strong moral support to demands for reform, including the transfer of the Congo from Leopold's personal sovereignty to that of the Belgian government. International action was urged in a memorandum from the Senate Committee on Foreign Relations to Secretary of State Elihu Root, who came around to the view, late in 1906, that the United States had grounds for intervention. In London, an American diplomat informed the British government that President Theodore Roosevelt "was moved by the deep interest" in the Congo question among all classes of the American people, and that the United States would cooperate with Britain if it decided to call for international action to improve conditions in the Congo. In the Senate, Henry Cabot Lodge sponsored a resolution which would have asked the President to support international measures. Such action proved unnecessary, however, when the Belgian Parliament decided to take over and reform the administration of the Congo Free State, which became the Belgian Congo on November 15, 1908.

POSTWAR TERRITORIAL SETTLEMENTS

Finally, the United States took an active part in two major African territorial settlements—the disposition of the German colonies after World War I and of the Italian colonies after World War II. African issues at Paris in 1919 have been described by George Louis Beer in his *African Questions at the Paris Peace Conference.* A specialist on colonial problems, Beer was on the American delegation at Paris and was slated to head the mandates section of the League of

[4] Quoted by C. T. Brady, Jr., *Commerce and Conquest in East Africa*, Salem, 1950, p. 205.

Nations Secretariat if the United States had joined the League. At the peace conference, President Woodrow Wilson was adamant in his rejection of British, French, and South African demands for annexation of German colonies in Africa. In a final compromise, the powers concerned agreed to place the disputed territories under the mandates system while Wilson agreed to weaken the League controls he had originally envisaged.

For several years after World War II, the great powers argued over the disposition of the former Italian colonies in Africa. The Russians at one point asked for a trusteeship over Tripoli. Britain, conscious of its relative weakness among the Big Three and embarrassed by wartime promises that the colonies would never be restored to Italy, was interested in a settlement that would safeguard its lifeline to the Far East. France, hypersensitive and harassed by Indochinese uprisings, was inclined to support Italy's claims for return of its colonies; trusteeship over Italian Africa, the French feared, might serve as a precedent for trusteeship over Indochina. The Arab League, although focusing most of its energies on Palestine, demanded independence for Tripolitania and Cyrenaica. Eritrea and Italian Somaliland were formally claimed by Ethiopia. Amidst this confusion of claims and counterclaims, the United States was uncertain whether the colonies should be placed under an international trusteeship administered by the United Nations or under Italian administration supervised by the U.N. Trusteeship Council. When all negotiations proved fruitless, the Big Four finally agreed to turn the disposition of the problem over to the U.N. General Assembly. On November 21, 1949, the Assembly decided on independence for Libya, a 10-year trusteeship under Italian administration for Italian Somaliland, and the federation of Eritrea with Ethiopia.

These few historical highlights indicate that the development of trade with Africa was our predominant interest until late in the nineteenth century. Numerous American fortunes in New England and New York were built on the slave trade during the eighteenth century. On the eve of the Declaration of Independence in 1776, there were already half a million slaves in the 13 states. Thereafter, "legitimate" trade, such as the Salem trade with Zanzibar in cotton goods, expanded until the Civil War, when we had 25 American commercial agents resident in Africa. After Europe took over Africa in the last quarter of the nineteenth century, the expansion of American trade was curtailed for many decades.

SELF-DETERMINATION

Meanwhile, moral factors were also at work on American opinion. The corrupt and brutal traffic in African slaves was outlawed in 1808, and slavery itself was abolished in the 1860s. The work of missionary societies in Africa began to attract more interest, and the mistreatment of Africans in the Congo aroused American indignation after 1900. Woodrow Wilson's popularization of the principle of self-determination stimulated the idealism of many Americans, as did the Four Freedoms of Franklin D. Roosevelt and the Atlantic Charter of August, 1941.

The political factors which dominated our Africa policy after World War II had their origin in the late–nineteenth-century conquest of Europe by Africa. By 1919, when the first Pan-African Congress met in Paris, African protests against European rule were mounting and African leaders from several territories were petitioning the peacemakers for help. Wilson's clash with Clemenceau and Lloyd George over the disposition of the colonies taken from Germany is perhaps the first major example of the American dilemma in dealing with Europe over the colonial question in Africa.

Many Americans believe that the people of the United States have an "instinctive" urge for or a moral faith in the "right of self-determination." This view is so widely held that it merits testing against the record of our history. When this is done, one finds as much myth as reality, although the myth has acquired real force through Fourth of July orations, the schoolbook version of the American Revolution, and the periodic attacks on the British Empire in certain newspapers.

Jefferson's faith in the "consent of the governed," a forebear of the right of self-determination, was the basis of the ideology used to rationalize the American rebellion against England. When the Revolution ended, however, Americans tended to lose their interest in the eighteenth-century philosophy of the rights of man and to become more concerned over preserving the fruits of victory. As Carl Becker has pointed out in his book *The Declaration of Independence*, the nineteenth century in America and Europe was basically an antirevolutionary period in which emphasis was placed on the idea that the basis of democracy was the "power" rather than the "natural right" of the majority to rule. Many Americans came to regard the old Jeffersonian truths as fallacious. The eighteenth century belief that all men, when they form a social compact, are equal in rights was changed in several state constitutions in the South to read all *freemen*. The validity of self-determination as a right of all men was further beclouded when Southern whites were prevented from exercising it by the Civil War. At the end of the nineteenth century, moreover, we went on a small imperialist binge of our own. President McKinley's celebrated rationalization of why we took the Philippines equals the best of Rudyard Kipling.

Woodrow Wilson was able to rekindle enthusiasm for self-determination, but his views and actions had many critics. His conservative-minded Secretary of State Robert Lansing attacked it as a "phrase loaded with dynamite," which would raise hopes that could never be realized; "It will, I fear, cost thousands of lives. In the end it is bound to be discredited. What a calamity the phrase was ever uttered! What misery it will cause!"[5] Wilson himself later testified before a Senate committee that he did not believe the principle could be successfully applied to all territories throughout the world which were seeking full self-government and independence.

Although President Franklin D. Roosevelt and Secretary of State Cordell Hull are sometimes said to have been idealists unrestrained in their advocacy of self-determination, the fact is that on July 23, 1942, Hull said that "all peoples . . . *who are prepared, and willing* to accept the responsibility of liberty, are entitled to its enjoyment,"[6] and in 1948 he said that "our great nation should stand always for the *progressive* attainment of self-government and *eventual* independence by dependent peoples *when they are ready for it. . . .*"[7]

[5] Robert Lansing, *The Peace Negotiations*, Boston, 1921, p. 97.
[6] Cordell Hull, *Memoirs*, 2 vols., New York 1948. Vol. II, pp. 1484–1485, 1738. (My italics.)
[7] Cordell Hull, *op. cit.*, Vol. II, p. 1738. (My italics.)

THE AMERICAN DILEMMA OVER THE
COLONIAL QUESTION

By 1950, therefore, when the State Department began to develop an Africa policy, it had numerous precedents for placing qualifications on the principle of self-determination. Official spokesmen were careful to emphasize that self-determination was a "principle," not an unqualified "right," even in Article 1 of the U.N. Charter. Many observers continued to stress the "deep American faith" in the principle, an idea the government also publicized. By this time, however, our older economic and moral interests in Africa had been supplemented by new political and military interests. When the cold war with the Soviet bloc began to dominate American thinking, the dilemma of the United States over "the colonial question" emerged at once as the major preoccupation of American policy toward Africa. This dilemma was the conflict between our interest in supporting the principle of self-determination and our need for a strong NATO alliance. The essence of the problem was quite simple: we needed friends in both Europe and Africa, and whatever we did to please one group angered the other.

For this reason, all American policy statements from 1950 to 1958 contained certain paragraphs to placate Europeans and others to appeal to Africans. The basic principle of the policy was a qualified support for self-determination: "The United States supports the goal of self-government or independence for all peoples who have the desire and the capacity for it." The two qualifiers, *desire* and *capacity*, in one version or another, were seldom missing. The United States walked this tightrope until Europeans and Africans themselves resolved a large proportion of their quarrels over the timing of independence.

The dilemma is clear in the 1950 statement by Assistant Secretary McGhee, but the classic masterpiece of American ambiguity on the colonial question is found in our second major policy declaration made three years later by McGhee's successor, Henry A. Byroade. From a technical point of view the Byroade address of October 30, 1953, was so skillful a production that it has been commended by persons with diametrically opposing views of colonialism. If we strip away the excess verbiage in which the essence of the statement is obscured, however, we will find the following ten passages remaining, five of which tend to nullify the other five:

1. This movement toward self-determination is one of the most powerful forces in twentieth century affairs.
2. We ourselves believe that peace, prosperity, and human freedom can be assured only within a concert of free peoples . . . .
3. We hope that the peoples now seeking self-determination will achieve it . . . .
4. We recognize that the disintegration of the old colonialism is inevitable. We believe that much blood and treasure may be saved if the Western world determines firmly to hasten rather than hamper the process of orderly evolution towards self-determination.
5. The clock of history cannot be turned back. Alien rule over dependent peoples must be replaced as rapidly as possible by self-determination. Of this there can be no question.

And now the reverse:

1. It will be one of the great tragedies of our time if the peoples of Asia and Africa, just as they are emerging from generations of dependence, should be deluded by the fatal lure of the new [Soviet] imperialism and return thereby to an age of slavery infinitely more miserable than they have ever known before.
2. It is a hard, inescapable fact that premature independence can be dangerous, retrogressive and destructive.
3. Unless we are willing to recognize that there is such a thing as premature independence, we cannot think intelligently or constructively about the status of dependent peoples.
4. Premature independence for these peoples would not serve the interests of the United States nor the interests of the dependent peoples themselves.
5. . . . let us be frank in recognizing our stake in the strength and stability of certain European nations which are our allies. They share many common interests with us. They will probably represent, for many years to come, the major source of the free world defensive power outside our own. We cannot blindly disregard their side of the colonial question without regard to our own security.

The casual reader, of course, would find the contradictions in the Byroade statement less flagrant than they appear above, where they are deliberately stripped bare in order to dramatize the tortured efforts of the State Department to rationalize the dilemma. The dilemma was real enough, and our policy to meet it excusable. Nonetheless, the Byroade version of our Africa policy to some extent exposes the weakness of "government by committee compromises." As noted earlier, the widespread governmental process of policy making by committees is today under severe attack by many critics who contend that it stresses avoidance of risk rather than boldness of conception. From the double talk in the Byroade statement, one may deduce that it was drafted by an officer who knew, from long experience in the art of committee compromises, what had to be said in order to obtain the necessary clearance from officers with conflicting views. For the policy proposals emanating from the Department's African Bureau had to be cleared by other bureaus as well, notably that of European Affairs.

Despite this cautious hedging, the Byroade statement of 1953 does strike a note of its own which differs from that of either the Mc-Ghee statement of 1950 or a subsequent Africa policy declaration made by Assistant Secretary George V. Allen on April 21, 1956. The careful reader will note that the first five passages quoted above pay appropriate tribute to the principle of self-determination in rational but colorless prose. In the second five passages, however, the "dangers of premature independence" are heavily stressed in emotion-laden words which give the speech its tone—"fatal lure," "blindly disregard," "infinitely more miserable," "hard, inescapable fact," and "dangerous, retrogressive and destructive."

In a natural reaction against unthinking support of the abstract principle of self-determination, the pendulum of Department thinking had swung too far in the opposite direction toward an emotional attachment to another vague abstraction called "premature independence." The phrase "dangers of premature independence" does not appear in the McGhee policy of 1950, and in later declarations it withers away, making its farewell appearance in an address by Julius C. Holmes on May 29, 1958. It seems reasonable to conclude, therefore, that the Byroade statement of 1953 represents the high-water mark of the influence of the Bureau of European Affairs on Africa policy. By the time the British took the crucial, precedent-setting step of giving independence to Ghana on March 6, 1957, it was obvious to even the most conservative officials that the United States could not be more royalist than the Queen.

In the State Department our qualified support for self-determination was euphoniously termed a balanced or middle-of-the-road policy of constructive moderation. The public called it fence-sitting. There was truth in both descriptions. In any event, it was a frustrating policy which dissatisfied everybody—the American people, our friends in Africa and Asia, our European allies, and even the officials who formulated it. It was attacked as a "crisis" policy, a "crash" policy, "no policy at all," or in a more sophisticated version as a "policy to have no policy." Whether this middle-of-the-road posture can be called a *policy* is a semantic quarrel which can be left to others. The important point is that it was not something the State Department blundered into by accident, but a carefully weighed decision which was repeatedly examined from year to year and emerged unchanged for nearly a decade.

Those who blamed Western defense interests for the ambiguity of American policy were only partly right. The State Department was also inclined to caution because postwar colonial policies, particularly in Britain and France, were building the political, economic, and educational foundations needed for independence. The arguments tossed into the continuing debate over American policy contained numerous red herrings. The contention that we must attack colonialism in order to keep Africans and Asians from turning to the Soviet bloc was misleading because it ignored the economic and racial sources of friction which would still exist in a world of rich and poor states. Another non sequitur was the counterargument that independence in Africa would lead to chaos and Communist domination. The oft-heard view that we need not worry about the reaction of our Western allies because "they had no place to go" was wrong in its implication that the leader of a democratic coalition can hold its members even if it ignores their interests. The contention that we should have done what was "right" instead of trying to please friends was of little value to government officials who had to make decisions on fluid problems in which there was seldom a clear answer to what was right and what was wrong at any given moment. The widely used response that the United States should seek "respect" instead of popularity was equally inadequate because its exponents failed to produce convincing explanations of how we could be respected if we were unpopular.

The public sometimes blamed the fence-sitting of the United States on the conservatism of "striped-pants" Foreign Service officers who didn't know anything about Africa. It is worthy of note, therefore, that the State Department bureau which had the action responsibility for handling African issues in the U.N. did not fit this stereotype. Instead, it contained few career Foreign Service officers in the mid-1950s and many Ph.Ds who had been brought into the Department from the academic world when this new U.N. bureau was established. In the Office of Dependent Area Affairs which initiated the position papers on U.N. trusteeship and non–self-governing territories, six of the top officers had this kind of background. Although they differed from time to time on the proper tactics to employ and frequently looked for ways and means of squirming off the fence, they were unanimous in the basic conclusion that the needs of the United States in the mid-1950s required a "balanced" policy to meet conflicting interests. They were aware that this policy irritated everybody, but they could find no better policy available at the moment.

These officers no doubt acquired some of the conservative bias which seems inherent in all bureaucratic positions. Since I was one of them for a time, the passing of judgment on whether a better policy really was available had best be left to others who were not involved. Fortunately, the rapid march of Africans to independence brought this particular dilemma toward its end faster than was generally expected. The damage done to American prestige by our equivocation was great, but it was not as disastrous as often contended. African leaders were sometimes more sophisticated than American critics in their recognition of the conflicting interests and obligations of the United States. They knew the United States was at least "squirming," no matter how it voted in the United Nations. In the independent states of Africa in 1962, the United States still had a large reservoir of friendship despite its U.N. voting record on colonialism. If this friendship is lost, it will be because of what the United States does in the future, not what it did in the past.

In addition to qualified support for self-determination and a heavy emphasis on the dangers of premature independence in a world threatened by communism, several other main points emerge from the three policy declarations on Africa by Assistant Secretaries McGhee on May 8, 1950, Byroade on October 30, 1953, and Allen on April 21, 1956. These include (1) an appeal for an open door for American trade in Africa, a kind of hangover from the past which appears only in the 1950 McGhee statement; (2) an emphasis in all three declarations on the need to continue mutually beneficial economic and other relationships between Africa and Europe; (3) a cautious approach to racial problems in areas of white settlement—to quote Allen, "It behooves us, in view of our own experience, to approach the problem of race elsewhere in the world in all humility"; and (4) an occasional mention of our support for United Nations efforts to advance Africans.

It is worthy of note that McGhee and Byroade give the U.N. only limited attention and Allen does not even mention it. This seems puzzling, since it was U.S. voting on African issues in the U.N. that was causing the United States its biggest headaches. The explanation lies partly in the fact that the Department bureau headed successively by McGhee, Byroade, and Allen did not have the action responsibility for preparing positions on African issues in the United Nations; this was done in the offices dealing with United Nations affairs. It was not until 1958 that a United Nations adviser was assigned exclusively to the Africa office. Consequently most officers in it were rarely able to follow African issues in the United Nations closely enough to develop adequate knowledge of them.

THE EFFECT OF PUBLIC POLICY STATEMENTS

Since the conflicting interests of the United States made it impossible for the State Department to produce really effective declarations of policy at the height of the colonial era, certain critics have suggested that officials should have kept silent. "You don't have to explain something you haven't said," President Calvin Coolidge is reported to have replied when asked why he was so laconic. This was impractical in the 1950s, however, because participation in the United

Nations obligated the United States to take public positions on many African issues. This in turn aroused American and other critics to attack unsatisfactory positions, thereby prodding the Department to justify its conduct. Those who prepared the policy declarations might nonetheless have done better if a manual of do's and don't's for Africa speech writers had been available. This would have enabled them to avoid such unnecessary statements as a reference to African capitals as "hardship posts," which appeared in an official statement as late as January 27, 1958. It might also have made possible a more discriminating recognition of the fact that speeches to American audiences were read by Africans as well as Europeans.

Many of.the ideas and phrases which helped to win public support and congressional appropriations at home were likely to be unconvincing if not offensive in Africa, where the United States Information Agency gave them wide publicity. One example is the report to the President made by Vice-President Richard M. Nixon on his March, 1957, visit to eight African capitals. The mission was a timely move because it symbolized the friendship of the United States to the hundreds of thousands of cheering Africans who greeted Nixon. The Vice-President made several valuable policy recommendations, but the tone of his report occasionally bordered on the paternalism which characterized the colonial relationship. This undermined its effectiveness for African readers. The cliché "battle for men's minds," which Nixon repeated, may sound good to Americans, but Africans have minds of their own which they have no intention whatever of losing to either the United States or the Soviet Union.

The language in which the Vice-President described the Communist threat also made better reading in the United States than in Africa. While he acknowledged that Communist domination was not a present danger, he called Africa a "priority" target for Communists, who are "desperately" trying to win African support and are "without question putting their top men in the fields of diplomacy, intrigue and subversion into the African area."[8] To Africans these words seemed badly out of focus if not inaccurate. More important, the stress of the Communist threat tended to publicize the idea that

[8] *The New York Times*, April 7, 1957.

we were interested in Africa not for its own sake but because we were going all out to win the "battle for men's minds."

In fairness to Nixon and those who drafted his report, it should be repeated that this kind of language did help to bring the importance of Africa to the attention of a wider segment of the American public. While many observers criticize the government for justifying its aid programs in Africa on the grounds of military needs and the Communist threat, there is another way of looking at it. No doubt the United States ought to be helping Africa for sounder reasons, but the important fact is that we are doing it. Ironically, therefore, perhaps Africans should be grateful to the Soviet Union for scaring Americans into meeting their international responsibilities. In fact, if the world can muddle through without a third world war, the cold war may at least have had the advantage of forcing both great powers and other "have" nations to help the "have-nots" of Africa.

Public statements were more questionable when made in Africa by consuls about local conditions in the territories to which they were posted. Such remarks were always slanted, consciously or unconsciously, to meet the limited mental horizon of European colonials. The American consul general in Salisbury, for example, made a speech on November 30, 1955, in which he praised the establishment of the Federation of Rhodesia and Nyasaland as "a great act of statesmanship." Although the consul general prodded his white audience to move faster "to assure the continued cooperation of responsible African leaders in the times and trials that lie ahead," the local press naturally headlined his praise of the "great act of statesmanship." This hardly endeared the United States to those African readers, especially in Northern Rhodesia and Nyasaland, who had strongly opposed the Federation from the beginning and were still fighting it in 1962.

In a speech on the eve of his departure from Leopoldville in 1958, another American consul general came close to apologizing to a Belgian audience for American criticisms of colonialism. "Such criticisms are always made by private individuals . . . ," he said, but "I have not yet heard a single . . . official spokesman criticize what Belgium has accomplished in the Congo." The consul general's remarks were so pleasing to Belgians that they were printed in the January, 1959, issue of *Belgian Congo*, the monthly propaganda bulletin of the Belgian Congo and Ruanda-Urundi Information and Public Relations Office.

American policy toward Africa was hamstrung by indecision over the colonial question until late in the 1950s. In their obsession with their own dilemma, Americans tended to forget that the democratic governments of Europe were also confronted by a difficult choice. The direct responsibility for governing Africa was theirs, not ours. Believing in democratic values, they considered their new policy of gradual development toward self-government to be in the best interests of Africa and America as well as Europe. But they soon discovered that it could not be carried out without resorting to the undemocratic practice of suppressing African nationalists. When they were no longer willing or able to use force, they had to abandon the policy. That is why many new African states were able to emerge without violence in their fight for independence.

THE TIMETABLES ISSUE IN THE U.N.

Meanwhile, during these years of "qualified" American support for self-determination, a restless Republican maverick at the U.S. Mission to the United Nations in New York was attempting to get rid of the qualifiers. Mason Sears came to the world of diplomacy with a background in business and Massachusetts state politics, where he had been an adviser to Henry Cabot Lodge. On numerous occasions during his eight-year service as U.S. representative on the United Nations Trusteeship Council, his unconventional behavior made him a thorn in the conservative flesh of the State Department and a disturbing force to British, French, and Belgian officialdom.

One of the highlights of Mr. Sears's career as a diplomat was his important role in the heated United Nations dispute over the setting of timetables or target dates for colonial independence. This quarrel lost its fervor when African colonies began getting their independence faster than timetables could be set for them. For the five years between 1952 and 1957, however, it was a major issue which precipitated bitter arguments. Many U.N. discussions of it involved complicated procedural maneuvering, particularly on the part of the colonial powers as they sought to eliminate controversial clauses from General Assembly and Trusteeship Council resolutions to which they objected. The details of this bickering are not worth recounting, but the major aspects of the controversy will now be described at length for two reasons: they provide a fascinating case study of U.S. policy during the height of the controversy over the colonial question, and they foreshadow the transition to a new policy.

The timetables dispute first arose in 1952 when Haiti, India, Lebanon, the Philippines, and Yemen introduced Joint Resolution 558(VI) at the sixth session of the General Assembly in Paris. This resolution invited the administering authority of each trust territory to include in its annual report to the United Nations information on "the period of time in which it is expected that the Trust Territory shall attain the objective of self-government or independence." From the word "attain" in this resolution the issue came to be known in the United Nations as "the attainment question."

The Philippine representative who introduced the resolution suggested that in view of the 10-year time limit set for Somaliland trusteeship, a 10-year period would not be unreasonable for other territories. Several other anticolonial delegations gave it enthusiastic endorsement as a historic and constructive proposal. The efforts of the administering authorities to eliminate objectionable clauses were unsuccessful, and it was adopted on January 18, 1952, by a vote of 38 to 8 with 11 abstentions. The United States did not speak in the debate, and abstained in the vote. The essence of the colonial powers' opposition to the proposal was stated by the Belgian representative, former Congo Governor General Pierre Ryckmans:

> The possibility of fixing a time for the attainment of self-government had been fully explored during the preparation of the Trusteeship Agreements, and the inherent difficulties had led to the conclusion that it would be impossible. Some territories were likely to reach the ultimate objective earlier than others. Moreover, although certain goods could be clearly foreseen, there were economic factors which were wholly outside the Administering Authorities' control. It should be recognized that premature emancipation would not be of advantage to the peoples con-

cerned, while fixing of an over-distant date might, on the other hand
tend to retard rather than promote development.[9]

When the administering authorities failed to provide the requested
timetables in their next annual reports, the anticolonial group re
turned to the attack in a resolution adopted by the General Assem
bly on December 9, 1953, this time by a vote of 46 to 9 with 5 ab
stentions. It reaffirmed the earlier resolution and in addition brought
pressure on the Trusteeship Council by asking it to include in its
annual reports to the Assembly a separate section dealing with the
implementation of the two Assembly resolutions. The United States
again abstained, but its representative made an interesting declaration:

My government has carefully studied that request and would say in
reply that with the recent history of the Philippines and Puerto Rico
in mind, the period of time in which United States territories will attain
self-government or independence will depend as much on the desires of
the inhabitants themselves as on anything else. . . . The United States
is always guided by its traditional interest in encouraging and promoting
political freedom for all people in all parts of the world whenever conditions are such that their freedom will not be jeopardized by internal and
external pressures. At the moment, however, because of the widely differing stages of development in the various parts of the Trust Territory of
the Pacific Islands, no specific time can be forecast for the attainment of
the objective of self-government or independence for the territory as a
whole.[10]

In other words, no timetables for U.S. territories! This statement was
notable because of the history of the popular timetables idea in the
United States. Numerous Americans, recalling that in 1935 Congress
passed a law setting July 4, 1946, as a date for Philippine independence, had suggested that other administering authorities should do
likewise. President Roosevelt and his secretary of state, Cordell Hull,
supported the idea, although with enough qualifications to suggest
that in the climate of opinion of the early 1950s their position would
have been substantially the same as that of the Truman and Eisen-

[9] United Nations, General Assembly, *Official Records*, Seventh Session, 4th
Committee, 240th Meeting, January 9, 1952.
[10] Verbatim text of statement by Frances P. Bolton in the 4th Committee, 8th
Session of the United Nations General Assembly, December 1, 1953 (mimeo.).

hower Administrations. After the war, a number of popular books and articles endorsed the idea. And in the United Nations, the Philippine Delegation put the United States on the spot by repeatedly praising the American precedent in establishing a timetable for Philippine independence. As a result, certain liberal groups were urging the State Department to support the concept of timetables.

In Washington, however, the absolutely rigid opposition of the colonial powers made a strong impression. Their convictions were too strongly held to be overcome by reasoned arguments. Moreover, the decision to reject a timetable for its own trust territory—where the United States had important strategic base facilities—added another element to the American dilemma. Still anxious to avoid being stereotyped as a supporter of colonialism, however, the United States abstained on the Assembly's "attainment" resolutions in 1952, 1953, and 1954.

Meanwhile, a startling new development was in the making. The Trusteeship Council in 1954 appointed United States Representative Mason Sears as one of four members of its visiting mission to East Africa. Like the Council itself, visiting missions are equally balanced between nationals of administering and nonadministering countries, with the idea in mind of preventing the adoption of proposals which were unacceptable to one group or the other. The State Department was surprised, therefore, when Sears joined the two non-administering mission members to recommend that Belgium formulate a program for self-government for Ruanda-Urundi in 20 to 25 years and to express the belief that self-government was within the reach of Tanganyika much earlier. The fourth member, from New Zealand, who was also chairman of the mission, expressed strong disagreement with these views.

When the Trusteeship Council received the mission's report at its fifteenth session in 1955, the United States was in hot water. The press publicized the fact that the administering authorities concerned made strong representations in private to the State Department. They also denounced the mission's view publicly in the Council. Under this pressure the United States reconsidered the matter, and Mr. Sears had to tell the Council that his own view differed to some extent from that of his government, which would not support the timetable principle for Tanganyika and Ruanda-Urundi although it recognized the merit of target dates for self-government in cases where the territory concerned was close to attainment of that status. Many an eyebrow was naturally raised at this statement, which appeared to be a State Department reversal of its representative. However, visiting mission members were appointed by and legally responsible only to the Trusteeship Council, not their governments. This made it theoretically justifiable, though not very practical, for Sears to say different things in his two capacities as mission member and U.S. representative in the Trusteeship Council. At any rate, after an acrimonious debate, the evenly divided Trusteeship Council failed to adopt any resolution on the attainment question at its fifteenth session.

INTERMEDIATE TARGET DATES

A new stage in the quarrel began a year later at the seventeenth session of the Trusteeship Council, when the United States supported a controversial and widely misunderstood proposal for the establishment of target dates for the achievement of intermediate goals in the field of political as well as economic, social, and educational advancement. The General Assembly had meanwhile adopted by a vote of 43 to 11 with 9 abstentions another timetables resolution which expressed regret at the Trusteeship Council's inaction. In this Assembly vote the United States had been more negative, departing from its previous abstentions and voting against an Assembly resolution on the attainment question. When the Trusteeship Council resumed discussion of the problem early in 1956, the atmosphere was strained, and one of the worst wrangles in the Council's history occurred. The end product was an obscurely worded resolution to meet the Assembly's request for a separate section on the attainment question in the Council's annual report.

Certain of the administering authorities were relatively satisfied with this resolution because they believed it might bury the issue for the time being. They were therefore dismayed to hear United States Deputy Representative Benjamin Gerig, in explaining his position after the vote was already taken, interject another controversial idea into the discussion. He said:

We favor, whenever we think it helpful, the establishment of target dates for the achievement of intermediate goals, not only in the field of economic, social and educational advancement, but for political advancement as well. . . . A series of targets to which successive political, economic and social development plans and programs can be aimed will, we believe, tend to induce an atmosphere of understanding and confidence in which the territories involved will be able to move more rapidly and harmoniously ahead.[11]

He went on to say that "specific long-range target dates for independence are generally too rigid and usually will achieve little that cannot be achieved by the imposition of short-range intermediate target dates." And in concluding his statement, he referred to recent declarations by the Indian Delegation in favor of intermediate target dates as "some evidence that the position of the Indian and United States Delegations on the application of a timetable for the achievement of self-government, at least in the field of intermediate target dates, is drawing closer."

Despite the careful distinction drawn by the United States between final time limits for independence and intermediate target dates for specific political advances, the United States position was widely misinterpreted both at home and overseas as a reversal of the position adopted a year earlier. There was a considerable outcry in the Belgian press; and in the United States, the *New York Herald-Tribune* reported that the United States had decided to favor long-range timetables for independence, a distortion which it subsequently corrected at the request of the United States Delegation.

When the intermediate target dates formula began to be applied to specific territories by the Council about two weeks after the U.S. statement, a bitter debate ensued. Attempting to placate the British, Mr. Gerig praised British policy, and said that he doubted "if any of us sitting around this table are in a position to offer much advice to the United Kingdom on the subject of developing free and stable governmental institutions. . . . In fact," he added, "we are sometimes quite amazed at the advice which we hear so freely prof-

[11] U.S. Mission to the United Nations, *Statement by Mr. Benjamin Gerig, Deputy States Representative to the Trusteeship Council, on the Use of Target Dates and Timetables*, Press Release No. 2369, New York, March 16, 1956.

fered. . . ."[12] Explaining what the United States meant by favoring intermediate targets for political advancement in Tanganyika, he mentioned such examples as the setting in advance of dates for widening the suffrage, for granting additional powers to legislative and executive bodies, and for the building of representative institutions.

The British response was immediate and angry. Sir Alan Burns, the United Kingdom representative, said that he found it "hard to understand the motives of those delegations which seek to provoke a head-on clash with the administering authority." Timed political development was "unthinkable" because it would have to be "absolute guesswork" and "there could be no physical or factual basis" on which it could be calculated.[13] Other administering authorities were equally obdurate. Having already committed itself, however, the United States went on to vote with the nonadministering members for recommendations to the administering authorities of several territories to "indicate such successive intermediate targets and dates in the political, economic, social and education fields as will create conditions for the attainment of self-government or independence." The recommendations were approved by 8 votes to 5, with Italy abstaining. Italy's voting position was influenced by the U.S. stand and by the fact that its trust territory of Somalia already had a 10-year timetable for independence. The impact of these votes in which the United States broke with the other administering authorities on matters they considered of great importance was quite impressive. To the anticolonial group it appeared that the United States had moved away from the negative position which in 1949, for example, had resulted in many tie votes in the Trusteeship Council in a dispute involving the trust territory of French Togoland.

The sequel to this episode came at the next session of the General Assembly, in 1957, when the Soviet Union succeeded in exploiting the issue by getting the General Assembly to adopt a Soviet resolution on colonialism for the first time in 11 years. In its original form,

[12] U.S. Mission to the United Nations, *Explanation of Vote . . . on Intermediate Targets . . . in Tanganyika*, Press Release No. 2383, New York, April 2, 1956.

[13] United Nations Trusteeship Council, *Official Records*, 17th Sess., 697th Meeting, April 2, 1956, p. 338.

this Soviet proposal called for steps to be taken to proclaim African trust territories and New Guinea independent within three to five years. In contrast to its usual rigidity, however, the Soviet Delegation indicated its willingness to modify its proposals if there were disagreement on the period of time proposed. As it turned out, the resolution was so drastically altered by amendments that the Italian representative remarked that the Soviet representative could not vote for the revised draft without contradicting himself unless he withdrew his introductory statements. In its final form, the resolution was similar to others already adopted by the Assembly, and it was approved by a vote of 45 to 14 with 16 abstentions, the United States voting against it.

The Soviet Union thereby scored something of a propaganda victory over the United States. The United States might have forestalled the Soviet success by following up on its own initiative and introducing a more moderate resolution along the lines of its intermediate target dates formula. The failure to do so cost it much of the advantage it gained by supporting intermediate target dates in the Trusteeship Council. It would be difficult to maintain, however, that the Soviet Union gained more than a temporary advantage from its maneuver.

From this case history, moreover, it is evident that the United States was in such difficulties with its European allies after its proposal in the Trusteeship Council that it could not have taken the initiative in the General Assembly without antagonizing them even further. The surprised and angry reaction of the administering authorities suggests that their irritation was magnified because the United States had not informed them of its intentions before it introduced the target dates idea.

THE REAL ISSUES

Before passing judgment on United States behavior, one must clarify what the real issues were. First of all, there was never any suggestion that the United Nations itself should usurp the functions of the administering authority by setting the timetables or target dates.

Not even the Soviet Union would suggest this. The nonadministering members wanted the colonial powers to set the dates so that the U.N. could criticize them, not the reverse.

Second, the U.N. proposals were only recommendations, which means that the administering authorities could have informed the Trusteeship Council that, after considering the recommendations, they found them impractical for their territories. In that event, the General Assembly would presumably have repeated the recommendations, and the colonial powers could have stuck to their refusals. It would have made little difference to Africans because the pace of their political advance was already so rapid.

In the third place, it is essential to appreciate the difference between the setting of final time limits for independence and the setting of intermediate target dates for political advance. In their attacks on both proposals the administering authorities deliberately tried to obscure this difference by implying that they were one and the same thing.

Finally, it is imperative to distinguish between intermediate target dates as a problem in African administration and as an issue in U.N. politics. For some time, the administering authorities had already been setting intermediate target dates in the economic, social, and educational fields, with numerous successes. Moreover, although it is less well known, the British had themselves used intermediate target dates for political advancement. More than 30 years ago a distinguished governor of the Gold Coast, for example, set a specific target date to increase by a certain percent the number of Africans in senior posts in the administration. More recently, the governor of Uganda in a statement to his Legislative Council on April 24, 1956, set a five-year target date for introduction of direct elections on a common roll. He said:

> The Uganda Government's aim is that, if there is a general desire for them throughout the country, direct elections of representative members of the Legislative Council on a common roll should be introduced in 1961, provided that arrangements for doing so can be recommended which are acceptable to the United Kingdom Government.

Moreover, the governor himself drew a clear distinction between final time limits and intermediate target dates by adding that "if di-

ect elections on a common roll are introduced in 1961, this will be
a positive step towards self-government, but 1961 has in no sense
been accepted a target date for self-government." The British representative who told the Trusteeship Council that timed political
development was "unthinkable" is therefore belied by the policy of
his own government. The contention of the administering authorities
that final time limits and intermediate target dates are the same
thing is therefore obviously unacceptable. This does not mean that
intermediate political targets were necessarily a good practice in African administration, a point that can be argued either way, and perhaps depends on the particular circumstances in each case.

It may be concluded, therefore, that the major reason the administering authorities opposed intermediate political targets was not so
much that they were inherently bad but because it was the U.N.
which was proposing them. The colonial powers were reacting in
accordance with their basic principle that the U.N. had become a
"necessary evil" and that any extension of its activities must be re-
sisted as a slippery slope to something worse. This point was made by
the British representative, in fact, when he said to the Trusteeship
Council that the setting of successive targets and dates in the political
field would be used to apply direct pressure on the administering authority from the moment such targets and dates were set. And there
can be no doubt that this was indeed one of the reasons the anticolonials found the intermediate targets formula attractive. Again,
however, the point was more valid in theory than in practice, because
the trust territories concerned were getting independence too fast for
target dates.

EVALUATION OF U.S. TACTICS

What can be concluded about United States tactics on this issue?
At the outset it seems clear that the basic objective of the maneuver
was not to help African political advancement but to improve the
U.S. image in the eyes of the anticolonials. This seems evident from
the aforementioned policy declarations, which indicate that the Department was worried over the possibility that Africa was moving
toward independence too fast for political and economic stability.

Gerig had attempted to justify his proposal with the argument that intermediate target dates would "induce an atmosphere of understanding and confidence in which the territories involved would be able to move more rapidly and harmoniously ahead," and would "give a sense of purpose and direction to peoples who are on the way to the final goal." But this was largely the rationalization of and not the reason for the U.S. position.

American officials were worried about the growing stereotype of the United States as a supporter of colonialism, and were looking for ways and means to change this image. While the U.S. voting position had frequently differed from that of the other administering authorities, it had previously voted with them on nearly all the really controversial issues. Their rigid refusal to make any concessions to the view of the majority of U.N. members on the attainment question had placed the United States in an extremely frustrating position. The intermediate target dates formula was therefore appealing as one positive step the United States might take without doing real injury to the vital interests of its closest allies. In addition, the adoption of the moderate formula for intermediate target dates might have improved the position of the United States and the other administering authorities in the General Assembly by forestalling a more extreme resolution, at least for the time being.

A further irony is the fact that the United States had not in the past applied the intermediate target dates principle in its own territories. U.S. territorial administrators did not consider it practical, although they later presented a few inconsequential intermediate target dates to the U.N. An amusing aftermath of the affair was the jocular wish of British officials that they had accepted the U.N. request to set a final time limit for Tanganyika's independence so they could have held on to Tanganyika longer!

Although Benjamin Gerig was the initial spokesman for the United States on the intermediate target dates proposal, Mason Sears was its strongest advocate. His indefatigable efforts undoubtedly helped to modify the African image of the United States as a supporter of European colonialism. In this respect he was a valuable forerunner of new Africa policy trends which emerged in 1958.

18

Africa Policy Since 1958

THE year 1958 marks a turning point in Africa's international relations and a consequent shift in American policy toward Africa. The independence of Morocco, Tunisia, and the Sudan in 1956 and of Ghana in 1957 made possible a dramatic series of precedent-setting international conferences held *in* Africa *by* Africans in 1958. For the first time, Africans from eight independent states and many colonies were able to assemble together in different regions of their own continent to observe and discuss each other's problems on the spot, instead of relying on student meetings in faraway London or Paris. Before the year ended, Guinea joined the independent states.

Bringing many hundreds of African political, labor, educational, and other leaders together, these jubilant international meetings included the *first* Afro-Asian Peoples Solidarity Conference which ended in Cairo on January 1, 1958; the *first* Conference of Independent African States in Accra in mid-April; the *first* Conference of North African Political Parties in Tangier at the end of April; the *first* Pan-African Students Conference at Makerere College in Uganda at the beginning of July; the *first* Conference of the Confederation of North African Students in Tunis in August; the *first* meeting of the Pan-African Freedom Movement for East and Central Africa in Tanganyika in September; and the *first* All-African Peoples Conference in Accra in December. Also in 1958 the important U.N. Eco nomic Commission for Africa began to operate from its headquarter in Ethiopia, and the CCTA moved from London to Lagos.

In what way do these African conferences symbolize a turning point in Africa? The answer lies not only in their numbers or in the batteries of anticolonial resolutions they adopted; more important is the fact that all of them established permanent bureaus or secre tariats to carry on the fight for their goals. The exchange of ideas and emotions through new contacts was an invigorating and fortifying experience. The conferences no doubt helped to stimulate African na tionalists from the Rhodesias, Nyasaland, the Congo, Angola, and perhaps South Africa to plan the events which sparked violence in these areas in 1959, 1960, and 1961. A new force in African history thus made its appearance—the power of Africans to speak for them selves in world councils rather than having to rely on outsiders to speak for them.

The impact of the events of 1958 stimulated both the Soviet Union and the United States to accelerate their diplomatic, economic, and propaganda offensives in Africa. By October, 1958, the State Depart ment's declarations of Africa policy were presented in a tone quite different from that of the previous five years.

THE TRANSITION

Like most transitions, this shift in policy was gradual. It was fore shadowed by the notable improvement in the Africa policy machine in September, 1956, when the separate Africa unit described in Chap ter 16 began to operate. For two years, however, the new unit had to mark time under an interim regime while awaiting congressional au thorization for the appointment of an Assistant Secretary of State for African Affairs—the main stumbling block being certain Southern members of the House Committee on Foreign Affairs. The delay in the House was regrettable because a forward-looking leader, equipped with the full prestige and authority of the new post, was much needed.

The two career officers who headed the Africa unit during this interim regime from mid-1956 to mid-1958 were Deputy Assistant Secretary of State Joseph Palmer, II, and Julius C. Holmes, who was given the title of Special Assistant to the Secretary of State. Palmer effectively organized and improved the operations of his office. On the substance of policy, however, his statement of October 16, 1957, adhered too closely to the "dangers of premature independence" line in the 1953 Byroade address quoted in the last chapter. Since Ghana had already been independent for seven months, with others soon to follow, it was clearly time for a new tone. Yet Palmer warned that "in the long run premature independence may contain as many dangers for Africa and Africans as the denial of the status." He repeated the oft-quoted November 18, 1953, statement by Secretary of State John Foster Dulles that "there is no slightest wavering in our conviction that the orderly transition from colonial to self-governing status should be carried resolutely to a completion," but he added that it is "a matter of the greatest importance that the word 'orderly' be emphasized in this connection." Only in a politically stable Africa, he said, "will responsible, moderate, and positive elements emerge—in contrast to the extremist, disruptive, and negative nationalism which poses such dangers for us all."

It was not until mid-1958 that Department policy declarations began to acknowledge the imminent end of the colonial era. After a two-and-a-half-month trip through Africa to groom himself for the post of assistant secretary of state, Julius C. Holmes returned to Washington in January. Palmer went to Salisbury as consul general, and Holmes assumed command. On January 27, 1958, in the first of three addresses during a short tenure of six months, Holmes clung to "the dangers of premature independence" thesis. However, in two addresses he made in May, shortly after the first Conference of Independent African States in Accra, the first glimmering of a more relaxed American attitude appears. Speaking at an American Assembly meeting on the United States and Africa on May 1, 1958, Holmes affirmed that while there were a few resolutions at Accra "which might have been wiser and more constructive had they been somewhat less unrestrained," the United States was nevertheless in the "happy position of finding itself in broad agreement—or at least broad understanding—with much of what emerged." We may "confidently anticipate," he added, that the political, economic, and social systems developed "in time" by Africans to express their "distinctive African personality" would "preserve the essentials of democracy and the universal concept of the dignity of man." This was indeed a new tone. The bond with the past was still so strong, however, that Holmes felt it necessary to warn again of the dangers of premature independence and of "territories rushing pell mell toward local autonomy and eventual self-determination." In his swan song four weeks later in New Orleans on May 29, Holmes moved a step further away from the old policy. Aside from a final warning on the dangers and "pitfalls" of premature independence, he concentrated on the constructive work of the United Nations, and on multilateral and bilateral aid to develop Africa. In July, 1958, the post of assistant secretary of state for African affairs was finally authorized by Congress, but Holmes unexpectedly disappeared from the African scene, reportedly because of opposition expected from certain senators if he were named to the new post.

The Foreign Service officer who was suddenly appointed was Joseph C. Satterthwaite. Like his predecessors, he was a man of cautious disposition, but his advent nonetheless marked the start of a new period in American policy making for Africa, at least as far as public declarations of policy are concerned. Satterthwaite's first policy statement, made at Lake Arrowhead, California, on October 9, 1958, sounded quite different from earlier declarations. For the first time the shop-worn admonition against the "dangers of premature independence" disappeared. No mention was made of the need of the United States to support its NATO allies. Instead of the old negativism, Satterthwaite was quite affirmative, stressing the constructive role of the United Nations and the notable expansion of American aid to Africa. These and other themes of his October, 1958, policy statement were developed in further declarations during his 30 months in office. Considering them as a whole, along with statements by President Eisenhower and other top officials, one notes the emergence of four new trends in policy, all of which were relatively well outlined before the Kennedy administration assumed power in January, 1961.

FOUR NEW POLICY TRENDS

The first trend was the more sympathetic official position toward independence in Africa. Not only were the "dangers of premature independence" dropped, but even the two traditional qualifiers on the right of self-determination became more innocuous. Although Secretary Dulles retained them in a Cleveland address on November 18, 1958, his tone was much warmer: "The United States supports political independence for all peoples who *desire* it and are *able* to undertake its responsibilities. We have encouraged and we *rejoice* at the current evolution."[1] By April 8, 1960, Assistant Secretary Satterthwaite was able to make a statement that would not have been cleared five years earlier: "As to their 'readiness' I believe history has shown that this is almost an academic question. Peoples tend to acquire independence, ready or not, according to a timetable of their own making." Six months later, on October 24, in addition to dropping the qualifiers entirely, he said that "we welcome every step taken by the governing metropoles to promote both a readiness for and a realization of self-government."

The new posture, of course, did not mean that the Department of State was no longer worried about political instability. It only meant that many officers had belatedly recognized that in an Africa soon to be composed of independent states it was not in the United States's interest to continue harping on the dangers of premature independence. The later chaos in the Congo has often been interpreted as a vindication of those who argued against "premature independence." This is only part of the truth, however. The collapse of order in the Congo was a unique situation precipitated by (1) the unexpected mutiny of the Force Publique, (2) the consequent departure of skilled Belgian technicians and administrators, and (3) the earlier failure of the Belgians, despite more than a decade of warnings in the United Nations, to follow the British and French practice of developing a sizable corps of leaders with higher education and political experience to whom power could be transferred. In new states where these factors were absent, the transition to independence was orderly.

[1] My italics.

The second important change was the new emphasis on economic aid to Africa. The meagerness of American help in earlier years re sulted partly from the fact that the European powers were loath to accept any significant amount of foreign assistance in preparing col onies for self-government and partly from the fact that American aid officials preferred to focus attention primarily on the few independent countries. The birth of new states drastically altered this situation Many of their leaders, eager for aid and for less economic dependence on their former rulers, now looked to the United States.

Meanwhile, the valuable spade work of many national voluntary organizations had alerted a wider sector of the public to the fact that foreign aid was not just a temporary postwar device for the recon struction of Europe but was a continuing necessity for strengthening new states. This made it easier for congressmen to approve larger appropriations for the Africa program of the aid agency, the expendi tures of which rose from $13,000,000 in the fiscal year 1956 to $73,000,000 in fiscal 1958, $139,000,000 in fiscal 1960, and $204,700,000 in fiscal 1961. At the same time, the United States was contributing the largest share of financial support to the expanding Africa pro grams of the United Nations and its specialized agencies.

A third alteration of the substance of Africa policy by 1960 was the abandonment of the earlier inclination to regard neutralism as "immoral." Although this attitude was initially directed toward Asia rather than Africa, it was partially reflected in two of the Holmes statements of 1958 in which "neutralist uncertainty" was almost equated with "Communist enslavement" as threats which must be combated. By the end of 1958, however, criticism of neutralism or positive nonalignment in Africa largely disappeared, indicating that the Department felt obliged to respect the strong attachment of Africans for their independent posture in international relations. This is particularly evident in the spirit of the notable proposal made by President Eisenhower in a personal appearance before the General Assembly on September 22, 1960. He asked that all United Nations members pledge "to respect the African peoples' right to choose their own way of life and to determine for themselves the course they choose to follow," and that they "refrain from intervening in these new nations' internal affairs . . . by subversion, force, propaganda, or any other means." In the new attitude there was even a growing appreciation that neutralism was at least a partial asset in the worldwide struggle against communism.

At the same time, however, the Republican Administration proved highly sensitive about neutralists whom it judged anti-Western in orientation. The most open demonstration of this occurred after President Nkrumah's address to the General Assembly on September 23, 1960. Nkrumah's deep anticolonialism had prompted him to denounce Western policy in the Congo as "imperialist intrigue stark and naked," a "policy of divide and rule," a "desperate attempt to create confusion," and a "concealed intention" of setting up "clientele-sovereignty, or fake independence" in the Congo.[2] When questioned about these remarks at a press conference the same day, Secretary of State Christian Herter responded that Nkrumah had "marked himself as very definitely leaning toward the Soviet bloc." Nkrumah promptly expressed surprise, saying that "Mr. Herter was, in fact, the last person from whom I would expect such a remark."[3] The incident indicated that the Eisenhower Administration's tolerance of African neutralism was not unlimited.

Finally, the government gradually developed a more affirmative attitude toward the expansion of the role of the United Nations in Africa. When Africa was largely colonial, the United States frequently supported the administering powers in resisting efforts to expand certain United Nations activities in Africa. This position was based to a large extent on the argument that the European powers might boycott the U.N.'s colonial machinery if they felt themselves pushed to unreasonable lengths. The early lack of interest in developing the U.N.'s potentialities was also reflected in the fact that the U.N. was not even mentioned in Vice-President Nixon's policy recommendations to the President after his March, 1957, trip to eight African capitals.

A major change in this attitude became necessary when so many African states entered the United Nations. The new interest in the U.N. was evident in Satterthwaite's declarations, and was even

[2] Kwame Nkrumah, *I Speak of Freedom: A Statement of African Ideology,* New York, 1961, pp. 263–265 (complete text of Nkrumah's address of September 23, 1960, on pp. 262–280).
[3] *The New York Times,* September 24, 1961.

better demonstrated by a statement made on March 25, 1960, by Francis O. Wilcox, Assistant Secretary of State for International Organization Affairs, who had visited Africa in January and February. Wilcox pointed out that nearly one-third of the 123 resolutions adopted at the fourteenth General Assembly in 1959 dealt specifically with African affairs, and that African states would soon be the largest single regional group in the U.N. "There is great opportunity within the framework of the United Nations," he declared, "for cooperative efforts between ourselves and the African states to advance our mutual interests." After describing both U.S. and U.N. contributions to Africa, he expressed the belief that American efforts "can be complemented in an important way by an expansion of United Nations activities in Africa."

NEW ATTITUDE TOWARD AFRICAN ISSUES IN THE U.N.

In U.N. voting on South African issues, the United States had already become more affirmative, swinging to yes votes on General Assembly resolutions criticizing *apartheid* on January 30, 1957, and October 30, 1958. In the latter resolution, adopted 70 to 5 with 4 abstentions, regret and concern were expressed that South Africa had not yet responded to the Assembly's appeal that it reconsider policies which impaired the ability of all racial groups to enjoy the same rights and fundamental freedoms.

In April, 1960, when South African issues were first brought to the Security Council, the United States went much further. It joined in a 9 to 0 vote, on which France and the United Kingdom abstained, for a resolution deploring *apartheid* and the Sharpeville shooting, calling upon the Union to abandon such policies and requesting the Secretary General, in consultation with the South African government, "to make such arrangements as would adequately help in upholding the purposes and principles of the Charter and to report to the Security Council when appropriate." In supporting the resolution, U.S. Representative Henry Cabot Lodge declared:

We deeply deplore the loss of life which has taken place in South Africa. . . . It is clear that the source of the conflict from which the recent tragic events have flowed is the policy of *apartheid*. . . . We appeal once again to the Government of the Union of South Africa that it reconsider policies which prevent people of certain races from enjoying their God-given rights and freedoms.[4]

The U.S. vote was hailed in many circles as an important shift in American policy.

A high point in the new attitude toward the United Nations came in the September 22, 1960, statement of President Eisenhower to the General Assembly proposing a five-point program of United Nations activities in Africa, including a promising plan for aid to African education through the family of U.N. organizations. This was followed at the eleventh General Conference of UNESCO in December, 1960, by a special pledge of $1,000,000 from the United States as an extra contribution to an enlarged UNESCO program for African education.

The new interest in the United Nations recalls to mind the early postwar years when support for the U.N. was sometimes said to be the cornerstone of our foreign policy. Point One of the 1949 Truman inaugural address which gave birth to the Point Four program is usually forgotten. In it, he had pledged "unfaltering support to the United Nations." During much of the 1950s, however, both the Truman and Eisenhower Administrations seemed to lack real confidence in the U.N. In 1960, somewhat ironically, the United States seemed to be returning to the United Nations, not because of greater confidence in it but because we couldn't find a better way to deal with the new situation in Africa.

From the foregoing analysis it is clear that significant shifts in American policy which are sometimes attributed to the Kennedy Administration were actually under way before Eisenhower left office. The revolutionary change in Africa rather than the advent of President Kennedy was the basic cause of the modification of American policy.

THE "NEW FRONTIER" LOOK IN AFRICA

One must pay full tribute, however, to the admirable image of youthful vigor and progress conveyed by President Kennedy and his

[4] *The New York Times*, April 2, 1960.

advisers, a valuable asset in Africa where the American image was tarnished. The change of administration provided an opportunity for renegotiation, for new faces, and for additional steps to attune ourselves to the dynamism of the African revolution. Untainted by equivocation on colonialism, the enterprising Kennedy-Rusk-Williams team was able to make an auspicious beginning in giving American policy toward Africa a "New Frontier" look. A Nixon-Herter-Satterthwaite team could not have done this.

The tone of the New Frontier was clear in the warmth of the President's remarks to African ambassadors at a reception in the State Department on African Freedom Day, April 15, 1961:

> We also are a revolutionary country, and a revolutionary people, and therefore though many thousands of miles of space may separate our continent from the continent of Africa, today we feel extremely close.
>
> I think that the preoccupation of the United States with the cause of freedom not only here but around the world has been one of the most important facets of our national life. All of our early revolutionary leaders I think echoed the words of Thomas Jefferson that "the disease of liberty is catching." And some of you may remember the exchange between Benjamin Franklin and Thomas Paine. Benjamin Franklin said, "Where freedom lives, there is my home." And Thomas Paine said, "Where freedom is not, there is my home." I think all of us who believe in freedom feel a sense of community with all those who are free, but I think we also feel an even stronger sense of community with those who are not free but who some day will be free. . . .[5]

This presidential tribute was a striking departure from the practice of the previous administration, which had felt unable to risk European irritation by celebrating African Freedom Day.

President Kennedy's interest in Africa was already well known. In the Senate he had been chairman of the Subcommittee on Africa of the Foreign Relations Committee in 1959–1960, although it should be added that his Committee met only three times in 1959 and not at all in the election year 1960. In earlier speeches he had made clear his deep antipathy for colonialism. In 1957 he angered the French and aroused the enthusiasm of the rebel FLN by a strong plea for Algerian self-determination. On June 2, 1956, he made a

[5] Office of the White House Press Secretary, *Remarks of the President at the African Freedom Day Reception*, April 15, 1961.

striking statement at Rockhurst College in Kansas City, Missouri. In this speech, which was inserted in the *Congressional Record* on June 6, Senator Kennedy called for a policy in which "we shall no longer abstain in the United Nations from voting on colonial issues—we shall no longer trade our votes on such issues for other supposed gains—we shall no longer seek to prevent the subjugated peoples of the world from being heard." And in a ringing peroration, he declared,

. . . we can never escape the fact that we are dependent on the decisions of people who have hated, as their ancestors before them for centuries hated, the white men who bled them, beat them, exploited them, and ruled them. Perhaps it is already too late for the United States to repudiate these centuries of ill will. . . . But we dare not fail to make the effort.

Presumably Kennedy as President would not feel able to use the language he did as a Senator, nor were his remarks a valid description of the attitude of all Africans toward whites. His emotional statement nonetheless seems quite apt when one thinks of impassioned African leaders like Patrice Lumumba. In the Congo Parliament on the jubilant occasion of Independence Day, June 30, 1960, after hearing King Baudouin speak and President Kasavubu thank him, Lumumba jolted his listeners with a vehement comment that seemed to confirm Kennedy's 1956 view:

We are no longer your monkeys. We have known ironies, insults and blows which we had to undergo morning, noon and night because we were Negroes. . . . Who will forget the rifle fire from which so many of our brothers perished, or the jails into which were brutally thrown those who did not wish to submit to a regime of injustice, suppression, and exploitation?[6]

Lumumba's strong feelings were echoed by President Nkrumah of Ghana when he told the U.N. General Assembly on September 23, 1960, that Africa's sons "languished in the chains of slavery and humiliation" while her exploiters "strode across our continent with incredible inhumanity without mercy, without shame, and without honor."[7]

[6] Pierre de Vos, *Vie et mort de Lumumba,* Paris, 1961, pp. 195–196.
[7] Kwame Nkrumah, *op. cit.,* p. 263.

When he took office President Kennedy further demonstrated his concern for Africa by frequent talks with African leaders. On more than one occasion when an African chief of state rose to leave after the usual short meeting, the President asked him to stay for another half hour or more. In such frank talks the President often explained his own problems in dealing with Congress on aid to Europe and Latin America as well as Africa, or in dealing with Portugal on the Azores base. Sir Abubakar, the Federal Prime Minister of Nigeria, was particularly impressed by the amount of time the President devoted to him, as well as by the President's knowledge of Africa.

When President-Elect Kennedy began to select his advisers, the public was fascinated to find him putting the cart before the horse. He appointed Governor G. Mennen ("Soapy") Williams Assistant Secretary of State for African Affairs even before he designated Dean Rusk Secretary of State. The Williams appointment indicated that the President considered African problems second to none in importance. He chose a man of stature, already baptized in the fire of Michigan politics on political, racial and social issues—a man with direct access to the President and a seasoned politician and administrator who was more than a match for the Assistant Secretaries for Europe and other areas in the State Department. Governor Williams also had the kind of warm and outgoing personality the administration needed for its dealings with the young leaders of Africa. The Williams philosophy of personal diplomacy is set forth in a volume which he published in 1961 after twelve years in a governor's office:

. . . people are people and there is no substitute for genuine personal contact. There is no finer response than the smile on the face and the light in the eye of a person with whom you are shaking hands.[8]

The genial and unorthodox shirt-sleeve diplomacy of the intelligent and colorful former Governor of Michigan raised the eyebrows of numerous tradition-minded career officers, but it won many African friends for the United States. During his first year in office, Williams and his wife made three trips through Africa, and he delivered twice as many public speeches in the United States as all his predecessors combined during a whole decade. Thirty-six of his addresses in 1961

[8] G. Mennen Williams, A Governor's Notes, Ann Arbor, 1961, p. 6.

were made available as Department of State press releases. At the same time he was busily engaged in reorganizing and strengthening the personnel of the Bureau of African Affairs, and in private efforts to win congressional support. Another unprecedented step was his decision to bring a New Frontiersman, J. Wayne Fredericks, into the Bureau of African Affairs as Deputy Assistant Secretary of State to ensure coherence and continuity in the implementation of a new Africa policy. Under Williams's direction, the Africa Bureau also adopted a more relaxed attitude about receiving African visitors. In earlier years, for example, it had been the policy of government officials not to see rebel leaders from the Algerian FLN. The Williams team received FLN leaders in the State Department and arranged for them to meet American officials in Tunisia. The President and the Governor also spent much time and effort in recruiting higher calibre American officials for our key diplomatic posts in Africa. Because of the inherent limits of foreign policy, the manner in which diplomats operate is all the more important. Convinced that many of the older tradition-minded Foreign Service officers were unsuitable for African posts, Kennedy and Williams searched for men who had some of their own qualities of vigorous personality and flexible leadership. They also demonstrated an acute and thoughtful awareness of the significance of the younger generation of Africans who will sooner or later take over from the leaders who won independence.

Although the admission of 16 newly independent African states to the United Nations in the year before President Kennedy's inaugural took the edge off his advocacy of self-determination, officials of the new Administration were nonetheless vigorous in calling for political change in the remaining colonial areas and South Africa. A vivid example of this was the celebrated contretemps in which Williams became involved in Kenya where the white press attacked him for allegedly advocating "Africa for the Africans." When a group of Conservatives in the British Parliament asked their government to make an official protest to the United States about Williams's behavior, the Boston *Globe* of February 24, 1961, produced a magnificent 2-inch front-page banner headline: "BRITISH IN LATHER OVER SOAPY."

According to the most unbiased version available, what actually happened in Kenya was this. At an airport press conference when Williams arrived, a reporter asked him what the general policy of the United States toward Africa was. Williams replied that the United States favors self-determination for all the peoples of Africa. In answer to a follow-up question as to whether this included Europeans, he replied in the affirmative. He was therefore surprised the next morning to find the two leading newspapers in Nairobi damning him for saying "Africa for the Africans." It seems clear that the extreme sensitivity of Kenya whites, already severely buffeted by the wind of change, made them misinterpret his remarks. In any case, when the Governor was blasted by Kenya Europeans, poked in the nose by an irate white in Northern Rhodesia, and refused an official visit by the rigid *apartheid* Government of South Africa, his stature naturally rose throughout black Africa, bringing American prestige up along with it.

The New Frontier posture on self-determination and human rights is particularly evident in the United Nations, where American delegations have been taking stiffer positions against *apartheid* in South Africa and against Portuguese policy in Africa. Although the United States had already voted with the Assembly majority on resolutions against *apartheid* since 1957, a Kennedy representative in the General Assembly, Francis T. P. Plimpton, delivered the most sweeping condemnation of *apartheid* ever made by the United States on October 24, 1961. Passages which especially angered the South Africa government were:

The United States abhors . . . *apartheid*. . . . We rejoice in the bravery of the men and women of South Africa who . . . fight on day by day for racial justice. My Delegation is happy that one of the most distinguished sons of South Africa, Chief Albert John Luthuli, has just been awarded the Nobel prize for his fight against *apartheid*. . . . We must persevere, remembering that no man, no groups of men, no government is strong enough to resist indefinitely the conscience of mankind. How and when the South African Government will abandon its hateful racial policies we cannot know, but abandon them it will.[9]

[9] U.S. Delegation to the General Assembly, *Statement . . . on Apartheid*, Press Release No. 3811, October 24, 1961.

As a further sign of its dislike of *apartheid,* the Kennedy Administration refused to sell jet fighters and other arms to South Africa because they might be used against nonwhites. And it gave serious consideration to ways and means of bringing indirect economic pressure on the Nationalist government. The United States abstained, however, on a 1961 General Assembly resolution calling for economic sanctions against South Africa—a resolution which failed to obtain the necessary two-thirds majority in the Assembly plenary, after adoption in the Assembly's First Committee by a vote of 50 to 29 with 22 absentions.

Another new emphasis is found in the way the Kennedy Administration called on the colonial powers, Portugal in particular, to increase their preparations for self-determination. On May 13, 1961, in Milwaukee, Williams termed the pressure against colonialism "irresistible," and declared it "imperative that we take planned, deliberate action to make certain that the new countries achieve independence under the most favorable circumstances." Speaking on the Portuguese territories in the Security Council on March 15, 1961, Ambassador Adlai Stevenson called for "step-by-step planning," and said, "its acceleration is now imperative for the successful political, economic and social advancement of all inhabitants under Portuguese administration . . . toward full self-determination."[10] His vote the next day for a Security Council resolution condemning Portuguese policy was widely applauded as an indication that our policy on colonialism was no longer hamstrung by such military considerations as the American base in the Portuguese islands of the Azores. This was one of the most crucial early decisions, and it took the strong team of President Kennedy, Governor Williams, Adlai Stevenson, Chester Bowles, and other New Frontiersmen to put it through.

The Kennedy Administration has also sought to expand economic aid to Africa further. In Boston, on October 26, 1961, Assistant Secretary Williams emphasized that American aid to Africa will have to be "substantial and widespread," and "increased from all sources," government and private. "It is too little realized," he added, "that we lag far behind Europe in assistance to African nations. The historical basis for this imbalance has radically altered with the emer-

[10] *The New York Times,* March 16, 1961.

gence of African states to independence. Yet French aid to Africa last year was much larger than our own."

Despite the competing demands for aid to Latin America through the Alliance for Progress, funds for Africa also increased. The AID program for Africa in the fiscal year 1962 totaled about $250,000,000, including $100,000,000 in loans, $97,000,000 in grants, and the balance in "supporting assistance." The most dramatic examples of the new program for Africa were the Nigeria and Ghana arrangements announced in December, 1961. Nigeria was allotted $225,000,000 in grants and loans over the next five years for its new development program—the largest single commitment the United States had made to an African state.

President Kennedy's decision to go ahead with the long-considered support for the Volta River project in Ghana was not announced until shortly after the Nigerian decision, a timing which was deliberate. The assistance to Ghana took the form of $37,000,000 in loans for the Volta River dam project and about $100,000,000 in loan assistance to the private American consortium which will build and operate the proposed aluminum smelter. The arrangement also included about $50,000,000 in U.S. government guarantees for American investors.

The Kennedy team has also been more sympathetic than its predecessor toward African neutralism. In his Boston speech on October 26, 1961, Assistant Secretary Williams asked, "[Is it] fair to expect African states to forego diplomatic relations, trade and other contacts with the Communists when even their former colonial mentors engage in such activities?" It is better to be "realistic," he said. "We welcome Africa's new independence. We think it is a positive force. We do not wish to control or direct it."

Moreover, Williams's way of expressing "the danger of Soviet penetration" was more appropriate than the overdramatized declarations of the past decade. Let us not underestimate the "old black bag" of inflammatory, disruptive, and subversive Communist tricks, he said, "but let us avoid a fixation about it. . . . Some commentators would apparently feel comfortable about Africa only if the new nations there pretended never to have heard of the Soviet Union, and invariably crossed the street to avoid ever striking up an acquaintance."

Like the Eisenhower Administration, President Kennedy and his advisers were nevertheless sensitive about neutrals who might be leaning too far to the left. When President Nkrumah again vigorously criticized Western actions during the Belgrade Conference early in September, 1961, American sympathy for neutralism was put to a severe test. President Kennedy reacted to Belgrade by stating on September 5 that in the administration of aid funds "we should give great attention and consideration to those nations who have our view of the world crisis."

In October, however, the President sent Clarence Randall to Ghana to review the Volta project and reportedly to seek reassurances about Ghana's ability to meet its share of the costs and about the political orientation of the Nkrumah government. After the decision to extend the requested assistance to Ghana was finally announced in December, Williams commented in Washington on January 8, 1962: "We have calculated our risks with great care in deciding to assist the Volta project in Ghana and are confident that our national interest, as well as African advancement, is served by this decision."[11]

Finally, the Kennedy Administration carried further the trend toward more support for United Nations activities affecting Africa. In the speech on May 13, 1961, cited above, Governor Williams praised the U.N. as a "mirror of reality," and a place where we must stand up and be counted:

It is no longer possible to avoid choices on such difficult problems as Algeria and Angola. The United Nations forces an opinion for concrete action from us on every conceivable issue. I believe this is a good thing. Unpleasant and difficult as it sometimes may be to choose—particularly when the choice is between an ally and a cherished principle—our position of world leadership demands that we seek to influence constructively the course of events. The U.N. forces us to carry out a duty, to make decisions, which we might otherwise be tempted to avoid.

Such statements as this were useful in improving the American posture, whether or not "it is a good thing" for the United Nations

[11] *Washington Post*, January 9, 1962.

to force us to choose. There is much to be said for the view expressed in November, 1959, to the Senate Foreign Relations Committee by a group of about 20 foreign policy specialists assembled by the Council on Foreign Relations: "The essence of successful diplomacy on such issues will be the avoidance of absolute choice between Europe and Africa and the promotion of a peaceful transformation of relationships which prevents such choices from arising."[12] This policy fails, of course, when stubborn governments like those of Portugal and South Africa reject overtures for peaceful change.

THE CONGO AND GOA CRISES

The most striking example of the new attitude toward the United Nations was the Kennedy policy in the Congo crisis. In this case the United States went beyond "declaratory" policy to tangible support. It backed the Security Council resolution of February 21, 1961, urging the U.N. Command to use force if necessary and in the last resort to prevent the occurrence of civil war; and it later supported the U.N.'s military action to secure the U.N. position in Katanga against the forces of Moise Tshombe, who was using white mercenaries to lead his army. The decision to supply up to 21 additional cargo planes, announced in Washington on December 6, 1961, was enthusiastically applauded by many Africans and Asians as a token of American sincerity and integrity.[13]

The latter was a difficult decision for President Kennedy, not only because it was opposed by our major allies but because American conservatives chose to make a political issue out of it. It was widely attacked by Republicans, including former President Hoover, former Vice-President Nixon, and Senators Goldwater and Dirksen. On December 19, 1961, Nixon denounced the Administration's action as "the worst foreign policy blunder since its handling of the

[12] U.S. Congress, Senate Committee on Foreign Relations, *United States Foreign Policy—Compilation of Studies*, 87th Cong., 1st sess., Document No. 24, Washington, 1961, p. 652.

[13] For the details of the Congo crisis see especially Robert C. Good, "Congo Crisis: The Role of the New States," *Neutralism*, A. Wolfers, ed., Washington Center of Foreign Policy Research, June, 1961, pp. 1–46; and Stanley Hoffman, "In Search of a Thread: The U.N. in the Congo Labyrinth," *International Organization*, Spring, 1962, pp. 331–361.

Cuban invasion," an "incredible mess" which "might have the result of liquidating Tshombe, the strongest anti-Communist leader in
the Congo." Khrushchev, Nixon added, "got exactly what he wanted
and we are paying for it."[14] Other arguments tossed into the battle
were that the U.N. was supposed to keep the peace, not make war;
that Tshombe's Katangans had the same right of self-determination
as other Congolese; that the U.N. was violating its own Charter by
interfering in the internal affairs of the Congo; and that Tshombe
ran the only stable government in the area. Fuel was added to the
flame by the Senate Democratic whip, Hubert Humphrey, who tartly
remarked that he didn't intend "to aid Mr. Khrushchev in his efforts
to weaken, control or destroy the U.N. . . . If the right-wing crowd
in this country wants to climb in bed with Khrushchev, I hope they
fight over the covers and freeze."[15] The attack on the State Department grew more dangerous on December 20 when Thomas J. Dodd, a
Democratic senator who had recently visited Katanga, called for a
Senate inquiry into American support for the "naked aggression" of
the U.N.

Fortunately, a carefully reasoned explanation of American policy
had been made the day before by Under Secretary of State George
Ball in Los Angeles. Ball pointed out that the Adoula government in
Leopoldville was a broadly based coalition under the leadership of
an outstanding non-Communist African nationalist; that the issue in
Katanga was not self-determination but the threat of armed secession; that the Kennedy Administration would support Adoula in
keeping not only Katanga from seceding but also the Stanleyville
area of Antoine Gizenga, the "Communist-chosen instrument"; and
that Katanga secession would "threaten the entire Congo with chaos
and civil war and lead to the establishment of a Communist base in
the heart of Central Africa."

Ball's statement helped Americans to form a more balanced view
of the Katanga decision. The situation became more confused, however, when Administration officials justified the policy in different

[14] Richard M. Nixon, "It's Time for Change in U.S. Congo Policy," *Washington Post*, December 19, 1961 (sixth in a series of articles copyrighted by Richard
M. Nixon and the Times-Mirror Syndicate, Los Angeles).
[15] As reported by Robert C. Albright, *Washington Post*, December 21, 1961.

ways. In a Philadelphia speech on December 27, 1961, Deputy Assistant Secretary of State for Public Affairs Carl T. Rowan exaggerated the role of Michael Struelens, a former Belgian civil servant heading the Katanga Information Service in New York. "By spreading around at least $140,000 over the last year," Rowan said, "Mr. Struelens has gotten some extremely vocal help in dispensing a string of myths and a stream of misinformation about Katanga and the Congo."

Rowan's remarks were untimely because the Department was at the moment seeking Belgian and *Union Minière* support for its policy. In a television interview on December 31, Under Secretary George C. McGhee therefore pointed out that Rowan's speech "was not cleared at the top of the State Department," a statement designed to correct an erroneous report in *The New York Times* two days earlier. Those at the top level, McGhee added, probably "wouldn't have engaged in a recriminatory type of attack at this particular juncture."[16]

Numerous Americans who opposed Kennedy's Congo policy had never heard of Struelens, and were motivated by other reasons than those peddled by the Katanga propaganda machine. They were annoyed at being termed "the right-wing crowd," and it appeared for a time that public support for the policy might be jeopardized. The incident demonstrated anew the importance of having a well-informed public. Secretary of State Dean Rusk told the Senate Foreign Relations Committee on December 20 that he had no objection to "a full examination of the full story." Fortunately, by the time an inquiry began on January 18, 1962, in the Senate African Affairs Subcommittee under the chairmanship of Senator Albert Gore, the reasons for the policy were more widely understood and appreciated and the policy itself appeared to be succeeding. Because of the delicacy of the problem, the Senate hearing was wisely closed to the public.

The firm stand of the Kennedy administration in the Congo crisis was the most important achievement of its first year of Africa policy-making. Because of the significance of the Congo in 1961, it was in a symbolic sense the key to our whole Africa policy. If the United States had equivocated in the Katanga crisis, it would have jeopard-

---

[16] From the verbatim transcript of "Washington Conversation—As Broadcast over the CBS Television Network," December 31, 1961, pp. 2–3.

ized the good will won by its new policies elsewhere and might have ended up on the wrong side of other African issues. Many African leaders would have increasingly focused their energies on destroying Tshombe. With the support of the Soviet bloc, they would have continuously denounced an independent Katanga as a Western puppet which must be obliterated along with other vestiges of colonialism and neocolonialism.

The Africa policy achievements of the Kennedy Administration's first year may be summed up as a positive contribution which injected a new and much needed spirit into our relations with Africans, and carried further several trends of the last 18 months under Eisenhower. The Kennedy team soon found, however, that it was only moving from old dilemmas to new. In place of choosing between Africa and Europe, it soon had to decide whether it wanted to choose Adoula or Tshombe, Morocco or Mauritania, and the Casablanca or Monrovia group. One wonders if Secretary of State Dean Rusk did not look back with nostalgia on "the good old days" when, as undersecretary to Dean Acheson, the only Africa dilemma he had to worry about was our fence-sitting on the colonial question.

Moreover, the policy of the United States in other areas often undermined its success in improving relations with African leaders. The pleasure of Africans at the new United States policy toward Portugal, for example, was soon offset by the Cuban invasion fiasco. The welcome decision to supply planes for U.N. forces in the Congo was soon clouded by the sharpness of American opposition to the Indian invasion of Goa. Our policy on Goa and Cuba led many Africans to question the sincerity of American devotion to self-determination. Nkrumah sent Castro a message in April, 1961, congratulating him on his "successful crushing of the recent invasion of Cuba" and "his heroic resistance to colonialism," for "we see the same danger threatening the peace and security of Africa today."[17]

The African reaction to the attitude of the United States in the Goa case was quite indignant. After the Security Council on December 19, 1961, quashed a resolution calling for the immediate withdrawal of Indian forces from Goa and two other Portuguese territories, U.S. Representative Adlai Stevenson declared that the United

[17] Embassy of Ghana, Press Release No. 113, Washington, April 26, 1961.

Nations was "witnessing the first act of the drama which will end in its death."[18] To Africans, however, Stevenson's emphasis was quite misplaced. In their view India had liberated Goa from the worst colonial power in history.

This time it was not "radical" Ghana but "conservative" Liberia which objected. Liberia was the only African state on the Security Council, and it joined the Soviet Union, Ceylon, and the United Arab Republic in voting against the resolution calling for Indian withdrawal. In a later explanation of his country's attitude, Liberian Ambassador S. Edward Peal remarked:

We were unable to regard the Indian entry into that territory as an aggression against Portugal because, like most of the other members of the U.N., we had never accepted the fiction that Goa was an integral part of Portugal and not a colony. Portugal had stubbornly refused to submit reports on Goa as a non–self-governing territory and had ignored a number of U.N. resolutions which were designed to encourage her to adopt a more enlightened colonial policy. It was odd, therefore, that she should turn for help to an organization which she had constantly flouted. Like the rest of the Portuguese Empire, Goa was a dangerous and irritating anachronism.[19]

It also seems probable that the Kennedy Administration will encounter growing trouble over the rising economic expectations of African leaders. The nature and extent of the diplomatic efforts of Assistant Secretary Williams, who made his fourth trip to Africa in April and May, 1962, did much to improve the image of the United States in Africa, but posed a greater challenge to Americans to follow up this new approach with real assistance. By 1962 numerous African leaders who had welcomed Williams's visit in 1961 as a portent of great things to come were beginning to wonder whether the New Frontier was all public relations and no real help. At home, meanwhile, resistance to the Kennedy-Williams approach to Africa was building up in several governmental circles, such as the Department of Defense and the State Department's Bureau of European Affairs, as well as among certain nongovernmental critics including Dean Acheson.

[18] *The New York Times,* December 20, 1961.
[19] Embassy of Liberia, *Liberian Letter,* Washington, February, 1962.

19

American Aid to Africa

MUCH of the preceding analysis of United States
policy toward Africa has been based either on policy declarations
from Washington or on voting positions and explanations by U.S.
Delegations at United Nations meetings. In Africa itself, the United
States was meanwhile expanding three major foreign policy operations—foreign aid, information or propaganda activities, and educational exchange.

These three programs are often considered separately. Advocates
of foreign aid sometimes contend that all else will fail unless African
countries can be brought to the "take-off" point for self-sustaining
economies; friends of the USIA argue that our future depends on
whether we win the "battle for men's minds"; and devotees of educational exchange point out that aid and propaganda often backfire,
while exchange of persons builds contacts and friendships of lasting
value.

Perhaps the main conclusion to be drawn from these differing
views is that aid, information, and exchange are not only all essential
but are inseparable. Their interdependence is easier to understand if
one realizes that the aid agency also conducts information and exchange activities, while the Information Agency has aid and exchange
operations, and the State Department's exchange program has important aid and information aspects. All three are vital arms of our

Africa policy. Without them, policy declarations in Washington and votes in the United Nations would be gestures with little meaning.

THE AGENCY FOR INTERNATIONAL DEVELOPMENT

The Agency for International Development (AID) was established in the autumn of 1961 to revamp, rejuvenate, and expand the foreign aid program. It is thus the latest in the line of postwar aid agencies which includes the Economic Cooperation Administration, the Mutual Security Administration, the Technical Cooperation Administration, the Foreign Operations Administration, and the International Cooperation Administration. The new Agency also took over the operation of the Development Loan Fund and certain local currency dealings of the Export-Import Bank.

The administrator of AID is responsible, subject to the approval of the secretary of state, for the formulation and execution of foreign assistance policies and programs. His instructions go through our ambassadors in AID countries to the directors of AID missions. In the 1961 reorganization, many officers were shifted from functional offices to four new regional bureaus, each headed by an assistant administrator. The assistant administrator for the Bureau for Africa and Europe has a legal adviser, a Development Planning Office, a Technical Support Office, a Management Operations Office, and Geographic Area Offices which include East-South African Affairs, Central African Affairs, West African Affairs, and Mediterranean Affairs.

In his foreign aid message to Congress on March 22, 1961, President Kennedy said: "In the 1960's, there exists an historic opportunity for a major economic assistance effort by the free industrialized nations to move more than half the people of the less developed nations into self-sustained economic growth, while the rest move substantially closer to the day when they, too, will no longer have to depend on outside assistance."[1]

The President's statement was perhaps more hope than fact, for no one really knows how many African countries can be developed to the take-off point for self-sustained economic growth. One con-

[1] Complete text in *Washington Post*, March 23, 1961.

flicting view even maintains that foreign aid retards growth. Nonetheless, the aid program will have a better chance of long-range support and success if the American public grasps the central fact that we give aid not to "buy friends" but to build economic and educational foundations for political stability.

The crucial foreign aid debate of 1957, which focused on the congressional appropriations for fiscal 1958, helped to sharpen the issues and prepare the way for a better program. Among the 11 private research groups which prepared reports for the Senate Special Committee To Study the Foreign Aid Program, the most influential came from the Center for International Studies at the Massachusetts Institute of Technology. The well-known MIT thesis is set forth in a 1957 book by Max F. Millikan and Walt W. Rostow, *A Proposal: Key to an Effective Foreign Policy*, which called for a program of about $10,000,000,000 over 10 years to help underdeveloped countries reach a take-off point for self-sustained economic growth. They also sought to divorce aid from political and military considerations and make it available strictly according to the "absorptive capacity" of recipients, about 80 percent in loans.

In the April, 1961, issue of *Foreign Affairs*, J. K. Galbraith refines these and other ideas by stressing the importance of certain crucial political and social preconditions for economic growth. Criticizing American aid for its "incoherence, discontinuity, dispersal of scarce energies . . . and waste," Galbraith advocates removing "all of the barriers to advance" by setting specific economic and cultural targets for each country receiving aid, particularly "a specified gain in national income, a specified improvement in its distribution, a specified advance in literacy, and improvement in other areas of education." In Galbraith's view, "the present procedures on foreign aid in a very large number of countries are acceptable only because we have so resolutely avoided measuring the results."[2]

Rostow and Galbraith have been brought into government service by President Kennedy, and many of their ideas are reflected in his 1961 foreign aid message to Congress, which called for a unified Agency for International Development with high-quality personnel,

[2] J. K. Galbraith, "A Positive Approach to Economic Aid," *Foreign Affairs*, April, 1961, pp. 450, 453, 457.

individual country development plans, long-term financing, special emphasis on development loans repayable in dollars, special attention to countries willing and able to mobilize their own resources and make necessary economic and social reforms, a multilateral approach in concert with other industrialized nations, and separation of economic aid from military assistance.

TOTAL U.S. AID TO AFRICA: 1945–1961

The student who seeks to discover the total amount of United States government assistance to Africa since World War II will find his search confusing. The best available source is the March 21, 1962, publication of the Agency for International Development, entitled *U.S. Foreign Assistance and Assistance from International Organizations, July 1, 1945–June 30, 1961 (Revised)*. In this and most other government publications on American aid to Africa, however, the statistics on aid to Algeria and South Africa are not included, and Egypt is listed with the Near Eastern and South Asian countries.

During the 16 fiscal years from 1946 through 1961, the United States government made available a worldwide total of $90,500,000,-000 in foreign aid, a figure which includes $29,000,000,000 for military assistance. The continent of Africa, including Egypt and South Africa, received only $1,800,000,000 or 2 percent of the total aid. More than 95 percent of the aid to African countries was economic assistance, however, only $81,500,000 being for military assistance. Of the grand total for Africa, $993,400,000 was in the form of grants and $873,000,000 in loans. It came from the following sources:

International Cooperation Administration	$652,000,000
Public Law 480 (agricultural surplus disposals)	528,000,000
Export-Import Bank loans	320,100,000
Development Loan Fund	155,800,000
Military assistance administered by the Defense Department	81,500,000
Other economic programs	71,900,000

This $1,800,000,000 does not include that portion of the aid to France used for the postwar reconstruction of French North Africa, which has been estimated at about $365,000,000. Nor does it take into account the fact that the United States contributed about 35 percent, approximately $335,000,000, of the $968,800,000 of aid to Africa from the United Nations and the specialized agencies by June 30, 1961. If these two contributions are added to the total, the United States made $2,500,000,000 available for aid to Africa during these 16 years. The $1,800,000,000 that can be accurately identified is distributed among more than 33 African countries, as shown in Table 17.

TABLE 17.   United States Foreign Assistance to Africa: Obligations and Loan Authorizations from Fiscal 1946 Through Fiscal 1961 (in Millions of Dollars)

Country	Economic Aid Grants	Economic Aid Loans	Military Aid Grants	Military Aid Loans	Total Aid
United Arab Republic (Egypt)	$157.4	$227.0			$384.4
Morocco	109.3	192.9	a	a	302.2
Tunisia	202.7	51.9	a		254.7
Ethiopia	57.2	67.4	55.8		180.4
Libya	166.8	8.5	$ 3.7	a	179.0
South Africa		155.7			155.7
Liberia	28.1	85.0	1.0	$1.4	115.5
Sudan	41.2	10.0			51.2
Rhodesia-Nyasaland	0.9	32.4			33.3
Ghana	6.4	20.0			26.4
Nigeria	15.4	3.9			19.3
Congo (Leopoldville)	13.3				13.3
Somalia	11.1	2.0			13.1
Mozambique		12.5			12.5
Kenya	7.3				7.3
Tanganyika	2.5	1.9			4.4
Guinea	4.0				4.0
Senegal	3.6				3.6
Dahomey	3.1				3.1
Mali	2.5		0.6		3.1
Cameroon	2.2				2.2
Ivory Coast	2.1				2.1
Upper Volta	2.0				2.0

TABLE 17. United States Foreign Assistance to Africa: Obligations
and Loan Authorizations from Fiscal 1946 Through Fiscal
1961 (in Millions of Dollars) (*Continued*)

Country	Economic Aid Grants	Economic Aid Loans	Military Aid Grants	Military Aid Loans	Total Aid
Niger	2.0				2.0
Togo	1.9				1.9
Mauritania	0.2	1.4			1.6
Uganda	1.0				1.0
Sierra Leone	1.0				1.0
Malagasy	0.5				0.5
Chad	0.1				0.1
Gabon	0.1				0.1
Congo (Brazzaville)	0.1				0.1
Central African Republic	0.046				0.046
Sterling areas	0.7				0.7
Portuguese possessions	0.3				0.3
French Community	6.0				6.0
Regional	3.3		15.4	3.6	22.3

a Classified information.

SOURCE: Data taken from Agency for International Development, *U.S. Foreign Assistance and Assistance from International Organizations, July 1, 1945–June 30, 1961 (Revised)*, Washington, March 21, 1962, pp. 87–115, and p. 58 on Egypt.

The "Economic Aid" in this table includes assistance through the Public Law 480 agricultural surplus disposal program.

To carry out its program, AID had 1310 U.S. nationals in Africa on May 30, 1962. At the same time, about 750 Africans were training in the United States or third countries. The African countries with the largest complements of American aid personnel were:

Nigeria	190
Ethiopia	182
Liberia	172
Sudan	117
Libya	106
Tunis	59
Somalia	59
Morocco	59
Egypt	47

If one compares this list with the list of grants and loans in Table 17, he will note that Egypt and Morocco are the largest recipients of aid but have the smallest number of AID officers. This is partly because of political difficulties and partly because well over half of the aid to these two countries was made in the form of cash grants and loans, or in agricultural surplus disposals, rather than in programs involving U.S. technicians. It was not until 1962, it should be noted, that Nigeria jumped to the top of the list of countries with the largest number of AID personnel.

Mention should be made of one other general point, namely, the growth pattern of grants and loans to Africa. This is illustrated in Figure 3 by a chart from the aforementioned 1962 AID publication on *U.S. Foreign Assistance*. Since the total aid to Africa in the seven years from 1946 through 1952 was so small, the chart does not begin until 1953.

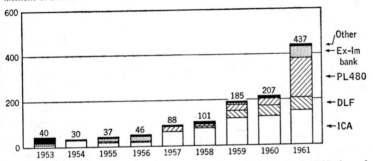

Fig. 3.   Growth of U.S. economic assistance to Africa from fiscal 1953 through fiscal 1961, excluding Egypt and South Africa (in millions of dollars).

Source: Agency for International Development, *U.S. Foreign Assistance and Assistance from International Organizations, July 1, 1945–June 30, 1961* (Revised), Washington, 1962, p. ix.

This brief chapter on American aid to Africa makes no attempt at a country-by-country description of the details of our assistance program. Many of its main characteristics have been summarized, particularly in the two old states of Liberia and Ethiopia and the two new states of Ghana and Guinea, by John D. Montgomery in a September–October, 1961, booklet in the Foreign Policy Association Headline Series entitled *Aid to Africa: New Test for American Policy.*

In many African countries, priority is given to the improvement of education and agriculture. Other important fields of technical assistance are health and sanitation, industry and mining, public safety, public administration, community development and social welfare, housing, and labor. The general character of these programs is well known from the voluminous literature on the political, economic, and cultural factors in the development process. In most African countries, American aid programs are too new for meaningful analysis. In several states, however, we have had sufficient experience that detailed country studies of the totality and the interrelations of United States diplomatic, aid, information, exchange, and other activities might now be undertaken with profit.

PROBLEMS FACING AID PROGRAMS

A number of major problems are more or less common to all American aid programs. The basic difficulty is the underdeveloped character of Africa. Although the coastal areas are generally more developed than the hinterland, most African countries lack the preconditions for economic growth. Illiteracy is high, skilled labor scarce, health standards low, and transportation in a rudimentary stage of development. A related part of the problem is inherent in the fact that economic development produces cultural change, which is inevitably complex, uneven, and slow. As we have learned from our oldest aid programs in Liberia and Ethiopia, it takes considerable money and effort and quite a period of time for aid to bear fruit. Whether this will be equally true of the new countries remains to be seen. One important difference is the driving and determined spirit of progress among many new African leaders. This was most noticeable to me in Tunisia in 1958, where the Tunisian people had a spirited and constructive energy far different from what I had seen under the colonial regime on a visit in 1950. The extraordinary vigor and determination with which they were tackling the education problem was quite impressive. When I once ventured a pleasantry to the effect that, as a professor, I was somewhat sorrowful to hear that the teachers had been forced to give up their summer vacations, the answer came back quickly, even somewhat tartly, that "we are a *new* country where everyone must *work, work, work,* all the time!"

A second problem confronting AID technicians in Africa is that the inadequate supply of trained Africans forces Americans to play an operational as well as an advisory role, performing many tasks themselves. Governments lack the trained personnel to draw up national development plans and to formulate aid projects which meet our stringent requirements. AID officers therefore become involved in helping on these subjects. This may cause friction over the attaching of "economic ropes," if not "political strings." AID officials are in a delicate position when they advise Africans to put their fiscal houses in order, or that they do not need a national airline.

Another difficulty is to find an appropriate balance between economic and political considerations. There are times when the United States must undertake projects with a view to their political impact on the government leaders or the populace as a whole. While it must try to avoid merely responding to Communist offers of aid for Africa, it cannot ignore them. In 1961, for example, when Emperor Haile Selassie requested aid for a new university which, in the American view, did not fit well into the educational pattern of Ethiopia, his request received careful attention because of concern that the Russians might build it. The Russians are already constructing a secondary school in Ethiopia which will use Soviet teaching materials and which may one day be staffed in part by Soviet teachers.

A fourth problem of AID personnel in Africa is that of dealing with officials of former colonial powers, some of whom are sensitive about American intervention. A French civil servant seconded to an African government or a British expatriate working in an African ministry may play a decisive role in determining aid priorities. He may pass on to his African colleagues a subconscious distrust of Americans and their methods. AID officers must respect the skill, integrity, and dedication of many of these European administrators and technicians who have worked hard to build political, economic, and educational foundations for modern states. Their experience is a valuable asset which cannot be lightly disregarded.

American technicians have an obligation, however, to step in and assert their convictions when necessary. In the Sudan, for example, education officials wanted British-type boarding schools throughout the country because they considered them a superior means of education. An American aid official dissuaded them by drawing up figures to show that the cost would be excessive.

The effect of this colonial legacy is much deeper than differences of view between American and European technicians. Patterns of technical cooperation with the former metropole may already be operating along well-established lines. American technical and financial assistance must therefore concentrate on supplementing rather than competing with European programs. This has limited our work in constructing roads, dams, ports, and other basic facilities.

Another thorny problem is the determination of what states to aid and how much aid to give them. In general, foreign assistance tends to strengthen the government in power, which may not always be in our interest. For example, many Americans ask whether we have not become too closely identified with the ruling Americo-Liberian oligarchy in Liberia, whose policies have been less than progressive. Others were uneasy when our assistance was instrumental in putting down the palace revolt in Ethiopia in December, 1960, which was in part a libertarian reaction against a semifeudal regime. Yet Liberia and Ethiopia have two of our oldest and most extensive aid programs. Even greater criticism has been leveled at giving aid to Guinea because of the Marxist orientation of its leadership, and to Ghana because of such measures as preventive detention which enables the government to detain opposition leaders up to 5 years without trial.

The main problem of this type, however, is whether the United States should help African states which take anti-Western positions on international issues and appear to have pro-Communist leanings. Aid to such countries has been challenged not only by outright opponents of all aid, like Senator Goldwater, but by the more rational arguments of such seasoned observers as George Kennan who, in his book *Russia, the Atom and the West* suggests that when we are told that if aid is not forthcoming states will go Communist, our answer should be: "Very well, then, go. Our interests may suffer, but yours will suffer first." One of Kennan's former colleagues on the State Department's policy planning staff also believes that the United States should develop a firmer posture on foreign aid, with a clear implication that aid to states which lean too far to the left will be discontinued. In his view, a state which cannot discriminate in favor of its friends cannot have a policy at all. Similar views are elaborated by George Liska, in whose view indiscriminate support for all neutralists could be more damaging than our sweeping condemnation of neutrality a decade ago. To halt a "drift" from nonalignment to "ever more virulent" and anti-Western forms of "militant neutralism," Liska believes that the United States "must differentiate and scale or graduate its commitments," and "deny assistance to some non-Communist governments . . . ." If both the United States and the Soviet Union reward anti-Westernism, he writes, "the non-aligned countries will have no alternative course to tempt them."[3]

It is easier to state such a theory than to apply it in practice to specific states. Our major experiment with a tough-minded attitude toward aiding "unfriendly neutrals" was the action of John Foster Dulles in refusing help to construct Egypt's Aswan Dam. Not only did he fail to topple Nasser, but Soviet technicians rushed in to replace Americans. At the time, many critics termed it a catastrophic diplomatic blunder, although in retrospect it seems to have done less damage to American interests than anticipated.

A somewhat comparable debate occurred over the question of lending money to Ghana for the Volta Dam. Most critics felt that the United States should continue aid to Ghana, but many did not approve of giving so large a sum to a country which had adopted anti-Western positions on international issues. The grant was apparently made in order to avoid the unpleasant political consequence of appearing to be punishing Nkrumah's militant brand of neutralism.

This new dilemma of American policy may not turn out to be as difficult in the long run as it now appears. The best balancers of Soviet and American aid may prove to be the African states themselves. If any of them decides that either the Western or Soviet bloc is gaining too strong an influence on its policy, it is likely to turn to one great power to countervail the other.

A final AID problem is that of the seemingly inevitable blunders resulting from inefficient administration. Scientific equipment has rusted on tropical wharves for want of delivery, and unsheltered bags

[3] George Liska, "The Rationale of Non-Alignment," in Arnold Wolfers, ed., *Neutralism*, Washington Center of Foreign Policy Research, June, 1961, p. 83.

of cement have turned to stone in the rain. AID is not alone in maladministration. UNICEF milk has been fed to cattle because mothers and children disliked its taste, and prize breeding boars delivered under the Colombo Plan have been consumed at banquets for visiting Western dignitaries. Enemies of foreign aid exploit such incidents as reasons for doing away with it. Their energies could be better spent on improving it.

IMPROVING AID PROGRAMS

The important question, therefore, is not whether to give aid but how to improve it. Since good personnel is essential to success, a number of steps toward this end might be taken, such as developing a permanent career service for technical and economic assistance overseas, sending to Africa whenever possible only those officers who want to go there, providing additional African area and language training for American technicians, and posting officials to African countries for longer periods. AID officials must have a high degree of skill and tact in attaining the happy medium between economic requisites and psychological factors.

A second essential of an effective aid program is a continually increasing degree of international cooperation. African leaders like this idea because multilateral assistance neutralizes the political impact of aid. By joining with other nations in giving aid, the United States not only demonstrates its disinterestedness but it runs less risk of being singled out for criticism when things go wrong.

Cooperation in aid projects might take several forms. One is to continue to support larger economic and technical assistance programs of the United Nations and the specialized agencies. Perhaps special support might be given to projects of the U.N.'s Economic Commission for Africa. Even among U.N. officials, however, it is considered essential that the United States and other Western powers also extend all possible bilateral help. What is needed from the West is an equal willingness to make the maximum effective use of U.N. facilities. The task is more than big enough for both.

A second type of multilateral approach is to join with other aid-giving nations and African recipients in new forms of cooperation—a

Colombo Plan or Alliance for Progress for Africa. Psychological barriers continue to make tripartite cooperation with Europe and Africa difficult, but the experiences of the past decade have helped to clear away much of the deadwood of outmoded conceptions and suspicions that obscure the main issue. African leaders who look to the U.N. for help now realize the need for assistance from other sources as well, as long as it does not jeopardize their internal political positions. A number of British Labor and other leaders have been interested in the idea of Anglo-American-African cooperation since 1958, and in 1962 the Bow Group of younger members of the Conservative Party published a pamphlet on *The New Africa* calling for an Alliance for Progress among all givers and receivers of aid in Africa.

The key to the success of such a multilateral development plan, however, is the willingness of Africans not only to accept it but even to take the initiative in proposing it. During the past five years the idea has been slow to gain support because certain critics term it an attempt to bypass the U.N., while others contend that there are already too many aid organizations. Several African leaders, however, have now made public statements favoring a Colombo-type plan for Africa, a flexible multilateral arrangement for assessing needs and resources and for helping to secure the necessary aid from outside sources.

The Colombo Plan, however, was restricted to the Commonwealth and could therefore build upon pre-existing economic and political ties. In the Alliance for Progress, the United States is the only major donor nation, and does not have to compete with European nations having a vested interest in certain recipient countries. The major multilateral assistance ties with Africa are those of European powers through the European Economic Community and the Commission for Technical Cooperation in Africa South of the Sahara. If the United Kingdom integrates even part of its own aid with that of the EEC, the multilateral aid program of the latter would become even larger. If other countries also join the EEC, they too will be under pressure to shoulder a proportion of the aid burden, even if they have no specific commitments in Africa.

A third form of multilateral assistance might be by working through regional organizations which the African states establish among themselves. It is in the interest of the United States to promote such groupings because they provide a means for a more rational allocation of scarce skills and resources and for more efficient and effective economic planning. At the moment, however, Africa is divided into rival groupings, which makes this difficult.

Meanwhile, multilateral cooperation on a lesser scale has already proved successful. An excellent illustration of the potentialities of tripartite cooperation was the nine-man team of three Nigerian, three American, and three British experts who produced the Ashby report analyzing the higher educational needs of Nigeria.

A final way of improving our aid policy is to relate it to our trade policy regarding tariffs and commodity price stabilization for African products. Africans are acutely concerned over the mounting surpluses of coffee, cocoa, and other tropical commodities and the consequent depression of world market prices. As one of the largest consumers of tropical produce, the United States must be ready to participate willingly and creatively in commodity price stabilization discussions. Our tariffs on African products are at present generally low and cause little friction, since African exports do not compete with our own production. However, Africa's development will lead to industrialization and the export of low-cost manufactured goods. American aid will be of limited value if we are not ready to open our markets to finished products from Africa, even if they compete with our own domestic industries. Finally, our aid program requires an imaginative use of agricultural surpluses. In Morocco and Tunisia, American surplus foods have been used to pay workers on national development projects, and extensive famine relief has been given to the Congo, and to East African countries which suffered from devastating floods in the fall of 1961.

THE PEACE CORPS

The Peace Corps is a unique combination of aid, information, and exchange, with the accent on youth. Unlike members of the Foreign Service, USIS, or AID, the Peace Corps volunteer is not an official of the United States government. Instead he is a private citizen who is expected to perform valuable aid services and to help dispel misunderstanding.

The Peace Corps was created and given temporary status as an agency within the Department of State by an executive order of March 1, 1961. It selects projects proposed by host countries and trains its own volunteers. In April, 1962, it had teachers and technicians in 12 countries, 4 of which were African. Another 136 were still in training. Peace Corpsmen numbered 51 in Ghana, about 100 in Nigeria, 37 in Sierra Leone, and 35 in Tanganyika. Agreements had been reached with 20 other states for nearly 2000 additional volunteers.

After initial hesitation on the part of many Africans and Americans, the Peace Corps was generally well received. In Nigeria, despite early adverse publicity which led to popular demands for the expulsion of the Corps, the government soon requested 350 more teachers, 10 times as many as in the original group. In April, 1962, Congress granted the President's request for $63,750,000 to expand the Peace Corps to 9970 by the fall of 1963. In his request, the President commented that the Peace Corps would "supplement technical advisers by offering the specific skills needed by developing nations." They will help provide the skilled manpower, "acting at a working level and serving at great personal sacrifice."

The Peace Corps has not only managed to overcome a widespread initial skepticism, but the idea is spreading. In March, 1962, Dennis Vosper, head of Britain's new Department of Technical Cooperation, was reported to have proposed the establishment of a British equivalent of America's Peace Corps.

THE REASONS FOR AID TO AFRICA

In conclusion, why should we aid Africa? This is the most vital question of all, because American taxpayers will not continue to pay the bill unless they know the answer. Public opinion studies have shown that support for this country's economic and military assistance programs declined from about 80 percent in 1945 to only 55 percent in 1957 and 51 percent in 1958. Recently the opponents of aid acquired a political leader in the person of conservative Republican Senator Barry Goldwater. On December 8, 1960, Goldwater told the National Association of Manufacturers that one of the most important tasks today was "to stop foreign economic aid." *The New York Times* quoted him as saying that "the United States should begin acting like a world power and quit grovelling on its knees to inferior people who like to come to New York."[4]

One answer to the question of why we should help Africa was given by the new director of the Agency for International Development, Fowler Hamilton, who called foreign aid "the most effective arsenal we have in the cold war."[5] This kind of argument influences most Americans, but it sometimes arouses objections from Africans and from those American liberals who contend that we should help Africa for the sake of humanity rather than out of self-interest. Since Africans talk so much about keeping the cold war out of Africa, Mr. Hamilton's choice of the words "arsenal in the cold war" was not the best. But, his central point—that we give aid because it is in our own interest to do so—is correct. As George Liska has demonstrated in his book *The New Statecraft—Foreign Aid in American Foreign Policy*, foreign aid is wholly inseparable from politics and is always an economic instrument of foreign policy.

There is no country in which the majority of taxpayers would give continual support to foreign aid if it were only a benevolent obligation of the rich toward the poor. American aid to Africa will be most dependable and effective when both parties understand that it is in their mutual interest. Aid has the economic objective of developing African countries, but we give it for the political reason that we are seeking to build free and viable societies which, in the long run, will help to strengthen international order and stability.

It is also essential for Americans to realize that we cannot "buy friends" with aid. This is lesson number one in the elementary ABCs of aid programs. Liska has compared "the plight of aid-givers today" to that of "money-lenders to sovereigns" at the dawn of the capitalist era.[6] Early evidence of this came from Bolivia where, in March, 1959,

<hr/>

[4] *The New York Times,* December 9, 1960.

[5] *Washington Post,* December 1, 1961.

[6] George Liska, *The New Statecraft: Foreign Aid in American Foreign Policy,* Chicago, 1960, p. 11.

after $177,000,000 worth of American aid, rioters attacked the aid office, partly because of the feeling that too many North Americans were present in programs that were not living up to expectations.

Since all people tend to look for scapegoats in hard times, the vulnerability of the United States to criticism mounts in direct proportion to the expansion of the American presence through aid programs. A sign of the times is the cartoon portraying an Arab giving street directions to another Arab passing by. "It's only a stone's throw from the American Embassy," the first Arab says as he points down the street. Throwing stones at American embassies has become a worldwide pastime. We have even had the distinction of being stoned by Europeans in one place and Africans in another on the same day. This was on December 10, 1961, when Belgian whites, shouting "Kennedy to the gallows," attacked the American Embassy in Brussels while Katanga blacks stormed the American Consulate in Elizabethville.

Africans do appreciate American aid, but they don't like to be "bought." The vicissitudes of local politics will inevitably produce anti-American attitudes from time to time and place to place. Aid to Africa will succeed only if Americans are patient and intelligent enough to endure occasional hostility. We should expect not to purchase unwanted alliances but to help states develop sufficient economic and political strength to become real and willing participants in the mutual task of building a stable world of free peoples.

The danger of American disenchantment with Africa is matched by the danger of African disillusionment with America. The high expectations aroused among Africans during the successful struggle for freedom have not been realized because of lagging economic development. Julius Nyerere has changed his Tanganyika slogan from "Freedom" to "Freedom and Work," but if foreign aid fails to produce results, popular pressures for radical innovations will mount. Numerous African youth, student, and labor organizations are already agitating for more authoritarian movements, which might grow philosophically closer to the Soviet bloc even if they do not go Communist. If this happens, American and other Western investments and access to Africa's raw materials and markets might be threatened and Western political freedom placed in jeopardy. In view of these dangers and notwithstanding our heavy commitments in Asia and Latin America, the United States ought to give Africa far more aid in the future.

In the foreign aid program for fiscal 1962, $100,000,000 is provided for loans and $150,000,000 for grants to Africa. Is this enough for the whole continent of Africa? African leaders want to inaugurate large-scale development plans quickly. President Sylvanus Olympio of Togo made a special appeal to 11 congressmen among the guests at a White House luncheon on March 20, 1962, telling them that "whatever the United States does [for] us, even though we may not be able to pay you back, I am sure it will help the United States. . . ."[7] His plea has been echoed by so many other African leaders that the present scale of grants and loans is hardly adequate.

For the fiscal year ending June 30, 1963, however, the AID has asked Congress for an appropriation of $3,378,500,000, perhaps $365,000,000 of which would be allocated to Africa, not including Egypt or the U.S. contribution to the U.N. program for the Congo. If one adds to this $365,000,000 an estimated $185,000,000 of assistance through PL 480, and an estimated $35,000,000 in Export-Import Bank loans, American aid to Africa would rise to about $585,000,000 in fiscal 1963. Comparable figures for the three preceding years were $207,000,000 in 1960, $437,000,000 in 1961, and $509,000,000 in 1962. If Egypt and the U.S. contributions to all U.N. and Specialized Agency assistance to the Congo and the rest of Africa are included, the total aid from the United States to Africa in 1963 could rise to more than $850,000,000.

In a thoughtful article on "Diplomacy for our Times," in the Winter, 1962, issue of the SAIS Review, Renzo Sereno presents the reasons for aid in a stimulating way. Pointing out that the old diplomacy is out of date, he remarks that in the bipolar world of today we must extend and multiply our relations with the many new states of Africa and Asia because we are one of the poles. Unless we do this, "We will have no ties at all." In this sense, foreign aid is not an economic but a political operation, and it is neither "foreign" nor "aid." It is an indispensable policy which "must be conceived as our way of taking our place in the world." The "alternative . . . is isolation."

[7] Washington Post, March 21, 1962.

20

Information and Exchange Programs

W HEN the Senate Foreign Relations Committee held hearings in March, 1961, on the confirmation of Edward R. Murrow, President Kennedy's appointee as Director of the United States Information Agency, Senator Homer E. Capehart remarked that "just as a salesman's job is to sell a Buick . . . or Cadillac," the man selling America abroad should never breathe a suggestion that there could be any weakness in the product. To this comment Murrow replied that "we cannot be effective in telling the American story abroad if we tell it only in superlatives." Both strong points and flaws should be reported honestly, he added, or else the weak spots "will be reported by others."[1]

THE USIA

The United States Information Agency has become an essential part of our Africa policy machinery. In the use of propaganda as an

[1] *Washington Post*, March 15, 1961.

instrument of foreign policy, the Department of State in 1945 inherited the staff of the Office of War Information. In the effort to make the information program more effective, it was expanded and reorganized five times between 1945 and 1953, when the USIA became autonomous. Its Africa operations were slow in gaining momentum. In 1953 only one USIA officer in Washington was assigned exclusively to the African area, although there were already 17 USIA posts in 12 African countries, including Cairo and Alexandria under the Middle East section and Algeria under the European Division.

The wind of change hit the USIA in 1957, however. Despite a budget cut which forced a retrenchment of its operations in other areas, it decided to expand in Africa. By the end of September there were 4 officers in the Africa section handling 19 posts in 14 African countries. In 1960 the Africa section achieved the status of a separate division with 14 officers. In addition, it had a research branch for Africa composed of 4 officers. The United States Information Service, the foreign service of USIA, hoped to have 133 American officers assisted by 476 local employees in 43 information centers in 31 African countries by the end of fiscal 1962. To ensure coordination with other U.S. agencies, all major USIA programs are implemented by these officers only after review by either the State Department or the "country team" on the spot, or both. The country team is headed by the American ambassador and composed of the senior me.nbers of other U.S. agencies in the host country.

The USIA tells the American story in Africa through four principal media—radio, libraries, films, and the press. The introduction of television offers a new opportunity. Algeria already has an estimated 62,000 television sets, including 10,000 owned by Moslems. New stations are now operating in Southern Rhodesia for 23,000 sets, in Nigeria for 10,000, and in Morocco for more than 5000. Seven thousand Libyan sets receive programs from Wheelus Air Base and from Italy, and 1000 sets in Ethiopia can tune in to U.S. Armed Forces Asmara. By 1963, Kenya, Tunisia, Ghana, Sierra Leone, Liberia and the Sudan also expect to have television.

The USIA is considerably handicapped by budgetary limitations, however, as shown in the following comparative figures, set forth in millions of dollars:

	1957–1958 Total Budget	1959–1960 Total Budget
ICA (Mutual Security)	1622.8	1728.3
Military assistance	1600.0	1400.0
Department of State	206.2	268.3
USIA[a]	100.1	104.9
USIA (Africa Division)	2.2	3.9

[a] Includes reimbursements from other agencies.

By fiscal 1962, USIA's planned obligations for Africa, including obligations under Title I of PL 480 but not including reimbursements from other agencies, had risen to a total of $11,200,000, out of total USIA obligations of $122,700,000. The USIA has no vigorous lobby supporting it, and it is prohibited by law from publicizing its programs within the United States. In the view of T. S. Repplier, President of the Advertising Council, "At a time when this country is spending $48 billion for military hardware which we pray may never be used, we are spending the price of just one Polaris submarine for the ideological war which may decide this country's fate."[2] This is $20,000,000 less, he added, than one company spends in the United States alone to sell its automobiles.

In addition to budgetary hardships, the USIA in Africa has been handicapped by several other factors. At the height of the controversy over the colonial question, it was extremely difficult to make palatable propaganda out of U.S. fence-sitting in the United Nations. The racial discriminations to which American Negroes are still subjected are even harder to explain to Africans. Since the Soviet Union, in contrast, has escaped identification with racialism and colonialism, American propaganda about Soviet "colonialism" and the threat of communism in Africa has little effect, and in fact is often regarded by Africans as deceptive counterpropaganda to conceal American support for Western colonialism.

Other obstacles to USIA operations in Africa include the low literacy rate, which means that greater emphasis must be placed on expensive visual aid material; the intensifying nationalist and ideological suspicions which have induced African governments to restrict USIA activities in such countries as Ghana, Guinea, and Mali;.

[2] *Washington Post*, December 17, 1961.

and the inadequacy of roads and other communications facilities needed for dissemination of information materials.

A few highlights of its work will illustrate the radio, library, film, and press activities in Africa. Radio is perhaps the most important communications medium in Africa, both present and potential. At the end of 1961, there were an estimated 5,286,600 radio receiving sets in the Arab world, 3,220,300 in non-Arab Africa, and 5,385,300 in all of Africa excluding Egypt. A substantial increase is expected as the economic level of Africa rises and as transistor radios, which operate without household electrification, become available at lower cost. To reach this audience, special English and French programs for Africa are now being broadcast regularly, and Swahili and Hausa occasionally. A "Voice of America" relay station being constructed near Monrovia, Liberia, is scheduled to go on the air by the end of 1963. This should resolve the problem presented by frequent complaints of poor VOA reception in Africa. Supplemental coverage of West Africa will be provided by a powerful relay station being constructed at Greenville, North Carolina, for operation at the end of 1962.

The impact of USIA libraries in Africa is particularly notable. Their influence is difficult to evaluate because the effect of reading miscellaneous American books and magazines is more intangible than radio, press, and film programs specially tailored for Africans. It is nonetheless significant that 1,700,000 persons attended USIA libraries in 30 African cities during the last six months of 1960 and the first six months of 1961. These libraries are small, normally containing from 1000 to 5000 volumes, but in many towns the USIA library is the only free library, in some it is the only library, and in every case, including in South Africa, it is open to all races. In 1957, in order to demonstrate American interest in Africa, a collection of 60 books and other publications on Africa by American authors was added to a number of these libraries. This collection is regularly updated. When a USIA library was first opened in Blantyre, Nyasaland, on March 21, 1961, several hundred Africans were waiting outside the door. Within a month, 600 of the library's initial 750 volumes had been checked out—at a time when the library was open only two and a half hours a day, with a staff of one person!

The film program of USIA includes documentaries on American life, newsreel coverage of significant events, and special films on such subjects as President Nkrumah's 1958 visit to the United States. The USIA's most popular film product, the monthly newsreel *Today*, is produced in English, French, and Arabic. By the end of 1961 it was being shown in some 710 theaters in 20 African countries to an estimated annual audience of 33,000,000. *Today* attempts to illustrate Africa's problems and progress and to connect these experiences with democracy in America. USIA films are also shown in African villages through the use of mobile van units, 40 of which were operating in Africa in 1961.

In its press and publications program, its fourth principal activity, the USIA publishes its own materials, and radioteletypes daily news in English and sometimes in French to Africa for the use of American officials and for release to local editors and others. Several African posts publish newspapers and magazines in the host countries. Outstanding among them is the *American Outlook*, published in Accra, a monthly journal of 16 pages which had a circulation of 114,000 in 1961. In the fall of 1960 a companion paper entitled *Perspectives Américaines* was launched for French-speaking Africans. Especially tailored for students is the *Nigerian American Quarterly* which, for example, publicizes such programs as the new African Studies Center at the University of California at Los Angeles.

In January, 1960, the Press Division of the USIA stepped up its Africa output by inaugurating a daily radioteletyped report especially prepared for about 15 monitoring posts in Africa. It planned to reach 29 country posts by the end of June, 1962. This USIA "Wireless File" to some extent supplements such commercial agencies as the Associated Press and United Press International, and provides among other things a daily account of important policy statements in Washington. It also endeavors to counter the effect of some of the news releases of the British agency, Reuters, which is conspicuous for disseminating throughout Africa stories of racial incidents in the United States. The USIA does not deny such incidents, but stresses the progress made in the United States in improving race relations.

In addition to these radio, library, film, and press activities, USIS officers operate the State Department's exchange of persons program in the field and foster a number of other activities, including a promising program of teaching English to selected groups of adults in 19 countries of non–English-speaking Africa. At the Bourguiba school in Tunis, the USIA teaches English to some 400 students. In the fall of 1961, a third of the 136 members of the Somali National Assembly were enrolled in English classes, as were 40 of the 51 members of the national legislature in Togo. The USIA English-language operation in Morocco is the largest in Africa. Four American teachers and about 25 local teachers give courses to almost 1500 students in Rabat, Casablanca, Fez, Marrakech, and Tangier. Students include many of the country's top government officials.

Under a special President's Fund Program, outstanding American athletes and artists are brought to Africa. They not only arouse enthusiasm but give an incentive to African talent. American performing artists who have toured Africa under this program include the Westminster Singers, the Herbie Mann Orchestra, Louis Armstrong, William Warfield, Camilla Williams, Phillipa Schuyler, and Wilbur de Paris. Outstanding athletes were the American Olympic competitors Mal Whitfield and Jack Davis. When Mal Whitfield, the Negro Olympic star, came through Lusaka, Northern Rhodesia, in 1955, I happened to be present in an enthusiastic African audience watching him instruct African secondary-school runners, and then run a handicapped quarter-mile race against a field of Africans and two whites. The occasion was a real success.

An interesting sidelight on the USIA's work was recounted to a Boston audience on October 25, 1961, by Edward V. Roberts, the Agency's assistant director for Africa. As Africans take control of their own affairs, they show considerable interest in the American experience in government, and USIA has responded to many requests about it. When Libya set out to form a constitution, every member of the constitutional convention was given a copy of the American constitution in Arabic. In Guinea a few months after independence a cabinet minister requested 1000 copies of a USIA pamphlet outlining the organization and functions of the U.S. government. In Nigeria on the eve of independence many requests for information on federalism were received. Kenya and Rhodesia parliamentarians in 1961 were also studying American constitutional precedents. In

Salisbury, when the High Court ruled in October, 1961, that segregated municipal swimming pools were illegal, it based its findings largely upon American legal experience and decisions of the Supreme Court. The American material cited in the ruling was provided by the USIA.

How effective is the USIA? Certain critics have taken it to task for having too many officers and for doing an ineffective job; for having inferior and poorly trained personnel who are transferred before they become well acquainted locally; for a news service less complete than the British News Agency, Reuters, and with less African news content than Agence France Presse; for having poorer technical radio transmission than Radio Moscow and Radio Peking; for having personnel in Africa who find it too difficult to adapt to the African environment; for overstressing material progress at the expense of cultural achievements; for excessive anti-Communist polemics; and for a generally uncoordinated hit-or-miss performance. No doubt there is validity in some of these criticisms. A sound judgment on them, however, would have to be based on a country-by-country analysis of USIA targets, achievements, and failures. Part of the trouble may result from inadequate USIA study of each African country with a view to clarifying and establishing proper targets, and adapting USIA material to African audiences.

USIA operations need improvement, but their value is clear. One of the highest priority needs is better personnel. This is particularly true because of the public relations nature and purpose of USIA work. An outstanding officer in an African post can do more than can be accomplished by any number of changes in organization or program. With this in mind, the USIA has attempted to recruit better junior officers, and has given Africa area training to a limited number of midcareer officers at the Foreign Service Institute and in the Program of African Studies at the Johns Hopkins University School of Advanced International Studies.[3] This kind of training is essential for the most effective work in Africa, and should be expanded.

The ability of the USIA to attract a sufficient number of well-

[3] I am indebted to one of these midcareer trainees, W. C. Powell, for research assistance in preparing the section on USIA.

qualified officers would be enhanced if it could give them career status. In 1958 the American Assembly at its session on the United States and Africa expressed the opinion that USIA personnel should be given career status, a recommendation that was repeated in 1959 by the United States Advisory Commission on Information. On January 11, 1961, President Eisenhower's Committee on Information Activities Abroad, after a nine-month study, stressed the "urgent need for substantial increases in the critical areas of Africa and Latin America."[4] A career system therefore seems all the more necessary.

In conclusion, however, it should be re-emphasized that the American people must set a high example for the USIA to publicize. As George V. Allen told the Agency's employees when he became their Director in 1957, "I have long been convinced that ninety per cent of the impression which the United States makes abroad depends on our policies and that not more than ten per cent, to make a rough estimate, is how we explain it—whether we say it softly, or loudly, or strongly, or belligerently, or with dulcet tones."[5]

EDUCATIONAL EXCHANGE

A third major United States operation in Africa is the educational exchange program, which is the responsibility of the State Department's new Bureau of Educational and Cultural Affairs established in April, 1960. It deserves higher priority in foreign policy. Public and private educational exchange projects which bring Africans to the United States and send Americans to Africa are a broadening and deepening experience of immeasurable value. The more Africans who know Americans as personal friends, the more unlikely their countrymen are to accept stereotypes of the United States as a money-grubbing giant with no appreciation of aesthetic and spiritual values. Like economic aid and propaganda, educational exchange occasionally backfires, but this should not deter us. We should consider it an integral part of our foreign policy, not a mere "fringe benefit."

Philip H. Coombs, who came from the Ford Foundation to become the Kennedy Administration's first Assistant Secretary of State

[4] *Washington Post*, January 12, 1961.
[5] *Remarks by George V. Allen . . . to USIA Employees at the Interdepartmental Auditorium*, Washington, November 21, 1957 (mimeo.).

for Educational and Cultural Affairs, declared on February 8, 1962, that his "central conclusion" after a year on the job was that educational and cultural affairs were "the most underdeveloped area of American foreign relations." Though costing far less, these operations were "on a parity of importance with military and economic assistance and with conventional diplomacy."[6] From the end of World War II to June, 1961, Coombs remarked, the United States invested $84,700,000,000 in economic and military assistance to other nations while spending less than 0.5 percent of this amount on the educational and cultural exchange programs of the Department of State.

The Fulbright Act which launched the program was once described as "the most fabulously profitable investment ever authorized by the Congress of the United States." Whether or not it merits this encomium, it was an imaginative bill which authorized the United States government to sell for local currencies the American equipment left abroad after World War II and to apply the proceeds to scholarships abroad for Americans. Under the companion Smith-Mundt Act, the operation of which was integrated with the Fulbright Act, foreign students, teachers, and scholars have been able to visit the United States. During the first 15 years of this combined program, more than 22,000 grants were made to Americans and more than 58,000 to foreigners.

The widespread appreciation of the value of exchange programs was demonstrated in the summer of 1961 when both Houses of Congress adopted by overwhelming majorities a new Fulbright-Hays Act. This Mutual Educational and Cultural Exchange Act, signed by the President on September 21, authorized a coordinated expansion of exchange activities. Important new features of the Act are provisions for government-sponsored orientation, counseling, and English-language training for foreign students; government assistance for foreign artists and athletes to visit the United States on nonprofit tours; and government assistance for American representation at international nongovernmental educational, scientific, and technical meetings as well as foreign representation at similar meetings, if under U.S. sponsorship, here and abroad. Several other provisions

[6] Speech in New York, February 8, 1962. Issued as State Department Press Release No. 89.

authorize greater flexibility in the use of funds. Unfortunately, this wider foundation for expanded exchange operations was not supported with a commensurate increase in funds at the very time African educational developments were offering a unique opportunity to make use of the broader authority granted by the Fulbright-Hays Act. Exchange initative, therefore, has been moving to agencies like AID and the Peace Corps whose larger budgets are making it possible to increase American exchange operations significantly at virtually all levels.

Coordination of government exchange activities is particularly essential because not only the State Department but the Agency for International Development and, to a much smaller extent, the United States Information Agency are involved in moving persons between countries. Though they have different purposes, these agencies operate in many of the same countries and, in numerous instances, in the same subject matter. In addition, a number of American foundations and other private organizations conduct similar activities, as do the United Nations and its specialized agencies. Moreover, as indicated earlier, the State Department program is handled in the field by USIS officers. To cope with the resulting overlap, the Department of State on January 25, 1957, requested each chief of mission overseas to set up a coordinating mechanism composed of appropriate diplomatic, technical assistance, and information personnel. This coordinating mechanism was not working well, however, and late in May, 1961, President Kennedy instructed each of our ambassadors to take complete charge of all our growing operations in his country. Program initiative and operational control still tend to remain where the money is, nonetheless, and the State Department's exchange budget remains disproportionately small.

The phrase *educational and cultural affairs* has come to encompass more than educational exchange of students, teachers, and scholars. Journalists, business and labor leaders, women leaders, creative artists, and others have been added to the exchange of persons program. The interchange of cultural products, including not only performing artists but books, films, photographs, and paintings as well, has also grown. Scientific and technical knowledge has been exchanged through both individuals and publications. Finally, the development of educational and cultural enterprises overseas has been added, including seminars in American studies and support for American-sponsored schools and colleges.

Exchange grants for Africa were slow in getting under way. In the nine years from 1949 through 1957, only 224 government grants were given to Africans for study or consultation in the United States, while only 107 grants were made to Americans for study in Africa (not including 384 Egyptians who came to the United States and 161 Americans who went to Egypt). In 1958 a change occurred, and a general expansion of America's African activities began. This is evident in the State Department's 1958 budget for educational exchange, which provided for 299 exchanges with Africa at a cost of $1,679,517. Even with this increase, however, the cost of exchanges with Africa was still only 8 percent of the total exchange budget. Meanwhile, our diplomatic and consular posts in Africa began making more and more specific requests for exchanges, and it soon became clear that the Department of State could easily have spent in 1958 twice the funds it was able to allocate to Africa.

As a result of these and other pressures, the budget for African educational exchanges doubled between 1958 and 1961. In 1960 the State Department financed 362 African and 62 American visits, the International Cooperation Administration supported 456 visits by Africans and 585 by Americans, and the Defense Department financed the visits of 65 Africans and 6 Americans—all at a total cost of $15,500,000.

Meanwhile, the number of Africans in American colleges and universities was rising sharply, from 1515 in the academic year 1957–1958 to 2831 in 1960–1961. The total has tripled within a decade and, at the present rate of increase, may reach 8000 by 1970. Africans still constitute only 5 percent of the total number of foreign students in the United States, however. Table 18, prepared from statistics in *Open Doors 1961*, a publication of the Institute of International Education, shows the number of African students, their country of origin and their financial support, and their academic class and fields of study.

While there is general agreement on the value of exchanges of graduate students and older persons pursuing training programs,

TABLE 18. African Students in the United States

	Algeria	Congo (Brazzaville)	Egypt	Ethiopia	Federation of Rhodesia and Nyasaland	Ghana	Guinea	Kenya
Students								
Total Students	12	11	840	171	61	160	13	332
Male	12	10	720	149	54	148	13	289
Female		1	120	22	7	12		43
New Students	2	9	362	68	36	46	11	184
Financial support[a]								
U.S. government	5		109	51	10	14	1	24
Foreign government		3	236	59		39	1	10
Self		2	124	7	16	13	1	54
Other private	2	5	151	28	24	66	2	202
U.S. government and private			5	1	6	2		13
Foreign government and private			12	1	1	2		3
Academic status[a]								
Undergraduate	4	5	140	65	31	77	13	283
Graduate	5	2	634	76	23	64		33
Special	2		39	24	6	12		11
Field of study[a]								
Agriculture			51	8	1	13		10
Business administration		1	70	18	2	5	3	24
Education			51	26	5	11		20
Engineering	3	2	171	19	3	24		13
Humanities	3	5	99	23	15	26		38
Medical science	1		73	11	4	14		33
Physical and natural sciences	4		170	21	13	25	7	63
Social sciencies	1	2	129	41	17	40	2	124
All others			7	4				

[a] Some students did not report these particulars.

Liberia	Libya	Morocco	Nigeria	Sierra Leone	South Africa	Sudan	Tanganyika	Tunisia	Uganda	Others[b]	Total
166	38	64	343	60	244	109	62	54	40	51	2831
125	37	51	324	44	208	106	56	53	30	47	2476
41	1	13	19	16	36	3	6	1	10	4	355
43	20	24	136	19	106	62	40	42	19	27	1256
18	9	37	24	1	18	63	6	47	8	15	460
77	12	2	62		21	5	9	1	4	4	545
20	3	6	57	22	65	4	3		4	10	411
25	2	8	145	31	101	12	30	1	18	16	869
			3	1	4	1	4	2	4	1	47
4	1	1	11		4		4				44
102	20	40	225	43	104	28	47	2	20	32	1281
46	11	12	94	16	123	38	11	4	16	14	1222
11	7	9	15	1	9	38	4	46	4	4	242
11	7	3	5	3	12	22	4		2	1	153
17		2	8	5	22	2	2	41	3	1	226
15		2	28	2	11	6	4			4	185
20	6	9	52	6	21	23	4	1	3	7	387
27	6	15	40	9	51	9	13	5	11	17	412
11	4	3	41	7	31	2	2	1	4		242
14	4	11	70	12	61	13	9	1	5	5	508
35	9	14	82	12	33	20	24	5	11	12	613
7						8				3	29

[b] "Others" include students from Angola, Basutoland, Congo (Leopoldville), British Cameroons, Republic of Cameroon, Dahomey, Ivory Coast, Malagasy Republic, Mauritius, St. Helena, Senegal, Somalia, South-West Africa, Swaziland, Togo, and Zanzibar.

numerous Americans are concerned over the problems of the large number of African undergraduates in American universities. Some observers have contended that we should not have so many undergraduate students because they are too often inadequately prepared, poorly financed, sent to the wrong universities, and antagonized by racial slights in this country. Such problems were studied in a 1949 Phelps-Stokes Fund survey of African students in the United States, and more recently have been fully documented in a 1961 survey sponsored by the Institute of International Education.[7]

The IIE study, conducted by a University of Michigan team, was based on a questionnaire returned by 1010 African students, along with interviews of 208 African students and 112 institutional administrators on 43 campuses. It found four types of difficulties encountered by African students: general, academic, financial, and social. The general difficulties were mostly temporary problems of first-year students in adjusting to American food and communicating in American English. Academic difficulties were reported by numerous students who were unaccustomed to the American system of "elective" courses; they complained that they did not know what courses to take. This indicated inadequate counseling services in the United States and the absence of definite plans at home for employing the American-trained student upon his return. Nearly four-fifths of the students reported, however, that they were satisfied with their academic programs, and 84 percent thought they were doing about as well or better than most foreign students.

On financial problems, three-fifths reported that they managed well or very well financially, while the balance said they had "many difficulties" or "barely enough to live on." Forty-seven percent earned money through summer employment. No relationship was discovered, however, between the extent of a student's financial problems and his grades.

The most important information elicited by the survey concerned the response of Africans to their personal relationships with Americans. On the one hand they liked American friendliness, while on the other they resented American racial discriminations. They ex-

---

[7]·James M. Davis, Russell G. Hanson, and Duane Burnor, *IIE Survey of the African Student: His Achievements and His Problems*, New York, 1961.

pected discrimination and encountered it. In the North it was worse than anticipated, while in the South it was not much worse than they expected. Africans were quite critical of whites who treated them better after they had identified themselves as Africans rather than American Negroes. The Africans were also disappointed in American Negroes, who seemed to lack interest in them. Twenty-seven percent of the Africans in Negro colleges reported that they had no friends among American Negroes. In the North, 45 percent said they had no Negro friends.

These details should alert private citizens to an important problem they can do something about. Local communities in which Africans live could each perform a real service by systematic planning to ease African students' difficulties. The IIE survey lists the number of African students in some 366 colleges and universities located in 48 states and the District of Columbia. The largest numbers are 164 in California, 130 in New York, and 123 in the District of Columbia.

The reaction of African students to their American environment is not particularly surprising. All foreign students, in fact all students, have similar problems. Despite difficulties, most African students have shown considerable sophistication in their reactions to America. They do not generalize that America is entirely bad because of its racial situation. Many admire the friendly qualities of Americans and are impressed by American attitudes toward labor when, for example, they see their own professors painting their houses in the summer or doing other manual work. A large number have become leaders on their return home, and many of them carry a warm feeling toward Americans with them. The alumni association of Nigerian graduates of American universities is a living proof of this. The active branch of more than 50 members in Ibadan is known as the Nigerian American Society. And President Nkrumah of Ghana, despite criticisms made of him by some Americans, retains a warm memory of America formed in his own student days. One of Ghana's postage stamps portrays Nkrumah looking at the Lincoln Memorial in Washington, a much happier bit of symbolism than if it were Lenin's Memorial in Moscow.

Africans educated in the United States and Europe could also become the most effective force in the inevitable process of blending traditional and modern ways. It is essential, therefore, to win the confidence of African leaders, because they set the pattern for other Africans to follow. It should not be forgotten that Communist strategy and tactics place a high priority on winning student movements along with the intellectuals who set student fashions. For these reasons the presence of a growing number of African students and other African visitors in the United States represents a significant challenge to American intelligence and good will. If properly handled, its advantages to both Africans and Americans should far outweigh any disadvantages.

One useful step in tackling the problems of African students was announced on July 1, 1961. A Council for Educational Cooperation was formed by six private agencies—the African-American Institute, the African American Students Foundation, the African Scholarship Program of American Universities, the Institute of International Education, the Phelps-Stokes Fund, and the United Negro College Fund. Because it was financed by two grants totaling $125,000, which came from the Department of State, the Council was successful in tackling two short-range problems—the provision of 147 scholarships for East African students and the development of arrangements to meet the 1961 summer employment needs of African students already in the United States. However, when it attempted to deal with larger issues and long-term problems for which it had no administrative or program funds, the Council floundered. Before it can resume effective operations, it must have more funds.

The African-American Institute, in addition to its regular scholarship program, has a special grant from AID for a 1960–1963 program to select and place about 150 students from the Republic of Guinea in American higher-education institutions. The African American Students Foundation was formed to promote and continue the better-known "Kenya Airlift" operation to bring East Africa students to American colleges on scholarships solicited largely by Tom Mboya. In 1960, its second year of operation, it received a grant of $100,000 from the Joseph P. Kennedy Foundation, which enabled it to raise to 289 the number of students it transported. Still another group is the African Scholarship Program of American Universities (ASPAU), a better-planned effort of 192 American universities and colleges which initially brought 24 Nigerian students over in 1960. The following year, ASPAU expanded its operation into 17 African countries and raised its number to 300 students. Its four-way support includes maintenance and living costs from AID, travel costs from the African governments participating in the program, administrative support from several American foundations, and room and board costs of the students, which are borne by the colleges themselves.

In the fall of 1961, a total of 679 new African students arrived under various forms of U.S. government assistance. Confronted with the prospects of a continued increase in the flow of African students, the Institute of International Education has proposed opening field offices in Africa to assist in the selection of suitable candidates and to serve as a source of information on opportunities available in American higher education. Under this plan, the IIE would also furnish data to American institutions on the priority and manpower training needs of African states, and would provide information on the education systems of the African countries from which students come. However, the successful implementation of this attractive idea will depend upon the availability of funds from both private and government sources.

It is also vital to the United States to have more and more Americans visit and revisit Africa. This is an essential element in the process of broadening and deepening American knowledge. Despite the progress of African studies in American universities during the past decade, there are still very few Americans with more than a superficial understanding of Africa. The rise of Africa has been so sudden that educational curriculums in the American primary- and secondary-school system have yet to catch up with it. Furthermore, the flow of American professors, teachers, and research scholars to Africa is still a trickle compared to that going to Europe, Latin America, and even Asia. Finally, few American students are to be found on the rapidly developing university campuses of Africa. Until more Americans make Africa a primary area of interest and concern and introduce themselves personally to its challenges and opportunities, much of the American image in Africa will remain that of the Hollywood film and the newspaper headline.

SUMMARY

In summing up the aid, information, and exchange programs described in these two chapters, it is pertinent to recall that their combined budgetary allocations for Africa in the fiscal year ending June 30, 1961, including Egypt, amounted to $206,800,000 for the ICA, $6,500,000 for the USIA, and $3,300,000 for the State Department's educational exchange program—a total of about $216,600,000. In addition, our agricultural surplus disposals in Africa totaled $262,000,-000. A small amount of military assistance, valued at $11,600,000, was also provided. It should not be forgotten that about 70 percent of all dollars for foreign aid are spent in the United States. Can such an investment be considered a heavy financial drain on the American people, who spend a billion dollars a year on pets? An AID official has pointed out that although our nation is 150 percent richer than when we launched the Marshall Plan, each American is contributing less than half as much for economic aid as he did between 1946 and 1951. Moreover, when aid is calculated as a percentage of gross national product, the United States ranks not first but fifth among the top ten countries contributing aid.[8]

[8] Frank M. Coffin, "Allies Are Carrying Their Share of Aid," *Washington Post*, June 3, 1962, pp. E1, E5.

21

The Impact of Africa
on International Relations

T HIS analysis of Africa's relations with the outside
world has focused primarily on the impact of external pressures on
Africa. Simultaneously, Africa was having a profound effect on international relations. Within a single decade, the disintegration of
the colonial system gave rise to so many new and troublesome issues
and attitudes that it altered the scope and character of world politics.
Since these changes are still under way, their meaning and ramifications are not entirely clear. In the search for a unifying theory to
give meaning to this turbulent period, Robert C. Good has termed
it the postcolonial era. Colonialism has almost ended, but the process
of mental decolonization is far from complete. The thinking of
many of us, both black and white, is still suffering from a severe
colonial hangover.

The decline of colonialism, however, was not an exclusively post-
World War II phenomenon. The number of independent states had
increased for a century and a half, despite the building of great
colonial empires. Quincy Wright once calculated that 33 of the
states which agreed to the U.N. Charter in 1945 had become independent since the middle of the eighteenth century, 12 of them
since the mid-nineteenth century, and 6 since 1930. The new states

of the past 15 years are different, however, in one important respect: they are all "non-Western" states whose political disagreements with the "white" states of the West sometimes have a racial tinge. Let us hope that the postcolonial era does not turn into a "racial era" in international relations.

THE INFLUX OF NEW STATES

The most obvious impact of Africa on international relations is the great increase in the number of states. The 45 states whose representatives signed the United Nations Charter in 1945 quickly grew to 60. After a decade of operation as a 60-member organization, the U.N. suddenly expanded to 82 states when a "package deal" on the admission of new members was agreed to by the Soviet Union and the United States. The second influx of new states began in 1960; Africa brought the total to 104 by the end of 1961, with possibly another 20 colonies on the road to independence. This striking increase obviously complicates international relations. It creates not only substantive problems but organizational difficulties for all the foreign offices of the world. It brings forth a large group of untrained and inexperienced diplomats dealing with unfamiliar tasks.

The efforts of African leaders to develop independent foreign policies raise significant questions for research and analysis. It is too early for a comprehensive study comparable to Russell H. Fifield's 1958 book, *The Diplomacy of Southeast Asia: 1945–1958.* Fifield's book is useful to Africanists, however, because it portrays the new states of Southeast Asia with many of the same characteristics that one observes in Africa. The shaping of foreign policy is largely in the hands of a few leaders, while the ordinary citizen has little knowledge of or interest in it. Most leaders have had only limited experience, and often rely on Western diplomatic practice for precedents. They are basically preoccupied with domestic problems and are seldom profound in their knowledge of world affairs. They tend to react to foreign policy questions on a day-to-day basis. They are extremely sensitive to foreign pressure and they are inclined, with their eyes on local reactions, to make public pronouncements which do not always reflect their personal convictions.

Since the new leaders do not yet have experienced foreign service officers abroad, they are often unable to obtain the information and advice needed for the best policy decisions. Their foreign offices are small, but the foreign ministry is often a key post, and the head of state often predominates in the making of foreign policy. The leaders attach real importance to the United Nations, which served as a valuable training school for some of them. And they tend to unite in declaring that the major problem of our times is not the struggle between democracy and communism but the fight against colonialism in all its forms. None of the new heads of state, however, is strong enough to lead the others in foreign policy.

Fifield's generalizations for Southeast Asia would have to be carefully tested in Africa, but there is abundant evidence that African leaders tend to use foreign policy opportunities to magnify and strengthen their own positions at home. They find it useful to exploit anticolonialism, Pan-Africanism, and racialism, the last especially in South Africa, for this purpose. Their tendency to use foreign policy as a response to local political needs is not surprising, but it does raise obstacles to stability in international relations.

It is worthy of special note, however, that Africans have attempted to remedy their lack of training and experience in international relations. The most notable effort was made by Nigeria. During the three years before its independence, it undertook to train 40 diplomats to step into the first diplomatic posts it planned to establish. This training was given in several centers. In Washington it began in October, 1957, under the supervision of Reginald Barrett, a British employee of the Nigerian government who headed the Nigerian Liaison Office, an autonomous branch of the British Embassy. Six midcareer Nigerians with experience in government service were given the title of assistant secretaries in the Nigerian Federal Department of External Affairs and sent to Washington with their wives for training. Others were attached to British embassies elsewhere to obtain practical experience.

The Nigerian trainees in Washington received a well-organized combination of practical experience and instruction in relevant subjects, including diplomatic procedures, international relations, protocol and social usage, and the French language. The United States

Department of State and the British Embassy in Washington made officers available to give lectures and discuss practical problems with the trainees, some of whom also took a regular course called African Issues in International Relations at the Johns Hopkins School of Advanced International Studies.

During their program, the participants spent a period of time in New York at the United Nations, where they served as members of the British Delegation. Their wives were given a special short course on what foreign service wives need to know.

The success of the Nigerian program attracted considerable interest. In the autumn of 1960 when Nigeria attained its independence, the better known Carnegie Endowment Programs in Diplomacy began under Barrett's direction. It was open to diplomatic trainees from all the new states of Africa and Asia. Financed by a grant from the Rockefeller Foundation to the Carnegie Endowment for International Peace, the program began in Geneva, New York, and Washington and later spread to other centers in Europe, Asia, and Africa.

In addition to their lack of experience in foreign affairs, the new states of Africa are all handicapped by weak and vulnerable economies and by the lack of enough African administrators and technicians to deal efficiently with the intricate problems of relatively large and modern states composed of peoples with different languages and backgrounds. In many of the new states there is a tendency toward despotism, more or less benevolent. Such regimes may stabilize the situation temporarily, but they do not necessarily solve the basic economic and educational problems. Their benevolent character may disappear and instability may again arise. In international relations this fosters confusion and uncertainty.

Another possible upsetting element might be the future development of arms and armies in Africa. Armies take money which is needed for economic growth, but numerous African states may feel increasingly compelled to build up their military forces, at least to some extent, if only as a token of their sovereignty. Guinea, with a population of 3,400,000, appropriated $8,500,000 or 25 percent of its total budget in the calendar year 1961 for an armed force of 3300 men; a police force of 2100, and a republican guard of 1200. Nigeria, with a population of 40,000,000, appropriated $26,400,000 or 17.9 percent of its budget in the fiscal year ending March 31, 1962, for an armed force of 8000 men and a police force of 12,800. And Ghana allocated $28,500,000 or 10.4 percent of its budget in the fiscal year ending June 30, 1961, for an army of 7700 men and a police force of 7500 for its population of 6,800,000. President Nkrumah has proclaimed July 1 as Armed Forces Day, and on the occasion of its first celebration he declared that "we are determined to build the best equipped and most efficient Armed Forces in modern Africa."[1] In an obvious reference to Ghana, President Houphouet-Boigny of the Ivory Coast remarked in February, 1962, that "a neighbouring country that is not at all faced with any threat of aggression—immediate or eventual—is busily piling up armaments many times more than her limited manpower of trained technical nationals require."[2] In 1962, however, there was no real evidence that African leaders intended to use their armies for aggression. The Ghanaians and Nigerians take considerable interest and pride in the role of their troops in the U.N. force in the Congo.

When American military assistance is requested, the United States judges each request on its merits but generally attempts to dissuade African leaders, except in North Africa, from developing military forces beyond the minimum requirements of defense. During his visit to the United States in July, 1961, Nigerian Prime Minister Abubakar Tafawa Balewa asked Secretary of State Dean Rusk for a jet fighter squadron of the latest type. In responding to this request, Rusk pointed out that the cost of such a squadron and its maintenance would be so great that it might equal the cost of educating up to 5,000,000 Nigerians. In 1961 the Department of State also refused to approve South Africa's request for jet fighters, but for a different reason: it was afraid the planes might be used by the government during the suppression of possible internal disturbances.

The advent of new African states also poses the possibility of irredentist movements and conflicts over international boundaries. The Somali unification movement has affected five territories. The Ewe and Togoland unification movement shows signs of revival in the

[1] Embassy of Ghana, Press Release No. 153, Washington, July 17, 1961, p. 2.
[2] "Ivory Coast Foreign Policy," West Africa, February 17, 1962, p. 185.

form of Ghanaian ambitions to absorb the Republic of Togoland or at least its Ewe-speaking peoples. Morocco's desire to "reintegrate" Mauritania creates another problem. South Africa may still cherish lingering hopes of bringing Basutoland, Bechuanaland, and Swaziland as well as the former South-West Africa mandate within its political system. And many other African states and territories are inhabited by peoples who have kinsmen living on the other side of arbitrary boundaries established by colonial powers in earlier times.

Thus far, however, the borders of the colonial period have been preserved by the new states. Long-established boundaries are hard to change, and they may cause fewer disputes than is sometimes feared. Part of the difficulty might be resolved by another new development in international relations—the wide variety of regional movements and organizations described in the chapters on Pan-Africanism. To the extent that these regional efforts succeed, potential international boundary conflicts might be transformed into less-dangerous border adjustments or into tariff, currency, and other common economic arrangements.

RACE RELATIONS BECOME INTERNATIONAL RELATIONS

A second principal impact of the rise of Africa has been its effect in transforming race relations into international relations. The United Nations has become the main mechanism through which racial issues become international disputes. Under the old rules of diplomacy, race relations were considered domestic matters. But the new players from Asia and Africa are making new rules. Although many Western observers deplore this trend as impractical and injurious to international relations, the approaches and conventions of the old diplomacy are no longer adequate. The deep feelings of many new leaders on racial matters can no more be disregarded than the explosive power of nuclear missiles.

To Americans, a notable aspect of this injection of racial issues into international relations is the way it has helped to break down racial segregation in the United States. This is because the rise of Africa and Asia, along with the cold war, focused universal attention on American racial problems. On October 25, 1961, a Ghanaian diplomat at the Africa Conference of the U.S. National Commission for UNESCO described 10 recent cases of racial discrimination against African diplomats in the United States. He pointed out that when a Nigerian diplomat was refused service in a Charlottesville, Virginia, restaurant in December, 1960, the National Council of Nigeria and the Cameroons issued a statement calling the United States "a country devoid of respect for human dignity, a country with completely bankrupt racial policy, a country which still lives in the dark ages, has no claim to leadership of free men."[3]

This was by no means the first African attack on American racism. A decade earlier, when seven Negroes of Martinsville, Virginia, were convicted and executed for rape of a white woman, West Africa's most reknowned nationalist newspaper, *The West African Pilot* of Lagos, made the following editorial comment on February 20, 1951: "By killing these men for a crime in which no white person had ever been condemned, America has lowered its prestige in the world more effectively than any Communist propaganda." In the same year an episode even more striking occurred in Paris in the Assembly of the French union. This parliamentary body, composed of 102 representatives of metropolitan France and 102 representatives of French territories overseas, mostly from Africa, is reported to have observed one minute of official silence in the memory of Willie McGee, a Mississippi Negro who was convicted and executed for rape of a white woman. Such adverse propaganda had already begun to worry numerous American officials before the Till murder trial, the Clinton school segregation affair, the Autherine Lucy case, and especially the Montgomery bus boycott were picked up by the world press. And it penetrated the top echelons of government when the Little Rock crisis burst into the headlines as the most heavily reported U.S. story abroad in 1957.

As Harold Isaacs has pointed out in his stimulating writings on the impact of world affairs on U.S. race relations, the Russians were quite clever in exploiting it. When they launched Sputnik I, they mock-

[3] E. M. Debrah, "The Effect of the Existence of Segregation in the U.S. on the American Image in Africa," U.S. National Commission for UNESCO, Press Release, Nat. Conf. 8/18, October 25, 1961.

ingly included Little Rock in the daily itinerary they issued to announce the towns it passed above as it circled the globe. When Vice-President Richard M. Nixon and his wife were attacked in Venezuela, the angry crowds shouted at them, "Little Rock! Little Rock!" Local Communists often helped to incite racial feelings. American embassies and consulates abroad flooded Washington with cabled reports of the damage Little Rock was doing to the American image around the world, and the propaganda machinery of the United States Information Agency was mobilized to produce additional defensive explanations and justifications.

The dispatch of federal troops to Little Rock raised a major issue in the old constitutional dispute over the respective powers of our federal and state governments, but when President Eisenhower appeared on television to explain his action to the nation, he emphasized the damage Little Rock was doing to the United States abroad, a point that was also stressed by the Secretary of State and by most American newspapers.

By focusing world publicity on American racial difficulties, the rise of Africa and Asia thus stimulated federal intervention to help American Negroes in their long fight against discrimination. It also had something of a tendency to reinvigorate their struggle, helping to induce at least some Negroes to undertake "positive action." The emotional welcome of Kwame Nkrumah in 1956 by Harlem and Chicago Negroes surprised many observers. The Negro passive resistance leader, Reverend Martin Luther King, Jr., who led the bus boycott in Montgomery, Alabama, told an enthusiastic Negro youth conference, according to *The New York Times* of April 17, 1960:

This is an era of offensive on the part of oppressed people. All peoples deprived of dignity and freedom are on the march on every continent throughout the world. The student sit-in movement [which swept the South after February 1, 1960] represents just such an offensive in the history of the Negro peoples' struggle for freedom. The students have taken the struggle for justice into their own hands!

Speaking to Howard University students three years later, on April 8, 1962, King urged American Negroes to "wake up" and participate in the "great social revolution" that is sweeping imperialism out of Africa and segregation out of the United States.

By thus associating themselves with a worldwide movement, the new radical Negro leaders could think of themselves as more than a small minority, only a tenth of our population. They could consider themselves "a segment of the power of Bandung." They sometimes attacked the older National Association for the Advancement of Colored People as a "black bourgeois club." Occasionally this new Negro consciousness fostered violence. On the night of April 3, 1960, three young Negroes in Portland, Oregon, pulled up in a car and assaulted several whites, one of whom died. When questioned by police, the Negroes said they "had been reading about South Africa and troubles in our own South, and just went out to do something about it."[4]

The rise of Africa also helped to strengthen the extremist Black Muslim movement in the United States, which contends that the white man has deliberately "written the Negro out of history." In his book *The Black Muslims in America*, Eric Lincoln writes that the desire of Black Muslims to have their children learn something about the past is surprisingly strong in the Black Muslim parochial schools in Chicago and Detroit, particularly since African states have gained their independence.

The impact of Africa on American race relations is most direct in the case of the African diplomats who were denied service in restaurants along Route 40 as they traveled back and forth between their embassies in Washington and United Nations headquarters in New York. When K. A. Gbedemah, Ghanaian Minister of Finance, was turned away from a Howard Johnson restaurant in Dover, Delaware, on October 7, 1957, President Eisenhower invited him to the White House for breakfast, and Howard Johnson called at his New York hotel to apologize in person. Johnson also sent letters to all his 550 restaurants reminding them that it was company policy to serve whoever entered; 60 percent of the chain, however, were locally owned restaurants under franchises which did not contain nondiscrimination requirements.

Similar incidents of discrimination along Route 40 and elsewhere continued until the Kennedy Administration took more vigorous steps in 1961 to prevent it. When William Fitzjohn, Sierra Leone chargé

[4] *Star* (Johannesburg), April 4, 1960.

d'affaires, was refused service at a Howard Johnson restaurant in Hagerstown, Maryland, on March 9, 1961, Angier Biddle Duke, the State Department's Chief of Protocol, sent a letter of apology to Fitzjohn and a letter to Howard Johnson asking for another explanation of the chain's policy. A White House official requested the Department of Justice to determine what legal powers the government might have to avert discrimination against diplomats. The Hagerstown restaurant announced on April 10 that it was dropping its racial barriers immediately and, in a unique aftermath, about 200 leading Hagerstown citizens, including 30 Negro couples, held a banquet on June 23 in Mr. Fitzjohn's honor. According to Cabell Phillips in *The New York Times* of June 24, it was "the first such mixed social event here in the memory of citizens."

Other efforts were also made by federal officials in 1961. The White House drew the attention of the governors of Maryland and other states to the seriousness of the situation, and Under Secretary of State Chester Bowles invited Maryland editors to a luncheon meeting at the State Department where he asked for their help. Two hundred leaders of communities along Route 40 were called to a meeting at which a personal plea from President Kennedy was read. On September 13, 1961, the State Department took the unusual step of sending Pedro Sanjuan, Assistant Chief of Protocol, to testify before the Legislative Council of the General Assembly of Maryland in support of a bill to outlaw discrimination in public accommodations. In a vigorous plea, Sanjuan declared:

Recently during a period of two weeks four African ambassadors were humiliated by private restaurant owners on Route 40 in Maryland. One of them was refused a cup of coffee while he was en route to present his credentials to the President of the United States. I would like to put this in the clearest terms possible—that when an American citizen humiliates a foreign representative or another American citizen for racial reasons, the results can be just as damaging to his country as the passing of secret information to the enemy.

The idea that they were damaging American foreign policy by "refusing to serve a sandwich to a passing Negro" seemed incredible to many small cafe proprietors along Route 40 who had run a "white only" business for years. As one of them is said to have remarked, however, "I really don't want to serve Negroes, but if the President of the United States tells me I should, well, I guess I should."[5] In his mind, this pressure from the federal government seemed more influential than the simultaneous sit-in and picketing demonstrations being waged along Route 40 by American Negro and other groups.

The impact of the rise of Africa on American race relations is quite clear, particularly in the changing attitudes of whites. Many Americans have long had a "sense of guilt" about our failure to live up to our democratic and Christian ideals, as psychologist Gordon W. Allport has pointed out. In his words, this sense of guilt was "sharply enhanced" when the United States learned that "its greatest handicap in dealing with the colored nations and colonial peoples of the world is its treatment of American Negroes."[6] The impact of Africa on American Negro attitudes is more speculative. Ernest Dunbar and other Negroes have pointed out that their fight against racial discrimination began long before the rise of Africa. We have seen that certain Negro leaders do exploit the rise of Africa to arouse further enthusiasm for the fight against discrimination in the United States, but it is difficult to judge its significance for the American Negro population as a whole. It is perhaps less important than it sometimes appears.

POLITICAL INTERPRETATION OF INTERNATIONAL LAW

This transformation of domestic racial issues into world affairs helps to explain a third impact of Africa on international relations. It is influencing international law by breaking down the old distinction between domestic and foreign affairs. This is especially obvious in U.N. disputes over Article 2(7) of the Charter, the "domestic jurisdiction" clause: "Nothing contained in the present Charter shall authorize the United Nations to intervene in matters which are essentially within the domestic jurisdiction of any state." Despite this clause, the United Nations has frequently discussed North African and South African matters which, in the view of French, South

[5] Quoted by Robert E. Baker, "Bowles Pleads with Md. Editors to Aid Cafe Bias Fight," *Washington Post*, September 27, 1961.
[6] Gordon W. Allport, *The Nature of Prejudice*, Toronto, 1958, pp. 329–330.

African, and other delegations are outside the legal competence of the U.N. The statements and votes of United States delegates, among others, are steadily whittling away at the limitations of Article 2(7). The deliberate vagueness of the article, which contains such ambiguities as "intervene," "essentially," and "domestic," is said to be partly the work of John Foster Dulles at San Francisco in 1945.

When the item on race conflict in South Africa arose in the General Assembly's Ad Hoc Political Committee in 1952, the United States representative declared on November 15 that the United States believed that the Assembly enjoyed under the Charter the full right of discussion of relevant matters and that the exercise of that right did not contravene the restriction imposed by Article 2(7). He went on to explain the rationale of the United States position as follows.

My Delegation . . is frankly concerned not to see the door of legality bolted in a way which would prevent adequate consideration of the vital and far-reaching problem of human rights in this changing world; but we are equally concerned not to open the door at this time to every sort of proposal. Wise statesmanship suggests that we leave the door ajar and neither close it tight nor open it wide. That conclusion flows out of our own experience under a written constitution. It was the broad construction of the United States Constitution by Chief Justice John Marshall which gave that document vitality and permitted the nation under it to grow and mature.[7]

The United States representative then questioned the "practical wisdom" of South Africa's *apartheid* policy, but urged the Assembly to affirm its respect for human rights "in general terms," calling on all members to work toward this goal. This, he said, would "avoid the vexing issue of competence and avoid also the danger of the stability of this organization inherent in singling out for direct action special legislation of a Member State."

Calling attention to the fact that the Assembly had no power to enforce change but "only the power to urge in order to persuade," the United States representative concluded in these terms:

We would leave enforcement to the lively conscience of each country and to the power of the public opinion of the world. This course may

[7] U.S. Delegation to the General Assembly, Statement by the Honorable Charles A. Sprague in the Ad Hoc Political Committee, Press Release No. 1585, November 15, 1952.

not satisfy those eager to crack down on a Member whom they regard as delinquent. It will not satisfy those who, not recognizing the limitations of this organization, want the United Nations to *do something* about distressing situations. But in the long run, this course may accomplish far more than abrupt and direct action. Let us not impute evil purpose or lack of intelligence to the people of South Africa. Rather our attitude should be one of neighborly helpfulness in working out just solutions to the difficult problems they face in the field of race relations in their country.

As already pointed out, the United States later stiffened its attitude toward South Africa for political reasons. From the beginning it took the position that U.N. controversies over Africa were essentially political rather than legal problems. In the view of the State Department's legal advisers, Article 2(7) does not bar the discussions authorized under Article 10, which says that the General Assembly may discuss any question or any matters within the scope of the Charter. In this view, intervention presumably means some kind of enforcement action rather than simply discussion or even recommendations. Certain international lawyers even go beyond this position and maintain that enforcement action is not necessarily barred by Article 2(7).

During the discussion cited above, an enterprising representative from Pakistan quoted relevant American views expressed in the United States Senate *Hearings* on Chapter IX of the Charter in which Articles 55 and 56 on human rights and related matters are found. When a senator asked whether he was correct in thinking "that any racial matter, any of these matters we are talking about, that originate in one country domestically and that [have] the possibility of making international trouble, might be subject to the investigation and recommendations" of the U.N., the State Department representative replied: "I should think so, because the Organization is created for that."[8]

The domestic jurisdiction clause was derived from a similar formula in Article 15, Paragraph 8, of the Covenant of the League of Nations. In League days, the clause was given what has been called a legal

---

[8] U.S. Delegation to the Seventh General Assembly, *Verbatim Text of the Statement of the Delegate of Pakistan . . . at the 15th Meeting of the Ad Hoc Political Committee, November 13, 1952,* US/A/AC.61/4, November 13, 1952.

interpretation. The League's Council was careful, in deciding whether a case was within its competence, to base its decision on customary international law and relevant treaties rather than on moral obligations and the pressure of world opinion.

In the United Nations, however, a less objective and more political interpretation has been given to the domestic jurisdiction clause. The difference between legal and political interpretations is elaborated by John Howell in an article on "The French and South African Walkouts and Domestic Jurisdiction" in *The Journal of Politics* for February, 1956. In practice, the U.N. interpretation has come to mean that a matter is no longer domestic if a sufficient majority of the U.N members decide that a U.N. organ is competent to deal with it. Those delegations which have attempted to justify this position have developed what has been called a doctrine of international concern. In the first year of the United Nations, the Australian representative in the Security Council said:

> When you look at the internal affairs of a country you start off with the postulate that it is no business of any other nation to concern itself with how the people of that country govern themselves . . . , but if the facts indicate that that regime, by its nature, by its conduct, by its operations, is likely to interfere with international peace, and likely to be a menace to its neighbours, then the existence of that regime is no longer a matter of essentially domestic concern.[9]

This doctrine appears to make potential as well as actual threats to the peace a matter of international concern. The substitution of *concern* for *jurisdiction* further confuses the matter. Certain delegations, moreover, tend to support the strictly legal concept to keep the United Nations out of their own affairs while supporting the loose political interpretation to get the United Nations into African problems. The Soviet bloc fosters still another interpretation of domestic jurisdiction, contending that if a state has a political organization competent to deal with a matter, it is domestic. The Mindszenty case, which came before the Assembly, was domestic because there were laws for settling it, but the race conflict in South Africa is not domestic because there are no laws capable of settling it! More-

[9] Quoted by John M. Howell, "The French and South African Walkouts and Domestic Jurisdiction," *Journal of Politics*, February, 1956, p. 98.

over, a Polish representative contended that the problem of Negroes in the Southern United States was not domestic because although

> . . . the domestic jurisdiction of the United States was based on that country's Constitution . . . the legislation of the Southern States was, on that point, in contradiction with the Constitution. The Government of the United States could answer that it was not in a position to interfere with the legislation of the Southern States, but, in so doing, it would be proving that all matters in the Southern States did not come under national jurisdiction and that some of them should therefore be settled by a decision of the United Nations.[10]

The conflict over the domestic jurisdiction clause in certain African disputes aroused great bitterness, and induced French and South African delegations to walk out of U.N. discussions more than once. Occasionally it was suggested that the International Court of Justice be asked for a ruling on the applicability of Article 2(7) to certain cases, particularly the item on race conflict in South Africa. There was little enthusiasm for this idea, however, the general feeling being that it was better to let the General Assembly "feel its way," allowing it to grow through experience.

Whether rightly or wrongly, the old legal interpretation of domestic jurisdiction has thus been successfully challenged in the United Nations by a less objective and more political interpretation. And it is the emergence of African issues which has led to this change, particularly two of those three hardy perennials from South Africa which blossom forth on the General Assembly's agenda every September.

TUMULT IN THE U.N.

A fourth and related impact of African controversies has been the weakening of the United Nations by breaking down the spirit of cooperation necessary to make it work with maximum effectiveness. Speaking on the Congo crisis in his first major address to the United Nations Security Council on February 15, 1961, Adlai Stevenson declared, "The issue is simply this: Shall the U.N. survive?" As he spoke, a flying wedge of about 30 American Negroes overpowered two U.N. guards and stormed into the packed public gallery, shouting, "Lumumba! Lumumba!"

[10] *Ibid.*, p. 101.

The 1961 dispute over U.N. policy in the Congo came after a decade of quarreling on other issues. During these earlier controversies the French and South African delegations had temporarily walked out or refused to participate in General Assembly discussions affecting them, the Belgians had permanently withdrawn from the Committee on Information from Non–Self-Governing Territories, and the United Kingdom and Australia had indicated that they would no longer cooperate if the Assembly took certain objectionable steps in the colonial field. In India, Prime Minister Nehru told the House of the People on June 12, 1952, that if "the whole of Asia and Africa combined cannot get a subject discussed [Tunisia was in his mind] because two or three great powers object, then the time may come when the Asian and African countries will feel that they are happier in their own countries and not in the U.N."

By the early 1950s, many Europeans had already developed the negative philosophy that the U.N. was nothing more than a necessary evil, at least as far as Africa was concerned. For most of this decade, however, the Western powers could muster enough votes for the necessary one-third plus one needed to defeat Assembly resolutions to which they took strong exception. It was not until 1960, when the African and Asian states became almost a majority of the Assembly membership, that the West appeared to be losing this position.

On December 18, 1961, British Foreign Secretary Lord Home told the House of Commons that the United Nations could reach a point in the Congo where Britain would have to withdraw its support. In a public address 10 days later, he spoke of a "crisis of confidence" in the United Nations, where " a number of countries have voted publicly and without shame in favor of the use of force to achieve national ends."[11] These widely publicized statements precipitated an important debate in the House where, on February 5, 1962, the leader of the Labor Party called for a motion of censure against Conservative Party leadership because of Home's criticism of the U.N. During the debate on the motion, which was rejected, Prime

[11] British Information Services, Reference and Library Division, *Text of the Speech by the Secretary of State for Foreign Affairs*, T. 49, December 29, 1961, p. 2.

Minister Macmillan clarified three major British complaints against the U.N.: (1) the increase in the influence of the Secretary General and the Secretariat "in ways not envisaged in the Charter or in the minds of the founders"; (2) the unforeseen development of the General Assembly because of the frustration of the Security Council by 100 vetos, and because of the growth of the Assembly to 104 members; and (3) the bias and "double standard" of the Assembly which led it to adopt many resolutions on its favorite topic of anti-colonialism while proposing very few "against the true imperialists— the dictatorships, which have seized much of Europe and Asia." Because of the conflict between communism and the free world, Macmillan said, "the whole foundation on which the United Nations was built has been undermined."[12] The press devoted less attention to the fact that both Macmillan and Home also called attention to the constructive work the U.N. was still doing.

Shortly afterward, on February 23, 1962, the British found that they were no longer able to win sufficient votes to defeat a resolution instructing the Assembly's new Special Committee of 17 members to consider whether Southern Rhodesia had attained a full measure of self-government. The vote was 57 to 21 with 24 abstentions. Britain's representative had earlier warned the Assembly's Trustee-ship Committee that such a step would be an "entirely unnecessary and unwise intervention that would be outside the U.N.'s competence." The special autonomous status of Southern Rhodesia, he said, had repeatedly been recognized internationally. This U.N. action in 1962 symbolizes the vast change since 1953 when, after a warning from the British Delegation, India and other anticolonial powers had backed away from an Indian proposal for Trusteeship Committee discussion of Rhodesian affairs.

During 1961, a further impact of Africa on the United Nations seemed to be the growing tendency to insist on purely African solutions for African problems, with Africans regarding the U.N. as a vehicle for this purpose. This is evident in the predominantly African composition of the U.N. Advisory Committee on the Congo; in the large number of African contingents which originally participated in

[12] Great Britain, *Parliamentary Debates, House of Commons*, Vol. 653, No. 48, February 5, 1962, 46–57.

the United Nations military presence in the Congo; in the work of the Special Committee of Seventeen set up by the 1961 General Assembly to study the implementation of the 1960 Assembly's Declaration on the Granting of Independence to Colonial Countries; and in the United Nations Commission appointed to advise on the problems of Ruanda-Urundi. In 1962, moreover, it appeared that the Special Committee of Seventeen would become so active that it would overshadow both the Trusteeship Council and the Committee on Information from Non–Self-Governing Territories.

France's President Charles de Gaulle has condemned General Assembly meetings as "tumultuous and scandalous," and Portugal's Premier Antonio de Oliveira Salazar was even angrier at the U.N.'s failure to support him against India's seizure of Goa. He told the Portuguese National Assembly on January 3, 1962, that he did not know "whether we shall be the first country to abandon the United Nations, but surely we will be among the first. . . . Meanwhile we shall refuse them our collaboration in everything that is not in our direct interest."[13]

It is quite clear that sharp conflicts over colonial and racial issues have broken down the spirit of cooperation and weakened the United Nations, at least in the short run. It is not so clear what the long-run consequences of this discontent and frustration will be. An Assembly of more than 100 members is cumbersome, but it still gets its work done. Despite Soviet efforts, the Assembly is most certainly not a Communist tool. Nor do the 54 African and Asian states control it. They have differences as well as similarities, and they seldom vote as a bloc. The charge that African and Asian states are irresponsible on the issue of colonialism is misleading. Certain delegates make quite radical statements, but the final texts of anticolonial resolutions are usually couched in relatively moderate language. Africans have refused to support certain extremist Soviet resolutions, and Asians have sometimes toned down or helped to defeat African resolutions which have gone further than the Asians consider appropriate. The United States can still obtain the majorities it seeks for many resolutions of importance to itself.

Numerous observers have recently taken a position of "controlled

[13] *The New York Times,* January 4, 1962.

optimism" about the impact of Africa and Asia on the United Nations in order to counter the "uncontrolled pessimism" in other quarters. Several of them participated in a 1961 symposium held by the Johns Hopkins School of Advanced International Studies and the Brookings Institution. In a resulting book, Lincoln P. Bloomfield contends that "the final passing of the colonial issue will profoundly transform the European-United Nations relationship, just as it will transform European-African relations over-all." Moreover, although the African and Asian states "still do not hold the parliamentary whip-hand," their strength constantly forces both the Soviets and ourselves to reappraise our diplomatic priorities.[14] Inis L. Claude, Jr., expresses approval of the new "preventive diplomacy" in which the United Nations sends military units supplied by states other than the great powers into crisis areas like the Suez and the Congo. Ernest A. Gross, in response to the European view that the United States must choose between supporting U.N. debate and supporting its European friends, finds it "closer to the truth" to state the matter just the other way around. "If the approach of our friends is wrong," he writes, "it is they who face a choice of either accepting debate or undermining our common interest."[15] And Harland Cleveland adds that "the Congo operation has helped to develop the law, the tradition, the practice, that mutual involvement in internal affairs is of increasing importance in less-developed areas."[16]

These affirmative views raise the interesting possibility that when the present tumult subsides, the rise of African states might prove to have been a more constructive force in international relations than it now appears.

IMPACT ON THE BRITISH COMMONWEALTH

The effect of African controversies on the British Commonwealth of Nations is a fifth impact of Africa on international relations. It is not easy for British representatives in the United Nations to sit and listen as they are publicly berated by fellow members of their

[14] Lincoln P. Bloomfield, in Francis O. Wilcox and H. Field Haviland, Jr., eds., *The United States and the United Nations*, Baltimore, 1961, pp. 57–59.
[15] *Ibid.*, p. 85.
[16] *Ibid.*, p. 135.

own Commonwealth. The representative of Pakistan, for example, once accused Britain and the other colonial powers of having "a beautiful front and a very large and stinking back yard" extending over the whole continent of Africa.[17]

Britain has nonetheless had notable success in its constructive effort to transform the Commonwealth from a white into a multiracial organization. By 1961, when the "club" lost its biggest troublemaker, South Africa, the remaining four original members had been joined by nine others—four from Asia, four from Africa, and Cyprus. The colored members thus had an eight-to-five majority, with the expectation that they would be joined by Jamaica and Uganda in 1962 and numerous others in later years. The traditional flexibility of the Commonwealth has enabled India, Pakistan, and Ghana to become republics, a status which Tanganyika and others are also expected to obtain. Canada is not in the sterling area although in the Commonwealth, while Burma is in the sterling area but not in the Commonwealth.

The relationship between Britain and the older dominions had its unity in their common ideas and ideals, traditions, feelings, interests, and symbols. The Asian and African members of the new Commonwealth, however, have not only a different color and a different cultural background but a deep antipathy to colonialism, which has a disruptive effect on the Commonwealth when Britain has trouble with white settlers in such areas as Kenya and the Rhodesias.

The task of building the multiracial Commonwealth would be difficult enough even if the only problem were to resolve tensions and disagreements over racial and colonial issues in private discussions at the conference table. But the existence of the United Nations has injected a new factor into the problem, namely, the airing of Commonwealth differences before the eyes and ears of the world. In the General Assembly, where orators speak to a world audience including their own supporters at home, the temptation to go beyond the bounds of propriety sometimes proves too great.

[17] U.S. Delegation to the Seventh General Assembly, *Verbatim Text of the Statement of the Delegate of Pakistan . . . at the 15th Meeting of the Ad Hoc Political Committee, November 13, 1952*, US/A/AC.61/4, November 13, 1952.

It has been argued that U.N. disputes over colonialism provide a safety valve which permits Commonwealth members with divergent views to let off steam that might otherwise explode. While this view contains an element of truth, it is a risky asset which is sometimes offset by the additional tensions created through intemperate controversy. Britain's reservations about U.N. armed intervention in Katanga, for example, aroused African ire and suspicion of British integrity.

Africans nonetheless find several specific advantages in Commonwealth membership. Politically it gives Africans another forum, different from the U.N. but sometimes effective, in which to make known their strong opposition to colonialism and racialism in Africa. Economically it makes an important amount of aid available to Africa, including the resources allocated to the Special Commonwealth African Assistance Plan and to the new British Department of Technical Cooperation. Between 1957 and 1961 Britain doubled its total overseas assistance program, and the government hopes to maintain the flow of aid at a level not less than the figure reached in 1961; in the United Kingdom, there is no anti–foreign-aid lobby comparable to that in the United States. Culturally the Commonwealth appeals to at least some Africans because of its common language, literature, culture, and education system. And psychologically membership in the Commonwealth brings to Africans the symbolism of belonging to a larger group with prestige and tradition, in which African states are equals. The importance which President Nkrumah attached to the Queen's visit to Ghana, at a time when he was under heavy criticism, is a further indication of the psychological value which the Commonwealth attachment can have for Africans. In a joint communiqué signed on October 4, 1961, Nkrumah and Duncan Sandys, British Secretary of State for Commonwealth Relations, declared their conviction "that the Commonwealth as a multiracial association of free peoples could play a unique part in providing a bridge between races and continents and in helping to create trust and understanding between them."[18]

[18] British Information Services, Press Division, *Ghana: Nkrumah/Sandys Statement*, New York, October 6, 1961, p. 11082.

It is uncertain how British admission to the Common Market would affect the Commonwealth. President Nkrumah has attacked the Common Market as a species of Eurafrican neocolonialism, and it is even said that Ghana will leave the Commonwealth if Britain finally joins Europe. Canada, Australia, New Zealand, India, and Pakistan are also reported to have raised objections. The United Kingdom hopes, however, that the transition to Common Market status will be so gradual that it will not prove unduly troublesome. The British further contend that their participation in the Common Market would strengthen the British economy and thereby help to ensure the continuation of their Commonwealth assistance program on an increasing scale.

The success of the multiracial Commonwealth is important to Britain because of its economic and strategic assets as well as its prestige and symbolism. To the West as a whole, moreover, the new Commonwealth provides a valuable link with Africa and Asia. It is one of the major constructive forces of our times. Let us hope that the political inventiveness of the peoples concerned will be equal to the task of continuing its effectiveness. Their talent for flexibility is demonstrated anew in a proposal by Kenneth Robinson in the November, 1961, *Journal of Commonwealth Political Studies*. Robinson calls attention to the fact that the present constitutional delays involved in changing a country's status within the Commonwealth could act as an unnecessary "irritant" which might prejudice the development of a new state's friendly association with the Commonwealth. If new states want to be republics, he asks, "would it not be better for this form of government to be adopted straight away?"

NEW TENSION AMONG WORLD POWERS

A sixth effect of the emergence of Africa was the wide range of new disagreements among the major powers. The resulting tension has already been elaborated in several earlier chapters, and needs only brief recall here. It jeopardized friendly relations between the United States and its allies during critical years in the North Atlantic Treaty Organization. It provoked friction among the colonial powers themselves, particularly French suspicions of British policy in West

Africa. Moreover, the rise of Africa had a significant impact on the ideological rivalry of the Soviet Union and the United States. It stimulated them to step up their efforts, both by increasing their propaganda and by refining their ideas and goals. At the same time, both superpowers were confronted by appeals from African leaders to settle their major cold war disputes.

Finally, the transition of Africa from colonialism to independence has forced us to search for new ways and means of stabilizing international relations in the postcolonial era. Despite its injustices, colonialism had its constructive aspects. From the point of view of economics, it was the galvanizing force which awakened Africans to their opportunities. From the point of view of education, the new ideas it brought to Africans were a modernizing force of revolutionary significance. And from the point of view of international relations, the colonial system tended for a time to maintain a semblance of international order and stability. It provided a worldwide imperial network which made possible a system of law and economic organization which functioned effectively at least part of the time.

When World War II ended, the revolution in great-power relationships transferred to the United States a large part of Britain's earlier role in using power with restraint to maintain international peace and stability. Not only was the United States handicapped by lack of experience, but it inherited its new role during a period of unprecedented change and turmoil. As a result it made numerous mistakes.

The rapid changes in Africa were particularly complex. In fact, they even produced a natural reaction against change, which stimulated a resurgence of tribalism. The word *tribalism*, it might be added, is to some extent a trap for loose thinking; it is used to cover such widely varied phenomena as Tshombe's desire to spend the wealth of Katanga in Katanga, the Mau Mau movement in Kenya, the useful social security activities of the new tribal associations in the towns of Africa, the desire of Hutu farmers in Ruanda-Urundi to escape exploitation by the Tutsi aristocracy, the desire of the Baganda to preserve a political structure they like, and the fear of Ashanti chiefs that Nkrumah would destool them.

DEMANDS ON U.S. STATESMANSHIP, PRESENT AND FUTURE

This confusion over the meaning of tribalism re-emphasizes the complexity of the new Africa and the far-reaching dimensions of the problem of developing a new and effective system of international order and stability. An effective American policy in this extraordinarily fluid situation will require continuous and simultaneous action on four main fronts—in Africa, in Europe, in the United Nations, and at home. Bold programs on each of these fronts will help from time to time, but steady progress on all of them is the main requirement. Promising steps taken in one area can so easily be undermined by missteps elsewhere.

The main needs of our policy in Africa itself were outlined in the two chapters on aid, information, and exchange. For the reasons stated therein, an expansion of all three of these programs is essential. In Europe continual diplomatic overtures are required for better political understanding and for more effective tripartite cooperation with Africans in economic development endeavors. The problem of dealing with Portugal and South Africa is particularly difficult and important. In the past they were partially protected from foreign intervention by the screen unintentionally provided by British, French, and Belgian power in Africa. Today, in their defiance of world opinion, Portugal and South Africa stand naked and alone. Despite their extreme sensitivity to external pressure, the United States cannot keep silent about their misbehavior. Their policies can only lead to trouble for Africa, for themselves, and for the rest of the world. No doubt other policies would also create problems, but Portugal and South Africa will have to move with the trend of the times sooner than they think. Much will depend on how and when they reconcile themselves to this fact, and American diplomacy ought continually to impress it upon them.

In the United Nations, African and Asian members are now so numerous that it is even more important for the United States to avoid being stereotyped as a supporter of colonialism. A belated jump to the front of the anticolonial bandwagon would be somewhat hypocritical, however, and of little lasting value. An independent posture, keeping the door to both groups open, may still prove valuable in the difficult period ahead. In the past American Delegations have perhaps focused too much on the details of each issue and not enough on the significance of the total U.S. voting pattern. United States representatives might profitably relax a little more over the exact wording of resolutions and the occasional intemperance and obduracy of other delegations.

In general, it remains desirable to support as broad an interpretation of the United Nations Charter as practicable. The maintenance of United States support for the expanding U.N. economic and technical assistance programs is also essential. Despite the failures caused by the cold war and by the excessive nationalism of its members, the U.N. is still a valuable forum for discussion, a major center for multilateral diplomacy, a peace-keeping machine useful in certain cases, and a growing economic development agency.

Moreover, despite the bad press on the U.N.'s Congo operation in 1961, a nationwide Gallup poll released in February, 1962, revealed that 80 percent of those Americans questioned felt we should not give up our membership in the U.N., 78 percent thought the U.N. was doing a good or fair job, and 83 percent considered it "very important" to make the U.N. a success. These encouraging statistics should strengthen the determination of American delegates to demonstrate to Africans that Americans share their faith in the value of the United Nations.

At home, our knowledge of Africa and our machinery for dealing with African affairs still need much improvement, but perhaps most of all the United States needs to repair its tarnished image as the land of the free and the home of the brave. As Representatives Hays, O'Hara, and Church reported to the House Committee on Foreign Affairs after their 1957 trip to Africa, they found that "our handling of the race problem is a more decisive factor in shaping African attitudes toward us than many of our high level policy statements and extensive programs."[19] This conviction was echoed by Senators

---

[19] U.S. Congress, House Committee on Foreign Affairs, *Report of the Special Study Mission to the Near East and Africa*, by Representatives Hayes, O'Hara, and Church, 85th Congress, 2nd Session, Washington, 1958, p. 37.

Church, McGee, and Moss in their report on a 1960 mission to Africa. The central fact, they reported to the Senate, is that even those Africans who understand our problems and respect our efforts to end segregation "quite naturally cannot help but react emotionally to widely advertised instances of racial intolerance or violence in this country. . . . This reaction is especially intense when an African diplomat or visiting dignitary is affronted."[20]

Improving the American image is more than a race problem, however. Our reputation as a free land with a pioneering spirit developed in the nineteenth century when the United States was borrowing money from Europe and when its borders were open to immigrants from all the world. Today, the United States is the world's greatest creditor, a situation that endears it to no one. We restrict immigration and are unwilling to make any fundamental change in this policy. We are paying the penalty of all successful political and economic systems by our natural tendency to concentrate on preserving our successes at the cost of the ardor and pioneering spirit which gave them birth. In 1961 and 1962, the new "thunder on the right" made Africans wonder whether the reactionary spirit of McCarthyism was reviving.

The overseas image of American *immobilisme* which Barbara Ward reported after a recent world tour is a real handicap. That is why President Kennedy's attempt to get America "moving ahead" is significant. There is no easy way of doing it. It involves the maintenance of a strong and thriving American economy; continuous efforts to improve the position of the Negro; a more liberal immigration policy; a more liberal passport and visa policy; a freer trade policy, which should help our aid program; and a public more sophisticated in matters affecting international relations.

Particularly important because it affects every step we take on all four of these fronts—in Africa, Europe, the United Nations, and at home—is the underlying need to develop the right general attitude toward Africa and Africans. This applies not only to government

---

[20] U.S. Congress, Senate Committee on Foreign Relations, *Study Mission to Africa, November-December 1960*, Report of Senators Church, McGee, and Moss, 87th Congress, 1st Session, Washington, February 12, 1961, p. 3.

officials but as well to educators, businessmen, religious leaders, labor leaders, and congressmen.

What are the main elements in such an attitude? First of all, an active policy with a sense of urgency is needed, but it must be carried out in a spirit of patience and forbearance. Second, we must recognize our own limitations and, in particular, the limits of foreign policy as a means of changing things outside our control. Third, the new Africa is certain to be full of surprises for all of us (including Africans), and we must not be overly disappointed and succumb to cynicism when today's policy proves to be out of date tomorrow.

Most important of all, Americans must acquire a deeper understanding of the basic fact that Africans are not inferior beings. One of the West's best friends in Nigeria, Obafemi Awolowo, has warned us that "in their heart of hearts the white people, especially those of the Western world," still regard African societies as "inferior."[21] We can hardly expect success until we outgrow this immature persuasion, which is contradicted by the capabilities so many Africans have already demonstrated as doctors, bishops, judges, artists, technicians, U.N. officials, and prime ministers. The bias of Westerners is a habit of mind rooted deep in the history of slavery and reinforced in the last century by racist theories of "social Darwinism." Today it expresses itself in attitudes more condescending than arrogant, but the mixture often proves "even more nauseating than the plain article."

Our white superiority complex subtly and unconsciously induces us to prescribe what Africans ought to have, and keeps us from giving adequate recognition to African wishes. It makes us intolerant of Africa's efforts to develop its own types of political and economic systems, and it fosters exaggerated fears over one-party states and Socialist types of economic planning. It keeps us from grasping the fact that most of the traditional societies of Africa have complex forms of law and organization and do not at all conform to the Western stereotype of simple and savage tribes. And it retards our appreciation of the extensive cultural heritage of Africa, which includes music and dancing with complex rhythms, many kinds of

[21] Obafemi Awolowo, *Awo: The Autobiography of Chief Obafemi Awolowo*, Cambridge, England, 1960, p. 302.

songs and singing styles, a rich collection of folk tales, proverbs and riddles, along with elaborate mythologies, and in western Africa a long tradition of arts and crafts including skilled woodcarving, leather-work, weaving, and cire perdue casting and other metal work. The art of Nigeria and certain other regions of Africa is today recognized by specialists as a major world cultural resource.

In the rediscovery of their own culture and values, many thousands of Africans are now visiting museums in Abidjan, Abomey, Accra, Douala, Lagos, Livingstone, Nairobi, and elsewhere. At the same time, Africans are expressing themselves in new forms of creative art in painting, drama, and literature. The arts have been sorely neglected in our aid and exchange program because of the priority given to economic and educational development. Both government and private agencies ought to do much more to stimulate American appreciation of African history and cultural achievements in order to help over-come the bias which handicaps us.

Africans are "just such a strange mixture of good and evil as men are everywhere else," David Livingstone concluded after many years of observing their behavior and misbehavior. The right attitude to-ward Africans is admirably reflected in this perceptive remark. The principle of racial equality, it is true, has already won the lip service of policy-makers. But do they really believe in it?

In Washington in 1961, I participated in numerous private discus-sions of African foreign policies by a group of highly trained specialists in international relations, men with both government and academic background. One of those present opined that African leaders were inferior; another said that they were behaving like "children"; and a third commented that African behavior was "paranoidal." These views brought back to my mind a warning that "half-truths" can be-come "mortal errors," an admonition that came not from a modern behavioral scientist but from a wise old colonialist, Pierre Ryckmans, who devoted 40 years of his life to the Congo and Ruanda-Urundi. In a penetrating address entitled "Demi-vérités et mortelles erreurs," de-livered to a Belgian audience in Brussels in 1934, well before most Americans had even discovered Africa, Ryckmans exploded the clichés .that Africans are "lazy" and "like children." What he learned from Africans led Ryckmans to tell his countrymen that if he had to sum up all his experience in one simple formula, he would say, "Try then to treat them as *men!*"[22]

In learning to deal with the new leaders of Africa, we are handicapped by our habitual impulse to brand them "wrong-headed," or still worse, "pro-Communist," when they minimize or disagree with the values we tend to regard as "absolutes" for all the world—the superiority of free enterprise, the virtues of Western democratic forms, and the righteousness of the Western position on Berlin, nuclear testing, and other cold war crises. After long years of having to accept decisions made by Europeans, African leaders feel a strong compulsion to form their own judgments, not only about Africa but about the outside world as well. Their attitudes toward us will be more and more affected by our ability or inability to understand their view of the world. Naturally we want them to appreciate our view of the world too. In the long run, however, it is the prosperous West, not impoverished Africa, which has the most to lose from misunderstanding.

The mood of the new Africa is a volatile mood, angry at times and eager for experiment. The history of revolutions suggests that radical change has not yet completed its leftward course. Sooner or later, a new generation of leaders, more African in education and less Western in pattern, will come to power. When, and how, is unpredictable, but many surprises and reversals are likely. Perhaps "radical" Ghana may even become the bulwark of stability in West Africa, while "conservative" Nigeria reverts to the forgotten position of earlier years when it produced the extremists of African nationalism.

We must attune ourselves to this revolutionary spirit in Africa and Asia and view it as affirmatively and sympathetically as we can. If we fail in the effort, we may find our present system of international security collapsing all around us within the next decade.

[22] Address on October 30, 1934, to the Conference du Jeune Barreau de Bruxelles, reprinted in Pierre Ryckmans, *Dominer pour servir*, Bruxelles, 1948, pp. 176–189.

Appendix

List of Sources

CHAPTER 1. THE RISE OF AFRICA IN WORLD POLITICS

Batuta, Ibn, *Travels in Asia and Africa, 1325–1354*, trans. H. A. R. Gibb, Cambridge, England, 1929.

Bovill, E. W., *The Golden Trade of the Moors*, London, 1958.

Coleman, James S., "Nationalism in Tropical Africa," *American Political Science Review*, June, 1954.

Dike, K. O., *Trade and Politics in the Niger Delta, 1830–1885*, Oxford, 1956.

Fage, J. D., *An Introduction to the History of West Africa*, Cambridge, England, 1955.

Fortes, M., "The Impact of the War on British West Africa," *International Affairs*, April, 1945.

Hailey, Baron William M., *An African Survey—Revised 1956*, New York, 1957.

Huizinga, J. H., "Africa—The Continent of Tomorrow's Troubles," *United Empire*, March–April, 1950.

Hodgkin, Thomas L., *Nationalism in Colonial Africa*, London, 1956.

Langer, Willard L., *The Diplomacy of Imperialism, 1890–1902*, 2 vols., New York, 1935.

Newbury, C. W., *The Western Slave Coast and its Rulers*, Oxford, 1961.

Oliver, Roland A., *Sir Harry Johnston and the Scramble for Africa*, London, 1957.

Ponsonby, C. E., "African Colonial Administration," *United Empire*, September–October, 1945.

Rudin, Harry R., *Armistice 1918*, New Haven, 1944.

Sithole, Ndabaningi, *African Nationalism*, Cape Town, 1959.

Toynbee, Arnold J., "The Psychology of Encounters," *The World and the West*, New York and Oxford, 1953.

Toynbee, Arnold J., "The Siege of the West," *Foreign Affairs*, January, 1953.

U.D.A. *London Letter*, March 8, 1947.

CHAPTERS 2, 3, AND 4. AFRICA AND THE UNITED NATIONS

Arden-Clarke, Charles, "Southwest Africa, the Union and the U.N.," *African Affairs*, January, 1960.

Armstrong, Elizabeth H., and William I. Cargo, "The Inauguration of the Trusteeship System of the United Nations," *U.S. Department of State Bulletin*, March 23, 1947.

Bailey, Sydney D., "The Future Composition of the Trusteeship Council," *International Organization*, Summer, 1959.

Bates, Margaret L., "Tanganyika: The Development of a Trust Territory," *International Organization*, February, 1955.

Bunche, Ralph J., "Trusteeship and Non–Self-Governing Territories in the Charter of the United Nations," *U.S. Department of State Bulletin*, December 30, 1945.

Burns, Sir Alan, *In Defence of Colonies: British Colonial Territories in International Affairs*, London, 1957.

Chidzero, B. T. G., *Tanganyika and International Trusteeship*, Oxford, 1961.

Chowduri, R. N., *International Mandates and Trusteeships Systems: A Comparative Study*, The Hague, 1955.

Coleman, James S., "Togoland," *International Conciliation*, September, Summer, 1959.

Eagleton, Clyde, "Excesses of Self-Determination," *Foreign Affairs*, July, 1953.

Fletcher-Cooke, J., "Some Reflections on the International Trusteeship System, with Particular Reference to Its Impact on the Governments and Peoples of the Trust Territories," *International Organization*, Summer, 1959.

Fox, Annette Baker, "International Organization for Colonial Development," *World Politics*, April, 1950.

Fox, Annette Baker, "The United Nations and Colonial Development," *International Organization*, May, 1950.

Gilchrist, Huntington, "Colonial Questions at the San Francisco Conference," *American Political Science Review*, 1945.

Haas, Ernst B., "The Attempt to Terminate Colonialism: Acceptance of the United Nations Trusteeship System," *International Organization*, February, 1953.

Hailey, Baron William M., *The Future of Colonial Peoples*, Princeton, 1944.

Hall, H. Duncan, *Mandates, Dependencies and Trusteeship*, Washington, 1948.

International Bank for Reconstruction and Development, *The World Bank in Africa*, Washington, July, 1961.

International Development Association, *First Annual Report, 1960–1961*, Washington, 1961.

Kelsen, Hans, *The Law of the United Nations*, New York, 1950.

King, Joseph, "Chapter XI of the U.N. Charter in Action," *American Journal of International Law*, January, 1954.

Kozicki, Richard J., "The United Nations and Colonialism," in R. Strausz-Hupé and H. W. Hazard, eds., *The Idea of Colonialism*, New York, 1958.

Logan, Rayford W., *The African Mandates in World Politics*, Washington, 1948.

Lugard, F. J. D., *Times* (London), January 10, 1945.

Mitchell, Sir Philip, *African Afterthoughts*, London, 1954.

Mortimer, Molly, *Trusteeship in Practice: A Report to the Fabian Colonial Bureau*, June, 1951.

Reyher, Rebecca, *The Fon and His Hundred Wives*, London, 1953.

Riggs, Fred W., "Wards of the U.N.: Trust and Dependent Areas," *Foreign Policy Reports*, June 1, 1950.

Rivlin, Benjamin, *The United Nations and the Italian Colonies*, New York, 1950.

Roche, Jean de la, and Jean Gottman, *La Fédération française—Contacts et Civilisations d'outre-mer*, Montreal, 1945.

Sady, Emil J., *The United Nations and Dependent Peoples*, Washington, 1956.

Sayre, Francis B., "Legal Problems Arising from the United Nations Trusteeship System," *American Journal of International Law*, April, 1948.

Stanley, Colonel Oliver, *British Information Services Press Release* ˙R4286, January 19, 1945.

Toussaint, Charmian E., *The Trusteeship System of the United Nations*, New York, 1956.

United Nations, Department of Economic and Social Affairs, *Five-Year Perspective, 1960–1964*, E/3347/rev.1, Geneva, 1960.

United Nations, *Economic Commission for Africa Annual Report, February 7, 1960–February 18, 1961*, Economic and Social Council Official Records, 32nd Session, Supplement No. 10, E/3452/rev.1 and E/CN.14/109/rev.1, New York, 1961.

United Nations, Office of Public Information, *The United Nations and Africa*, New York, February, 1962.

United Nations, *Official Records of the Economic and Social Council*, New York, 1946–1961.

United Nations, *Official Records of the General Assembly*, New York, 1946–1961.

United Nations, *Official Records of the Security Council*, New York, 1946–1961.

United Nations, *Official Records of the Trusteeship Council*, New York, 1947–1961.

United Nations, Special Fund, *The Priorities of Progress*, Sales No. 62. I. 2, New York, 1961.

United Nations, Special Fund, *Status of Projects Approved by the Governing Council as of 31 March 1962*, SF/Reports, Series A, No. 19, New York, March 31, 1962.

U.S. Department of State, *United States Participation in the United Nations*, Washington, annual report by the President to the Congress.

Van Langenhove, F., *Le Problème de la Protection des Populations aborigènes aux Nations Unies*, Leyden, 1956.

Van Langenhove, F., *The Idea of the Sacred Trust of Civilization with Regard to the Less Developed Peoples*, June, 1951.

Wainhouse, David W., and Philip A. Mangano, "The Problem of the Former Italian Colonies at the Fourth Session of the General Assembly," *U.S. Department of State Bulletin*, May 29, 1950.

Wright, Q., *Mandates Under the League of Nations*, Chicago, 1930.

CHAPTER 5. THE IMPACT OF WORLD OPINION ON SOUTH AFRICA

This chapter is based primarily on an analysis of the following South African newspapers from July, 1959, to July, 1960. They are listed in the order of their circulation figures.

Sunday Times	Johannesburg	317,000
Star	Johannesburg	170,000
Dagbreek en Sondagnuus	Johannesburg	124,000
Rand Daily Mail	Johannesburg	114,000
Cape Argus	Cape Town	95,000
Cape Times	Cape Town	66,000
Die Vaderland	Johannesburg	48,000
Die Burger	Cape Town	43,000
		60,000 weekend
Die Transvaler	Johannesburg	41,000

The Bow Group, *The New Africa*, London, 1962.

Calvocoressi, Peter, *South Africa and World Opinion*, Oxford, 1961.

Hepple, Alex., *Censorship and Press Control in South Africa*, Johannesburg, 1960.

Keppel-Jones, Arthur, *When Smuts Goes—A History of South Africa from 1952–2010, First Published in 2015*, Pietermaritzburg, 1953 edition.

MacCrone, Ian D., "Human Relations in a Multi-Racial Society," *Race Relations Journal*, January–June, 1958.

Nkosi, Lewis, "Robert Sobukwe: An Assessment," *Africa Report*, April, 1962.

CHAPTERS 6 AND 7. PAN-AFRICANISM

Allen, Samuel, "Tendencies in African Poetry," in John A. Davis, ed., *Africa Seen by American Negroes*, Dijon, 1958.

Apter, David E. and James S. Coleman, "Pan-Africanism or Nationalism," manuscript presented at Third Annual AMSAC Conference, Philadelphia, June, 1960.

Baldwin, James, "Princes and Powers," *Encounter*, January, 1957.

Beier, Ulli, "In Search of an African Personality," *Twentieth Century*, April, 1959.

Bisheuvel, Simon, *Race, Culture and Personality*, Johannesburg, 1959.

Carey, A. T., *Colonial Students*, London, 1956, especially chap. VI, "The Colonial Students' Unions."

Césaire, Aimé, *"La pensée politique de Sékou Touré,"* *Présence Africaine*, December, 1959.

Cronon, Edmund D., *Black Moses*, Madison, 1955.

Decraene, Philippe, *Le Panafricanisme*, Paris, 1959.

Decraene, Philippe, *"Panafricanisme et Grandes Puissances,"* *Politique Étrangère*, No. 4, 1959.

Desmond-Smith, Captain, *United States of Africa*, a 64-page pamphlet with no place or date of publication.

Dodge, Bayard, *Al-Azhar—A Millenium of Muslim Learning*, Washington, 1961.

"Dr. Nkrumah Suggests Two Houses of Parliament for United Africa," *Ghana Today*, February 14, 1962.

Drake, St. Clair, "Pan-Africanism, Négritude and the African Personality," address to the U.S. National Commission for UNESCO biennial conference on Africa and the United States: Images and Realities, October 25, 1961. (mimeo.)

Drake, St. Clair, "Rise of Pan-African Movement," *Africa Special Report*, February, 1958.

Du Bois, W. E. B., *The World and Africa*, New York, 1947.

Emerson, Rupert, "Pan-Africanism," *International Organization*, Spring, 1962.

"From Accra to Addis," West Africa, July 2, 1960.

Garigue, Philip, "The West African Students' Union," Africa, January, 1953.

Garvey, Amy-Jacques, ed., The Philosophy and Opinions of Marcus Garvey, New York, 1923.

Gillespie, Joan, "Africa's Voice at the U.N.," Africa Special Report, June, 1959.

Good, Robert C., "Four African Views of the Congo Crisis," Africa Report, June, 1961.

Halpern, Manfred, "Egypt Discovers Africa," Africa Report, April, 1961.

Hempstone, Smith, The New Africa, London, 1961.

Henry, Paul-Marc, "Pan-Africanism: A Dream Come True," Foreign Affairs, April, 1959.

Hodgkin, Thomas, "Panafrica, Eurafrica, Malanafrica," Spectator, March 26, 1954.

"Independent African States at Addis: I," West Africa, July 2, 1960.

"Independent African States at Addis: II," West Africa, July 9, 1960.

Isaacs, Harold R., "Du Bois and Africa," Race, November, 1960.

Kahin, G. M., The Asian-African Conference, New York, 1956.

Kiano, Gikonyo, "The Pan-African Freedom Movement of East and Central Africa," Africa Today, September, 1959.

Kloman, Erasmus H., Jr., "African Unification Movements," International Organization, Spring, 1962.

Kohn, Hans, "Pan-Movements," in Encyclopedia of the Social Sciences, New York, 1937, vol. II.

Kraft, Louis, "Pan-Africanism: Political, Economic, Strategic and Scientific," International Affairs, April, 1948.

Legum, Colin, Pan-Africanism—A Short Political Guide, New York, 1962.

Lloyd, William B., "The Significance of the Bandung, Cairo and Accra Conferences," Race Relations Journal (Johannesburg), October–December, 1959.

Logan, Rayford, "The Historical Aspect of Pan-Africanism, 1900–45," ms. presented at Third Annual Conference, American Society of African Culture, Philadelphia, June, 1960.

Lomax, Louis E., The Reluctant African, New York, 1960.

Mphahlele, Ezekiel, "The Cult of Négritude," Encounter, March, 1961.

Mphahlele, Ezekiel, John Reed, and I. I. Potekhin, "Is Négritude Relevant?" Current, September, 1961.

Nasser, Gamal Abdel, Egypt's Liberation: The Philosophy of the Revolution, Washington, 1955.

Nkrumah, Kwame, The Autobiography of Kwame Nkrumah, Edinburgh, 1957.

Nkrumah, Kwame, I Speak of Freedom—A Statement of African Ideology, New York, 1961.

Padmore, George, *Pan-Africanism or Communism? The Coming Strug-gle for Africa*, New York, 1956.
Rowan, Carl T., "Has Paul Robeson Betrayed the American Negro?", *Ebony*, October, 1957.
Shepperson, George, "Notes on Negro American Influences on the Emer-gence of African Nationalism," *Journal of African History*, Vol. I, 1960, p. 2.
Smith, Edwin W., *Aggrey of Africa*, London, 1929.
Wright, Richard, *Black Power*, New York, 1954.

CHAPTERS 8 AND 9. EURAFRICA, THE COMMON
MARKET, AND TECHNICAL COOPERATION

Ansprenger, Franz, *Politik in Schwarzen Afrika: Die moderner politischen Bewegungen im Afrika*, Cologne, 1961.
The Bow Group, *The New Africa*, London, 1962.
Caine, Sydney, *Collaboration in Development in the New Africa*, The Africa Bureau Anniversary Address, London, 1958.
CCTA, *Conférence interafricaine pour les Sciences humaines; 1ère ré-union: Bukavu, 1955*, London, n.d.
CCTA and CSA, *Inter-African Scientific and Technical Co-operation, 1948–1955*, London, n.d.
CCTA, CSA, and FAMA, *Africa*, London, 1961.
Cousté, Pierre-Bernard, *L'Association des Pays d'outre-mer à la Com-munauté Économique Européene*, Paris, 1959.
de Montsabert, General, "North Africa in Atlantic Strategy," *Foreign Affairs*, April, 1953.
DeLattre, Jean-Michel, "Organisation Africaine et Malgache de Coop-ération Économique," *Politique Étrangère*, No. 6, 1960.
Delauze, Pierre, "Nouvelle Étape vers L'Eurafrique," *Communauté Euro-péenne*, May, 1962.
Delorme, Jean, "Colonies françaises," *Vie Industrielle*, June 6, 1941.
Frank, Isaiah, *The European Common Market*, New York, 1961.
Gambelli, Enrico, "La coopération internationale en Afrique et la CEE," *Civilisations*, Vol. X, No. 2, 1960.
Gordon, Lincoln, "The Organization for European Economic Coopera-tion," *International Organization*, February, 1956.
Guernier, Eugène, *L'Afrique—Champ d'expansion de l'Europe*, Paris, 1933.
Guernier, Eugène, "L'Eurafrique et la Communauté Européene," in *L'Eurafrique et le Marché Commun*, Académie des Sciences d'Outre-Mer, Vol. XVIII, May–June–July, 1958.
Henry, Paul-Marc, "The European Heritage: Approaches to African De-velopment," *Africa Today*, ed. C. G. Haines, Baltimore, 1955.

Henry, Paul-Marc, "The United Nations and the Problem of African Development," *International Organization*, Spring, 1962.

Hurd, Volney D., "Eurafrica Re-echoes," *Christian Science Monitor*, March 21, 1957.

Hurd, Volney D., "Eurafrica Skirts Hurdle," *Christian Science Monitor*, February 21, 1957.

Hurd, Volney D., "Eurafrican Dream Given Fresh Shine," *Christian Science Monitor*, April 22, 1957.

"The Impact of Western European Integration on African Trade and Development," E/CN.14/72, December, 1960.

Lalanne, Philip, "For a United Eurafrica," *Western World*, October, 1959.

Landstrom, Hans O., *Capital Movements and Economic Integration*, Leyden, 1961.

Lefebure, Jacques, "Perspectives des territoires d'outre-mer dans le marché commun," *Civilisations*, Vol. VIII, No. 3, 1958.

Moreira, Adriano, *Politica Ultra Marina*, Porto, 1956.

Moussa, Pierre, *Les chances économiques de la Communauté franco-africaine*, Paris, 1957.

Moyal, Maurice, "What Prospect for Eurafrica," *New Commonwealth*, August 5, 1957.

Organization for European Economic Cooperation, *Report of the Overseas Territories Committee*, Section XV of Volume III, December 31, 1958.

Pick, Hella, "Nkrumah Molds Ghana in His Image," *Washington Post*, April 15, 1962.

"Qu'est-ce que la CCTA?" *Afrique Nouvelle* (Dakar), July 26, 1961.

Sarraut, Albert, *La Mise en valeur des Colonies françaises*, Paris, 1923.

Servoise, René, "La répercussion du 'Marché Commun Européen' sur les pays tiers (régions intertropicales)," *Civilisations*, Vol. VIII, No. 3, 1958.

Soper, Tom, "Africa's Economic Links with Europe after Independence," *Optima*, September, 1960.

Soper, Tom, "The European Economic Community and the Underdeveloped Countries in Africa and Asia," *Western World*, February, 1960.

"Soviet Views of Eurafrica," *Mizan Newsletter*, September, 1961.

The Development of Africa, Report of the Group of Experts Presented to the Consultative Assembly of the Council of Europe, September, 1957.

United Nations, Economic Commission for Africa, E/CN. 14/72.

Vedovato, Giuseppe, "La coopération internationale en Afrique, sur les plans économique, financier et technique," *Civilisations*, Vol. X, No. 2, 1960.

Verdier, E. T., "CCTA–CSA and International Cooperation in the Field of Education," *Civilisations*, Vol. X, No. 2, 1960.

Viard, René, *L'Eurafrique pour une nouvelle Économie européene*, Paris, 1942.

Willcox, Sally H., "Africa and the EEC: Prospects for 1962," *Africa Report*, August, 1961.

Zischka, Anton, *Afrique, Complément de l'Europe*, Paris, 1952.

CHAPTER 10. AFRICA AND INDIA

"Aga Khan," *Reporter—East Africa's Fortnightly Magazine* (Nairobi), May 13, 1961.

Awolowo, Obafemi, *Path to Nigerian Freedom*, London, 1947.

Berkes, Ross N., and Mohinder S. Bedi, *The Diplomacy of India—Indian Foreign Policy in the United Nations*, Stanford, 1958.

Bruwer, J. P. van S., "The Asians in Africa," *Digest of South African Affairs—Supplement*, March, 1956.

Calpin, G. H., "An Indian State in Africa?" *East African Standard*, January 5, 1951.

Calpin, G. H., *Indians in South Africa*, Pietermaritzburg, 1960.

"Commissioner Deplores Article in Local Paper," *Kenya Daily Mail*, January 11, 1951.

Current Affairs Publications, *Nehru on Africa*, New Delhi, 1954.

Dart, Raymond A., *The Oriental Horizons of Africa*, Johannesburg, 1954.

Dilley, Marjorie Ruth, *British Policy in Kenya Colony*, New York, 1937.

Fredericks, Wayne, "The Department of African Studies—University of Delhi," *African Studies Bulletin*, May, 1960.

Gandhi, M. K., *Satyagraha in South Africa*, Stanford, 1954.

Geyer, A. L., "Asia Resurgent," *Digest of South African Affairs—Supplement*, February, 1956.

Hollingsworth, L. W., *The Asians of East Africa*, London, 1960.

Indian Council of World Affairs, *India and the United Nations*, New York, 1957.

Kuper, Hilda, *Indian People in Natal*, Pietermaritzburg, 1960.

Murarka, Dev, "Indians in Africa," *Africa Trade and Development*, February, 1961.

"Nehru on Africa," *Africa Diary* (Delhi), August 26–Sept. 1, 1961.

Oliver, Roland, *Sir Harry Johnston and the Scramble for Africa*, New York, 1958.

Palmer, Mabel, *et al.*, *The Indian as a South African*, Johannesburg, 1956.

Palmer, Norman, "Indian Attitudes Toward Colonialism," in R. Strausz-

Hupé and Harry W. Hazard, eds., *The Idea of Colonialism*, New York, 1958.

Rao, P. Kodanda, "Indian Interest in Africa," *Current History*, July, 1953.

Singh, Khushwant, "Frank Conversation at an Empty Table," *UNESCO Courier*, October, 1960.

Van Heerden, W., "Africa's Role Between East and West," *Digest of South African Affairs—Supplement*, February, 1956.

Williams, R. Denton, "The Indians in Africa," *African World*, December, 1953.

Wright, Peter, "Rising Indian Interest in Africa Seen in New Educational Ventures," *African News*, May, 1956.

Zinkin, Taya, "Indian Foreign Policy: An Interpretation of Attitudes," *World Politics*, January, 1955.

Zinkin, Taya, *Manchester Guardian*, June 16, 1956.

CHAPTERS 11, 12, AND 13. SOVIET POLICY ON AFRICA

"African Studies in Moscow," *Mizan Newsletter*, April, 1961.

Beloff, Max, "No Peace, No War," *Foreign Affairs*, January, 1949.

Bird, Christopher, series of articles on Soviet writings on Africa, *Africa Special Report*, October, 1957, November, 1957, December, 1957, March, 1958, April, 1958, and August, 1958.

Bird, Christopher, "Scholarship and Propaganda," *Problems of Communism*, March-April, 1962.

Bulletin de la Société d'Études et d'Information Politique, May 16–31, 1950 (article on the Rassemblement Démocratique Africain).

Cattell, David T., "Communism and the African Negro," *Problems of Communism*, September–October, 1959.

Césaire, Aimé, "*La Pensée politique de Sékou Touré*," *Présence Africaine*, December, 1959.

"Classes in African Society," *Mizan Newsletter*, June, 1961.

"The Communist Party in South Africa," *Africa Report*, March, 1961.

"Des Africanistes Russes parlent de l'Afrique," *Présence Africaine*, Winter, 1960.

Hodgkin, Thomas, "Soviet Africanists," *West Africa*, October 3, 10, and 17, 1959.

Holdsworth, Mary, *Soviet African Studies, 1918–1959—An Annotated Bibliography*, issued in two parts, Chatham House Memoranda, Oxford, March, 1961.

Idenburgh, P. J., "Soviet Russia's Interest in Africa," *International Spectator*, January, 1960. (mimeo. trans.)

Kolarz, Walter, "Communism in Africa—The West Africa Scene," *Problems of Communism*, November-December, 1961.

Laqueur, Walter Z., *Communism and Nationalism in the Middle East*, New York, 1956.

Laqueur, Walter Z., "Communism and Nationalism in Tropical Africa," *Foreign Affairs*, July, 1961.

Legum, Colin, "Soviets Sag Lower in Africa," *Washington Post*, April 15, 1962.

Lemin, I., "The Colonial Policy of the Labour Party and the Position of the Workers in Africa," *Problems of Economics*, No. 2, 1949. (mimeo. trans.)

London, Kurt L., "Red China in Black Africa," *Problems of Communism*, July, 1962.

Marshall, C. B., *Two Communist Manifestos*, Washington Center of Foreign Policy Research, 1961.

Mildenburger, Kenneth, "African Studies and the National Defense Education Act," *African Studies Bulletin*, December, 1960.

"More Soviet Thoughts on African Nationalism," *Mizan Newsletter*, June, 1961.

Morison, David L., "Communism in Africa—Moscow's First Steps," *Problems of Communism*, November-December, 1961.

Munger, Edwin S., *Communist Activity in South Africa*, Africa ESM, New York, August, 1958 (American Universities Field Staff, 1958).

Nokwe, Duma, "The Great Smear: Communism and Congress in South Africa," *Africa South in Exile*, October–December, 1961.

Okonkwo, T., A. R. Amar, and M. Ayik, "An Open Letter to All African Governments," *America*, December 17, 1960.

Padmore, George, *Pan-Africanism or Communism? The Coming Struggle for Africa*, New York, 1956.

Pistrak, Lazar, "Soviet Views of Africa," *Problems of Communism*, March-April, 1962.

Potekhin, I. I., "Africa Looks Ahead," *Supplement to Mizan Newsletter*, Moscow, April, 1961. (abr. trans.)

Potekhin, I. I., "Études Africaines en Union Sovietique," *Présence Africaine*, Winter, 1960.

Potekhin, I. I., "The Stalinist Theory of Colonial Revolution and the National Liberation Movement in Tropical and South Africa," *Soviet Ethnography*, No. 1, 1950. (mimeo. trans.)

"The Present Stage in Soviet African Studies," *Mizan Newsletter*, February, 1961.

Roux, Edward, *Time Longer Than Rope*, London, 1948.

Schwarz, Solomon M., "Revising the History of Russian Colonialism," *Foreign Affairs*, April, 1952.

Smirnov, S. R., "The British Policy of 'Indirect Rule' in Southeast Nigeria," *Soviet Ethnography*, 1950. (mimeo. trans.)

Sonnenfeldt, Helmut, "Nigeria as Seen from Moscow," *Africa Report,* January, 1961.

Sonnenfeldt, Helmut, "Soviet Strategy in Africa," *Africa Report,* November, 1960.

Stolte, Stefan, "Africa Between Two Power Blocs," *Bulletin of the Institute for the Study of the U.S.S.R.* (Munich), May, 1961.

Stolte, Stefan, "The Moscow Declaration and the Underdeveloped Countries," *Bulletin of the Institute for the Study of the U.S.S.R.,* January, 1961.

Stolte, Stefan, "The Soviet Union, Communist China, and the Underdeveloped Countries," *Bulletin of the Institute for the Study of the U.S.S.R.,* August, 1960.

"The 22nd CPSU Congress," *Mizan Newsletter,* November, 1961.

Tucker, Robert C., "The Psychology of Soviet Foreign Policy," in Alexander Dallin, ed., *Soviet Conduct in World Affairs,* New York, 1960.

USSR Academy of Sciences, Africa Institute, *Information About the General Meeting of the Department of History (USSR Academy of Sciences) Devoted to African History,* Moscow, 1962.

Von Stackelberg, Georg A., "Anti-Islamic Propaganda in the Soviet Union," *Bulletin of the Institute for the Study of the U.S.S.R.,* May, 1960.

Von Stackelberg, Georg A., "Changing Soviet Views on Arab Unification," *Bulletin of the Institute for the Study of the U.S.S.R.,* April, 1960.

Von Stackelberg, Georg A., "Peaceful Coexistence Between the Communists and the National Bourgeoisie," *Bulletin of the Institute for the Study of the U.S.S.R.,* July, 1960.

Von Stackelberg, Georg A., "Soviet-African Studies as a Weapon of Soviet Policy," *Bulletin of the Institute for the Study of the U.S.S.R.,* September, 1960.

Von Stackelberg, Georg A., "Soviet Afro-Asian Policy Enters a New Stage," *Bulletin of the Institute for the Study of the U.S.S.R.,* November, 1960.

Von Stackelberg, Georg A., "The University for the Friendship of Peoples," *Bulletin of the Institute for the Study of the U.S.S.R.,* April, 1960.

Yergan, Max, "The Communist Threat in Africa," in C. G. Haines, ed., *Africa Today,* Baltimore, 1955.

CHAPTER 14. AMERICAN INTERESTS IN AFRICA

Bennett, Norman R., "Americans in Zanzibar, 1825–1845," *Essex Institute Historical Collections,* July, 1959.

Bennett, Norman R., "Americans in Zanzibar, 1845–1865," *Essex Institute Historical Collections*, July, 1961.

Bennett, Norman R., "Americans in Zanzibar: 1865–1915," *Essex Institute Historical Collections*, Vol. 98, 1962.

Brady, C. T., Jr., *Commerce and Conquest in East Africa*, Salem, 1950.

Committee on the University and World Affairs, *The University and World Affairs*, December, 1960.

Dunbar, Ernest, "The Image of Africa in the United States," address to the U.S. National Commission for UNESCO biennial conference on Africa and the United States: Images and Realities, October 24, 1961. (mimeo.)

Hill, Adelaide, "A Survey of American Voluntary Organizations in Africa," background paper for the U.S. National Commission for UNESCO biennial conference on Africa and the United States: Images and Realities, October, 1961. (mimeo.)

Howard, Lawrence C., "The United States and Africa—Trade and Investment," in John A. Davis, ed., *Africa Seen by American Negroes*, Dijon, 1958.

Leakey, L. S. B., *Defeating Mau Mau*, London, 1954.

Levallois, Maurice, "Les tendances anti-colonialistes des Etats-Unis, de l'U.R.S.S. et de la Chine," *Renaissances*, October, 1945.

Lincoln, C. Eric, *The Black Muslims in America*, Boston, 1961.

Shepherd, George W., "The Conflict of Interests in American Policy on Africa," *Western Political Quarterly*, December, 1959.

Springer, Maida, "African Labor at the Crossroads," *Africa Report*, August, 1961.

Sutton, Francis X., "The Ford Foundation's Development Program in Africa," *African Studies Bulletin*, December, 1960.

U.S. Congress, Senate Committee on Foreign Relations, *United States Foreign Policy—Africa, a Study Prepared by the Program of African Studies, Northwestern University*, 86th Cong., 1st sess., Washington, October 23, 1959.

U.S. Department of Labor, Bureau of International Labor Affairs, *Report on the Overseas Activities of American Trade Unions. Section II: Activities of United States Labor Unions and Labor Federations, Organized on an Area by Area Basis with Special Note as to Certain Countries*, Washington, 1960. (mimeo.)

U.S. Department of State, *African Programs of U.S. Organizations—A Selective Directory*, ER-53, Washington, June, 1961.

U.S. National Commission for UNESCO, *Africa and the United States: Images and Realities—Background Book* (8th National Conference, Boston, October 22–26, 1961), Washington, Department of State, 1961.

U.S. National Commission for UNESCO, *Africa and the United States:*

Images and Realities—Final Report (8th National Conference, Boston, October 22–26, 1961), Washington, Department of State, 1962.

Wickert, Frederick R., "American Universities and Africa," *African Studies Bulletin*, December, 1960.

Yarmolinsky, Adam, "How to Run a Small Foundation," *Harper's Magazine*, April, 1961.

CHAPTER 15. OUR "NATIONAL INTEREST" IN AFRICA

"Africa," *Foreign Commerce Weekly*, September 12, 1960.

Awolowo, Obafemi, *Awo—The Autobiography of Chief Obafemi Awolowo*, Cambridge, 1960.

Baldwin, Hanson W., "Cape Route's 'Guardian'—An Analysis of South Africa's Increased Importance Because of the Suez Crisis," *New York Times*, September 18, 1956.

Beard, Charles A., *The Idea of National Interest—An Analytical Study in American Foreign Policy*, New York, 1934.

Beard, Charles A., *The Open Door at Home—A Trial Philosophy of National Interest*, New York, 1934.

Becker, Carl, *Modern Democracy*, New Haven, 1941.

Bell, Philip W., "Colonialism as a Problem in Foreign Policy," *World Politics*, October, 1952.

Blankenheimer, Bernard, "Africa Looks to New Kind of Investor," *Foreign Commerce Weekly*, May 7, 1962.

Conolly, Admiral Richard L., "Africa's Strategic Significance," in C. G. Haines, ed., *Africa Today*, Baltimore, 1953.

de Montsabert, General, "North Africa in Atlantic Strategy," *Foreign Affairs*, April, 1953.

Eliot, George Fielding, "Africa—Key to Western Security," *American Mercury*, April, 1955.

Herald, G. W., "Africa, Strategic Prize of the Century," *UN World*, February, 1952.

Irion, F. C., "Specialized Groups," *Public Opinion and Propaganda*, New York, 1952.

Kennan, George F., "How New Are Our Problems?" and "The National Interest of the United States," *Illinois Law Review*, March-April, 1951.

Lefever, Ernest, *Ethics and United States Foreign Policy*, New York, 1957.

Mason, Edward S., "American Security and Access to Raw Materials," *World Politics*, January, 1949.

May, Stacy, "Private Enterprise and the Future of Africa," Address to the U.S. National Commission for UNESCO Biennial Conference on Africa and the United States: *Images and Realities*, October 23, 1961. (mimeo.)

Morgenthau, Hans J., "United States Policy Toward Africa," in Calvin Stillman, ed., *Africa in the Modern World*, Chicago, 1955.

Nyerere, Julius, "Will Democracy Work in Africa?" *Africa Special Report*, February, 1960.

Reitzel, Wm., Morton A. Kaplan, and Constance B. Coblenz, *United States Foreign Policy 1845–1955*, Washington, 1956, especially Chapter I and Appendix A on "Definition of Terms."

Report of the President's Commission on National Goals, *Goals for Americans*, American Assembly, New York, 1960.

Rivkin, Arnold, "Why This U.S. Interest in Africa?" *Central African Examiner*, November 22, 1958.

Steubel, Heinrich, "The Strategic Significance of South and Central Africa," *Military Review*, November, 1955.

U.S. Congress, House Committee on Foreign Affairs, *Mutual Security Act of 1958*, Hearings on . . . HR 12181, February 18–March 13, 1958, Parts I–VIII, Vol. 1, Washington, 1958.

U.S. Congress, Senate Committee on Foreign Relations, *United States Foreign Policy*, 86th Cong., 1st sess., Document No. 24, Washington, 1961, especially Study No. 4 on "Africa," and Study No. 7 on "Basic Aims of United States Foreign Policy."

"U.S. Exports to Africa Indicate Rising Importance of Minor Markets," *Foreign Commerce Weekly*, September 16, 1957.

Wallerstein, Immanuel, "What Happened to the Opposition?" *West Africa*, November 25, 1961.

CHAPTERS 16, 17, AND 18.   AMERICAN POLICY ON AFRICA

SELECT LIST OF OFFICIAL STATEMENTS ON AFRICA

For those addresses which were issued as U.S. Department of State press releases, the press release number is indicated in parentheses after the date of the address. When an address has no title, the name of the group to which it was delivered is given.

Date of Speech	Speaker	Title of Address	Place
May 8, 1950 (469)	George C. McGhee	"United States Interests in Africa"	Oklahoma City
June 28, 1951 (564)	George C. McGhee	"Africa's Role in the Free World Today"	Evanston

Date of Speech	Speaker	Title of Address	Place
October 16, 1952 (814)	Dean Acheson	Address to the U.N. General Assembly	New York
October 30, 1953 (605)	Henry A. Byroade	"The World's Colonies and Ex-Colonies: A Challenge to America"	Asilbomar, California
November 18, 1953	John Foster Dulles	"The Moral Initiative"	Cleveland
April 21, 1956 (206)	George V. Allen	"United States Foreign Policy in Africa"	Philadelphia
August 18, 1956 (442)	George V. Allen	Excerpts from an address to the 83rd Infantry Association	Washington
October 16, 1957	Joseph Palmer, II	"The Problems and Prospects of Sub-Saharan Africa: A United States Point of View"	Princeton
January 27, 1958 (32)	Julius C. Holmes	"Africa: Its Challenge to the West"	Philadelphia
May 1, 1958 (235)	Julius C. Holmes	"The United States and Africa: An Official Point of View"	Arden House
May 29, 1958 (292)	Julius C. Holmes	"Africa's Challenge to the Free World"	New Orleans
October 9, 1958 (590)	J. C. Satterthwaite	"The United States and Africa: Challenge and Opportunity"	Lake Arrowhead, California
January 17, 1959 (38)	J. C. Satterthwaite	"The United States and the New Africa"	Biloxi, Mississippi
March 20, 1959 (206)	J. C. Satterthwaite	"The Role of Labor in African Development"	New York
May 1, 1959 (298)	J. C. Satterthwaite	"The United States and West Africa: A Survey of Relations"	Richmond, Indiana

Date of Speech	Speaker	Title of Address	Place
May 15, 1959 (325)	J. K. Penfield	"The Role of the United States in Africa: Our Interests and Operations"	Chicago
March 25, 1960 (157)	F. O. Wilcox	"The New Africa and the United Nations"	Lexington, Kentucky
April 4, 1960 (167)	Christian Herter	"The Less Developed Areas"	Chicago
April 8, 1960	J. C. Satterthwaite	"Our Role in the Quickening Pace Towards Independence in Africa"	Philadelphia
May 15, 1960 (246)	J. K. Penfield	"Africa: A New Situation Requiring New Responses"	St. Paul, Minnesota
September 22, 1960	Dwight D. Eisenhower	Address to the U.N. General Assembly	New York
October 24, 1960 (610)	J. C. Satterthwaite	"The United States and the Continent of Africa"	Amherst
January 30, 1961 (41)	G. M. Williams	Address to the Americans for Democratic Action	Philadelphia
February 17, 1961 (74)	G. M. Williams	"The United States and Africa: Common Goals"	Addis Ababa
March 24, 1961 (156)	G. M. Williams	Address to the National Press Club	Washington
March 29, 1961 (171)	G. M. Williams	Address at the Conference on African Resources	New York
April 15, 1961	J. F. Kennedy	Remarks at African Freedom Day Reception	Washington
April 19, 1961 (237)	G. M. Williams	Address at the Patriot's Day Celebration	Lexington, Massachusetts
May 11, 1961 (310)	G. M. Williams	Address to the Foreign Policy Association	New York

Date of Speech	Speaker	Title of Address	Place
May 13, 1961 (313)	G. M. Williams	"United States Policy Toward Africa and the United Nations"	Milwaukee
May 17, 1961 (327)	G. M. Williams	Address to the New York Division of the American Negro Centennial Authority	New York
May 19, 1961 (332)	G. M. Williams	Address to the Wichita Urban League	Wichita, Kansas
May 19, 1961 (333)	G. M. Williams	"Africa's Challenge to America's Position of Free World Leadership"	Norman, Oklahoma
June 16, 1961 (398)	G. M. Williams	Address at the United Negro College Fund meeting	Detroit
June 21, 1961 (419)	G. M. Williams	Address to Operation Crossroads Africa	Washington
June 22, 1961	G. M. Williams	Address at Wayne State University	Detroit
July 5, 1961 (474)	G. M. Williams	Address to the Nigerian Economic Mission	Washington
August 25, 1961	G. M. Williams	"Basic United States Policy"	Salisbury
September 13, 1961 (629)	Pedro Sanjuan	Address to the Maryland Legislative Council	Baltimore
September 18, 1961 (641)	G. M. Williams	"Southern Africa in Transition"	Philadelphia
September 27, 1961	G. M. Williams	"Education—Africa's Greatest Need"	Baltimore
October 26, 1961 (737)	G. M. Williams	"New Impressions of Africa"	Boston
October 31, 1961 (751)	G. M. Williams	Address to the Overseas Press Club	New York
November 14, 1961 (784)	G. M. Williams	Address to the WHO Citizens Committee	Detroit

Date of Speech	Speaker	Title of Address	Place
December 1, 1961 (828)	G. M. Williams	"Africa's Challenge to American Enterprise"	Washington
December 14, 1961	G. M. Williams	Address to the NAACP	Washington
December 19, 1961	George W. Ball	"The Elements in our Congo Policy"	Los Angeles
December 27, 1961 (905)	G. M. Williams	Address to Sigma Delta Chi	Detroit
December 27, 1961	Carl T. Rowan	Phi Beta Sigma	Philadelphia
January 11, 1962	G. M. Williams	"Africa and the United Nations"	Washington
January 23, 1962	G. M. Williams	"The Role of Private Enterprise in Africa's Development"	Bethlehem, Pennsylvania
March 9, 1962 (158)	G. M. Williams	"The Challenge of Africa to the Youth of America"	Lancaster, Pennsylvania
March 19, 1962	G. M. Williams	Address at Farmers Convention	Denver
March 22, 1962 (180)	G. M. Williams	"Intergroup Relations in National and International Affairs"	New York
March 27, 1962	G. M. Williams	Address at the 50th Anniversary Dinner of the St. Louis Argus	St. Louis
March 29, 1962 (203)	G. M. Williams	"Change and Challenge in Africa"	Brighton, Massachusetts
April 11, 1962 (241)	G. M. Williams	"American Foreign Policy and the Emerging Nations of Africa"	Amherst, Massachusetts
April 13, 1962 (253)	G. M. Williams	"Aids and Obstacles to Political Stability in Mid-Africa"	Philadelphia

Date of Speech	Speaker	Title of Address	Place
May 4, 1962 (291)	J. Wayne Fredericks	"The Impact of the Emergence of Africa on American Foreign Policy"	Orange, New Jersey
May 14, 1962 (310)	G. M. Williams	Statement on African Trip upon Arrival Home	Washington
June 5, 1962	G. M. Williams	Address to AFL-CIO Convention	Grand Rapids, Michigan
June 15, 1962 (391)	G. M. Williams	"The New Frontier of Africa"	Los Angeles
June 20, 1962	G. M. Williams	"The Outlook on Ruanda-Urundi"	Washington
June 26, 1962 (417)	Lucius D. Battle	"The Educational and Cultural Exchange Programs of the United States: Their Role in Foreign Relations"	Washington
June 28, 1962 (424)	G. M. Williams	"The Future of the European in Africa"	Detroit

CONGRESSIONAL DOCUMENTS ON AFRICA

U.S. Congress, House Committee on Foreign Affairs, *Activities of Private United States Organizations in Africa*, Hearings, 87th Cong., 1st sess., Washington, 1961.

U.S. Congress, House Committee on Foreign Affairs, *Report of the Special Study Mission to Africa South and East of the Sahara*, by Representative Frances P. Bolton, 84th Cong., 2nd sess., Washington, 1956.

U.S. Congress, House Committee on Foreign Affairs, *Report of the Special Study Mission to the Near East and Africa*, by Representatives Hays, O'Hara, and Church, 85th Cong., 2nd sess., Washington, 1958.

U.S. Congress, House Committee on Foreign Affairs, *Staff Memorandum on the Republic of the Congo*, 86th Cong., 2nd sess., Washington, August 24, 1960.

U.S. Congress, House Committee on Foreign Affairs, *United Nations Operations in the Congo*, Hearings, 87th Cong., 1st sess., Washington, April 13, 1961.

U.S. Congress, Senate Committee on Foreign Relations, *Development*

Programs in Africa South of the Sahara, 84th Cong., 2nd sess., Washington, November 23, 1956.

U.S. Congress, Senate Committee on Foreign Relations, *Economic Aid and Technical Assistance in Africa*, report on a study mission by Senator Theodore F. Green, 85th Cong., 1st sess., Washington, February 21, 1957.

U.S. Congress, Senate Committee on Foreign Relations, *North Africa and the Western Mediterranean*, report on a study mission by Senator Mike Mansfield, 85th Cong., 2nd sess., Washington, January 30, 1958.

U.S. Congress, Senate Committee on Foreign Relations, *Study Mission to Africa, November–December, 1960*, report of Senators Church, McGee, and Moss, 87th Cong., 1st sess., Washington, February 12, 1961.

U.S. Congress, Senate Committee on Foreign Relations, *Study Mission to Africa, September–October, 1961*, Report of Senators Gore, Hart, and Neuberger, 87th Cong., 1st sess., Washington, January 14, 1962.

U.S. Congress, Senate Committee on Foreign Relations, *United States Foreign Policy—Africa, a Study Prepared by the Program of African Studies, Northwestern University*, 86th Cong., 1st sess., Washington, October 23, 1959.

U.S. Congress, Senate Committee on Foreign Relations, *United States Foreign Policy (Part 1), Hearings on United States Foreign Policy—Africa*, 86th Cong., 2nd sess., Washington, 1960.

OTHER SOURCES ON AMERICAN POLICY

The Africa League, *A New American Policy Toward Africa*, New York, February, 1960.

American Assembly, *The Secretary of State*, Englewood Cliffs, 1960.

American Assembly, *The United States and Africa*, New York, 1958.

Becker, Carl, *The Declaration of Independence: A Study in the History of Political Ideas*, 2nd ed., New York, 1942.

Bowie, R. R., "Analysis of Our Policy Machine," *New York Times Magazine*, March 9, 1958.

Bowles, Chester, *Africa's Challenge to America*, Berkeley, 1956.

Brady, Cyrus Townsend, *Commerce and Conquest in East Africa*, Salem, 1950.

Buell, Raymond Leslie, *Liberia: A Century of Survival—1847–1947*, Philadelphia, 1947.

Coleman, James S., "America and Africa," *World Politics*, July, 1957.

Coleman, James S., and Carl G. Rosberg, *New Perspectives on Sub-Saharan Africa*, Washington, Union for Democratic Action, n.d.

De Kay, Drake, "Slavery," in *Encyclopedia Americana*, New York, 1961.

De Kiewiet, C. W., "America's Role in Africa," *Education and Our Expanding Horizons*, ed. R. G. Macmillan, P. D. Hay, and J. W. Macquarrie, Pietermaritzburg, 1962.

Duignan, Peter, and Lewis Gann, "A Different View of United States Policy in Africa," *Western Political Quarterly*, December, 1960.

Elder, Robert, *The Policy Machine: The Department of State and American Foreign Policy*, Syracuse, 1960.

Enke, Stephen, "Seven Fallacies About Central Africa," *Central African Examiner*, April 9, 1960.

Good, Robert C., "Congo Crisis: The Role of the New States," in Arnold Wolfers, ed., *Neutralism*, Washington Center of Foreign Policy Research, June, 1961.

Howard, Lawrence, "The United States and Africa-Trade and Investment," in John A. Davis, ed., *Africa Seen by American Negroes*, Dijon, 1958.

Hull, Cordell, *Memoirs*, 2 vols., New York, 1948, especially vol. II.

Hunton, Alpheus, *Decision in Africa: Sources of Current Conflict*, New York, 1957.

Irwin, Ray W., *The Diplomatic Relations of the United States with the Barbary Powers, 1776–1816*, Chapel Hill, 1931.

Kitchen, Helen, "Africa and the Kennedy Era," *The New Republic*, December 12, 1960.

Lansing, Robert, *The Peace Negotiations*, Boston, 1921.

London, Kurt, with Kent Ives, *How Foreign Policy Is Made*, New York, 1949.

Marshall, C. B., *The Limits of Foreign Policy*, New York, 1954.

Muller, George F., "A Diplomatic History of the Congo Free State," unpublished doctoral dissertation, Johns Hopkins School of Advanced International Studies, 1948.

Murphy, Robert, "Africa and Asia in the World Community," Department of State Press Release No. 644, November 11, 1955; an analysis of the application of the principle of self-determination in international relations.

Nkrumah, Kwame, *I Speak of Freedom—A Statement of African Ideology*, New York, 1961.

Reitzel, William, Morton A. Kaplan, and Constance G. Coblenz, *United States Foreign Policy, 1945–1955*, Washington, 1956.

Ritner, P., *The Death of Africa*, New York, 1960.

Rosenthal, Eric, *Stars and Stripes in Africa*, London, 1938.

Van Essen, Marcel, "The United States Department of State and Africa," *Journal of Human Relations*, Spring and Summer, 1960.

de Vos, Pierre, *Vie et Mort de Lumumba*, Paris, 1961.

Williams, G. Mennen, *A Governor's Notes*, Ann Arbor, Institute of Public Administration, University of Michigan, 1961.

Young, Roland, "The Stake of the United States in an Independent Africa South of the Sahara," *Journal of Negro Education*, Summer, 1961.

CHAPTER 19. AMERICAN AID TO AFRICA

Beneviste, Guy, and William E. Moran, Jr., *African Development: A Test for International Cooperation*, Stanford, 1960.

Coffin, Frank M., "Allies Are Carrying Their Share of Aid," *Washington Post*, June 3, 1962.

Galbraith, J. K., "A Positive Approach to Economic Aid," *Foreign Affairs*, April, 1961.

Haviland, H. Field, Jr., "Foreign Aid and the Policy Process, 1957," *American Political Science Review*, September, 1958.

International Cooperation Administration, *Operations Report—Data as of June 30, 1961*, Washington, 1961.

Kennan, George F., *Russia, the Atom and the West*, New York, 1957.

Liska, George, *The New Statecraft—Foreign Aid in American Foreign Policy*, Chicago, 1960.

Liska, George, "The Rationale of Non-Alignment," in Arnold Wolfers, ed., *Neutralism*, Washington Center of Foreign Policy Research, June, 1961.

Millikan, Max F., "New and Old Criteria for Aid," *Aid Digest*, January 15, 1962.

Millikan, M. F., and W. W. Rostow, "Foreign Aid: Next Phase," *Foreign Affairs*, April, 1958.

Montgomery, John D., *Aid to Africa—New Test for U.S. Policy*, Foreign Policy Association Headline Series No. 149, September–October, 1961.

Rivkin, Arnold, *Africa and the West, Elements of Free-World Policy*, New York, 1962.

Rivkin, Arnold, "Proposed Multilateral Approach to Economic Development in Emergent Africa," *Africa Special Report*, September, 1958.

Sereno, Renzo, "Diplomacy for Our Times," *SAIS Review*, Winter, 1962.

CHAPTER 20. INFORMATION AND EXCHANGE PROGRAMS

Davis, James M., Russell G. Hanson, and Duane Burnor, *IIE Survey of the African Student: His Achievements and His Problems*, New York, 1961.

Dizard, Wilson P., *The Strategy of Truth—The Story of the U.S. Information Service*, Washington, 1961.

Elder, Robert E., *The Foreign Leader Program: Operations in the United States*, Washington, 1961.

Feld, Cora H., "New Horizons for U.S.-African Understanding," *African News,* May, 1954.

Gardner, John, "The Foreign Student in America," *Foreign Affairs,* July, 1952.

Institute of African-American Relations (African American Institute), *Views of African Students on Strengthening African-American Relations,* Washington, n.d.

Institute of International Education, *Open Doors,* New York, annual.

Institute of International Education, Committee on Educational Interchange Policy, *African Students in the United States,* New York, December, 1960.

Institute of International Education, Committee on Educational Interchange Policy, *The Foreign Student—Exchange or Immigrant,* New York, May, 1958.

Phelps-Stokes Fund, *A Survey of African Students Studying in the United States,* New York, 1949.

Robinson, Virginia, *Report on United States-South African Leader Exchanges,* Philadelphia, American Friends Service Committee, 1955. (mimeo.)

Sims, Albert G., "Africans Beat on Our College Doors," *Harper's Magazine,* April, 1961.

Sloan, Ruth C., "Educational Exchanges with Africa-Fallacies of Generalizations," *IIE News Bulletin,* November, 1949.

U.S. Department of State, *Coordination of the Educational Exchange Program of IES, Exchange Aspects of the Technical Training Activities of ICA, and Certain Cultural Activities of USIA,* Washington, December, 1957.

U.S. Department of State, "Educational and Cultural Exchange with Africa: The Program of the Department of State," *African Studies Bulletin,* May, 1961.

U.S. Department of State, *International Educational, Cultural and Related Activities for African Countries South of the Sahara,* Washington, August, 1961.

U.S. Department of State, *Program Planning Analysis of Educational Exchange and Related Exchange-of-Persons Activities for Libya, Morocco and Tunisia,* Washington, January 10, 1958.

U.S. Department of State, *Report on United States Government Assistance to Sub-Saharan African Students Seeking Higher Education in the United States,* Washington, January–September, 1961. (mimeo.)

U.S. Department of State, *Students from Africa Studying in the United States,* Washington, December, 1948. (mimeo.)

U.S. Information Agency, *The Agency in Brief,* Washington, January, 1962.

CHAPTER 21. THE IMPACT OF AFRICA ON
INTERNATIONAL RELATIONS

"Africa Speaks to the United Nations—A Symposium of Aspirations and Concerns Voiced by Representative Leaders at the U.N.," *International Organization*, Spring, 1962.

Allport, Gordon W., *The Nature of Prejudice*, Toronto, 1958.

Awolowo, Obafemi, *Awo—The Autobiography of Chief Obafemi Awolowo*, Cambridge, England, 1960.

Bell, Cora, "The United Nations and the West," *International Affairs*, October, 1953.

Becker, Carl, *How New Will the Better World Be?* New York, 1944.

Cohen, A., "The New Africa and the United Nations," *International Affairs*, October, 1960.

Courtney, Winifred F., "Focus on Africa: The 15th UN General Assembly," *Africa South*, April–June, 1961.

Cowan, Zelman, "The Contemporary Commonwealth: A General View," *International Organization*, Spring, 1959.

Dean, Vera Micheles, and J. Bartlet Brebner, *How to Make Friends for the U.S.*, Foreign Policy Association Headline Series No. 93, May–June, 1952.

Dunbar, Ernest, "The Image of Africa in the United States," address to the U.S. National Commission for UNESCO biennial conference on Africa and the United States: Images and Realities, October 25, 1961. (mimeo.)

Fifield, Russell H., *The Diplomacy of Southeast Asia: 1945–1958*, New York, 1958.

Gillespie, Joan, "Africa's Voice at the U.N.," *Africa Special Report*, June, 1959.

Good, Robert C., "Congo Crisis: The Role of the New States," in Arnold Wolfers, ed., *Neutralism*, Washington Center of Foreign Policy Research, June, 1961.

Goodwin, Geoffrey, "The Expanding United Nations Voting Patterns," *International Affairs*, April, 1960.

Hall, H. Duncan, "The British Commonwealth of Nations," *American Political Science Review*, December, 1953.

Herskovits, Melville J., "African Values in the World Scene," *The United Nations and the Emerging African Nations*, University of Wisconsin Global Focus Series, No. 2, Milwaukee, 1961.

Hoffman, Stanley, "In Search of a Thread: The U.N. in the Congo Labyrinth," *International Organization*, Spring, 1962.

Holmes, John, "The Impact on the Commonwealth of the Emergence of Africa," *International Organization*, Spring, 1962.

Howells, John M., "The French and South African Walkouts and Domestic Jurisdiction," *Journal of Politics*, February, 1956.

Isaacs, Harold R., "American Race Relations and the U.S. Image in World Affairs," background paper for the U.S. National Commission for UNESCO biennial conference on Africa and the United States: Images and Realities, 1961. (mimeo.)

Isaacs, Harold R., "World Affairs and U.S. Race Relations: A Note on Little Rock," *Public Opinion Quarterly*, Fall, 1958.

Kelsen, Hans, *The Law of the United Nations: A Critical Analysis of Its Fundamental Problems*, London, 1950.

Larson, Arthur, "Common Sense and the United Nations," *Saturday Review*, February 24, 1962.

Lomax, Louis E., *The Reluctant African*, New York, 1960.

Michie, Allan A., "The Growth of an African Power Bloc," *Reporter*, March 17, 1960.

Robinson, Kenneth, "Constitutional Autochthony in Ghana," *Journal of Commonwealth Political Studies*, November, 1961.

Rosen, Jane K., "Close-Up of the Afro-Asian Bloc," *New York Times Magazine*, December 17, 1961.

Spencer, John H., "Africa at the U.N.: Some Observations," *International Organization*, Spring, 1962.

Wallace, Terry, "U.S. Negroes Urged by Dr. King to Enlist in Social Revolution," *Washington Post*, April 9, 1962.

Wilcox, Francis O., and H. Field Haviland, Jr., *The United States and the United Nations*, Baltimore, 1961.

Index

Abbas, Mekki, 64
Abboud, Gen. Ibrahim, and Sudan unions, 214
Abdoulay, Diallo, 215
Abrahams, Peter, at fifth Pan-African Congress, 93, 101
Accra, FAO regional office, 33, 60
Accra *Daily Graphic*, 268
Acheson, Dean, 298, 312
Addis Ababa, 58–59, 64
AFL-CIO, 260–263
Africa Bureau (U.S.), 295
Africa League, 255
Africa Office (U.S.), role in State Department, 295–296
Africa Report, 254
Africa Society of India, 178
Africa Today, 254
African Advisory Committee of ILO, 60
African Affairs Society of America, 249
African-American Institute, 254, 394
African-American Students Foundation, 255, 394
African Common Market idea, 118
African Communist, The, 236
African Consultative Assembly, 116
African Defense Facilities Conference, 1951 meeting, 141
African Freedom Day rally, 265
African Issues in International Relations, 400
African Military High Command idea, 118
African National Congress, 76, 197, 208, 255
African Regional Organization (AFRO), 123
African Research Foundation, 255
African Scholarship Program of American Universities (ASPAU), 394, 395
African Service Institute, 255
African Students' Association of America and Canada, 101
African Studies Association, 254
African Studies Bulletin, 254
African Trade Union Confederation (ATUC), 123–124, 214, 215

African Wildlife Fund, 265
African Worker's University, 216
African Youth League of the Ivory Coast, 218
Africanism, 8
Africanity idea, 125
Africanization of Marx, 240
Afro-Asian Economic Conference, 104–105
Afro-Asian group in the U.N., 102–105
Afro-Asian Institute of Labor Studies, 262
Afro-Asian Organization for Economic Cooperation, 189
Afro-Asian Peoples Solidarity Conferences, 103–105, 216–218
Afro-Malagasy Economic Cooperation Organization (AMECO), 115, 155
Afro-Malagasy Union, 115
Aga Khan III in East Africa, 177, 188
Aga Khan IV on Indians in Kenya, 178
Agency for International Development (AID), 362, 366–371, 388–389
Aggrey, J. E. K., 125
Air Afrique, organized, 115
Al-Azhar University, influence, 107
Algeria, and U.N. Security Council, 29, 62, 116, 221
Algerian Communist Party, 207–208
All-African Peoples Conference, 94, 96, 110–111, 123, 218, 261
All-African Trade Union Federation (AATUF), 123, 214, 215, 261
Allen, George V., 322, 386
Allen, Samuel W., 124
Allport, Gordon W., on race relations, 407
Amar, Andrew R., reply to Soviet, 220
American Association of University Women, 254
American Colonization Society, 314
American Committee on Africa, 254–255
American Metal Climax Co., help to miners, 282
American Outlook, 383
American Society of African Culture (AMSAC), 254

457